What Other Writers & Researchers Have Said About This Book

"Amid the flurry in science about genes, neurons, and neuro-transmitters, another quiet revolution has been building for several decades. It involves a view of consciousness in which the mind is not confined to specific points in space or time, such as the brain, body, and the present. In this book, legendary psychologist and psi researcher Charles Tart assembles the pieces of this new picture. He is eminently qualified to do so, as he helped invent the new image of consciousness through five decades of meticulous research. Tart's inspiring, majestic image of consciousness will prevail because of two compelling reasons: it is built on good science and it more fully accounts for who we humans are and how we behave." — Larry Dossey MD, author of *The Power of Premonitions* and *Healing Words*

"Prescient! This book represents the next step in the geotrans-formational processes that are altering modern concepts of borders, social structures, wealth, and governance. The precepts are at once omnipresent and historical, yet often elusive or rejected. Buoyed by a confluence of cataclysmic socioeconomic upheaval, a growing awareness of paradoxes not explained by traditional science, and an innate human longing for understanding, Charles Tart succinctly provides a blueprint for metamorphosis to an evidence-based spiritual awakening for Western cultures." — John B. Alexander, Ph.D., counselor at the Society for Scientific Exploration

"If you would like a clear, readable, and eminently fair-minded introduction to some of today's most contentious scientific topics, here is a book for you." — Roger Walsh, MD, Ph.D., professor at the University of California, Irvine, and author of *Essential Spirituality*

"A remarkable tour de force that will hopefully end forever the argument that science and the spiritual are opposed to one another. This wonderful collection of facts and arguments, written in a good-natured, almost conversational style, makes it easy to loosen yourself from your preconceptions and enjoy seeing reality more clearly and completely. We have needed such a book for a long time."
— James Fadiman, Ph.D., author of *The Psychedelic Explorer's Guide: Safe, Therapeutic and Sacred Journeys*

"A truly seminal work based on lifetime of research and careful thought that not only challenges, but overturns the dominant scientific paradigm. Tart patiently explains the reasons for scientific resistance to parapsychology and spirituality, providing a comprehensive overview of the field and its implications for the nature of human existence. Compulsory reading for scientists and spiritual seekers alike." — David Lorimer, program director of The Scientific and Medical Network

"Charles Tart has distilled a wealth of knowledge derived from his empirical study of human experiences that points to the presence of the spiritual in the world. Tart's characteristic humor and sense of fun shine through the text again and again, but always against the background of his wisdom, acquired over a lifetime of pondering the mystery of what it means to be human. This is the book for those who value an approach to the spiritual that is both scientific and richly personal in tone." — Adam Crabtree, author of *Multiple Man* and *Trance Zero*

"This beautifully written book is not only a masterful survey of parapsychology and psychical research, but also a thoughtful analysis of scientific inquiry and how it can be used to explore and explain the spiritual aspects of human nature. Combining laboratory evidence, case studies, and his own extensive experience as a scientist and spiritual seeker, Charles Tart skewers the postulates of a materialistic worldview that for too long has ignored vast areas of the human potential." — Stanley Krippner, Ph.D., coeditor, *Varieties of Anomalous Experience*

"This book is an outstanding contribution to the emerging dialogue between science and spirituality. Tart makes a persuasive argument for questioning common assumptions about the nature of reality, thoroughly grounded in solid research. This is essential reading for anyone interested in the farther reaches of human awareness. — Frances Vaughan, Ph.D., psychologist and author of *Shadows of the Sacred*

"The Secret Science of the Soul is brilliant. This is the book Tart has obviously been working up to all his life." — Colin Wilson

"An extraordinary accomplishment in parapsychology by an enlightened experimental psychologist in the tradition of William James." — Eugene Taylor, Ph.D., executive faculty at Saybrook Graduate School, lecturer on psychiatry at Harvard Medical School

Other Books by Charles T. Tart

Altered States of Consciousness (editor and contributor)

On Being Stoned: A Psychological Study of Marijuana and Intoxication

Transpersonal Psychologies (editor and contributor)

States of Consciousness

Symposium on Consciousness (with P. Lee, R. Ornstein, D. Galin, and A. Deikman)

Learning to Use Extrasensory Perception

Psi: Scientific Studies of the Psychic Realm

Mind at Large: Institute of Electrical and Electronic Engineers Symposia on the Nature of Extrasensory Perception (C. Tart, H. Puthoff, and R. Targ, editors and contributors)

Waking Up: Overcoming the Obstacles to Human Potential

Open Mind, Discriminating Mind: Reflections on Human Possibilities

Living the Mindful Life

Body Mind Spirit: Exploring the Parapsychology of Spirituality

Mind Science: Meditation Training for Practical People

THE SECRET SCIENCE OF THE SOUL

CHARLES T. TART, PhD

FEARLESS BOOKS
NAPA CALIFORNIA

Second Edition
This book was originally published in hardcover with the title
THE END OF MATERIALISM by Noetic Books/New Harbinger
in 2009. This is the first paperback edition.

FEARLESS BOOKS
PO Box 4199 • Napa CA 94558
www.fearlessbooks.com

ISBN: 978-0-692-93769-3
Library of Congress Control Number:
2017952592

DESIGN & TYPOGRAPHY:
D. Patrick Miller • Fearless Literary Services
www.fearlessbooks.com/Literary.html

TABLE OF CONTENTS

Acknowledgments

This book is the culmination of a career spanning more than fifty years of work on the nature of consciousness, particularly altered states of consciousness, parapsychology, and transpersonal psychology, so there are many people I'm grateful to for support and guidance! I'll mention only the more obvious ones: my wife, Judy, who has given me such loving support and stimulation for so many years; Palyne Gaenir, my webmaster and computer guru; the late Irene Segrest, my devoted assistant for a decade; and the students in my Introduction to Parapsychology course at the Institute of Transpersonal Psychology in winter 2007, Jamal Granick, Maureen Harrahy, Josh Maddox, Daniela Mafia, Laurel McCormick, Matthew Metzger, Sean Saiter, Heather Schwenn, Goolrukh Vakil, Alison Wattles, and David Wilson, who gave me detailed feedback on an early draft of this book.

A number of institutions have supported my work over the years, so alphabetically, my thanks to the Fetzer Family Foundation; the Institute of Noetic Sciences; the Institute of Transpersonal Psychology; the National Institute of Mental Health; the Parapsychology Foundation, Inc.; and the University of California, Davis.

Various psychological and spiritual teachers have helped me become a little more insightful and mature over the years. I'll give thanks here to just the major ones whom I've had personal contact with, again listed alphabetically: Ernest Hilgard, Henry Korman, Claudio Naranjo, Jacob Needleman, Sogyal Rinpoche, Tsoknyi Rinpoche, Kathleen Riordan Speeth, Tarthang Tulku, and Shinzen Young.

Preface to the 2017 Edition

WHAT'S A respectable scientist like me doing by titling the second edition of his book *The Secret Science of the Soul?* Many scientists would practically shout "Blasphemy!" or "Heresy!" when a fellow scientist uses words like "secrecy" and "soul," and want to take away any symbols of authority, including the white lab coat or laboratory instruments...

But I'm delighted if I shock, and so get attention this way! I'm trying to provoke people, of course — especially if they stop for a moment to think in a way that's the essence of both common sense or science, namely "Yes, I have my *opinions* but maybe some actual *facts* should carry more weight than my opinions?"

The question of whether we have souls, or, to put it more generally, whether there is any reality to the spiritual realm, is vitally important in a world where materialistic greed contributes daily to the trashing of our planet and its life, including the human race. I don't think people should be effectively forbidden the scientific observations and knowledge that suggest — some would say *proves* — that there is indeed some kind of reality to "soul" and "spirit." Frozen attitudes that effectively act as a fundamentalist Church of Materialism tell us that spirituality is all delusion and imagination to soothe the ignorant, while the smart ones grab the wealth and power.

I care about doing science well and gaining knowledge, but I care about the well-being of us humans too. Not just to survive, but to have *meaning* in our lives, and the satisfaction that real meaning can provide without having to trash our planet and each other.

Many people, including scientists, believe that science long ago *proved* that all religion was basically false. There were no gods or goddesses, saints or devils, no miracles, and prayer was just talking to yourself.

Why am I claiming that science, while showing that some as-
-pects of religion and spirituality may indeed be delusory, actually
has high quality, but largely unknown and indeed *suppressed*
evidence that some of spirituality is *reality*?

A brief background story. I was intrigued by science from the
time I was a child with a chemistry and electricity laboratory in my
cellar. I was a Boy Scout and became a ham radio operator. I've always been fascinated by ideas, but I'm also very *practical*. I worked
my way through college, for example, as a Radio Engineer, keeping
commercial radio station transmitters running, and my wife Judy
and I built our own cabin.

I was raised to be a religious Lutheran. My grandmother, a
source of unconditional love for me, took me to Sunday School.
What was good enough for her was good enough for me! I believed
what they taught me in Sunday School, and I tried to be good (it
wasn't that easy!). At age twelve I was confirmed as a church member.

But when I was eight, my grandmother died unexpectedly, drop-
ping to the sidewalk from a heart attack. Not long after, I came down
with rheumatic fever. In those days there wasn't really any good
treatment for it, other than bed rest and hope. Most kids who had
rheumatic fever got permanent heart damage and died of heart failure sometime in their twenties. With the wisdom of hindsight, partially gained through an enormous amount of work on spiritual
growth and psychological understanding, I realized that my world
had turned so tragic with my grandmother's death that I wanted to
die — of a broken heart, no less — and go to heaven to rejoin her.

As an adult, I can see how illogical that unconscious decision
was, yet I have a deep respect for my earlier self who loved that much.

As I became a teenager, I realized that adults were pretty hypo-
critical in the way they practiced their religion. More importantly, I
recognized that *science was in conflict with much of religion*. Indeed,
science seemed to think that religion was nothing but superstition
and even insanity. How to reconcile that conflict with a basic faith

in a God and a loving universe that was still so much a part of me?

This book, originally published in hardcover in 2009 as *The End of Materialism* (Noetic Books/New Harbinger), is a result of more than a half-century spent looking for the soul, looking for what truth there is in religion and spirituality, based on my and colleagues' studies in parapsychology and altered states of consciousness. As I grew older, I realized that science was right about many false and crazy-making aspects of religion, but science was also quite biased, ignoring the fact that various religions not only gave us deep meaning; *they also had some degree of factual support.* As a sophisticated adult, I now look much more sympathetically on religions as important attempts by human beings to find meaning, and to make sense out of the occasional deep spiritual or mystical experiences that people have. I also realized how often religion has been used as an excuse to indulge the worst of human instincts for dominance, greed, and power, so I can empathize with those who are very negative about religion.

Note in the previous paragraph that I was tempted to put the word "soul" in quotes to ease the shock of using it for scientist colleagues, many of whom are strongly conditioned to close down their minds and turn away when they hear that kind of word. While it's the best word I can think of in this context, we don't really understand what it means. But my white-coated friends and colleagues can relax, because I'm not going to try to convert you to anything in this book. But I will present you with a lot of facts and ideas that are *very* interesting, and challenging.

There, I've put myself in a scientifically cautious and respectable position! Except, unfortunately, I expect to be irrationally rejected by those for whom science has hardened into dogma, that is, a belief system that must not be questioned.

I never claim to be an authority on the spiritual, but I am well versed in essential science. Would it help us to have a more factual, a more "true" understanding of certain phenomena that provide the basis for much of religion and spirituality?

I certainly thought so by the time I was in my teens, and thus my eventual career as a scientist and psychologist has focused around themes like:

(a) what are real phenomena that provide some kind of basis for religion and spirituality;

(b) what kinds of things distort our understanding of religion;

(c) what kind of attitude toward religion encourages the best in it and helps us; but

(d) doesn't let us be carried away with superstition and prejudice, or

(e) overreact to the errors in spirituality or contemporary science such that we throw out the baby with the bath water?

There's no question in my mind that essential science has the potential to help us understand spirituality and perhaps make it more effective. But I haven't written this book simply as a scientist.

We tend to think of scientists as people who are seeking more accurate truths, but while believing that they shouldn't be (and aren't) personally engaged with their subject matter, in order to avoid bias. That's a noble and practical belief system, in many ways. We certainly have scholars of religion who pursue nothing but intellectual analyses (often very biased analyses), and we have social scientists who look at psychological and social consequences of various religious beliefs without ever asking anything about the truth of those beliefs *per se*. You can be socially accepted in the social hierarchy of organized science today if you assume, explicitly or implicitly, that religious experiences are all illusions of the brain. But it's OK and useful to investigate the consequences of people *believing* they are real. Useful knowledge can be gained that way — at the cost of implicitly denying any reality to spirituality without actually *investigating* that potential reality.

I consider science to be a noble calling, an attempt to improve our human condition by getting better knowledge of how the natural world and people function. But while the aim is noble, we scientists are still human. We are swayed by our hopes and fears, and can unthinkingly be deeply biased. Consider the story below, related to me by a trusted colleague. I have blurred some of the names and places, but I have had many experiences like it myself.

Two prominent parapsychological researchers had been invited to a debate for educating an audience of several hundred writers and reporters from a major media network. The first parapsychologist, a physicist by training, presented some information about the state of our knowledge of ESP, drawing primarily on experimental results published in refereed scientific journals. Then a prominent philosopher and "skeptic" got up and scathingly dumped all over the physicist's presentation, dismissing it all as stupid nonsense.

Then it was the turn of my colleague who told me of this incident. He pointed out to the philosopher that, ethically, one could not take such a strong and negative position on any area of knowledge without being fully conversant with the relevant literature. My colleague said that he assumed the philosopher knew the literature well, and suggested that he pick any study he liked and tell him and the audience what was wrong with it. Then it could be reasonably discussed.

Without even thinking, in a voice dripping with condescension, the prominent philosopher replied, "You don't think I read this stuff, do you?"

My colleague just let that statement hang in silence. After a bit there were snickers, then chuckles, then the room filled with guffaws from the audience. The philosopher suddenly understood what he had said, and turned bright red. There was a break soon, and he didn't come back from it.

This kind of incident is why, sadly, I feel there are almost no honest, genuine "skeptics" when it comes to parapsychological and related evidence that points toward a spiritual reality. The *Shorter Oxford English Dictionary* gives a major definition of a skeptic as "a person seeking the truth; an inquirer who has not yet arrived at definite convictions." The self-styled "skeptics" I have met are, for practical purposes, True Believers in a certain style of rationality who think they already know all important truths, so they simply dismiss anything that doesn't fit their worldview — without bothering with actual scholarly or scientific inquiry. Since being a scientist is a high-prestige role in society they claim to be scientifically trained and motivated, but they are not. The more adamant they are that the psychic and spiritual are all nonsense, the less they usually know about the scientific evidence. Why bother to waste their time becoming informed about what they already know is nonsense? So I have to call them *pseudo-skeptics*.

This book and many others I refer to in the Recommended Readings in Appendix 1 could give them serious factual evidence to think about it, but I doubt the pseudo-skeptics will bother to follow it up. As a psychologist — and as someone who has observed my own irrational defenses in many areas of life — I can understand this, but as a scientist it's pretty depressing.

I concluded in the first edition of this book that it was reasonable to be *both* scientific *and* spiritual in your approach to life. But that openness is not enough: *discrimination is always required.* That a writer accepts that psychic events and spirituality may have some reality does not necessarily mean that the specifics they write about are all true or accurate. This is currently illustrated in a series of reviews of a recent book that is being read by many people. The book bills itself as the *definitive* history of the US government's involvement in parapsychological research, but my colleagues who actually did the research criticize it as grossly inaccurate, ignoring things that did happen while describing things that didn't happen as if they were real. As one colleague who was an investigative reporter earlier in his career noted to me, if the author of this book were his assistant, he would fire her for not doing basic fact checking. These reviews can be seen in the *Journal of Scientific Exploration*, for summer 2017.

If you're wondering, dear reader, whether it's hard to research science and spirituality, yes. There is irrational dismissal on the one hand and imaginary "facts" on the other — but it's been a fascinating six decades of research for me! I have no regrets that I didn't stay on a safe, conventional career path and study only what was accepted by the Establishment.

I'm not just a person living only in my intellect. Much of the personal growth in my life has come about by realizing that ideas, and the feelings they generate, can be intoxicating. I'm an intellectual drunk, a thoughtaholic. But just because ideas make me feel good doesn't make them true. *All ideas should to be checked, as much as possible, against reality.* You can't do this for everything, of course; faith is important, but I prefer an informed faith to a blind faith.

So I have been personally involved in many spiritual practices throughout my life, blending these disciplines with my scientific and intellectual attempts at understanding. Not that I'm a "believer" in any particular religion or spiritual path. As much as I respect many spiritual paths and religions, I doubt that any of them have fully understood all the important truths about the universe and expressed them in ways that are eternally true. I've been misunderstood a million times in my own life when I've explained things in ways that I thought were perfectly clear and couldn't possibly be misinterpreted — but they were. Insofar as this can happen with relatively ordinary things, how much more so with things that touch on our deepest values and beliefs, or involve extraordinary ways of sensing and knowing?

Thus there's been a kind of back-and-forth in my life between deep involvement in particular spiritual practices, then deep involvement in study and experimentation from the scientific and scholarly side. Sometimes the two approaches help each other, sometimes they just make me more aware of how little I understand. But overall I've gotten some better understanding — at best with my heart, not only my intellect.

A few years ago I decided it was time to put what I and my colleagues had learned from studying altered states of consciousness, psychology, spiritual experiences, parapsychology, and all sorts of interesting but taboo areas together in a form that would be helpful to other people who are also trying to make sense out of life. Thus the first edition of this book, *The End of Materialism*. We have the beginning of a "science of the soul" but, unfortunately, what we've learned is being kept much too secret by those who believe that Total Materialism is the answer to everything. By repressing this growing science, many, many people have suffered unnecessarily, as they are told by the self-appointed Authorities that their profound spiritual experience is nothing but their brains acting crazy.

My decision to put what we've learned together does not mean that I think I have finally figured out the Truth about God, religion, spirituality and the like — just that we have some very useful information that can help us seek and find meaning in life. Such information is still subject to change, as I learn new things. These new learnings are expressed occasionally with essays on my ongoing blog (*http://www.blog.paradigm-sys.com*) that can supplement this book and my other writings.

The first edition of this book was well received, and finely produced, but marketed to a rather narrow range of readers, mostly psychotherapists and members of the Institute of Noetic Sciences, so most people didn't learn of it. Thus this second edition is intended to make the insights and information more widely available, and do a little updating on some of the sources and recommendations for further knowledge.

If you are curious about your nature, if you sincerely wonder whether there is anything more to life than:

(a) we and the whole universe came about through nothing but blind chemical processes;

(b) we live with no inherent meaning to life other than that which helps us survive, and then

(c) we die, period...

then you'll find this book quite interesting. If you are deeply involved in some particular religion or spiritual path, you may find the information presented here encouraging, but it may also stimulate useful questions about some aspects of your experience. If your personal spiritual path teaches that you should not ask any questions, then this book will be no more useful than it will be to a close-minded rationalist.

I look forward to the time when this book can be updated as *The Science of the Soul*, without all the secrecy!

— CHARLES T. TART
July 2017

Foreword

Charles Tart devotes so much of this interesting and absorbing book to substantiating its title — that is, to arguing that materialism has had its day and is done for — that we think this foreword can best serve the reader by reversing the usual order and beginning by telling the reader what the author is for.

Tart wants to reinstate the dignity and freedom of the human mind, defending it against the view that our noblest thoughts are simply secretions of chemical and electrical events in our brain tissue, and that our notion that we have some freedom of choice is an illusion. He contends that body and mind interact; it's a two-way street. Simply defined, materialism (also called reductionism) and scientism is the idea that everything will eventually be explainable in terms of electrical currents, chemical reactions, or yet to be discovered physical laws. Mind and spirit are mere epiphenomena.

Science begins when experience doesn't jibe with what we know or think we know. From that, an explanatory theory is spun, with hypotheses that can be tested under controlled conditions. Materialism is a theory that has been enormously fertile in the physical sciences, but its success in that realm has caused theory to harden into the dogmatic belief in materialism that dominates much of our culture. It's not a theory that accounts for all of human experience, such as the healing influence of loving, caring relationships. It's in such relationships that spontaneous psi events occur, but scientific tests for psi phenomena require laboratory controls, not simply personal narratives.

Because skeptics insist that there must be some physical agent that has been overlooked in the experiments, Tart describes experiments in extensive detail. Readers can scrutinize them for anything that might have been overlooked. Informed skeptics are taken seriously. When one suggested that the information in an experiment with telepathy or clairvoyance must've been transmitted by electromagnetic waves, for example, Tart's colleagues consulted physicists, who assured them that electromagnetic waves do not penetrate to five hundred feet below the surface of the ocean. The experimental subjects descended five hundred feet in a sub to repeat the experiment! The data was the same.

Science is an open-ended inquiry, not an answer, and yet it's in our nature to look for explanations. Materialism doesn't have all the answers: some can be found in the great religious traditions. Although such traditions use various names, they all teach that "being," "mind," or "spirit" is larger than the human mind — something larger than can be subjected to the laboratory, but it can be considered, and Tart is refreshingly open about his reflections on the great spiritual teachings and his own spiritual practice.

Not surprisingly, I (Huston) am reminded of some of my students at MIT, because Tart, too, was a student at MIT, and is thoroughly grounded in science and technology. I learned that some students were experimenting with water dowsing, trying to see if they could trace the water pipes under the university bookstore by moving a dowsing rod over the floor, and also experimenting with psychokinesis. For the latter they were floating buttered needles on water and attempting to influence the needles' movement by mental concentration. For MIT students this was play, and they would've acknowledged cheerfully that their experiments weren't flawlessly designed. When I expressed surprise that students dedicated to hard-nosed science were amusing themselves in this way, one of them said, "Oh, I know science. I got my first chemistry set when I was five years old. I do science. I just want to know what else is out there." They were like Aldous Huxley, who once commented to us that he was interested in the interstices between the pigeonholes of knowledge, those big questions for which we don't have equations, much less theories. Anyone who is equally curious and open minded, and likes an intellectual challenge will like this book.

The Secret Science of the Soul is the work of a complete human being sharing the breadth of his interests, speculations, and experiences as a scientist. There's a lighthearted seriousness about the author that sustains him in a discipline that's difficult because it's controversial and consequently poorly funded. No one is burned at the stake for questioning conventional "truth," but professional journals are wary of publishing research papers that imply the existence of psi phenomena or legitimatize it as a topic for scientific study. Yet Charles Tart is irrepressibly cheerful, sustained by his delight in finding out "what else is out there," and he retains his capacity for love and laughter.

— Huston Smith and Kendra Smith

Introduction

Noted science writer Sharon Begley, in her book *Train Your Mind, Change Your Brain: How a New Science Reveals Our Extra-ordinary Potential to Transform Ourselves* (2007, 131–32), reports how, while on a visit to an American medical school, His Holiness the Dalai Lama, the highest ranking lama in Tibetan Buddhism and winner of the Nobel Peace Prize, watched a brain operation. His Holiness has always been fascinated with science. He has enjoyed hours of conversations with neuroscientists over the years, and was fascinated by ways they had explained to him that all our perceptions, sensations, and other subjective experiences represent and are produced by chemical and electrical changes in our brains. If patterns of electrochemical impulses surge through our brain's visual cortex, for example, we see, and when such impulses travel through our limbic system, we feel emotions. These rivers of electrochemical impulses may be generated in response to stimulation from happenings in the external world or result from just thoughts in the mind alone. Consciousness, His Holiness remembered various scientists explaining with great conviction, is nothing more than a manifestation of brain activity. When the brain stops functioning, from injury or death, our mind vanishes — period, end of story.

But Begley reports, the Dalai Lama had always been bothered by the seeming certainty of this kind of "explaining away" of consciousness. Even if you accept the theory that our minds are what our brains do, that our emotions and thoughts are expressions of brain activity, isn't there more? Isn't some kind of two-way causation possible? Perhaps some aspects of whatever mind ultimately is might act on the physical brain, modifying its activity?

Could it be, as common sense seems to tell us, that mind might have an active reality rather than just be a by-product of brain activity? His Holiness voiced this question to the chief surgeon.

Begley reports that the brain surgeon hardly paused before authoritatively answering no — period. What we call consciousness or mind is nothing but a product of the physical operation of the brain.

The Dalai Lama is a very polite person, and he let the matter drop. He was used to hearing such absolute statements from people who were (supposed to be) scientists.

But, as Begley notes, "I thought then and still think that there is yet no scientific basis for such a categorical claim," His Holiness wrote in his 2005 book *The Universe in a Single Atom*. "The view that all mental processes are necessarily physical processes is a metaphysical assumption, not a scientific fact" (Lama 2005, quoted in Begley 2007, 132).

This book is a scientific, rather than a scientistic, answer to the Dalai Lama's questions. The difference between science and scientism, and the differing consequences of these approaches, will become clear as you read on.

Before I give a more formal introduction to this book, read and think about the following: In 1872 Richard Maurice Bucke, a Canadian physician and psychiatrist, had the following overwhelming experience. Since he thought of himself as a man of science, devoted to factuality and accuracy, he wrote about this experience in the third person in an attempt to be as objective as possible. Bucke coined the term "Cosmic Consciousness" to describe what happened to him as well as similar experiences of others. This is his account of his experience (Bucke 1961, 7–8):

It was in the early spring at the beginning of his thirty-sixth year. He and two friends had spent the evening reading Wordsworth, Shelley, Keats, Browning, and especially Whitman. They parted at midnight, and he had a long drive in a hansom (it was in an English city). His mind, deeply under the influences of the ideas, images, and emotions called up by the reading and talk of the evening, was calm and peaceful. He was in a state of quiet, almost passive enjoyment. All at once, without warning of any kind, he found himself wrapped around, as it were, by a flame-colored cloud. For an instant he thought of fire, some sudden conflagration in the great city; the next he knew that the light was within himself. Directly afterwards came upon him a sense of exultation, of immense joyousness, accompanied or immediately followed by an intellectual illumination quite impossible to describe. Into his brain streamed one momentary lightning flash of the Brahmic Splendor which has ever since lightened his life; upon his heart fell one drop of Brahmic Bliss, leaving thenceforward for always an aftertaste of heaven. Among other things he did not come to believe, he saw and knew that the Cosmos is not dead matter but a living Presence, that the soul of man is immortal, that the universe is so built and ordered that without any peradventure, all things work together for the good of each and all, that the foundation principle of the world is what we call love and that the happiness of everyone is, in the long run, absolutely certain. He claims that he learned more within the few seconds during which the illumination lasted than in previous months or even years of study and that he learned much that no study could ever have taught.

The illumination itself continued not more than a few moments, but its effects proved ineffaceable; it was impossible for him ever to forget what he at that time saw and knew; neither did he, or could he, ever doubt the truth of what was then presented to his mind.

Here are the kinds of questions this book is concerned with and moves toward answering, even if not answering in any final sense:

- How would you feel if you had such an experience?
- Would you like to have such an experience? I certainly would!
- What if...

...Bucke's experience is literally true?

...the cosmos is indeed not dead matter but a living presence?

...we have souls that are immortal?

...the universe is so built and ordered that, without any doubt, in spite of all the apparent evil in the world, all things work together for the good of each and all?

...the foundation principle of the world is what we call "love"?

...and the happiness of every one of us is, in the long run, absolutely certain?

• But what if, as contemporary science seems to tell us with certainty...

... Bucke's experience resulted from disordered brain functioning?

... the cosmos is basically dead matter, and life is merely an accidental, ultracomplicated chance arrangement of that dead matter?

... we have no souls or spirits; instead, we're but material creatures who'll die?

... there's no order in the universe but that of physical laws; no purpose, no working together other than what's forced by physical laws; and certainly no coordination or coordinator of these blind physical forces that cares a bit about the good or bad of each and all?

... the foundation principle of the world is nothing but mindless physical laws and properties?

... and the happiness of every one of us is nothing but the effects of chance events and various biochemicals circulating in our bodies?

Wouldn't you like to believe some version of Bucke's experience? I certainly would! On the other hand, do you hate to be fooled or feel foolish? I certainly do! We'll return to a modern version of Bucke's Cosmic Consciousness experience and our "what if?" questions at the end of this book.

Now, for my more traditional introduction.

Seeking the Spiritual as a Scientist

"Seeking" is a word commonly associated with spiritual pursuits, but "science" and "scientist" are usually associated with a materialistic view of the universe in which there's nothing real to the "spiritual," so how could a scientist seek the spiritual? Wouldn't such seeking lead to intellectual and emotional conflicts that could be confusing and invalidating, as well as a waste of time?

Indeed, that's how it is for a lot of people today. Something in them seeks, often desperately, something "spiritual" (so far, I'm being deliberately general as to what "spiritual" means) to make their lives authentic and worthwhile, yet no intelligent person can disregard modern science and its understandings without mentally harming themselves in various ways. But modern science, which has given us so much materially, tells "spiritual seekers" that they're, at best, softheaded folks unwilling to be completely scientific and, at worst, superstitious fools, perhaps having a serious psychopathology that drives them to seek the "spiritual."

This all-too-common situation easily makes for an ineffective and stuttering kind of spiritual search, two or three steps forward (that spiritual idea or experience rings true in my heart!) and two or three steps back (scientifically ridiculous — I must be stupid or crazy!). One day your heart and head open toward the spiritual, and then the next day your (apparently) scientific mind rules it out as illusion and delusion.

It was probably simpler in the old days: you believed or disbelieved the one religion given you in your village, and that was it. There wasn't much in the way of competing views. Now we have so much information! Here I am, for example, a constantly fluctuating mixture of scientist; father; husband; psychologist; parapsychologist; teacher; writer; carpenter; bulldozer operator; liberal; conservative; skeptic; and serious off-and-on student of Buddhism, Christianity, Sufism, Yoga, the Fourth Way, and aikido, believing we have the potential of gods, believing we're usually practically mindless robots, and so on. That's a lot of information and roles to balance! And besides just the ideas, many of these spiritual paths say it's not enough to just think about and believe or disbelieve their ideas but you can and should live your life so that you can have direct personal experience of them.

I've written this book to help those who've experienced conflicts between their spiritual and scientific sides, or who are simply interested in aspects of science and the spiritual. In my own life I've not only finally become comfortable with (and proud of!) being both scientist and spiritual seeker, but I also have a dream that someday these two aspects of human life will help each other rather than be in conflict.

This book is not a scientific book per se as are most of my earlier books and articles; I haven't loaded it down with hundreds of scholarly and scientific references to buttress every point, sophisticated caveats, or the very latest news about all sorts of things that might be relevant. Nor is it a spiritual book per se; I'm not a natural mystic inspired by deep experiences. This book is a product of seventy years of my full humanity and complexity: scientific, humanistic, spiritual, skeptical but open — and personal, when that helps illustrate points. What's worked for me is certainly not "The Way," but the conflicts I've experienced and the insights I've had are those of many others, so they can help some people, and are worth sharing.

In the following chapters we'll look at the ongoing conflict between spirituality and science (the conflict is actually between second-rate spirituality and second-rate science) and see how the implications of the most rigorous kind of research in scientific parapsychology shows that we humans have qualities that open to a reality of the spiritual. That's why we can be both scientific and spiritual, and not have to artificially separate the two. We'll look at research findings about most major parapsychological phenomena and some less-researched but farther-out phenomena, and think about their implications for creating a spirituality anchored in scientific facts. We're still at the very beginnings of applying science to the spiritual and a long way from making recommendations like, "Being a Baptist will produce more spiritual growth for this particular kind of person than being a Buddhist," but we know enough to say that it makes a lot of sense to seriously work on your spiritual growth. Knowing that, our growth may still be difficult but not so stuttering and not so deeply undercut by useless conflicts about whether or not we're totally deluded.

In the end, I hope that you, gentle reader, like me, can be comfortable with, indeed proud of, being both scientifically oriented and spiritually seeking. The combination makes for an interesting life.

With this book as a basis, I later hope to write another one sharing some of the things I've explored about actually practicing a spiritual life in modern times.

Spirituality and Religion

Before turning to our central subject matter, there's an important distinction to make: this is a book about science and spirituality, not about science and religion. What do I mean by that? There are at least two levels at which we can think (or, just as importantly, feel) about that. Let's take the scholarly or rational level first and then briefly look at the more-difficult emotional level.

Although they can't be totally separated in reality since the distinction oversimplifies a complex human situation, as I and many other writers use these terms, spirituality is primarily about life-changing, primary experiences that happen to individuals, experiences like Bucke's "Cosmic Consciousness," while religion is primarily about the social organizations and beliefs that develop and become relatively fixed and institutionalized. Such organizations and belief systems are usually initiated by spiritual experiences of the religion's founder, and these organizations and belief systems incorporate and develop (with more or less fidelity) those basic experiences into ongoing social structures, relationships, beliefs, needs, and customs.

Someone, let's call him John Everyman, for example, almost dies and, while apparently dead, has a numinous, "realer-than-real" vision of meeting a nonphysical being. Let's call this being Angelicus. Angelicus communicates with John telepathically and tells John the deep meanings of existence and how embodied life should be lived once he comes back to it. This is a "realer-than-real" revelation to John, the most powerful single experience of his life.

John revives, and is a changed man. He begins telling others about his vision and how they should live. John has enough charm, charisma, or whatever it takes in the particular times he lives in to strongly influence many people, and a small religious group, technically a cult, forms around the Laws of Angelicus and his prophet John Everyman.

Since any change in the social status quo threatens some who already have favored positions, and appeals to others who want to change their status, accommodations in action and doctrine develop to alleviate these tensions so that Angelicusism starts to fit into society even while changing it. By the time John Everyman has been dead for a few generations, his original teachings and those of his close, early followers have been worked over to various degrees (lots of committee meetings and politics), and Angelicusism is now a distinct religion, with its theology, rites, customs, political affiliations, and social agenda. Unapproved interpretations of John Everyman's visions are called heresy and condemned. If Angelicusism becomes politically powerful enough, this condemnation and suppression of other views can easily lead to violence.

The degree to which John Everyman, if he could come back a few hundred years later, would recognize his original spiritual vision in this new religion is an interesting question.

This book, then, focuses on the degree to which you can be scientifically oriented and yet seek and value personal spiritual experience and growth without the doubt and conflict generated by regarding yourself as "irrational," "unscientific," or "crazy." I won't attempt to work with all the psychological and social factors that enter in once spirituality becomes religion, but note that the distinction isn't quite as clear-cut as we might like it to be. We humans are social creatures, and this can affect, to some degree, the very spiritual experiences we have in the first place, as well as our ongoing interpretation and understanding of them afterward. Most of us, too (and I certainly include myself here), need some ongoing social support in our spiritual lives, so I doubt we'll ever have a "pure" spirituality unaffected by religion. It must also be the case that even religions that have changed considerably from the spiritual experiences that started them must still satisfy at least some people's spiritual longings if the religions are to survive.

That's the rational part of the distinction between spirituality and religion. Now, let's move on to the more difficult emotional level. I'll talk about my own feelings here, but I know that large numbers of people have similar feelings. Those who don't are probably lucky.

For me, the word "religion" connotes the particular church I was raised in (Lutheran), its doctrines, and the effects on my personality or self that I can now recognize from a wiser (I hope!), adult perspective. On the one hand, there were many good effects: a concern for the welfare of others; a basic belief in some kind of wise, loving, and caring intelligence in the universe; and numerous instances of experiencing kindness and care from adults in the church that helped shape me. On the other hand, a lot of my neurotic shortcomings stem from or were reinforced by church doctrines, such as feelings of being inherently sinful, a nagging feeling that no matter how good I am it'll never be enough, and a pervasive shame about my body and sexuality that has taken many years to largely overcome. In many ways I was forcibly brainwashed in being taught my religion when I was too young to really understand and make choices. So "religion," for me, is a complicated category with conscious, semiconscious, and undoubtedly unconscious strong feelings, positive and negative, that can create conflicts and tension. Do you recognize yourself in this description?

"Spirituality," on the other hand, has been a matter of relatively conscious choice on my part as an adult, and the aspects of it I've chosen to make central in my life have given me goals and guidance that have added much meaning and satisfaction.

So the rational distinction between spirituality and religion — primary, life-changing experiences of the spiritual versus institutionalized, socialized doctrines and practices — is important to make. But lurking in the background are all these emotional elements, tending to make spirituality a "good" word and religion a "bad" word for many of us. At bodily and emotional levels, when I hear "religion," I tend to get a little tense and defensive, and when I hear "spirituality," I relax and open. To the degree that I recognize these complexities and work on healing the emotional angles, I can be more rational and effective in what I write about and do.

I won't generalize more here, because there are so many varieties of religion, and aside from their formal beliefs and structures, there are enormous variations in the way different individuals absorb and react to particular religions. By the time some of us reach adulthood, our childhood religions are a useful, and perhaps the best, vehicle for promoting and integrating our individual spiritual experiences, which in turn would further enliven our religions. For others of us, our childhood religions are the enemy of our spiritual growth. How it is for you is a matter for you to discover and work with. In this book, though, we'll focus, as I said, on science and spirituality, not science and religion.

How This Book Is Organized

To adequately deal with our broad topic of science, spirit, and reality, we'll cover a lot of material in this book; we have to in order to adequately deal with this broad topic, and as I so often tell my students, in extensive writing, one has to be careful to not let the reader lose the forest for the trees. But here's a quick overview of what's coming. If you get too fascinated by the "trees" in this book — the very interesting facts and ideas — and lose track of the "forest," come back and review this guide.

We began by looking at the powerful "Cosmic Consciousness" experience of Canadian psychiatrist Richard Maurice Bucke, an experience many of us might like to have but whose validity modern science discards. From that perspective, reality isn't the way Bucke perceived it, loving and intelligent, no matter how inspiring or comforting his vision, so forget the spiritual; it's all nonsense. Science and spirituality — or its socialized form, religion — don't go together, on either an intellectual or emotional level.

I bring this dismissal home more strongly in the first chapter with Bertrand Russell's negation of spirit, noting that such dismissals by prominent authorities bias our perceptions so that we're even less likely to have spiritual experiences. It's so important to begin to realize how deeply this affects us moderns, even when we think we're spiritually oriented, that I introduce the Western Creed exercise, hopefully actively done with the online video (see chapter 1) rather than just considered intellectually. It's what I think of as a sadder-but-wiser exercise.

If science is wrong to so thoroughly dismiss the spiritual — and some of our traditional religious beliefs are undoubtedly wrong, so there's a reality basis in this dismissal — how would we find evidence for any reality to the spiritual? Chapter 2 discusses the nature of the essential scientific process, which is really refined common sense. The ways of knowing that I characterize as the Way of Experience, the Way of Authority, the Way of Reason, and the Way of Revelation can be skillfully combined to keep refining our understanding of anything, including the spiritual, and I give an example of how we might study whether prayer or psychic healing has any effects other than material and psychological ones. Essential science and common sense keep coming back to data, fact, and observation. Direct experience is always the final arbiter of what's the best truth. I argue that by using essential science, human beings occasionally have experiences and show certain behaviors that cannot be reduced to materialistic explanations, and that appear to be fundamental aspects of a spiritual nature.

I understand that some people would prefer to get right to what essential science has found that indicates we have spiritual aspects rather than look at how science works. But if you don't have some understanding of this, you remain a victim of misuse of the Way of Authority, with the scientists telling you that you're deluded.

But science is practiced by human beings, beings who, like the rest of us, are fallible, so chapter 3 looks at ways of not knowing, ways in which essential science ossifies into *scientism*, a rigid belief system, and in which genuine skepticism, an honest search for better truths, turns into pseudoskepticism, or debunking. As I've observed it in my career, and as I think psychologist Abraham Maslow would have agreed, science can be practiced in a way that makes it an open-ended, personal-growth system for the practitioner or one of the most effective and prestigious neurotic defense mechanisms available.

Having looked at how we refine our knowledge and how we avoid learning, we're ready to look into the psychic phenomena that undercut the materialistic rejection of spiritual possibilities. Since I intend this book as a personal story of how I, and potentially you, can be both spiritually seeking and scientifically oriented, I start with an example of a psychic experience of my own, the *"coup d'état"* case, showing the kind of psychic phenomena that can happen in ordinary life. To give a little idea of how deeply our psychological characteristics can affect such phenomena, I go into some analyses and speculations of how my hopes, fears, and conscious and unconscious conceptual processes may have affected my reactions and interpretations.

Now having looked at the science-versus-spirit conflict on several levels, seen how to use science and common sense to refine knowledge, and been reminded of some of the kinds of psychic events that happen to a majority of people, we're ready to begin looking at the body of actual scientific experimentation on psy-

chic phenomena. In chapter 5 we look at the basic way such experiments are done, particularly how we exclude alternative normal
material explanations for any effects we get and the importance of
objectivity in assessing results. Then we're ready to look at the
psychic phenomena, or psi phenomena, that I call the "big five" —
telepathy, clairvoyance, precognition, psychokinesis, and psychic
healing — for which we have so much experimental evidence that
we can take them as basic possibilities for humans. Later we'll also
look at some of the possible psi phenomena that I call the "many
maybes," ones with enough evidence to indicate they may be real,
but which aren't as well established as the big five.

Chapter 6, on telepathy, is the first of the big five, the transmission of information from one mind to another when there's
no ordinary way for that to happen. We see how a basic telepathy
experiment is done and then review the research findings. To
make this more concrete, I describe one of my own studies of
telepathy, designed to make it more reliable and then, to illustrate
the process of discovery in science, note how psi abilities seemed to
sometimes function unconsciously in my experiments. Sometimes
my fellow experimenters and I wanted to give an electrical shock
to the percipients, since it was obvious to us that some part of
them knew the correct answer and they weren't giving it! We also
look at why telepathy (and this applies to the other phenomena in
later chapters too) is "nonphysical," or doesn't make sense in the
ordinary view of materialism, and thus requires us to consider a
spiritual, nonphysical aspect to reality, rather than wait around with
faith in what philosophers have termed promissory materialism to
eventually explain these phenomena away.

The next four chapters on the big five describe findings about
clairvoyance, precognition, psychokinesis, and psychic healing. In
each case I overview the research findings and give examples. These
chapters include instances where I've had to struggle with the basic
rule of science that data always takes precedence over what you
prefer to believe, such as when strong precognition sneaks into my

own laboratory and I discover that I've totally forgotten what was probably a demonstration of very strong psychokinetic, mind-over-matter effects, because while I accepted these things intellectually, on a deeper level I have irrational resistance. Essential science isn't easy; our perception and thinking can be distorted by strong attachments to beliefs that we don't even know we have! Thus the scientistic materialists' rejection of the spiritual isn't a simple intellectual matter of assessing the evidence and finding it wanting.

This review of the big five leads me to conclude that rigorous essential science has collected hundreds of experimental findings showing that human beings can sometimes show mind-to-mind communication, clairvoyantly know about distant aspects of the physical world, precognize the future, and affect both nonliving and living things by willing alone. That is, human are the kinds of creatures that we might describe as having qualities of a spiritual nature.

With chapter 11 we start looking at some of the many maybes, those apparent psi experiences with enough evidence for them that it would be unreasonable to offhandedly reject them but not enough evidence for many folks to declare them definitely real, like the big five. This chapter starts with a fascinating case of apparent postcognition, psi perception of information from the past, and then looks at potential uses of psi abilities in archeology.

Chapter 12 focuses on one of the most powerful experiences you can have that would convince you that you're spirit as well as body, the out-of-body experience (OBE). We start with an example from my case files of a fairly typical OBE, and I then discuss six studies of OBEs I've carried out over the years. Some suggest that some OBEs are only simulations of being out of the body, that nothing has really left the body; others suggest that sometimes the mind may truly perceive the world from an outside location.

Even more powerful than OBEs in changing people's views are near-death experiences (NDEs), now experienced by millions of people due to advances in medical resuscitation technology.

NDEs involve an altered state of consciousness, different ways of perceiving and knowing, as well as OBEs. A particularly striking case reviewed is that of Pam Reynolds, who was undergoing surgery that involved draining all the blood from her brain at the time she apparently had the most significant parts of her NDE. Materially, she was dead, with no brain functioning whatsoever, yet some of her perceptions of events in the operating room were accurate. We can theorize that the mind has a spiritual, nonphysical, transpersonal aspect, even though it's normally deeply enmeshed in the workings of the brain and body.

Chapter 14 opens the topic of postmortem survival, one of the "many maybes" of enormous importance to us all. Some can take comfort in a traditional religious or spiritual belief system, but many can't in this modern world. We want evidence, not just faith. The big five provide a picture in which the mind is something more than the brain but that's only indirect proof of survival. Is there more-direct evidence? In this chapter we look at ADCs, after-death communications, where spirits of the deceased apparently appear to the living. ADCs are much, much more common than believed but still aren't quite direct evidence of survival, and of course, some of them, if not many, may well be just wish-driven hallucinations, yet they're quite powerful to those who experience them.

In Chapter 15 we look at the most direct evidence that some aspect of our minds and personalities survives death: claims by spiritualist mediums that they can contact the dead. I describe a case involving one of the world's greatest mediums, the late Eileen J. Garrett, in an event that, though now almost forgotten, in its time shook the world as our Challenger space-shuttle disaster did, namely the crash of the British R-101 dirigible. But the mediumship evidence is actually very complex, as the German diplomat case I review shows, especially given the fact that our unconscious minds can use psi phenomena to support beliefs that may not be true.

Reincarnation is another way of thinking that a self might survive in some form. Chapter 16 begins with the story of a bestselling book in the 1950s, The Search for Bridey Murphy (Bernstein 1956), which created enormous controversy. I then describe a much more recent case from a collection of thousands of such cases at the University of Virginia, cases in which a very young child starts talking about events in a previous life. Is reincarnation proven? I don't think so, but it's a fascinating example of a "maybe," and, again, one that has a lot of implications for how to live our lives. It's one thing if that nasty habit you have now might get you into trouble a few more times but then you die and it's all over, and quite another if it might get you into trouble lifetime after lifetime.

We'll have covered a lot by then, so it'll be time to bring the many threads we've followed together. I wish I could say I weave them all into a single, coherent tapestry of elegance, truth, and beauty, but reality is more complicated than that! So I close with several chapters emphasizing different aspects of our explorations.

Chapter 17, "So What Have We Learned?" is a fairly straightforward summary. We looked at how we gain and refine knowledge, distinguished essential science from scientism, applied essential science and found the big five and the many maybes, and thus got massive amounts of data pointing toward a picture of humans as having a lot of qualities that partially constitute what we mean by spiritual. (There are many vital aspects of spirituality not touched on in this book, of course, but here our focus is on whether "spiritual" means more than "imaginary.")

Chapter 18, "If I Believed the Western Creed," comes back to considerations of whether scientistic materialism is indeed a total truth, whether this inherently meaningless chemical accident we call ourselves is all there is. How would we live then? This isn't just abstract philosophy; this is about how you live your life. I focus on the implications for me, and things don't have to be exactly that way, but a lot of it will apply to you.

In Chapter 19 I continue to reflect on what this all means to me, not that I'm the model for how everyone should be — far from it! But I want to further illustrate that we haven't been talking about abstract philosophy and science; this material is about how we want to live. I have to, for example, honor my childhood religion but grow beyond it, discovering the negative psychological uses I've made of it, the projections onto the world that have distorted my perceptions and interfered with my being a fully functioning human. Being a "child of God" was fine when I was a child; now it's time to be an "adult of God." I give an example of my coming close to death and finding that the scientific data about postmortem survival discussed in this book helped me cope with the stress, and looking to the future, I give an example of how a more enlightened science could help make genuine spirituality more effective.

Finally, in chapter 20, I come back to Bucke's fantastic experience of Cosmic Consciousness that we began this book with. Could it literally be true that, for example, "… the happiness of everyone is, in the long run, absolutely certain" (Bucke 1961, 8)? This is too big a question for me to even venture to answer, but I present a modern-day case of Cosmic Consciousness by an agnostic physician, Allan Smith, that has so many parallels to Bucke's experience that one can't help but wonder.

And finally? I've said that I've written this book as a whole, complex human person, not simply as a scientist, but the scientist and professor in me wants to help you find more information, reliable information, if you wish, so that's why we have four appendices. The first lists some recent, authoritative books on parapsychological findings, the second some reliable websites. The third is a pointer to my TASTE website, where you can read the transcendent and psychic experiences of scientists, and the fourth is a brief introduction to the field of transpersonal psychology and its leading center, the Institute of Transpersonal Psychology. This shows some of the directions in which a properly used science could go in exploring and developing spirituality.

I can't emphasize enough that wherever you look for information, use your discrimination. A lot of opinions are out there, pro and con, but remember the foundation of essential science and common sense: keep coming back to data, to what actually happens, and make the theories and beliefs secondary. Make your best bets on that basis. As much as you can, ground your science and your spirit in reality.

— Charles T. Tart
Berkeley, California 2008

Chapter 1

Spiritual Seeking in a World
That Thinks It's All Nonsense

SPIRITUAL (Middle English [origin: Old French and Modern French "spirituel" from Latin "spiritualis," from "spiritus"; see spirit noun, "-al"]): (1) Of, pertaining to, or affecting the spirit or soul, especially from a religious aspect. (2) Standing in a relationship to another based on matters of the soul. (3) Of a person: devout, pious; morally good. — SHORTER OXFORD ENGLISH DICTIONARY, *6th ed., s.v. "spiritual"*

IN THE introduction, I said that modern science, which has given us so much, declares seekers or the spiritually inclined, at best, softheaded folks who are wasting their time because they're unwilling to be properly scientific in their view of what is and isn't real and, at worst, superstitious fools, probably with serious stupidity or a psychopathology driving them to seek the spiritual. (Actually it's not essential science that tells us this but scientism, a rigidified and dogmatic corruption of science that we'll have a lot to say about later.)

To illustrate the scientistic dismissal of the spiritual, here's what Bertrand Russell (1872–1970), one of the giants of mathematics, philosophy, and logic, and an important influence on the development of modern science, stated on the matter of the religious and spiritual (1923, 6–7):

That man is the product of causes which had no prevision of the end they were achieving; that his origin, his growth, his hopes and fears, his loves and his beliefs, are but the outcome of accidental collocations of atoms; that no fire, no heroism, no intensity of thought or feeling, can preserve an individual life beyond the grave; that all the labours of the ages, all the devotion, all the inspiration, all the noonday brightness of human genius, are destined to extinction in the vast death of the solar system; and the whole temple of Man's achievement must inevitably be buried beneath the debris of a universe in ruins — all these things, if not quite beyond dispute, are yet so nearly certain, that no philosophy that rejects them can hope to stand. Only within the scaffolding of these truths, only on the firm foundation of unyielding despair, can the soul's habitation henceforth be safely built.

If a really brilliant person like Russell believes this philosophy of total materialism, it's rather difficult to put much effort into practices like meditation and prayer, or even into the serious study of spiritual ideas. Most of what we think of as our higher values derives from spirituality and religion: are they all invalidated as nonsense? Is ethics truly the proper conduct of life? If materialism is really true, my reaction is eat, drink, and be merry (and don't get caught by others if they don't approve of your pleasures), for tomorrow we die — and life doesn't mean anything anyway.

If ideas like this were strictly a matter of formal philosophical and scientific theories, all believed, disbelieved, or argued about quite consciously and logically, they wouldn't have too much of a pathological effect on our lives. But when any philosophy or belief system, spiritual or materialistic, sinks below consciousness in much of its operation, simply shaping our perceptions and thoughts without our being aware of it, we tend to become enslaved by it. This is especially true because modern psychology has demonstrated over and over again that much of what we call "perception" is not a straightforward taking in of what's actually in the world around us, of reality, but rather a form of automatized, very rapid "thinking," a processing of perception that can be strongly biased by our beliefs and conditioning so that perception is slanted or biased to apparently validate what we already believe. We have the old adage, "Seeing is believing," but we have to include the opposite also: "Believing is seeing." Furthermore, the "reality" you obviously "see" is a major determinant of what you feel, so your slanted perception can strongly bias your emotions.

If you deeply and largely unconsciously believe, to use a simple example, that people are basically brutal and nasty, that they're mere chimpanzees at heart, you'll "see" instance after instance of it. It's not that you see some event and then consciously think about the fact that it could be interpreted as validating your belief that people are brutal and nasty; rather you tend to automatically see brutal and nasty events all around you, which naturally reinforces your basic beliefs that people are brutal and nasty. If you deeply and largely unconsciously believe, on the other hand, that people are basically good (although their goodness is often veiled in a difficult world), you'll tend to "see" instance after instance of people trying to do the right thing, even when it's difficult, again, reinforcing your basic beliefs.

I'm optimistic about people, and I realize that my belief system may well bias me in unrealistic ways to see evidence for this. I also firmly believe that we need to seek greater truth about people and the world as much as possible, whether we're optimists or pessimists, so self-knowledge, understanding how your own mind works, is vitally important, as important as — or in many instances, more important than — knowledge of external things. One of the things I like about essential science is that in the long run (but sometimes it seems way too long!), proper science, as we'll see in detail later, has self-correction processes built into it that filter out erroneous views and reinforce useful ones. Meanwhile, in the short run, we need to know ourselves as well as our world in order to live more effective lives.

As a psychologist I long ago became aware that many people had semiconscious or unconscious contradictions in their deep belief systems that interfered with their lives. In terms of our specific interests, spiritual possibilities, I've talked with innumerable people who consciously thought of themselves as spiritual seekers, who were often quite knowledgeable about spiritual matters but, nevertheless, had something in them holding them back, doubting, sabotaging, and invalidating their own spiritual experiences and knowledge.

To help people increase their self-knowledge in this area, I devised a belief experiment, the Western Creed exercise, to use in my occasional workshops. A belief experiment is basically a matter of consciously and temporarily believing something as best you can for a set period, while observing your emotional and bodily reactions to holding that belief.

I've taken widespread and popular materialistically based ideas (often thought of as scientific "facts") that are very current and powerful in modern culture, and put them in a form that sounds a lot like a religious creed. (In fact, I based this on the formal structure of the Nicene Creed, but note that this isn't intended as a comment on Christianity; rather it's simply making use of a form with religious overtones that's familiar to a lot of people.)

The best way to experience the Western Creed exercise is do it along with my students in an online video hosted by the Institute of Transpersonal Psychology (ITP):

http://www.westerncreed.com/Tart_ITP.html

If you can do that, I recommend that you stop reading this chapter now and go to the website. If you can't do that, you can do the written version in the remainder of this chapter, but you can probably get more of an experiential feeling for it by doing it with the online video.

If you've decided to do the written version, here we go, working with pretty much the same text as on the website.

WESTERN CREED EXERCISE

DISCLAIMER: Please note that the following exercise is a learning exercise and doesn't necessarily reflect my actual beliefs or values or those of any institution I'm connected with, nor is it intended as specific criticism of any religious or spiritual system.

WARNING: This experiential exercise was developed for use with mature spiritual seekers who deeply value truth and self-knowledge, and are willing to risk temporary or permanent challenges to their current belief systems in the course of seeking more truth. It's probably not suitable for children and those with excessive emotional and intellectual attachments to their current belief systems. It's not essential that you do this exercise.

Transpersonal psychology, still a very young and incomplete branch of knowledge, attempts, on the one hand, to take the spiritual heritage of humanity as being about something real and of enormous importance while, on the other hand, also considering all that we know about human psychology, our good and bad points. Its long-term goals include separating the real from the unreal in the spiritual area as well as discovering how psychological factors can both help and hinder the realization of the spiritual in actual life.

I was one of the founders of transpersonal psychology, and long ago I noticed that many people might consciously aim at high spiritual goals, but their progress toward realizing such goals was often seriously hindered by various psychological factors, ranging from conscious and unconscious attitudes developed by each of us in our personal lives, to general cultural attitudes and beliefs inculcated in and shared by most of us who live in the current era. In the early 1980s I designed this experiential exercise, the Western Creed, for my classes and workshops to sensitize spiritual seekers to some of the major cultural attitudes and obstacles we moderns share in our search.

When you don't know you have a semiconscious or unconscious attitude or obstacle that interferes with your search, it hinders you, and there's little you can do about it, because you tend to project the problem as being "out there." When you know that some of your beliefs and attitudes may be hindering your search, you have an opportunity to try to understand and do something about them.

The Western Creed exercise takes about twenty minutes to do. Ideally you should take part in it just as the filmed participants (students in one of my classes at ITP) in the online video do, standing at attention in front of your computer where you can see and hear the video and repeat the Western Creed exercise words aloud, according to the instructions I give there, and then sit quietly for a few minutes afterward, noting your bodily and emotional sensations and feelings. You can approximate this now by propping up this book so that you can read it while standing at attention in front of it. You might find it best to do this exercise alone or with friends who also participate rather than just watch you.

If this isn't a good time right now, it would be best to wait for the right time. The Western Creed exercise is most effective the first time you do it wholeheartedly, and it may dull with repetition.

Most people don't "enjoy" this exercise, for they see some of the contradictions in themselves, but almost all agree that they feel wiser about themselves and thus better able to continue their spiritual search.

You'll see the word "scientistic" a lot in this book. This isn't an erroneous spelling of "scientific" but, rather, a shorthand way of reminding us that beliefs in science can become psychologically rigid instead of open to experimental testing, as they always are in essential science. There's much to be said for being open and flexible about examining our own beliefs, any beliefs, testing them rather than letting them become rigid.

Your main task will be to observe your bodily and emotional reactions to doing the exercise. You needn't bother to intellectually analyze while it's going on; you can do that later, after you've observed your feelings.

You'll probably want to take some notes on your reactions, so you might get a pen or pencil and something to write on before going further.

This is an exercise in finding out what you believe. Every one of us is a philosopher, even though we don't know it. Every one of us has a set of beliefs about the way the world is, the way we are, what's a good life, and what's a bad life. In fact we have a lot of beliefs about things like that, and a lot of them, we don't even know we have. We've arrived at some of our beliefs consciously, thinking about our life experience and what we can make of it, but a lot of our beliefs have simply been imposed on us by virtue of being around at the particular times in the particular culture that we live in.

In transpersonal psychology, we're interested in spiritual and transcendent matters, and tend to think of ourselves as having spiritual belief systems of one sort or another. But we're also products of the twentieth and twenty-first centuries, where a kind of scientistic materialism is a dominant belief system that has many, many effects on us.

As a psychologist, I've become more and more convinced that the things we believe and know we believe can be intelligently used as tools, because we can see how well they work, question them if they don't work well, and think about changing them. Things that we believe that we don't know we believe, though, are like a set of chains. They just automatically affect our perceptions and thoughts, and trap us.

So one of the things that's important in any kind of psychological or personal or spiritual growth is becoming more consciously aware of what it is that you actually believe, especially if it's contradictory to what you previously thought you believed.

I often do workshops or classes for people who think of themselves as very spiritually oriented, who think they're not held back by materialistic ideas and can just move ahead into the spiritual realms with no conflict. And I can intellectually tell people that we all have certain beliefs just as a result of being part of our culture, but knowing it intellectually and knowing it more deeply at a bodily and emotional level is quite a different sort of thing.

This exercise, which I call a belief experiment, is something that I devised some years ago. A belief experiment is a process in which I ask you to believe something for a limited period, say, ten or twenty minutes. Then we do something in accordance with that belief system or further define that belief system while you believe it. But your job isn't to intellectually question the beliefs at that point; instead, it's to notice how your body and emotions feel as we go through the belief exercise. You're collecting data from this experiment. Then I usually ask people to share what some of these reactions were, because your own and others' reactions often tell you things you don't know about what you believe and disbelieve.

Now, how do you just go ahead and believe things? At first, that sounds like a ridiculous sort of idea. But, as an example, every time you go to a movie, you perform a belief exercise. You don't sit there in a movie saying, "Those aren't real images in front of me; those are just lights reflecting on a screen. I'm really just sitting here in this seat, and nothing's really happening." You believe in the movie; otherwise you don't enjoy it at all. Another example is anyone who's ever played a game like Monopoly; you have to be practiced in believing to enjoy playing it. For a short period, those little pieces of wood and paper are very important to you, and you get very excited about them.

It's the same with a belief experiment. You just "play the game," as it were, letting yourself get into it for the limited period that you have to do it.

To do this belief experiment, first ask your inner self, "Is it all right to take a chance on believing something that hasn't even been defined yet, in order to find out something about myself?"

1. Just close your eyes for a moment and ask your inner self, "Is it all right to do this?"
2. Take as much time as you need to get an answer.
3. If you get a yes, fine; open your eyes again.
4. If you get a no, bargain with your inner self a little. It's only for ten to fifteen minutes. It might be interesting. See if you get an "okay" or a "maybe" answer to that.
5. If you still get a no, you can just fake going through the motions of the belief experiment, because you can learn a lot from that also!
6. Take a few moments to get some kind of permission. (Wait for permission before reading on.)

To use some of the social conditioning we've been subjected to as an aid to making this belief experiment more alive and involving for you so that you can see things better, I'd like for you to stand up and erect, as if at attention, while continuing to hold this book. (If you're doing this in a group, it's best if all of you stand at attention in neat, orderly rows.)

Now we're going to do responsive recitation. In a group I'd read out a phrase or line from the Western Creed, and you'd then repeat it aloud. In this solitary book form, you'll silently read a phrase — a dash marks the pause between each phrase — and then repeat it out loud in a solid, formal way, as if you were pledging allegiance to your flag or reciting a creed in church.

For example — if a sentence were hyphenated like this — to illustrate the process, you'd read, "For example," pause a moment, say, "For example" out loud, pause several moments while observing your bodily and emotional feelings, then read "if a sentence were hyphenated like this" to yourself, pause a moment, read it aloud, pause several moments to observe, and so on. Note that some words are set in boldface or italics too, meaning that you should give them a little more emphasis when reciting aloud.

I've taken widespread and popular materialistically based ideas (often thought of a scientific "facts") that are very current and powerful in modern culture, and put them in a form that sounds a lot like a religious creed.

In fact, I based this on the formal structure of the Nicene Creed, but note that this isn't intended as a comment on Christianity; rather it's simply making use of a form with religious overtones that's familiar to a lot of people.

You'll read a phrase that's separated from others by dashes, pause a moment in between to silently observe yourself, and then repeat it aloud.

To further use our social conditioning to increase the intensity of the Western Creed exercise, now place your right hand over your heart, continuing to stand at attention, as if you were pledging allegiance to your country's flag. (The right hand over the heart is a specifically American version, but if you have another form from your own culture, feel free to use it.)

Don't intellectually analyze this Western Creed and your reactions as we go through it. I recognize that you may be a world-class intellect who can logically tear this Creed and exercise to bits or use a barrage of clever thoughts to shield you from the effects of what you're doing, but that's not the point: the point is to do it and observe your emotional and bodily reactions. After the belief experiment is over, you can intellectually analyze to your heart's content. For now, notice how your body feels and any emotional feelings, even if fleeting or faint.

Now we begin. Remember to pause a few seconds in between each phrase that's separated from others by dashes to note your bodily and emotional feelings.

THE WESTERN CREED

I BELIEVE — in the material universe — as the only and ultimate reality — a universe controlled by fixed physical laws — and blind chance.

I AFFIRM — that the universe has no creator — no objective purpose — and no objective meaning or destiny.

I MAINTAIN — that all ideas about God or gods — enlightened beings — prophets and saviors — or other nonphysical beings or forces — are superstitions and delusions — . Life and consciousness are totally identical to physical processes — and arose from chance interactions of blind physical forces — . Like the rest of life — my life — and my consciousness — have no objective purpose — meaning — or destiny.

I BELIEVE — that all judgments, values, and moralities — whether my own or others' — are subjective — arising solely from biological determinants — personal history — and chance — . Free will is an illusion — . Therefore, the most rational values I can personally live by — must be based on the knowledge that for me — what pleases me is good — what pains me is bad — . Those who please me or help me avoid pain — are my friends — those who pain me or keep me from my pleasure — are my enemies — . Rationality requires that friends and enemies — be used in ways that maximize my pleasure — and minimize my pain.

I AFFIRM — that churches have no real use other than social support — that there are no objective sins to commit or be forgiven for — that there is no divine retribution for sin — or reward for virtue — . Virtue for me is getting what I want — without being caught and punished by others.

I MAINTAIN — that the death of the body — is the death of the mind — . There is no afterlife — and all hope of such is nonsense.

From *The Secret Science of the Soul* (Fearless Books, 2017)

Okay, quietly sit down again, close your eyes, and take an inventory of your bodily sensations and emotional feelings. A comprehensive and sensitive inventory is what matters here. Ease or difficulty with particular parts of the creed is worth noting too. If you get sidetracked into intellectual analysis, thinking about what happened or what you just thought instead of sensing your feelings, let the thinking go for now — you can do it all you want later — and come back to observing your feelings. Taking brief notes on your reactions in a notebook or journal is a good idea, because though you may have had some insights now, they have a tendency to fade away as you get busy with ordinary life again. Read on once you feel you've adequately noted your experience.

Now let's think about the exercise. Remember that I didn't really "create" this Western Creed; I merely took beliefs that are widely held and taught over and over again in our culture, both explicitly and implicitly, and put them in a form like a religious creed to help make clearer the potential impact of these beliefs. To put it another way, if you don't like what you experienced when you did the creed, don't get mad at me; I didn't make the world this way! We can draw intellectual and practical conclusions from formal philosophies of materialism in a variety of ways, of course, but this Western Creed version is an easy way of thinking to follow for many.

Over the years, I've heard a wide variety of reports of what people have learned from doing the Western Creed. A rather small number of people, maybe 5 percent or less, report, for example, that they really enjoyed the creed, that it gave them a feeling of great relief! Since there were no moral or spiritual standards they had to live up to, they were free of the guilt of not measuring up! I suspect that at least some of these people may have been too thoroughly indoctrinated in the "You're a miserable sinner who has to try to be good but will never make it, because you're too flawed and weak, so you're going to Hell!" style of religion. Materialism, a total rejection of all spiritual ideas, would indeed seem to be a relief and an intelligent psychological defense maneuver in such cases.

The vast majority of people, though, find themselves sadder but wiser. They're often shocked to see that, while they consciously think of themselves as very spiritual people, parts of them believe much of the Western Creed, and that's pretty discouraging. Here are some typical responses from the class filmed for the online version of this belief experiment:

"I noticed that the part early on, when we heard that there's no God, made me very sad. And then, by the end, I found myself wondering, if people really believe this way, why do they stay alive?"

"I feel as if I don't even want to be in this body; it seems pointless. I'd just rather not be a part of this reality."

"I have a sunken feeling in my stomach; it feels weird there. And there was a point during the exercise when my mind refused to accept those words. I couldn't. At the beginning, I was able to repeat after you, and then at a certain point I couldn't; the words weren't going in at all."

"I feel very unmotivated. And I feel very selfish."

"I had sort of a similar experience, to the point where I started laughing at what I was saying. So actually I had a range of experiences. My body also felt the heat as somebody else reported feeling. The feelings were mixed up, and it seemed that there was a block that was almost provoking me to laugh at what you were saying. I had to concentrate harder to keep up and repeat. So there's a mix. There's kind of laughter and sadness and heat and ridiculousness — kind of funny."

"I felt that the world seemed easier, if perhaps less interesting; if there were no objective moral standard and no one could judge me, then I could do things more easily."

You may want to think about what you've observed in yourself for a few minutes. If you have Internet access, feel free to go back to the website to repeat the exercise and see what some other people's reactions were.

Are you ready to end the belief experiment, to go back to

believing whatever it was you believed before, but hopefully with a little more self-knowledge?

Assessing Your Reactions to the Western Creed Exercise

You've taken part in the Western Creed exercise. As mentioned on the website, you may return to your previous beliefs now; you're no longer "playing the game" of accepting the Western Creed as true.

Of course, you may have found that parts of you do indeed believe various aspects of the convictions expressed in the Western Creed, even if you seldom consciously acknowledge them.

Most people find this exercise temporarily depressing, for they see various ways in which they share common cultural attitudes of a materialistic dismissal of spirituality, attitudes and beliefs that interfere with their full commitment to the spiritual search they consciously value. Having some idea of what these attitudes and beliefs are, though, gives you a chance to question and change them. You might want to take some notes on what you've learned.

As previously mentioned, a few people find themselves greatly relieved after doing the Western Creed exercise. Further exploration usually reveals that they were raised in some harsh religion that left them feeling unworthy, sinful, or damned, so giving energy to the idea that all religion and spirituality are nonsense is indeed a relief! Better oblivion than eternal damnation; better meaninglessness than hopeless sin and failure. Such attitudes and beliefs also call for examination and possible change in the course of personal growth.

The Western Creed is printed on the previous pages. And you have permission to reproduce it in its entirety, which must include the copyright notice, for noncommercial purposes. That is, you can give it away, but you can't sell it. You may want to lead friends or students in the exercise the way I did, as a learning experiment. If so, be sure to allow time for people to share their reactions afterward, and to remind them at the end that they have permission to go back to their previous beliefs. Hopefully there'll be some long-term change in beliefs, though.

Note that the Western Creed exercise is an example of some of the experiential learning used at the Institute of Transpersonal Psychology to help students grasp important psychological realities at more than just a word level.

I hope the conflict between spirituality and scientism is now clear. So what can we do about it?

CHAPTER 2

How Do We Know the Spiritual Is Real?

KNOW (Old English [origin: Old English cnawan*]): (1) Recognize, admit. Recognize, perceive; identify; specifically perceive (a thing or person) as identical with something or someone already perceived or considered. (2) Distinguish; be able to distinguish (one thing) from another.* — SHORTER OXFORD ENGLISH DICTIONARY, *6th ed., s.v. "know"*

S O HERE you are, a human being with a yearning for something higher than simple material gratification, something "spiritual." Yet, modern science, the most powerful knowledge-refinement system in history, which has led to enormous power over the physical world, seems to tell you in no uncertain terms that you yearn for nothing but fantasy — superstitious, outmoded nonsense that will make you less fit to live in the "real" world.

This isn't a very comfortable position to be in. Something in us yearns for this higher thing we vaguely call "spirit," but we don't want to feel stupid or crazy. How can we clarify, expand, and refine our knowledge (that's basically what science is about) in a way that allows us to see how much of a reality basis we have for our spirituality, instead of being stuck in this dilemma?

I saw two common responses to this science-versus-spirit conflict as I was growing up. People had spiritual impulses to various degrees, usually expressed through the religions they were brought up in as children. As young children, they generally accepted their religions with few questions, but then conflict would begin as they began thinking for themselves and came in contact with the scientific, materialistic view of the world that invalidated their beliefs.

Such conflict is necessary and healthy in many ways, of course, because we need to start thinking for ourselves as we grow up. But it can certainly be distressing.

One major "solution" to the uncomfortable feeling of conflict was to "convert" to materialism. The reaction was kind of like this: "Right, my religion is an old superstition; science has proven that there's nothing in the world but matter and physical energy, so I'd better try to live as happy a life as possible within that world — and not think about death or such things as God or purpose or meaning." Everything I've learned in life, as a human being generally and as a transpersonal psychologist particularly, though, has shown me that while this "solution" usually diminished or eliminated conflictual suffering at a conscious level, people often paid a high price in becoming converted to a rigid materialism. They repressed some roots of deep meaning and satisfaction in life, the spiritual side of their humanity.

The second major "solution" I observed was one of psychological isolation or compartmentalization. Religion and spirituality were thought about and perhaps acted upon for a limited time, usually on one special day of the week, and the rest of life was spent in pursuing various material goals, but the two aspects of life were otherwise kept as mentally isolated as possible from one another.

If you don't consciously see that you have competing, clashing views of something, it won't feel as if you have a conflict. But, at a deeper, psychological level, your psyche is not whole when you do this; the conflict will exact a price from you on less-conscious levels.

I was lucky when I went through this conflict in my teens. I discovered the literature of scientific parapsychology (as it was then and is still called) and the older literature of its originating field, psychical research (a term still in use and with wider implications but not as widely known in the United States as parapsychology), and found that I wasn't the first to experience this kind of conflict between science and religion. Many intelligent people in the nineteenth and early twentieth centuries had struggled with this issue as science became more powerful and religion typically gave way to science. Early presidents of the London-based Society for Psychical Research included such luminaries as philosopher Henry Sidgwick, philosopher and later Prime Minister of Great Britain Arthur Balfour, psychologist William James, physicist Sir William Crookes, philosopher F. W. H. Myers, physicist Sir Oliver Lodge, physicist Sir William Barrett, physiologist Charles Richet, mathematician Eleanor Sidgwick, philosopher Henri Bergson, psychologist William McDougall, psychologist Robert Thouless, and psychologist Gardner Murphy.

Science is undoubtedly right about so many things, they reasoned. Religion is indeed full of factually false ideas about the physical world and some beliefs that are psychologically unhealthy, if not downright crazy. Yet our ethics and morality, our highest values, come from religion. Won't we be on the same level as the savage beasts, "red in tooth and claw," if we completely reject religion? And is everything in religion factually false? This was a real worry: there has never been a lack of historical and contemporary evidence of just how selfish and bestial people can be, and science has all too often been applied to vastly increase human suffering, as well as to alleviate it. Materialistic science gives no transcendent values at all to live by, yet it was replacing religion, the major source of values — not that formal religion guarantees that people will be kinder and more moral, of course; many horrors have been committed in the name of religion, but it at least usually provides a framework favoring the moral life.

I was lucky to have read writings on psychic research while I myself was in conflict, because some of these early researchers had a radical idea, which was just what I needed. Scientific method — as separated from the particular theories and findings accumulating from applications of the method at any particular time — had been used very successfully in the physical sciences to increase our knowledge of the world and our consequent ability to improve it. It had enabled us to reject many historical ideas about the world that were shown to be useless or false, and replace them with understandings that worked much better. The applications of the germ theory of disease, for instance, resulted in much better control over deadly epidemics than ringing bells to frighten away evil spirits. Could the same thing be done with religion? By applying essential scientific method to the phenomena of religion and spirituality, could we separate the wheat from the chaff — any real and important essence of spirituality from the superstitions and distortions of the ages? Could we thus create a refined spirituality and religion that would continue to give us a basis for human values, while leaving the superstitions, outmoded ideas, and psychopathologies behind?

By the time I was reading material on psychic research and parapsychology, in the early 1950s, some of this application of essential scientific method, without a philosophical or political commitment that all knowledge must be reduced to only material knowledge, had been done, and a certain reality to spiritual phenomena had been, to my then-teenage mind (and my current, more mature, adult mind), clearly demonstrated.

By "demonstrated," I mean that by the formal, rational rules of science, which have worked so well in understanding the physical world, human beings occasionally have experiences and show certain behaviors that cannot be reduced to materialistic explanations and that look like fundamental aspects of a spiritual nature.

So you can take a basically scientific stance toward life and still legitimately claim that, using rigorous kinds of scientific procedures, the human mind shows properties that underlie what we think of as spiritual. That's the underlying theme of this book. I took up as my life's work the challenge of applying science to refine our knowledge of the spiritual, dealing with my personal conflict by doing something practical about resolving this conflict while helping (I believed) others. It's been a most interesting and satisfying life, especially because my understanding of what "spiritual" is all about has increased and reflected back into my science and living.

What do I mean by words like "spirit" and "spiritual"? I don't think they can be precisely defined as material things can be (for example, refrigerators), but by "spiritual" I refer to a realm of values, experiences, realities, and insights that goes beyond the ordinary material world. This is still rather general, but what I mean will become clearer as we go along.

We'll take a look at just what this essential scientific method is, because it's very important for our personal peace of mind to stop confusing it, as most people (including many scientists) do, with what's commonly called science but is actually scientism. Scientism has uselessly hurt enormous numbers of people, and we must distinguish scientism from science if we want any hope of science and spirituality helping each other.

We'll also take a quick look, in a following chapter, at some of the many factors that keep us from getting more accurate understandings of self and reality, the things Abraham Maslow (1908–1970), the psychologist who was the main founder of both humanistic and transpersonal psychologies, called pathologies of cognition. These are pathologies that not only form a basis for the prejudiced scientistic rejection of the spiritual, but also operate as much in everyday life and spiritual life as they do in science, so we should be alert for them.

Then we'll consider an example in the next chapter of likely psychic functioning in everyday life, a striking experience of mine, the kind of event that stimulated scientific investigation into this area in the first place. The chapters after that will survey the basic findings of psychical research and parapsychology relevant to a basic understanding of the spiritual. This will help us understand why a spiritual life and spiritual growth can be about something real, not just an appealing but imaginary idea. We'll have to touch on most of this lightly in the small space of this book, but for readers who want to go more deeply and technically into the evidence and its implications, I can recommend my book, *Body Mind Spirit: Exploring the Parapsychology of Spirituality* (Hampton

Roads Publishing, 1997), which includes the collaboration of some bright colleagues in considering this issue, as well as the books on contemporary parapsychological research mentioned in appendix 1 and the various Web resources mentioned in appendix 2.

First, let's get clear on what actual, essential science is, as opposed to its all-too-common degeneration, scientism.

Ways of Knowing

Many of us have been hurt by what we believe is science, by the power of beliefs like those expressed in the Western Creed or in the earlier Russell quote, a widespread social putdown that has invalidated our spiritual hopes and dreams and told us we're fools. We've been hurt not only in the sense of feeling like fools but also in possibly feeling on a deeper level that we've missed out on what's really important, missed out on the higher things of life, or in experiencing neurotic suffering as the spiritually affirming and materialistically denying parts of our minds struggle. Consequently, there's a lot of understandable antiscience feeling and anti-intellectualism in our times. Many people thus tend to think that science is the enemy! But it's not the essential method of science that has hurt us; rather, it's scientism, a materialistic and arrogantly expressed philosophy of life that pretends to be the same as essential science but isn't. Until we learn to distinguish essential science from scientism, we remain vulnerable to false invalidation, which seems to have the full power and prestige of science behind it but is really an arbitrary, philosophical opinion. And we lose the ability to constructively apply essential science to increase our understanding of and effectiveness with spirituality.

To see what essential science is, it helps to start with a look at traditional methods of gaining knowledge about anything. I've long thought of them as falling in four main categories: the ways of experience, authority, reason, and revelation. These overlap in practice, of course, but it's useful to distinguish them.

The Way of Experience: The way of experience, of collecting the facts, is a matter of learning from your direct experience of something. What was it like, what happened when you tried various things, and what did you learn from it? If I want to understand and master, say, paddling a canoe, the way of experience is to get in one with a paddle, start paddling, try various styles of using the paddle, see what happens, and learn from the experience.

This is an excellent approach to learning, but as we all know, experience per se doesn't necessarily mean you learn much from it. Indeed, we all know friends (and perhaps have even had personal experience) who have had much experience with something but, sadly, haven't learned much at all. You may flail about a lot with your paddle, but your canoe doesn't go very far. I know: I played with paddling a canoe this way as a child sent to summer camp, and my canoe moved but not very well.

The Way of Authority: The way of authority is to ask for knowledge about what puzzles you from someone who's supposed to be an authority on the subject. For our example, I find an experienced canoeist and ask her, "How should I paddle a canoe?" She gives me instructions to apply next time I'm on the water. When I went on an extended canoe trip with the Explorer Scouts years later, for example, I got expert instruction on paddling, and moved a lot farther much more easily for the effort I put in.

As with the way of experience, consulting authorities can often be an excellent and efficient way of learning, getting the best ideas right away from the experts instead of floundering about, making our own mistakes over and over. But as we all too sadly know, authorities can be wrong or biased, and even lie to us. We've all experienced so much disappointment with authorities that the point needs no illustration!

The Way of Reason is to think things through logically: Here's my situation, with factors A, B, and C; if I do X to A, then I logically expect N will happen, so if I combine, and so on. A canoe is a long, slender physical object floating on the water (factor A); if I put my paddle (factor B) into the water on the right side of the canoe and pull it toward me, then ..., but if I push the paddle away from me, then...

As with experience and authority, logical reasoning can be an excellent aid to understanding in many situations, but often it doesn't work well in reality. A classic example I learned in college were the logical, mathematical calculations that showed that a steamship couldn't cross the Atlantic Ocean, because the weight of the coal required would sink the ship before it left port! A second was that one of the classical theories of aeronautics, useful in many ways for designing airplanes, logically showed that bumblebees couldn't fly! They didn't have enough wing area for their mass. Fortunately for bumblebees, they didn't understand the theory. A third occurred while I was in graduate school, getting ready to research dreams. I read a book by a prominent philosopher that showed, through sophisticated reasoning, that there were no such things as dreams. I had nightmares about it that night and then went on to do my dream research quite successfully. It was a good lesson to me on how we can tie our own minds in knots.

These three methods of knowing have been widely acknowledged for both their advantages and disadvantages for a long time, but I generally add a fourth way that's not always formally recognized.

The Way of Revelation or Noetic Knowing: This way of knowing involves getting into some altered state of consciousness (ASC) in which a new idea or understanding presents itself to you complete, as a revelation or a different kind of knowledge — noetic knowledge, noesis — rather than something you consciously work out step by step from experience, authority, or reason in your ordinary state. Richard Maurice Bucke's experience in the introduction was an ASC revelation to him. Some obvious ASCs in which this has happened to people are dreams, reveries, drug-induced states, and meditation states. The revelatory or noetic quality is that the understanding is experienced with suddenness, great force, clarity, and convincingness. It's not like an ordinary idea where you think,

"This seems plausible; let me think about it some more, run some variations on it, and check it out against the facts"; it's much more like "This is the truth!" If the ASC experience includes feelings of contact with the spiritual realm, this further adds to the convincingness: "God or the universe has told me that this is true!"

While a study of the history of science shows that many brilliant ideas came to people in some sort of altered state — dreams, for example, or drug-induced states — the way of revelation is seldom officially acknowledged as a creative method in formal science. The social stereotype of scientists as strictly rational is strongly identified with, so even altered-state revelations are frequently described, in retrospect, as if they were logical thinking.

In retrospect, some revealed ideas have worked out in ordinary reality, and the people who've had them are seen as creative geniuses. Some people, scientists and artists, for example, thus deliberately cultivate ASCs in the hope of receiving creative ideas. While most dramatic when they come suddenly, some "revelations" may gradually be learned in a repeated ASC. Many revealed ideas, though, turn out to either have no connection to a reality we can check them in, like physical reality, or are just plain wrong. The intellectual and emotional feeling, "This is true!" while intensely satisfying, is no guarantee that an idea is useful or true. Was Bucke's Cosmic Consciousness revelation "the truth" because it felt that way to him, because it was the deepest, most powerful feeling in his life? We'll let that question stay open for now.

When I was a child, for example, I learned to fly in my dreams. At first I had to dream of being in little airplanes, and then I learned to run and flap my arms to take off without the little airplanes. Finally, I learned to create a certain mental attitude so that I could just float up, and I got pretty good at that. I had deliberately cultivated a gradual learning in my dreams, a small revelation, a noetic knowledge of how to fly. But I was always disappointed when I woke up. I would stand in the middle of my bedroom floor and try to create that mental flying attitude, and it never worked!

This was an understanding or revelation that worked in dreams but just didn't transfer to ordinary, physical life. Was it "false" to begin with, just an illogical idea in my dreams? Or was it what I've called "state-specific knowledge" (Tart 1972, 1998a), true in the dream ASC but not in the ordinary state?

All of these four ways of understanding are useful, but any one of them can become a kind of cognitive shortcoming or pathology when it becomes an exclusive way of approaching reality. When you believe some authority even though the person's statements contradict experience or reason, for example, or insist that your reasoning is correct when it leads to predictions of things in life that don't work out, you aren't using your full abilities and are misusing what you do have.

Essential scientific method — which is really refined common sense — is a way of combining these various approaches to understanding so that their weaknesses tend to cancel each other out, but their strengths tend to add up.

Essential Science, Essential Common Sense

Modern science is generally seen as having been created in rebellion against too much power vested in the way of authority. The Roman Catholic Church was the most powerful institution in the West. It had its specifically religious doctrines that weren't to be questioned — to do so was heresy and could cost you your life — and its not-so-specifically religious ideas about the way the world worked, based on approved ancient authorities, that supported its core religious beliefs. So if you wanted to understand something about physical reality, for example, you read Aristotle. If you disagreed with an approved authority like Aristotle, you could be in trouble.

The ways of authority and reason well established, for example, that heavier bodies fell faster than lighter bodies. Science was a rebellion against oppressive authority, because it asked, "Can't we actually look at some falling bodies and see if heavy ones actually fall faster than light ones?" What I think of as the most essential aspect of science (as opposed to scientism) is this insistence on direct experience — on observation, data, and facts — as having the ultimate priority in understanding, even though supplemented and interpreted by reason.

The following figure diagrams my understanding of what the essential scientific process — and good common sense! — is all about. It's a way of starting from relatively poor knowledge of the facts about something and crude or misleading understandings as to why things relate (theory), and gradually getting more and more accurate facts and more and more accurate and useful understandings, or theories, about why the facts are as they are.

Figure 2.1 Basic Scientific Method

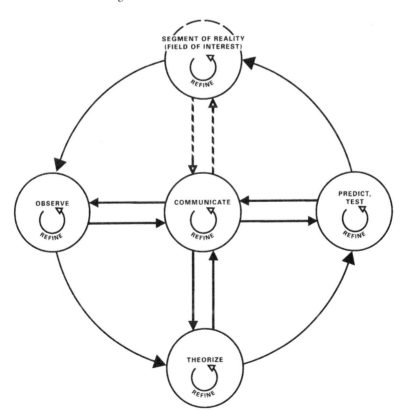

We commence with some area of reality of interest to us and begin by observing what happens there. This is application of the way of experience. The worst way to do it is to take a quick look and arrogantly assume we've now got all the information we need. To make it essential science or intelligent common sense, we practice being humble about our ability to observe, though, recognizing that we may be biased or lazy, or just not fast enough, smart enough, or sensitive enough to accurately observe some things. So we commit to not only getting all the facts that we can but also refining our methods for observing.

As an example, let's say we've heard that sometimes diseases are cured by a certain holy woman praying over an ill person, diseases we wouldn't expect people to recover from readily. Is prayer, or the god being prayed to, what's really effective in causing these reported cures, or might it be something else? Maybe some ill people just get better anyway, but we only hear about the ones who were prayed for. Or maybe these are just rumors; they didn't really happen. Or perhaps there's some other explanation.

So we embark on an observation program to start refining our knowledge. This could include (1) reading previously published accounts of cures attributed to prayer, (2) tracking down stories of such cures and interviewing the participants (healers and patients) to try to get a more detailed set of facts about what actually happened, (3) running an experiment in which we pray for some patients in a hospital and not others, (4) finding people with reputations as successful prayer healers and having them pray for some patients (the experimental group) and not others (the control group), or (5) any combination of the previously listed methods. And we'll have various outcome measures, such as percentage of patients who died within a certain time or length of hospital stay before release.

If we're humble enough to not automatically assume that we're perfect observers and fact gatherers, we would quickly discover that things are more complicated than we expected. Many, perhaps all, healers, for example, might pray for their patients, but they do a lot of other things besides that. Some spend a lot of time caring for the patient in conventional ways: some use "laying on of hands" with prayer, and others don't; some work cooperatively with medical personnel, while others tell their patients to refuse conventional medical treatment. Some healers pray silently or whisper in the patients' ears (who knows what they think and say?), while others dramatically pray aloud. A lot's going on!

So we've collected some data about prayer and healing, and know more than when we started. But we're not really that interested in the data, the facts in and of themselves; we're more interested in what the data means, in what the data suggests about the less-obvious forces and factors that control reality. We want knowledge that is general, and applies beyond our immediate situation in which we collected facts. We want to involve the way of reason, but reason based on facts, not just beliefs and assumptions. If we'd measured the breaking strength of various-sized wooden beams, for example, it's not that we cared about those particular beams, it's that we want to know how to design houses that wouldn't collapse, because we have general knowledge, accurate theories that predict how new beams of various sizes will stand up to stress. In general we want to know how the world works so that we can deal with new situations successfully.

In our prayer-study example, we now have some observations, data about healing prayer and outcome, but while that's a good start, it's going to be hard to discover general principles and theories about prayer and healing because there's so much variation in our data, so many factors that might affect it. Some of the stories we collected, for instance, seem to be (we don't know for sure) accurate accounts from reliable witnesses, but some make us suspicious that the witnesses and reporters weren't very attentive or might've had their perceptions distorted in the service of some belief system, such as giving credit to their particular religions as being responsible for successful healings. How do you tell who are the reliable observers and who aren't? How do you separate the facts, the data, from interpretations that are reported as if they were the data?

And how about the other things healers do besides pray? Isn't the laying on of hands, for instance, a powerful psychological intervention? Most of us find touch very personal. When a healer touches us, does the kindness conveyed by the touch facilitate the healing, rather than the prayer? Might the prayer for healing just be a psychological excuse for touching, which does the real healing? And the healers who pray loudly and dramatically — might this have a motivational effect on the hospital staff, who then unknowingly give the patient prayed for in this way more care than other patients get, promoting more healing through conventional medical treatments?

If you had plenty of time and resources, you might be able to let all these factors besides prayer run through all their natural variations and just try to analyze healing outcomes separately for various combinations of factors. But we seldom have unlimited time and resources, so we may strategically decide to simplify our observational and experimental situation to get a clearer look at some of the possibilities, let's say, one we could call factor A. If you get a clearer look at what factor A does, then you can add that into the big picture you finally get after you've gotten a clearer look at factor B, factor C, and so on. It's a classical strategy that reasons that if the situation is too complex to readily follow, reduce it down to simpler components that you can understand and then see if you can put together your better understandings of the simpler components to get a better overall understanding. This kind of reductionism can be tricky, of course, because things may not add up in a simple, linear way, but it's useful in many instances. (Indeed, overattachment to reductionistic explanations is one of the pathologies of cognition Maslow mentions; we'll come to that in the next chapter.)

So let's say you simplify your prayer-and-healing experiment by studying only the presence or absence of prayer for a group of patients versus controls, while eliminating things like touch, social interaction, and possible effects on the medical staff from dramatic prayer. You can have your healer do distant prayer, that is, the healer never actually meets the patients or is in the same room as them or the hospital staff but is simply told to, say, pray ten minutes for each of twenty patients whose names are provided. To avoid observational biases, neither the healer nor the medical staff knows who the experimental, prayed-for, patients are, nor who the control, unprayed-for, patients are. Then you specify, in advance, some particular measure of healing outcome, say, length of stay in the hospital, and look at the discharge records at the end of the study, and you have an objective way (usually by doing a statistical analysis) to see if the prayed-for patients had significantly shorter hospital stays than the unprayed-for patients. If they did, you've observed a relationship between "praying" (without specifying exactly how the praying was done) and healing outcome, and your first-level theory, your understanding, is that prayer is effective in speeding up healing. Further, since you know your healers had a variety of beliefs and practices, you might elaborate your theory that it's the intention to heal that brings about results rather than the specifics of the healers' belief systems and practices. Later, of course, you'd want to do studies to see if it's just intention and not specific healing or praying practices that are effective.

And, yes, these kinds of healing studies have often been significantly successful. We'll look at that in chapter 10.

The Happiness of Discovery

It's very satisfying, both intellectually and emotionally, to discover a relationship like this, to feel that we have a new, better understanding of some aspect of reality. We had a puzzle, scattered data that we weren't sure meant anything, and found a pattern and solved the puzzle; it fits!

At an ordinary, commonsense level, the puzzle-solving process, the reasoning, often stops here with this feeling of satisfaction. "I'm smart, I understand, and the job is finished!" Implicitly, you may realize that if you don't keep thinking about it, you can hold on to this feeling of being smart. Unfortunately (and also quite fortunately), a major function of the human mind is fitting patterns to data, and it feels good when that happens, but the fact that your theory makes you feel good and seems logically correct doesn't necessarily mean that this is indeed the way the world works.

This is where essential science and intelligent common sense require a new step, a way of disciplining your mind. You must test your reasoning, your theory, your explanation in new situations. The fit between your reasoning and your data in the original experiment could have been accidental, because you've mistakenly imagined or rationalized a relationship rather than reasoned out the true laws governing things. I've often stated this as the Law of Universal Retrospective Rationalization: in retrospect, we clever humans can always find a seemingly plausible reason why things happened the way they did; we're very, very smart pattern makers.

Whether or not this reason has anything to do with reality can only be determined by new application of the reasoning, of the theory, in differing situations. This is formally represented in figure 2.1 by the test and prediction process. You work the inherent logic of your theory and make predictions about new situations, and then go out and actually test those predictions. If the predictions turn out to be accurate, so far, so good for your theory!

For example, let's say your theories about the strength of beams predict that two-inch-by-six-inch beams of eight feet in length can safely bear loads of five hundred pounds, and some new two-by-sixes do indeed carry such loads without breaking*. But if your theory makes predictions that don't work, if it says given A, B, and C, you'll observe D, but you set up A, B, and C and observe E instead, too bad for your theory. It doesn't matter what your feeling about its deep truthfulness is or its apparent logicality, or whether it fits with the latest fashions in science and reason, or feels true in your heart. If it doesn't correctly predict what will happen in new areas, it's wrong. Perhaps it can be modified to work better, or perhaps it will just have to be discarded, and a whole new theory, a new way of understanding, devised. And that new theory will be subject to test also. If some of your two-by-six-inch beams crack under a five-hundred-pound load, something's wrong with your theory about the strength of wooden beams. (I'm just making these numbers up for illustrative purposes; don't build anything based on them!)

This is the discipline and strictness of essential science and common sense: you may love and be attached to the concepts, theories, and ideas you've created, but you have to keep coming back to the facts, the data. Data's always primary!

Look back at figure 2.1, which diagrams the whole process of essential science. Ignoring the middle process and circle with its information-flow arrows for a moment, we can now see how knowledge refinement takes place. We start with some area of reality that interests us and collect data about it. This leads us to an initial theory about why things happen the way they do. You don't rest (at least not for too long) in this feeling of satisfaction though; you work the logic of your theory and make predictions about new situations, related to but different from the situations where you initially obtained your data, go out and test the predictions of your theory against reality, and observe how well they do or don't work. Practicing intelligent humility, we work at improving all of these processes: how can I observe the facts more clearly and accurately? How can I be sure my reasoning is correct? Am I making the correct predictions from my theory?

If your predictions work out well, you might refine your theory to make it even more accurate and widely applicable. If they work out only moderately well — they're in the ballpark, perhaps, but not really accurate — perhaps you can modify your theory. If they work out very poorly, it's time to consider a whole new theory. The cycle of information and activity flows counterclockwise around this outer circle. You start from crude observations and theories, continually refine and replace them as new data comes in, and move toward more and more accurate observations of the facts and more and more comprehensive and accurate theories that predict how the world works.

This process can be practiced by a solitary investigator and can lead to major advances in understanding. But any one of us, while perhaps brilliant in many ways, is also biased and inadequate in various ways. You may simply not notice certain kinds of things, which is a mental color blindness of sorts. Your knowledge refinement can only go so far under such circumstances.

This is where the social nature of knowledge refinement, of essential science and common sense, come in. This is the central communication process in figure 2.1. You discipline yourself to have full and honest communication about each step of the process with peers, people who are also knowledgeable about and interested in the same areas that you are. You tell them exactly what you observed under what conditions, you share the steps of the reasoning that led to your theory and its logical structure, and you reveal what predictions your theory makes and how well these predictions are or aren't supported by new observations of data. As a reward for your sharing, your peers' observational and reasoning abilities supplement and extend your own. Yes, they may be biased in some ways also, but it's unlikely that (in the long run) they'll all have exactly the same biases you do, so some will see things you might miss.

I stress the need for complete honesty and integrity in the communication process. If a researcher lies about observations, for example, the whole process breaks down, and other researchers waste their time following false leads. Since scientists are human, there are, of course, occasional ones who lie about their data. They may be trying to please a superior by apparently getting expected results, or hoping to advance their own careers with apparent discoveries, even though these "discoveries" will fade later, when others can't replicate them. When deliberate lies are caught, though, the scientist is usually drummed out of the field. This is especially true in parapsychology, apparently more so than in conventional fields of science. I can remember a few instances in my career when someone was caught creating fraudulent data. This was widely reported to the active researchers in parapsychology, usually in the field's journals, and not only was the work in which the fraud occurred discredited, but all the researchers' previous work, unless independently replicated by others, was considered suspect.

Given full, accurate, and honest communication, your peers can then communicate things like, "I saw the same things you did but measured more precisely; here are better values," "Here's some data I collected with a different aim but that's quite relevant to what you're working on," "I didn't see what you said you saw; did you specify all the necessary conditions for seeing it?" "In step 7 of your theory, you have a calculation error," "Your theory could be joined to such-and-such theory and become more powerful," "It's not clear how that particular prediction really follows from the logic of your theory," or "I derived this new prediction from your theory and tested it, and it works."

The social, interactive aspects of science, then, make it much more powerful and, in the long run, self-correcting of errors. We start out with crude and distorted observations of the way things are, with rough and, often, quite wrong ideas, theories about why they're that way, but gradually we learn to observe more clearly and precisely, and our concepts and theories about why they're that way cover more and more of our observations accurately.

The "long run," though, can sometimes be very long — dozens or hundreds of years — when implicit, deep-seated attitudes affect the thinking and work of most scientists, as they often do. I've oversimplified the process of human beings actually practicing science, of course, but the process I've described is the ideal model of essential science. Let's look now at a more specific obstacle to knowing, resistance to knowing, especially with respect to the dominant philosophy of materialism.

CHAPTER 3

Ways of Not Knowing:
Distortions of Science and Intelligence

INTELLIGENCE (Late Middle English [origin: Old French and Modern French from Latin "intelligentia," formed as "intelligent"]): The faculty of understanding; intellect.
— SHORTER OXFORD ENGLISH DICTIONARY, *6th ed., s.v. "intelligence"*

I'VE FOCUSED on essential science as a formal system for gaining and refining knowledge, and scientism as a degeneration of essential science that harms many people by irrationally dismissing and pathologizing all aspects of the spiritual perspective. (Scientism hinders progress in all areas of science, of course, inhibiting new ways of thinking, but in this book we focus on its effects on our possible spiritual nature.) Real people, with all of their good and bad qualities, and individual differences, use systems, philosophies, and knowledge tools. I have no doubt that there are some materialistic practitioners of scientism, for example, who are kind, generous people who wish the best for others, just as there are practitioners of essential science or of various spiritual systems who are, for whatever reasons, mean spirited and derive some kind of pleasure from belittling and dismissing other people. So while we focus on these formal philosophies and systems of materialism and spiritual views, we have to remember that there are always important differences in the way real people use them.

Your motivations, personality, and other psychological factors interact with the formal characteristics of the knowledge system.

In terms of establishing how we would discover and refine knowledge about the spiritual, as well as progress in general, we'll take a brief look at some of the ways people use knowledge tools to actually avoid learning new things or getting better understandings of old things. If you sometimes recognize yourself in these descriptions, as I too often recognize myself — well, better to be embarrassed and learn than to remain ignorant!

> "...it is tempting, if the only tool you have is a hammer, to treat everything as if it were a nail" (Maslow 1966, 15–16).

Abraham Maslow, a pioneering psychologist who was the primary founder of both humanistic and transpersonal psychology, published a brilliant little book back in 1966, *The Psychology of Science: A Reconnaissance*. He focused on science since it was and remains prestigious and a highly influential way of knowing, but his insights into the psychology of knowing and not knowing — what real people may actually do when they try to expand their knowledge, as opposed to what they say they do — are vitally applicable to ordinary, religious, and spiritual life. His insights are a psychology of scientism, or just about any "ism."

I often sum up his insights in this way: Used correctly, science can be an open-ended, error-correcting, personal-growth system of great power. Used incorrectly and inappropriately, science can be one of the best and most prestigious neurotic defense mechanisms available. As Maslow (1966, 33) beautifully put it: "Science, then, can be a defense. It can be primarily a safety philosophy, a security system, a complicated way of avoiding anxiety and upsetting problems. In the extreme instance it can be a way of avoiding life, a kind of self-cloistering. It can become in the hands of some people, at least, a social institution with primarily defensive, conserving functions, ordering and stabilizing rather than discovering and renewing."

The same is true, in my experience, for spiritual systems. They can be open-ended, error-correcting growth systems, opening to new, vital knowledge and compassion for self and others, or they can be used as neurotic defense mechanisms, protecting users from real spiritual growth while allowing them to feel superior to ordinary people, and "spiritual" at the same time.

So what are these pathologies of cognition, both intellectual and emotional, that Maslow identified in *The Psychology of Science*? There are twenty-one of them, and I'll summarize them in a table later, but let's look at them more thoroughly now.

Pathologies of Knowing and Learning

A compulsive need for certainty is the first pathology. Many psychological studies have found that a tolerance for ambiguity — an ability to admit "I don't know" or "I'm confused by this" — is a sign of psychological maturity.

Premature generalization is one of the consequences of an excessive need for certainty. Your mind forces actual instances of life into general categories that eliminate much of life's richness and subtler differences, while giving you the impression that you know so much.

Hanging onto a generalization in spite of new information that contradicts it is something people may desperately and stubbornly do for the kinds of reasons just stated. You attach too much to what makes sense, what makes you feel good, what has worked before. Remember our discussion of essential science: theory is always subject to change if new data doesn't fit. When human experience doesn't fit into scientistic materialism, for instance, there's often a specious generalization invoked to make such potentially disturbing information go away. A common method is to invoke human fallibility: people are misled, superstitious, crazy, liars, or deluded, so you can stop paying attention to anything that doesn't fit your idea of the way the world works.

Denial of ignorance is another major obstacle to knowledge.

Because we all want to look good, of course, to ourselves and others, we're unable to say, "I don't know" or "I was wrong about that." Personally I've found that the sooner I can admit, at least to myself if not to others, that I don't understand something, the sooner I stop digging myself deeper into a messy mixture of ignorance and deluded pride about what I do know.

The need to appear decisive, certain, confident is often what covers such denial of doubt, confusion, or puzzlement. We're talking about an inability to be humble.

It's funny, here, I don't think of myself as a particularly spiritual person, and yet I sometimes think that I have, in my role as a "scientist," a great advantage over people recognized as "spiritual teachers." I can say I don't know something, whereas our social and personal expectations put those designated as spiritual teachers under enormous pressure to (pretend to) know everything. Various spiritual systems all make claims of knowing everything that's really important. (When was the last time you came in contact with a religion that said, "We have a few aspects of the truth but a lot to learn, so we may be wrong about some things"?) Add to this the need for teachers, as representatives of their spiritual traditions, to uphold their systems, and these folks are under enormous pressure to feel as if and act as if they always know whatever's required.

An inflexible, neurotic need to be tough is another expression of this. The person needs to be powerful, fearless, strong, and severe. That's the kind of person, the kind of scientist or spiritual teacher, we respect, isn't it? But these image investments, personas, are what are called counterphobic mechanisms by psychotherapists; they're defenses against fear and ignorance. As Maslow (1966, 27) put it, "Among scientists the legitimate wish to be 'hard nosed' or tough minded or rigorous may be pathologized into being 'merely hard nosed' or exclusively tough minded, or of finding it impossible not to be rigorous. There may develop an inability to be gentle, surrendering, noncontrolling, patient, receptive even when the circumstances clearly call for it as prerequisite to better knowing, e.g., as in psychotherapy."

A lack of balance between our masculine and feminine sides is another major obstacle to growing in knowledge. Science, religion, and most spirituality have been socially and historically shaped mainly by men, often with active suppression of women and the characteristics we usually consider feminine. Balance, full openness to knowledge, calls for the ability to be not only active, dominant, masterful, controlling, "in charge," and "masculine," but also noncontrolling, noninterfering, tolerant, receptive, and "feminine." Knowing which stance is appropriate for a given task is important, or, if you don't know what's best, being willing to experiment with different stances to see what each yields.

Rationalization is another major obstacle to knowing. The brain's emotional circuits often react and form a judgment before the more intellectual parts have even gotten the message that something's happening, something's being perceived. It's as if a controlling part of our minds said, "I don't like that fellow, and I'm going to find a good, logical-seeming reason why." Our enormous skill at rationalization, our ability to create an apparently logical connection between almost anything, regardless of whether that connection exists in reality, is why I stressed that in essential science we can't stop at the theory stage, feeling good because our explanations make so much sense; we've got to go on and make predictions, and see how our theories account for new input.

Intolerance of ambiguity, an inability to be comfortable with the vague and mysterious, is a strong personality trait of some people, despite that learning new things can often take a long time. So, to get more comfortable, their minds generalize or rationalize too soon or too broadly, or oversimplify by ignoring parts of reality.

Social factors biasing the search for knowledge should never be underestimated, of course. This pathology can manifest as the need to conform, to win approval, to be a member of the in-group. At an ordinary level, it feels a lot better to be an accepted member of a high-prestige group known as "scientists" or, in a much smaller subset of the population, "spiritual seekers" than to be a "crackpot" or a "weirdo."

I've struggled with such social factors throughout my career. On the one hand, I've taken pride in the model of Gautama Buddha, expressed in me in an attitude of "I, Charles T. Tart, on my own, am going to sit down under this tree and meditate or think until I have figured out everything important about the world! No mindless conformity for me!" (I'm not grandiosely claiming that the Buddha was like me, but instead I'm talking about the way we tend to perceive him as a solitary hero conquering the world of illusion.)

On the other hand, I've learned, often after considerable struggle, that I'm not only actually a very social creature and strongly influenced by the beliefs and attitudes of those around me, I need other people; social life is woven into the fabric of my being. Trying to accurately see where I am on the seesaw between these forces and ideals is important work for me, as I do want to get at the truth insofar as I can.

Grandiosity, megalomania, arrogance, egotism, and paranoid tendencies are among the faults that serve as additional human obstacles to refining knowledge. Obstacles that these factors are, the situation is often even more complicated by the deeper psychological factors that they might be covering up, like feelings of worthlessness.

Pathological humility, what Maslow calls a "fear of paranoia," is another extreme that people exhibit. For various reasons, conscious or unconscious, we can undervalue ourselves and thus try to evade our own growth as a defense; for example, "How can I, a mere everyday person, be seriously interested in spirituality and the paranormal when the real authorities, the scientists, have dismissed it all as nonsense?"

Overrespect for authority, for the prestigious institution, for the great man, and the need to mirror his opinion to (in your mind) keep his love is another pathology. These authorities can be troublesome! Maslow (1966, 28) sees this as "Becoming only a disciple, a loyal follower, ultimately a stooge, unable to be independent, unable to affirm himself."

Underrespect for authority is, of course, another extreme, and it often manifests as a compulsive need to fight authority. Then you're unable to learn from your elders or teachers. The way of authority, as discussed earlier, can be quite misleading if practiced in isolation from the other ways or by being influenced by authorities who happen to be wrong about some things, but it's very useful as part of the balanced process of essential science.

Overrespect for the intellectual powers of the mind also is another pathology, one where you have a need to be always and only rational, sensible, and logical. Bucke, in his description of his Cosmic Consciousness experience, showed a sensible respect for the intellectual in, for example, describing his experience in the third person because he felt it helped him be more accurate, but he certainly didn't make us feel as if intellectuality and rationality were the main points of Cosmic Consciousness or even the most important aspects.

Intellectualization is very tricky in general. Our ability to step back from the immediacy of experience, emotion, and bodily agitation to take a broader, more logical view of a situation is one of the greatest powers of the human mind. But considering it as always being the "highest" ability, using it (or, too often, being used by it) compulsively in all situations for all knowledge seeking, or both is maladaptive.

A particular style of psychopathology that psychotherapists often see used, for example, is an **automatic or compulsive (or both) transforming of the emotional or the bodily into the (apparently) rational**, "…perceiving only the intellectual aspect of complex situations, being satisfied with naming rather than experiencing, etc. This is a common shortcoming of professional intellectuals, who tend to be blinder to the emotional and impulsive side of life than to its cognitive aspects" (Maslow 1966, 28). I personally understand this all too well, and one of the major growth themes in my own life has been developing my emotional and bodily intelligence, and at least taking it into account, if not letting it lead when appropriate for situations, instead of having my life compulsively and automatically intellectualized.

Dominating, one-upping, or impressing people is a pathology for which your intellect may be a tool. Then, rationality frequently gets subtly shifted into rationalization in the service of power, often at the cost of part of the truth.

Fearing the truth and knowledge to the extent of avoiding or distorting it is hard to appreciate unless you've done a lot of self-discovery work. It's a scary, unknown world out there in many ways, and we all die in the end, so it's understandable that we create our own little "knowledge clearing" in the forest of reality, and are very reluctant to venture into the woods beyond the clearing. Like all these obstacles to increasing knowledge, if you consciously know you're doing it, you have a chance to alter things. When any of these obstacles become completely automatic and you don't even know you're using them and being used by them, you have little chance of changing, unless perhaps reality "hits you over the head" very hard, and even then you may just curse your fate instead of seeing difficulties as potential growth opportunities and calls for deeper insight into who you are and what your attitudes are.

Rubricizing, or forcing reality into categories that have an authoritative quality about them so that so we're hesitant to think about them any other way, is what a lot of intellectual and emotional activity amounts to. As with other obstacles to knowledge we've discussed so far, lack of flexibility in dealing with experience and reality always has costs.

Compulsively dichotomizing is one very common and general kind of forced categorization. With this, there are only two opposing values to everything: good or bad, yes or no, black or white. A spiritual tradition like Buddhism, for example, sees this automatic compulsive duality as a primary cause of our suffering. At times, reality may be good or bad, good and bad, neither good nor bad, or something in between, something else altogether.

A compulsive seeking of and need for novelty and the devaluation of the familiar is the opposite obstacle to knowledge of attachment to the familiar, to the known, mentioned above. Sometimes important truths are indeed commonplace, humdrum, just repeated over and over again knowledge.

Table 3.1 lists these obstacles to knowing in a shorthand way for convenience.

TABLE **3.1**
Pathologies of Cognition and Perception

Compulsive need for certainty	Unable to tolerate and enjoy ambiguity
Premature generalization	Derives from compulsive need for certainty
Compulsive attachment to a generalization	Ignoring information that contradicts beliefs you're attached to
Denial of ignorance	Inability to admit "I don't know" or "I was wrong"; need to look smart and tough
Denial of doubt	Refusing to admit puzzlement, doubt, confusion
Inflexible need to be tough, powerful, fearless, hard nosed	Can lead to counterphobic defense mechanisms

Only dominant, masterful, controlling; never non-controlling, non-interfering, receptive	Overmasculine, lack of versatility, rigidity
Rationalization masquerading as reason	The classic "I don't like that fellow and I'm going to find a good reason why"
Intolerance of ambiguity	Can't be comfortable with the mysterious, the unknown
Need to conform, to win approval	Be a member of the in-group
Grandiosity, egotism, arrogance	Often a defense against deeper feelings of weakness, worthlessness
Fear of grandiosity, egotism, arrogance	Evasion of one's own growth
Overrespect for authority	To be approved of by great men and considered a loyal disciple
Underrespect for authority	Compulsive rebelling against authority, inability to learn from elders
Compulsive rationality	Inability to be wild, crazy, intuitive, risk-taking when it's appropriate
Intellectualization, blindness to nonintellectual aspects of reality	Satisfaction with naming rather than experiencing

| Intellectual one-upmanship | Impressing people with your brilliance without regard to truth |
| Rubricizing, inaccurate categorizing and stereotyping | Easier than deep perception and thinking |

Now let's look more specifically at the dismissal of spirituality by scientism.

Skepticism and Pseudoskepticism

While this may seem odd to say, I've been personally bored for decades with the controversy about whether or not psi perceptions, aspects of the human mind that I'll argue for throughout this book, provide a sound basis for openness to the reality that at least some of the spiritual really exist. Indeed, I often feel that my parapsychologist colleagues who are still trying to provide evidence for the existence of basic psi phenomena, well-meaning as they are, could better spend their time on more fruitful pursuits, such as how psi abilities work, as well as their applications and implications for spirituality. I'll make some remarks about skepticism and pseudoskepticism so you can understand my position.

> SKEPTICISM (1646): (1) an attitude of doubt or a disposition to incredulity either in general or toward a particular object. (2) The doctrine that true knowledge or knowledge in a particular area is uncertain; (b) the method of suspended judgment, systematic doubt, or criticism characteristic of skeptics. (3) Doubt concerning basic religious principles (as immortality, providence, and revelation). Synonym: "uncertainty." — SHORTER OXFORD ENGLISH DICTIONARY, 6th ed., s.v. "skepticism"

I often think of myself as a skeptic in the sense of the second dictionary definition given in the inset box, namely that in many areas of life I'm unsure that our apparent knowledge is really accurate or complete, and I'd like better knowledge.

When people tell me about "psychic experiences" they had, for example, I listen carefully. Sometimes I then agree with their characterizations of the experiences as psychic; sometimes I suggest that they might be more plausibly explained as unusual experiences but not necessarily psychic; sometimes I indicate that it's a judgment call as to whether or not they were psychic experiences, because I could argue it either way but there's no definitive aspect to firmly place them in the psychic or nonpsychic category. Often, for the most interesting cases, I just suspend judgment; I don't know what to make of the experience. Sometimes I think that the personal growth possibilities in the experience are much more important to follow up on than categorizing it as genuinely psychic or nonpsychic. Or I read about colleagues' experiments to see how they might interpret the outcome the way they did but am skeptical that there isn't an alternative explanation that's also plausible, given what we currently know.

Being skeptical in general, or, at least where it matters, being a "skeptic," is a rational and sensible strategy in life. There's a lot of things we think we know that we may well be mistaken about. Being a skeptic is also an honorable, high-status social role, especially in intellectual circles. We tend to think of skeptics as smarter and sharper than those who just unquestioningly accept whatever they're told. Being a skeptic implies being a smart person who has looked more closely than most usually do and has investigated things more thoroughly, because he or she wants to know the truth, or at least a better approximation to the truth, about these things. You might characterize me as a skeptic about materialism, for example; not that I doubt the reality of the material world, but I doubt the kind of thinking that demands that everything must be totally explained in conventional material terms. I'm rather skeptical, in general, of any claim that everything can be explained in terms of any one particular system of thought; are we really that clever? And yes, my ego does think I'm pretty sharp for being like this.

The proper understanding and functioning of skepticism is greatly confused, though, by the existence and activities of numerous pseudoskeptics, people who claim to be skeptics — people interested in getting at the truth while doubting that current explanations are really adequate — but who are really adherents to and advocates of some other belief system that, they believe, already has all the necessary truth. Such pseudoskeptics call themselves skeptics because of the high prestige of that term, rather than more accurately labeling themselves as, say, "Believers in System M" who don't like the facts or ideas you're talking about and want to discredit you to defend System M. They're debunkers, missionaries, advocates. Believers, however, isn't a high-status word in intellectual circles, so they prefer to call themselves skeptics.

I have no difficulty relating to people who honestly label themselves believers in some system. If people say to me, "My religion R teaches such and such, and therefore, you must be wrong in what you say about X, even if you seem convincing," I accept that as their honest position. We can openly agree to disagree, but we're not fooling ourselves or anyone else about the nature of our disagreement. We're not doing science; we're doing personal beliefs. Dealing with a pseudoskeptic about parapsychological findings, however, is usually very frustrating.

The typical pseudoskeptic will argue that your parapsychological results must be wrong and the result of sloppy experiments, wishful misinterpretations, or downright dishonesty by your subjects or even by you, because what you're claiming is scientifically impossible.[1] The pseudoskeptic thus casts himself as not only a seeker of truth but also an expert in the relevant scientific disciplines for judging your work.

What makes someone a scientist, an expert in a particular discipline? I'll illustrate this from my own discipline, experimental psychology, which I know best, but this is typical of most scientific disciplines.

First, you complete, with high grades, a major in psychology as part of your undergraduate college education. Then follow three to five years of graduate school, which involves reading, analyzing, and criticizing hundreds of primary sources, journal articles rather than textbooks, and usually comprehensive examinations, both written and oral to satisfy the faculty that you both know the field factually and can intelligently reason about it. Graduate school is also often an apprenticeship as well as an education, in that you work closely with one or more faculty members on their research projects. For most, the doctoral degree is then the end of formal education, and they go on to teaching, clinical, or research positions, but for many, as in my own case, the doctoral degree is followed by a two-year postdoctoral fellowship, working closely with, and under the supervision of, an accomplished researcher in your specialty to further hone your skills. Such formal credentialing as a scientist in your field qualifies you to start working in it. How accomplished you actually become will then usually be judged on your research output, primarily published technical articles in journals where articles are accepted for publication only after being refereed and vetted by other acknowledged experts in the field, as well as books. So with the formal training, the advanced graduate degree, and a track record of publications in refereed journals, you become an expert in your field.

I have the credentials and this kind of track record in several areas of psychology, so I can speak with some expertise about aspects of these areas. That doesn't mean I know everything about those fields or that I can't be wrong about things in them, just that I'm much better informed than people with no training and experience in those fields.

Now would you like to hear me rant about how I'm skeptical of current directions in cancer research? Or the safe design of nuclear reactors? Or the best medical treatments for the common cold? Of course not! Although I am a good speaker, and know how to act as if I know a lot (and try never to fake it like that), I'd be lying if I presented myself as a qualified skeptic with respect to those fields. I don't have any formal training in them, and I certainly have no track record of refereed publications there; indeed, I've never done any relevant experiments at all. My practical knowledge of those areas is as lacking as my theoretical knowledge.

But, I might tell myself (although probably without admitting it to you), I don't need to bother getting the formal training, reading the experimental literature, or actually doing any experiments, because I already know that what those investigators are doing is impossible, so why should I waste my time? This is what I mean by saying that the pseudoskeptics aren't actually skeptics in a genuine sense; they're believers in some other system, out to attack and debunk what they don't believe in while trying to appear open minded and scientific, even though they're not.

Bringing this back to parapsychology, in the fifty years I've been studying and working in this field, there have been lots of attacks on it from pseudoskeptics. These debunkers are sometimes high-status scientists in other fields, but they don't bother to actually read the published reports of the experiments in parapsychology's refereed scientific journals, much less get their hands dirty by doing any experiments themselves. Indeed, I can only think of one longtime pseudoskeptic who has shown some knowledge in demonstrating he has actually read many of the reported studies, and too many colleagues have told me about times they got him to admit in public debate that he was wrong about some point, only to find him making the same point in his next public talk or article. It's discouraging.

Various media love to report on these controversies stirred up by pseudoskeptics, and usually give the pseudoskeptics high, "expert," status and make the arguments sound serious, either because (1) the people running a particular reporting medium are themselves pseudoskeptical, committed to scientistic materialism,

(2) as cynical media people have put it for decades, controversy sells more newspapers than accurate reporting, or (3) both.

This is not to say that there haven't been occasional serious shortcomings in parapsychological research, especially in some of the earliest research going back more than a century, when we were still learning how to do it the best way. Such real flaws, though, have in almost all cases been discovered and corrected by the people working in parapsychology, not the pseudoskeptics. (For those interested in the sociology and psychology of science in this area, I recommend articles by Collins and Pinch 1979, and Hess 1992.)

Review: Material vs. Spiritual Views of Life

Let's look more systematically at material and spiritual views of human life to clarify where they conflict and what kind of evidence we would need to support the usefulness of some kind of spiritual view.

Figure 3.1 maps a totally materialistic view of life and consciousness. We start with the most fundamental and real at the bottom of the figure: matter, energy, space, and time. Because they're what's most real in this view, indeed the only things that are "really" real, I've put them in the heaviest, boldest type in the figure. It's assumed that everything arises from the laws governing matter, energy, space, and time, so the best understanding of all of life that we can ever get will spring from our understanding of these most fundamental factors.

Within this material, reality, over time — zillions of years, to put it crudely — particular phenomena and configurations of the fundamental reality happen. I almost said "evolve," but materialists might object to the implicit implication of purpose in the unqualified word "evolution." It all just happened — the interactions of the phenomena we normally think of as physics and chemistry, the way the fundamentals of material reality manifest at this time in the history of the universe. A subset of chemistry and physics gave us biology. Again there's no "reason" as in having purpose; it's just the way things happened. Since we usually think of ourselves as the smartest beings in the universe, it's natural to see this as "evolution," but again it wasn't an evolution guided by a purpose, intending toward some goal; it just happened.

Figure 3.1 Totally Materialistic View of Consciousness

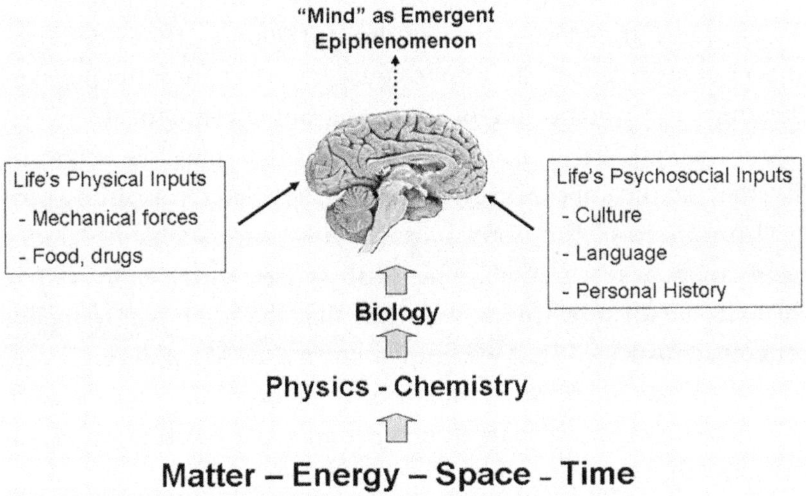

In a relatively short period — hundreds of millions of years — compared to the history of our universe, the materialist view goes on, particular physical and chemical events happened that we refer to as life and biology. Materialists reject the idea that there's anything special about life, something as real as matter but of a different nature, a "life force," or vitalism. Vitalism is a kind of dualism, so it can't be correct; there's nothing but material reality. Life simply means that when you get just the right combinations of physics and chemistry, you get self-sustaining, self-reproducing actions that constitute life as we know it.

Eventually, that life electrochemical reaction gets complex enough that we talk of brains and then the human brain. It's still basically controlled and limited by the laws of matter, and there are lots of direct material influences on its functioning during life, ranging from crude mechanical forces like a blow on the head to chemical inputs in the forms of foods, drugs, hormones, and so on. Curiously — and this is a real puzzle to materialists although they usually ignore it — this human brain develops consciousness, a mind or awareness that often believes that it isn't limited to just the material dimensions of life. Consciousness just emerges, it's believed, from the system properties of the brain. Although it's an item of faith in materialism that physical science will someday be able to explain exactly how consciousness arises from the physical structure and functioning of the brain, and so explain it "away," currently we have no useful scientific theory that does anything like that, so the appearance of consciousness from the purely physical processes of the brain is called the "hard problem" among contemporary researchers. This faith is frequently expressed in the extreme form by saying we know that the brain is responsible for consciousness. What we know in terms of essential science, of course, is that the brain is importantly involved in consciousness as it manifests in ordinary life, but that's not the same thing as knowing that the brain creates consciousness.

This emergent consciousness, an epiphenomenon in philosophical terms, a secondary manifestation of the really primary physical functioning of the brain, is subject to influences we normally classify, for convenience, as psychological, such as language, psychological and sociological events, and the whole cultural milieu in which our personal history evolves. But while it's convenient to talk of psychological and cultural factors at present, the dream or goal of materialism is to ultimately explain these, too, in terms of physics and chemistry, the most real, the only ultimately real, aspects of matter and energy. Thus today it may be the best we can do to explain someone's behavior using concepts like, for example, "He had a difficult childhood without adequate role modeling by his father, and this resulted in neurotic complexes." Ultimately, as good materialists, we want to be really precise and "scientific" by explaining the same behavior as something like, "excitatory activity of such and such chemical and electrical value in neural network #4,567,322 spreading to neural network #34,567,935 resulted in the behavior we observed."

Some of the emotional implications of a totally materialistic view in particular have, hopefully, emerged for you from doing the Western Creed exercise in chapter 1.

Figure 3.2 contrasts the material view with a kind of generalized spiritual view, generalized to include the basics of what I know of the essences of world religions rather than sticking to any one spiritual system.

Fig. 3.2 General Spiritual View of Life and Consciousness

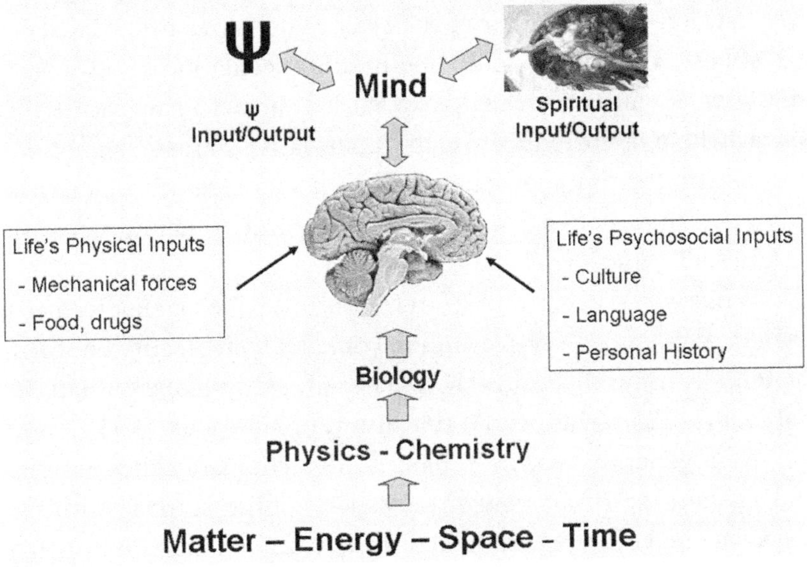

We again have all the elements of the materialist view, because I don't think any major spiritual system would be naive enough to ignore the importance of physical laws, and the structure and functioning of the brain and body in affecting us. But I've drawn "mind" in with large, bold letters as an independent reality of its own, just as important as matter, energy, space, and time. That's not to claim that mind isn't affected by the operations of the physical brain; it clearly is, in a multitude of ways. But mind, as we ordinarily know it, is here considered an emergent of both the operation of the physical brain and inputs from and outputs to something else, the qualitatively different realm postulated by emergent dualism. To be comprehensive, I've represented this something else as being psi (Ψ) inputs and outputs in general (detailed in later chapters) and, specifically, spiritual inputs and outputs in particular, using the Michelangelo painting. (I use the Michelangelo painting for artistic reasons, not because I believe Christianity has a better understanding of the spiritual realm than other religions do.)

Now, we come again to the crucial question of this book. We can conceptualize a dualist view of reality and draw nice diagrams about it, but is it real? From the materialist's perspective, aren't we, at best, just wasting our time in idle speculation or, at worst, indulging in fantasies that make us less able to survive in the real world? Or, to indulge in the materialistic dream, aren't we just exciting activity of such and such chemical and electrical value in neural network #4,567,322 spreading to neural network #34,567,935, and so on?

What would constitute strong scientific evidence that we need a wider, dualist perspective, and to consider some reality of a fundamentally different nature than material reality, along with material reality? And what would this different view look like?

As a general start, in Table 3.2, I've compared the material and a general spiritual view on six aspects of life, starting with the ways we can get information about the world and act on it, going on to our purpose in life, who we believe we are, our life span, and how we contact and interact with other beings. You can see that the general spiritual view includes all of the factors in the material view but adds ways of sensing, acting, and interacting with other "beings" over a longer and wider time span than the materialist view. These extra possibilities include various forms of psi (Ψ)abilities, such as ESP to gather information about the world, and PK and psychic healing to affect the world and create a bigger sphere of action: a "spiritual world" and possibly a much longer life span through postmortem survival or reincarnation to act in. We'll discuss these different forms of psi abilities in detail in later chapters. But how do we get scientific evidence to show we're not just speculating?

TABLE 3.2

Total Material vs. General Spiritual Worldviews

Function	Materialistic View	Spiritual View
Information input	Five senses, mechanical sensory amplifiers, and reasoning	Five senses, mechanical sensory amplifiers, reasons, and Ψ
Action on world	Muscles and tools	Muscles, tools, PK, psychic healing, "spirit" intervention, and action on "spirit world"
Identity	Biologically-based and body, and psychological overlays	Biologically-based ego and body, psychological overlays, plus "soul"
Purpose	Survival; no ultimate purpose	Spiritual evolution
Life span	Sixty to eighty years	Sixty to eighty years plus postmortem life, reincarnation, or both
Contact with other beings	Through physical senses	Through physical senses and direct Ψ contact

Notes

1. One of the early psychic researchers, the distinguished English philosopher Henry Sidgwick (1838–1900), noted, "We have done all we can when the critic has nothing left to allege except that the investigator is in [on] the trick. But when he has nothing else left to allege, he will allege that" (1882, 12). The pseudocritics began doing that a long time ago. I always take it as a compliment to my experimental design when they end up claiming that I must be incompetent or that my subjects or I must've cheated.

CHAPTER 4

Starting from the Natural World:
A Psychic *Coup d'État*?

Coup d'état *(origin: French, literally "blow of state")*: *A violent or illegal change in government. Formerly also, any sudden and decisive stroke of state policy. [More generally, an unexpected, sudden seizure of control.]* — SHORTER OXFORD ENGLISH DICTIONARY, *6th ed., s.v. "coup d'état"*

IF MATERIALISM is seen for what it actually is, a philosophy or theory of reality that's very useful in many areas but quite inadequate in others, it need not be at all psychologically damaging or invalidating. It's when it all-too-commonly hardens into dogma, into scientism, claiming to be the ultimate and final truth about everything, that the invalidation of our spiritual nature occurs and hurts us. This can happen with any philosophy or set of ideas, of course: rigidity has its costs.

There's no denying the power of the results of the physical sciences: this computer I'm typing on; the airplanes that fly overhead; the medicines that have kept me alive and healthy long after I'd probably be dead in the normal, historical course of events; and so on. I love physical science and am a happy nerd when it comes to technology, but without the meaning that spiritual experience gives life, I imagine I'd be quite depressed. "Of course, you could take an antidepressant and not worry about it," reply the dedicated materialists, "and someday we'll stimulate the relevant part of your brain directly, without needing to be so indirect as to use drugs, and make you as happy as you want to be." But I very much live my life as a scientist, for whom the facts always come first, not simply as a person who wants to avoid negative feelings and enhance positive ones, and my own and others' scientific work has convinced me that the spiritual perspective is a part of reality; we neglect and deny it at our peril.

The scientific work that shows us this (discussed in the next chapters) didn't spring up from nowhere, of course; it began because puzzling — yet often exciting and inspiring — events happened in real peoples' lives, events that implied something spiritual but called for closer examination. People who prefer to gain knowledge from deliberate, well-controlled experiments refer to these life events as "spontaneous" cases of "ostensible" psi phenomena, meaning they weren't a deliberate attempt to create psi effects under rigorous conditions. Calling them natural psi events would be more accurate than spontaneous, for they had, of course, their own causes, even if we don't know them in particular instances, just not deliberate experimental causes. There are many books collecting such events: one of the earliest great collections being the "Report on the Census of Hallucinations" (Sidgwick 1894; see appendix 1) carried out by the Society for Psychical Research, the latest excellent one being *The Gift* by Sally Rhine Feather (psychologist and daughter of the great parapsychologist J. B. Rhine of Duke University) and Michael Schmicker (St. Martin's Press, 2005; see appendix 1). These natural cases are usually fascinating reading (and often sad, since they so often involve apparent psi knowing of human tragedies involving loved ones), and this book could easily be filled with them. But in this chapter I share just one such real-life event that happened to me, to give the flavor of this kind of event in some depth and set the stage for looking at the scientific evidence for the reality of spiritual experiences in more detail. I draw heavily from my own published account of this from 1989.

Only Making Coffee?

On February 4, 1983, I was working in my office at home on a paper I was preparing to submit for presentation at a forthcoming Parapsychological Association convention (the international professional society of those who work in scientific parapsychology; see www.parapsych.org). At midmorning I took a break to prepare some coffee. While standing at my kitchen stove waiting for the water to boil, I found myself saying the phrase *"coup d'état"* aloud to myself.

I repeated the phrase aloud six to ten times, finding the rhythm of the sound appealing. I didn't know why I was thinking the phrase or saying it aloud. I had come across *"coup d'état"* in reading brief news items in newspapers and magazines, but it's not a topic I'd given more than passing thought over the years or had any particular interest in, and I'd probably never said the phrase aloud before.

It's rare for me to start saying a word or phrase aloud, much less over and over, when I'm alone. I've always been curious about my own psychological workings, so I was mildly puzzled as to why this phrase had popped into my head and, as it were, onto my tongue. I don't follow international news closely and could think of nothing in my immediate past that had anything to do with *coup d'état*s. In spite of being puzzled, I enjoyed saying the phrase aloud over and over, and started thinking about military dictatorships. I thought of cheering crowds when a *coup d'état* brought a military group to power and deposed a failing civilian government, and the crowd's later disillusionment. I thought that the sound of the phrase had a stimulating, rhythmic ring of power to it, appropriate for a military dictatorship. I thought about how a military government might come to power because a civilian government was too disorganized to run things, that the military might be the most organized group in the country and thus naturally take over.

After a minute I stopped saying the phrase but occasionally thought about it during the day, but I quickly forgot the specifics of these discursive thoughts.

The next morning, when I arrived at my office at the university, one of the first envelopes in my mailbox was from a Mrs. Coudetat of San Diego!

I was immediately reminded of my experience the day before, and thought: "Yesterday was probably the first time in my life that I ever said '*coup d'état*' aloud — it's not a word or a concept of importance in my life — and this is the first letter I've ever gotten from someone named Coudetat." Nor have I ever gotten a letter from someone of that name since, so as of 2008, this is a once-in-seventy-one-years occurrence.

Mrs. Coudetat's letter was as follows (I've made some subtle but psychologically irrelevant changes in certain facts to protect the privacy of the people involved here):

> "I am writing regarding my son, Robert Coudetat, who was in your altered states of consciousness class last semester.[1] I knew he came and spoke to you once, but after that I don't think he wanted to bother you, and he didn't really feel like approaching your assistant. He began to have very severe anxiety attacks with a variety of many symptoms: he was dizzy, he could not sleep well, and his whole digestive system seemed confused. It was hard for us to help him, long distance, and he was referred by the X Medical Facility to Dr. Y in Davis, whom he saw until Christmas. He struggled through, a fraction of his usual self.
>
> "After Christmas he returned to Davis, and shortly after registering he returned home feeling terrible. He was diagnosed as having mononucleosis, and now he has withdrawn from Davis. He is going to a psychiatrist here in San Diego, Dr. Z, who is helping him greatly. Dr. Z says it is a 'classic identity crisis and that Robert is very confused.'
>
> "My suggestion for you would be that in teaching your class, you make sure that students have readily available

channels for help, discussion groups, short conferences, or whatever might be needed. My son experienced extreme anxiety and fear. I myself am a student of metaphysics and parapsychology, so I appreciate very much the work in which you are engaged. But I now realize that some kinds of thoughts can be very threatening to young minds and need to be approached carefully."

I immediately wrote to Mrs. Coudetat, sympathizing with Robert's problems, describing sources of help available at the university, and suggesting a possible further source of therapeutic assistance in her community. I never heard any further from her, although I wrote a later letter of inquiry. I optimistically presumed Robert recovered soon after, because such cases are common among college students and seldom have prolonged consequences.

I wasn't sure I remembered Robert's talk with me. My altered-states class typically had 150 to 250 students in it, and many students from the class (as well as other students from all over the university) talked with me about all sorts of issues, so they tended to run together in my memory after a while. When students asked me clear questions, I usually answered them directly if I knew the answers, or suggested sources of information they could turn to. Occasionally, students were vague, and it was unclear to me what they wanted. If it seemed to be only an intellectual vagueness from not having thought out what was on their minds, I usually suggested that they think about it some more and come to see me later when it was clearer. If I felt that a student might have strong emotional disturbances (a rare occasion, fortunately), I usually suggested that he or she drop by the student health center for counseling.

Let's take it for granted for the moment that something interesting probably happened here, something with "psychic" or "spiritual" aspects to it, and think about it some more.

Predictive Psi

Although one can never be certain about just what is and isn't "coincidence" in everyday life events like this, given the overwhelming evidence for the existence of psi phenomena under controlled laboratory conditions, which we'll look at in the next chapters, I personally regard this *coup d'état* case as a clear instance of what we might call predictive psi phenomena. The unusualness of my speaking repeatedly aloud to myself with no discernible motivation to do so at the time, the great rarity of the phrase *"coup d'état"* in my life, and the immediate confirmation of its importance the following morning rule out coincidence as a good explanation in my mind. I call it "predictive psi phenomena" rather than precognition (see chapter 8), because the mechanism might just as well have been present-time telepathy (or clairvoyance) as precognition, since I'm sure Mrs. Coudetat was thinking about me and her letter to me, which was on the way to me at the time the phrase *"coup d'état"* popped into my mind. Whether this specific instance was genuine psi functioning or actually a quite unusual coincidence, it's similar to even more convincing cases of psi perceptions in everyday life, so the *coup d'état* incident is a useful basis for some theoretical thinking about psychic matters.

Why did the event happen? My speculation at the time was that it was important for Mrs. Coudetat to communicate with me, primarily out of concern for her son, plus concern for students who might be in a similar predicament in the future, and a mutual interest in parapsychology. Further, she probably accepted, to some degree, her son's feeling that I hadn't wanted to listen to him, so she would have a strong emotional investment in making sure I listened by writing to me.[2]

Could Mrs. Coudetat's need to communicate have provided the motivational "power" that resulted in my unusual behavior of not only getting the critical sound of her name but also saying it aloud repeatedly, thus sensitizing me to pay close attention to her pending letter? This line of reasoning seems adequate on a commonsense psychological level to provide a motive or "force" for telepathy to occur, and is probably mostly true.

Although exploring it will divert us from getting on to spiritual matters for a while, straightforward conscious motivation is seldom all that operates in our human minds, so we're going to take a little side trip into human minds in general, and my mind in particular. This will sensitize us to other relevant factors that may be useful in understanding the multiple psychological factors involved in the manifestation of psi phenomena and spirituality, and begin to illustrate why the application of science and psychology to spiritual matters may deepen our understanding and ability to use spirituality.

Analytical and Associative Overlay

Let us first look at analytical overlay. The concept of analytical overlay was introduced for understanding results of remote-viewing studies, described in detail in chapter 7, where a designated viewer attempts to use ESP or psi ability to describe the characteristics of some distant target, sensorially isolated from him or her (Puthoff and Targ 1976). Following initial psi-mediated impressions of the hidden target, impressions that may be correct and specific, there's often a tendency for the viewer or percipient to automatically and often unknowingly associate to, and intellectually analyze and elaborate on, his or her (hopefully) psi-mediated impressions.

If the target is a small jewelry store with a large plate-glass window that the outbound experimenter is standing in front of, for example, a viewer might start reporting impressions such as "seeing" images of light reflecting off something rectangular and shiny that's bright and hard, and sensing that there are many things behind or associated with this rectangular thing.

So far, excellent! Our ordinary minds are seldom content with "raw" experience, however: automated parts of our mental processing — what I've called the world-simulation process in other contexts explaining the nature of dreaming (Tart 1987) and the "biased quality of ordinary consciousness" (Tart 1986) — function in an automatized, semiconscious fashion to make raw experience meaningful in terms of a person's ordinary mind-set. Psychologist Ronald Shor (1959) called that automatized, background, interpretive network the generalized reality orientation, and I've renamed it the consensus reality orientation to emphasize how much our particular cultural upbringing influences what we think of as real and important.

So automatically wondering what these impressions mean, in this example, the viewer might find that the images remind him of a recent trip to a Macy's department store. The bright, hard, shiny rectangle is automatically analyzed as a display window or entrance to Macy's. This kind of automatic association seldom functions in the form of consciously thinking, "This resembles Macy's, so perhaps it's that," but rather as an immediate perceptual given: "This is Macy's." Now linked associations, memories, and apparently relevant images of Macy's, associative overlay, might modulate, suppress, and distort further psi reception of the actual target. The viewer might go on and describe a large building with long aisles, vast crowds, and busyness, completely losing the feel of the small, quiet jewelry store. As analytical and associative overlay increases, the salience of the original correct imagery can easily be lost, making it impossible for judges to correctly associate this remote-viewing report with the target it was intended for. Genuine psi functioning can easily drown in these kinds of noise, especially if the viewer or percipient isn't practiced in detailed observation of her or his own mental processes enough to be able to discriminate different qualities of mental events.

I believe the associations of military dictatorships, cheering crowds, and thoughts about efficient and disciplined organizations taking over when governments fail represent analytical and associative overlay following my initial psi impression of the word "coup d'état." In this case the initial psi impression was so unique that its correspondence to a later event wasn't smothered by the overlay, but suppose the student's name had been something like Coffee or Stove? An initial psi impression of Coffee or Stove could have easily been buried by "rational" associations to the coffee I was brewing on the stove.

In this case I was saved from letting further analytical and associative overlay obscure the original psi-relevant impression ("*coup d'état*") by the prosaic fact that my coffee was ready and I wanted to get back to work. I took my coffee back to my computer and began writing again, easily pushing the *coup d'état* incident aside to focus on writing. It's interesting to wonder how many psi (or spiritual) impressions in everyday life are lost because of analytical and associative overlay.

Theoretical Overlay

I wrote up a rough draft of this case, essentially as given above, within three days of the events, because I thought it was interesting in and of itself, as well as a good illustration of the problems of analytical and associative overlay. (There are more technical considerations along these lines in the published article from which this chapter is drawn than I go into here.) I suspected that the case might be richer than I perceived, though, so three days later, I mailed a copy to a colleague, the noted psychoanalyst and parapsychologist Jule Eisenbud (1908–1999), asking for his comments. While I don't go along completely with psychoanalytic explanations, I always found Eisenbud's ideas about psi phenomena provocative and stimulating (1970, 1982).[3]

Eisenbud wrote back and suggested that I consider the possibility of theoretical overlay, an interpretive bias he has often seen in parapsychologists, and apply it to the *coup d'état* case. The particular theoretical bias he emphasized was that parapsychologists, when psychological factors are clearly seen in psi cases, tend to interpret them as idealistically inspired by altruistic concern for others. In Eisenbud's clinical experience, by contrast, negative motivations and desires to hurt others are far more common.

My immediate reaction was on the order of "Me? Wanting to hurt someone? Hey, I'm one of the good guys!" But Eisenbud's suggestion clearly deserved more thought.

Psychological investigation immediately after the events with a skilled therapist is probably the best way to investigate motivations and theoretical overlays of parapsychologists like myself in these kinds of cases. This isn't generally possible, of course, for practical reasons. I've spent many years investigating my own mental and emotional processes (1986), however, so while some of my memories and feelings have undoubtedly been dimmed by the passage of time, I'll make some observations and speculations along the lines suggested by Eisenbud to illustrate a useful direction for the parapsychological and psychodynamic investigation of psi events — and this applies to our spiritual interests too! I hope this will inspire other investigators to undertake relevant self-examinations.[4]

Although I hadn't included the preceding material (as it wasn't clear to me at the time) in the original write-up sent to Eisenbud, I had thought of it as an additional motivational factor that might have made this psi manifestation more likely. In addition to Mrs. Coudetat's motivation, there might have been an unconscious, unresolved concern on my part about Robert, a consciously forgotten but still active feeling of frustration that a student had wanted some sort of help but I hadn't been able to see what he wanted and assist him. Similar situations had happened with too many students over my twenty-plus years of teaching. I generally have at least two negative feelings in reaction to such incidents, feelings that I prefer to avoid in the first place if possible, or to suppress as soon as possible if I do have them. One is a feeling of frustration that I can't do anything useful when asked for help. This also undermines my own feelings of being a competent person. The second is some anger and feeling of being put-upon: am I supposed to be able to solve everybody's problems about everything, especially when he or she won't even be clear about what the problem is? Such a lingering unconscious residue might have sensitized me to psychically perceiving information coming about Robert (like getting his mother's letter).

I believe this additional motivating factor has a high probability of being true in this case, given my general psychological knowledge of myself, even though I couldn't specifically recall Robert's visit to my office. Basically, I'm sometimes concerned about other people's welfare, and as a conscious ethical value, this has high priority for me. However, I also know that I have a positive bias in interpreting events, so I may indeed be manifesting an altruistic theoretical overlay in analyzing this case. Thus some reflections on possible negative psychological factors in this case are warranted.

I'm certainly selfish and concerned primarily about my own welfare much of the time, like most of us. (Is that last phrase a defensive rationalization on my part, as well as a realistic perception?) My conscious values are such that when I see such selfish factors operating in a way that would harm others or violate my values of friendliness and altruism, though, I usually try to change my behavior to a more positive form — but I don't always succeed. While I've always been interested in understanding my own motivations and the workings of my mind (1986), there are undoubtedly many instances where I'm not fully aware of my motivations.

Applying this to the *coup d'état* incident, I hypothesize that I may have had a continuing unconscious concern about Robert that was motivated as much or more by guilt or anger as by altruistic concern: guilt in that I have a harsh superego that expects me to succeed in everything I value, yet I hadn't been able to help Robert, and thus, from my superego's point of view, deserved to feel guilty; and anger in that he'd come and taken up my time, yet by not making himself clear, "wasted" it.[5]

I might also speculate that my psychic perception of the imminent and somewhat critical letter from Mrs. Coudetat constituted my own psychological *coup d'état* in defending me against possible guilt. In spite of the generally friendly tone of Mrs. Coudetat's letter, she does suggest that I should have better methods for protecting students against the adverse impact of unconventional, even if valid, ideas. Realistically, I do have methods, but by my own strict superego's standards, they can never be good enough. So Mrs. Coudetat's letter had the potential to make me feel guilty over my possibly inadequate teaching style. But, by having psychically anticipated the arrival of her letter, my conscious mind became focused on the interesting psychic aspects of the case, using up psychological energy that might otherwise have activated guilt.

Note, too, that Eisenbud's psychoanalytic investigations (1970, 1982) strongly suggest that psychic events are typically multiply determined rather than having a single cause. Thus, all of the above motivational considerations may be correct to various degrees. This consideration also made me think of another possible motivation for the event.

A few days before the Coudetat letter arrived, I had attempted to do some psychic healing, using shamanistic methods like those described by Michael Harner (1980) on a friend of mine who was scheduled for some life-threatening surgery. I've never told my friend about this activity of mine, because such activity is a very private part of my life. It would also have seemed egotistical to mention it, and I didn't know whether my attempts would have any effect anyway. (I'm ambivalent about mentioning it in this book and do so only for psychological completeness.) I had wanted to help a friend but had retrospective doubts about what I'd done. [6]

The *coup d'état* incident excited me. Although I've been firmly convinced about the reality of psychic abilities in general for many years on an intellectual and scientific level, I still have occasional emotional doubts, especially about my own possible ability to actually use a psychic ability in a particular instance. Thus the *coup d'état* incident strengthened my convictions. Since my friend is strongly interested in psychic abilities and hoped his own might help him through his surgery, I telephoned him and told him about the *coup d'état* incident a couple of days before his surgery was scheduled. I deliberately wanted to strengthen his faith in his own psychic abilities such that they might help him pull through the operation. Now I wonder if some part of me might have helped cause the *coup d'état* incident so that my own faith in psychic abilities might be strengthened, and thus retrospectively potentiate my attempts at healing my friend and strengthening his faith. (He came through the lifesaving operation just fine.)

This kind of event implies that there are normally hidden, non-material connections between us. I've looked at the possible deep psychological aspects of this particular experience much more than we're usually able to, because I'm convinced that when we understand these motivating and shaping psychological factors more thoroughly, we'll understand reality a lot better. And this process has also been a way for you to get more acquainted with the author rather than have me stay relatively invisible behind my store of knowledge and authority, as is more typical in this kind of writing.

Notes

This chapter was originally published in a slightly different form as "A Case of Predictive Psi, with Comments on Analytical, Associative, and Theoretical Overlay," *Journal of the Society of Psychical Research* 55(814):263-70, © 1989 by The Journal of the Society of Psychical Research Reprinted by permission.

1. This class, "Psychology 137: Altered States of Consciousness," was a large lecture course with a lot of conceptual material to cover, and I had little time to even suggest psychological exercises to the students, much less carry them out in class. There were two demonstrations I usually presented early in the course to demonstrate the constructed nature of perception, however, and either or both of these may be what Mrs. Coudetat was implicitly referring to. In the first demonstration, a homework exercise, you look in a mirror and mark the top and bottom of your head's reflection on the mirror, then step to the side and see that the size of your head as you marked it seems to be only half the size of the head you perceived in the mirror. Students usually find this quite amazing, for their heads were clearly normal size when they looked at their reflections! In the second demonstration, performed in class, we listened to

a tape created by consciousness researcher John Lilly that contained a single word, "cogitate," repeated over and over again, with instructions to listen for interpolated words and write them down. Actually there were no interpolated words, but normal people hear many because of auditory and cognitive fatigue. I taught then, and continue to teach, that much of what we take for granted as simply real, as a straightforward perception of reality, is a semi-arbitrary construction, so the things we take for granted should be systematically examined.

2. One of the puzzling and saddening experiences of my career as a university professor has been the degree to which students develop fantasies that professors don't want to talk with them. Perhaps some professors don't, but I've always been friendly to students in class, repeatedly conveying my office hours when students could drop in to chat, make appointments if those hours didn't work for them, and so on. A few students always took advantage of my office hours, and we had interesting chats, but I always found too many suddenly speaking to me after class at the end of the quarter who revealed that they'd long wanted to ask me about something or other but couldn't bring themselves to come by my office because they knew that professors didn't want to waste their valuable time with "dumb" students like them.

3. Sometimes it's hard not to play with the idea, without knowing whether or not I'm really serious, that the universe psychically plays with us. In preparing the final manuscript of this book, for instance, I kept semiconsciously puzzling over the two references to Disembody 1970 and Disembody 1982 in this text, copied from an earlier article—an odd name for a psychoanalyst, I thought. It was only when I reached the editing stage of completing the references and couldn't find anyone named Disembody in my reference database that I went back to the original printed journal article and found that Eisenbud had somehow been transposed by my computer into Disembody. Since Eisenbud died in 1999, he certainly is disembodied now.

4. I must sadly admit that my hope of inspiring other parapsychologists to explore and write about their deeper motivations and psychological characteristics has still not been fulfilled. In almost all published reports, parapsychologists implicitly present themselves as completely objective scientists motivated only by a desire for truth and pure intellectual curiosity. Since it's clear that the very idea of psychic connections between people makes experimenters integral parts of experiments, rather than

detached observers, all our literature is thus glaringly incomplete in its description of what happened.

5. Freud theorized that our minds can usefully be classified in three ways as ego, the realistic part of the conscious mind; as id, the instinctual, animal desires we have; and as superego, a kind of socially and individually conditioned watchdog above, "super" to the ego. The superego mechanically watches what we think, feel, and do, and can punish us with guilt and anxiety when we violate its norms.

6. When I performed this shamanic-healing procedure, my attitude was to suspend disbelief for the time being and do what I could. While I can sometimes suspend doubt fairly effectively in this way, intellectual doubt usually creeps in later, hopefully when it's too late for such doubt to block the effect I'm trying for.

CHAPTER 5

Extended Aspects of Mind:
The Big Five

*PSI (origin: Greek "psei"): (1) The twenty-third letter of the
Greek alphabet.*

*(2) Paranormal phenomena or faculties collectively; the
psychic force supposed to be manifested by these. Frequently
attributed as psi powers and so forth.* — SHORTER OXFORD
ENGLISH DICTIONARY, *6th ed., s.v. "psi"*

As I mentioned in the previous chapter, I became convinced of
of the reality of some psychic phenomena (the big five I mentioned in the introduction: telepathy, clairvoyance, precognition, psychokinesis, and psychic healing; we'll discuss these in
more detail later) as a result of reading the scientific literature
about it years before I'd ever had any personal experience of psi
phenomena. Although one can never be absolutely certain in any
particular case, the *coup d'état* incident probably was just what it
seemed to be: Mrs. Coudetat telepathically "reached out" (probably
with no conscious realization that she was doing so) and affected
some deeper level of my mind, and her intention was strong enough
that, while I was in a relatively "idling" mental state, putting aside
my focused thought processes about what I was writing while fix-
ing my coffee, the impression rose to the surface of my mind
strongly enough to start my talking aloud. Indeed, it suddenly
occurs to me that it was kind of a *coup d'état* on her part to seize
control like that from the usual processes governing my mind.

This is a classic kind of everyday psi event, and as I mentioned in the previous chapter, the interested reader can find thousands and thousands of such cases in print. Being in a distracted state of mind is often a favorable condition for psi phenomena to manifest, because your mind isn't preoccupied with some ordinary task and automatically rejecting everything outside that task. Many hundreds of such natural events have been personally reported to me over the years. A person, a percipient, (1) suddenly starts thinking about, seeing images, or getting impressions of another, distant person or event; (2) that person or event is usually of some importance to percipient, such as involving a loved one in distress; (3) there's no rational reason for the percipient to have such thoughts or images at that time; (4) but the percipient later finds out that these impressions provided information about the event that was too specific to simply put down to coincidence. In my case in the previous chapter, (1) the phrase *"coup d'état"* came to mind so suddenly and strongly that I started repeating it aloud; (2) I was important to Mrs. Coudetat, and she intended to make her and her son important to me; (3) *"coup d'état"* had no place in my life, so there was no reason for me to think about the idea or phrase; and (4) it's hard to dismiss as coincidence that the first time I ever said *"coup d'état"* aloud was when Mrs. Coudetat was thinking about me and trying to influence me in an ordinary way with the letter she'd sent.

So do these natural, ostensibly psi events prove that we have some spiritual nature, capable of engaging in psi ability, of sending telepathic messages and transcending space, when no ordinary way of communicating exists?

No, not in any absolute sense. They certainly provide strong evidence for the idea that we have a psychic or spiritual nature, but any particular natural case like this can be debated. The typical arguments against accepting their reality and implications are that they're just "stories," anecdotes, not solid scientific observations, and they come from ordinary humans who are prone to forgetting, imagining, exaggerating, and, sometimes, just plain lying. If this is all there is to these kind of spontaneous psi cases, though, the human race is in trouble, because most surveys show that a majority of people have had such experiences; what does that say if most of us are pretty unreliable and deluded or just plain liars?

Some of these spontaneous cases are of much better quality as evidence goes, like the *coup d'état* incident. It's not just a "story," for example; it's as clear a report as if I'd written that a certain kind of instrument in my laboratory read 4.52 volts at 7:45 p.m. on such and such date. It's not subject to much forgetting, because I wrote about it the next day, when I went to campus and picked up Mrs. Coudetat's letter. The existence of the letter makes it hard to believe I just imagined it all. As to exaggeration — well, maybe, but I am trained, as all scientists are, to describe factual events as clearly as possible. Perhaps I'm lying and made up the whole story? You'll have to take my word that it's true, of course, backed by my reputation as an honest researcher; and if you won't take my word for it, I suggest that it would be psychologically interesting to try to understand why you have such an extraordinarily high level of resistance and why you're reading this book.

How about just plain coincidence? Unrelated events do come together occasionally and we can see significance that isn't there in reality. So it could be a coincidence that the only time in my life I said the phrase *"coup d'état"* aloud just happened to correspond to when Mrs. Coudetat was writing to me and thinking about me. That fact that it could be coincidence is one of the main reasons I said that these kinds of spontaneous psi events don't prove anything about our spiritual or psychic nature in an absolute way, although they certainly are powerful evidence.

So how can we more solidly test, gather information for or against, the idea that mind can transcend brain and body, that "mind" or "soul" — whatever you want to call a supposedly spiritual part of us — can sometimes do things that are impossible for a material brain and body?

We've discussed the general procedures for refining and testing knowledge in the previous chapter, so now let's get more specific. Figure 5.1 diagrams how you set up a basic experiment to test the empirical reality of phenomena that in principle cannot happen if you accept materialism as a complete explanation of reality. Technically, I refer to this as testing the reality of paraconceptual phenomena; it's a little silly and inaccurate to call psi phenomena "paranormal" when a majority of the population believes they've experienced them, even though "paranormal" is the generally accepted term. (I've tried introducing more accurate terms than "paranormal" on many occasions in my career, and have almost always learned that old words have a life of their own, no matter how much we dislike their misleading implications or fuzziness. So I imagine these will be called "paranormal phenomena" forever.)

How do we test? Given our conceptions, theories, and beliefs about the way the world is, we set up a situation where nothing should happen if our concepts are indeed completely correct, but if something does happen, it's para: beyond our concepts.

Figure 5.1 Basic Paraconceptual Experiment

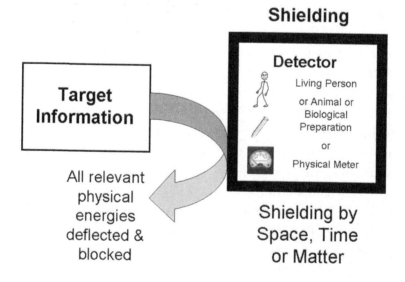

We set up some target that we want to get information about and some detector or detectors to pick up that information. The detectors could be people (percipients), animals whose behavior is observed, biological preparations like a cell culture, or some physical detection instrument that gives us some meter readings. The shielding could be (1) simple space, far away, for example; (2) time — the target will only exist in the future; (3) matter, a solid barrier between target and detector; or (4) some combination of space, time, and material shielding. Right now, for instance, we could say that this book is an unshielded target: it's full of information, and your eyes and mind are the detectors of that information. But — and it's an important "but" — for a paraconceptual experiment, we could shield the book target so that no information about it can reach the detectors, given what we know about the way the physical world works.

If some book, never before seen by you, were in a locked, solid metal box, for example, it wouldn't matter how much you looked at the box, weighed it, or shook it, given our beliefs and concepts about how the physical world works, there's no way for you to have any significant and specific idea of what's printed in the book. You could hazard a guess that the word "the" appears in it, but we wouldn't be impressed since the guess is too general and insignificant.

Thousands of such paraconceptual experiments — almost always described as "parapsychological" experiments — have been carried out, and indicated that some kinds of effects do occasionally happen, with significance beyond chance, in spite of our materialistic concepts that say they shouldn't.[1] Thus, there is experimental evidence for paraconceptual or parapsychological phenomena. These experiments rarely produce extensive, spectacular effects, such as someone correctly telling you all of the words, in order, on the pages of a book in a locked box — to stay with our hypothetical example. I didn't suddenly foresee that I was getting a letter from a Mrs. Coudetat about her son who'd been a student of mine, and exactly what his problems were. Rather, there's a detector output that shows some variation, usually mostly due to chance but also with significant departures from what we expect by chance; I'll clarify just what I mean by that shortly.

A Preference for Objectivity

Staying with our real-life *coup d'état* example, it wasn't a formal experiment; it just happened due to (perhaps many) causes outside of our complete understanding. Yet I assessed it as most likely being an example of some kind of natural psi ability, of telepathic intention from Mrs. Coudetat, perhaps a foretelling of the future — the letter the next day — on my part, or both. But suppose it had been less specific than the spoken phrase "*coup d'état*"? Suppose I had just thought about "*coup d'état*" for a moment but not spoken it aloud? Or found myself singing a folk song about the troubles of life? Or thought about the American Revolution, and the next day decided that a revolution is sort of a *coup d'état* and my thinking about it must've been related to the letter? Would something like that have made me suspect psychic impressions?

Probably not — I'm pretty strict in judging whether an experience of my own is psychic — but whatever I thought along those lines, it would've been a subjective judgment, and while we have to make a lot of subjective judgments in life, we usually prefer more objective ways of assessing reality when we can use them. We're all aware of how misleading wishful thinking can sometimes be.

The totally materialistic view of life dismisses spontaneous experiences like the *coup d'état* incident as indeed nothing but subjective judgments (or misjudgments), in which the wish to believe in something beyond the material interferes with our objectivity, making us interpret meaningless coincidences as "proof" of what we want to believe. People certainly do things like this all the time, in all areas of life! But, curiously, materialists almost never apply this line of reasoning — that we distort our perceptions and interpretations to support our prior beliefs — to their own dismissal of spontaneous psi events as meaningless.

I've met numerous self-styled "skeptics" — I more accurately call them "pseudoskeptics" for reasons discussed earlier — who are so committed to a philosophy of total materialism that they dismiss any evidence to the contrary, for the most spurious and unscientific reasons. (See *www.skepticalaboutskeptics.org* for information on prominent skeptics and pseudoskeptics.)

An essential aspect of any paraconceptual experiment, then, is a way of assessing outcomes as objectively as possible, as free from biases of the experimenter and reader — pro or con — as possible. The classical method that dominated parapsychological or paraconceptual research for decades was using multiple-choice tests in the form of card guessing, with the outcome then subject to statistical analysis.

For example, if I thoroughly shuffled a deck of ordinary playing cards, shielded them from you, and asked you to try to get a psi impression of whether each card was red or black and call it out to me or write it down, most of the time you'd just be guessing. (Research back in the 1930s and 1940s showed that about ten dovetail shuffles produce adequate mixing and randomizing of decks of cards.) This guessing is an example of the detector output that shows some variation, usually mostly due to chance, mentioned earlier. Given the materialistic null hypothesis (no psi phenomena) as a complete explanation of what could happen in this situation, you have a fifty-fifty chance of being right on any particular call, and for the fifty-two cards in a standard deck, we'd expect you to average twenty-six correct calls.[2] Sometimes you'd get a few more, sometimes a few less, but the more times you called through randomized decks, the closer your average score would be to twenty-six hits, or 50 percent. If you got all fifty-two correct — or none correct, for that matter — you wouldn't need statistics to tell you that that would be extraordinary, a far too improbable event to attribute to chance.[3]

In real life, percipients in experiments have called red or black with ordinary playing cards, or one of the five symbols of the classic Zener ESP test cards (see the following figure) that were commonly used for parapsychological studies. With the Zener cards your chances were 1 in 5 of being correct on any try by chance alone. Most of the time, results indicated that people were indeed just guessing, but a significant amount of the time, they got a few more hits than they should've by chance. That is, there's an occasional response due to psi perceptions mixed in with all the guessing. I won't go into the statistical details, but let me reassure you that they're solid statistics of the most basic sort used in all the sciences. If "There's got to be something wrong with the statistics!" as dedicated pseudoskeptics often loudly proclaim, most fields of science are in bad trouble, because they use the same basic statistics (Utts 1996).

Figure 5.2 Zener Cards for Testing Basic ESP Functions

So we can do paraconceptual experiments with a variety of objective procedures (for example, it's easy to count the number of hits in card-calling studies with complete reliability) that let us say something like, "The odds against this outcome's happening by chance alone are more than 100 to 1," or "The results are well within the range expected by chance variation." In psychology generally, odds of 20 to 1 or better against chance, the ".05 level," are considered a pretty reliable sign that something besides chance variation is happening.

So what happens when we try variations of this basic para-conceptual experiment to discover and understand various types of paranormal or paraconceptual phenomena that might form a basis for a more spiritual view of reality?

Notes

10. In a survey I did in 1979 among experienced parapsychologists (Tart 1979b), "occasionally" meant that about a third of their experiments produced significant evidence for various forms of psi phenomena, rather than one in twenty, expected by chance.

11. This procedure doesn't allow you to know whether or not you were correct on each call, of course, because doing that makes the statistics much more complicated since you'd obviously change your guesses to "black," for example, if you knew from feedback that most of the red cards had already come up.

12. If you really want to know, the exact probability (binomial calculation) of getting all fifty-two or none correct is 4,503,599,627,370,702 to 1, which we can round off as 4 quadrillion to 1. Thanks to Richard Shoup and York Dobyns, who calculated this for me.

CHAPTER 6

Telepathy

TELEPATHY (late nineteenth century [origin from "tele-"
+ "-pathy"]): The communication or perception of thoughts,
feelings, and so on by (apparently) extrasensory means.
— SHORTER OXFORD ENGLISH DICTIONARY, *6th ed., s.v.*
"telepathy"

W HEN people pray, they're basically attempting to communicate with some sort of being, God or god, saint, angel,
spirit, or ancestor. But that being, insofar as it exists, is
not physically present and does not have a physical form with ears
anyway, so from a materialist's perspective, praying, aloud or silently, is a waste of breath and time. But what if mental intentions
and information could be shown to travel across space to other
living human minds?

The basic idea of telepathy, a term coined by classics scholar
and early psychologist Frederic W. H. Myers in 1882, is that one
person's mind can pick up information from another person's mind.
Figure 6.1 shows the basic procedure for a telepathy experiment.
In an experiment, the target information is examined with the intention of mentally sending it by a sender or agent, so that we know
that the relevant target information exists in the mind of the person acting as sender. This sender is materially isolated from the
percipient, another living person who acts as the detector, by
distance or material barriers. If total materialism is correct and
there's indeed no such thing as telepathy, then the sender's
attempts to mentally send the information will have no effect:

the percipient's calls will be nothing but guesses, and results will merely reflect chance variation. If there's some kind of telepathic channel operating even intermittently, shown by the dotted line labeled ? (the Greek letter psi) in the figure, while there still may be lots of chance variation, it won't be only chance variation; there will be extra hits in identifying the target information.[1]

Telepathy implies, of course, that mind is somehow of a different nature than matter. We set up the experiment so that, given our knowledge of physical matter and reasonable extensions of that knowledge, nothing could happen; yet in practice something sometimes happens.

Figure 6.1 Basic Telepathy Experiment

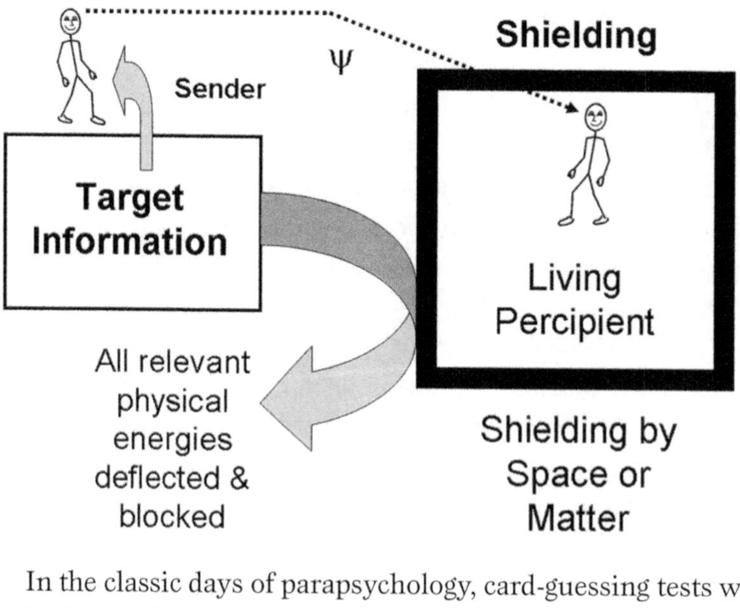

In the classic days of parapsychology, card-guessing tests were standard procedure. The sender would usually be in a separate room, perhaps even in another building, to be sure there were no relevant sensory cues about the cards given off by the sender. The experimenter (who was sometimes also the sender) would thoroughly shuffle a deck of target cards, and at a designated time, the sender would begin looking at the cards one by one, in sequence. He would look at each card for a designated length of time, say half a minute, while trying to send the identity of that card to a distant percipient. Starting at the same time, the percipient, in another room, would try to get an impression of what the card was and either write it down or tell it to an experimenter, who wrote it down. After completion, the order of the deck of target cards would be compared to the percipient's calls, hits would be counted, and a statistical evaluation made.

At this stage of our knowledge, we don't actually know how much the sender's efforts to send really matter. Many experiments formally designated as telepathy experiments might actually have their results due to clairvoyance or precognition, as described in following chapters. In spite of this lack of theoretical clarity, though, the idea of mind-to-mind communication, telepathy, is a commonsense idea that will undoubtedly stick with us. Its existence is especially important if we think that mind is of a different nature than body, resulting in some kind of dualism. Without getting into the theoretical complications, then, I'll continue to use telepathy in the commonsense way to mean that the relevant target information exists in someone's mind — who may or may not be actively trying to "send" — at the time the percipient is trying to get the information by some kind of psi perception.

Let me give you the flavor of a telepathy experiment by describing some of my own training in telepathic ability.

Figures 6.2 and 6.3 show the sender (a younger me, in this case) and a percipient or receiver (one of my students at UC Davis) in an extensive telepathy experiment I carried out in the 1970s (Tart 1976). Note that this was not an experiment designed to test the reality of telepathy per se, although it added to the evidence for the existence of telepathy. As I mentioned earlier, an enormous amount of evidence for the reality of phenomena like telepathy had been collected long before I came into the field. It's always been clear to me that nonacceptance of that evidence was almost always for irrational reasons, so I never saw the point in collecting more proof-of-existence evidence that would also be irrationally ignored. The purpose of my experiment was to try to see if people could be trained to use telepathy more effectively by giving them immediate feedback on how they were doing.[2]

As a result of my conventional psychological training, I'd thought about the basic telepathy-testing situation in a different way than parapsychologists usually conceptualized it. They thought of it as testing how much telepathic ability a sender and percipient team had. I reframed it as a situation in which the percipients (and agents) needed to learn what to do, instead of just being a matter of testing the level of a talent they already possessed. After all, if someone says, "Lift your right hand while wiggling your fingers," you can do that with ease and precision because you've long ago learned how to do that, but if the person says, "Read my mind," what are you supposed to do? Concentrate hard? Relax? Pray for success? Take a casual attitude? Stare at the ceiling? Pray for aid from the local nature spirits? Breathe deeply? Breathe shallowly?

In the almost universal procedures used in telepathy experiments that had been done before I came into the field in the late 1950s, a percipient in a telepathy, clairvoyance, or precognition experiment guessed at the identity of an entire deck of cards before receiving any feedback as to whether any particular guess were right or wrong. From a psychological perspective, this struck me as what psychologists term an extinction paradigm, a procedure that kills off any talent a person actually has in a given task through confusion and discouragement.[3]

Think of it this way: In classic card-guessing tests, on any given trial, you have to make a call as to what you think the target card is, so you hope for inspiration or some kind of feeling to guide you, and when (or if) it comes, you act on it. Or perhaps you just "guess," whatever internal psychological process "guess" means at a particular time. Then you have to make another call and another call and another call. By the end of a run through the cards, when the results of your calls through the target deck are scored and shown to you, you might find that you were right on, say, the third, seventh, fifteenth, sixteenth, nineteenth, and twenty-third trials. This is delayed feedback. Were those hits the ones on which you felt

Figure 6.2 Charles Tart Sending with Ten-Choice Trainer

especially confident, or were those the ones on which your body seemed to tingle? Or, what else? That is, the feedback of rightness or wrongness comes too late for you to begin accurately discriminating what kind of internal cues or feelings might indicate that your call was actually influenced by psi perception, versus those on which you were just guessing. So my experiment was designed to test whether providing immediate feedback to percipients who already showed some talent at this kind of procedure, such as in a screening test, would enable them to gradually increase their scores, instead of their scores gradually diminishing to chance, resulting in extinction of talent, as was, sadly, the normative result for repeated guessing studies. The commonness of the decline effect, a falling off of scoring with repeated trials until it often reached chance, was frequently cited as strong evidence for the reality of psi ability. Chance, after all, doesn't get "tired," "bored," or "confused"; it operates uniformly over time. People, though, get tired, bored, or confused.

In my procedure, the sender sat in front of a panel on which ten lights, each with a corresponding switch beside it, were arranged in a circle. An electronic random number generator (RNG) (the

Figure 6.3 Student Percipient Using Ten-Choice Trainer

little box on the right, on top of a somewhat larger box in figure 6.2) was used to select which of the lights would be lit and thus serve as the telepathic target on any particular trial.[4] When this target was selected and the experimenter or sender turned on the chosen target light, a "ready" light in the center of the circle on the percipient's panel (see figure 6.3), came on to show her that it was time to try to telepathically perceive what the correct target was and then indicate her response by pressing the appropriate button beside the light she thought was the target. Immediately, the correct target light came on, so the percipient got instant feedback on whether or not she was correct.[5] If incorrect, was she physically close to the correct target? If she was exactly correct, a pleasant chime also rang inside the apparatus. Percipients came to love the sound of that chime!

These were large-scale experiments. Working with student co-experimenters I trained in my experimental psychology class at UC Davis, in the first study we screened more than fifteen hundred students for psi ability, giving a group psi test in their classes and inviting those whose individual results looked significant to a confirmation study to see if their results held up or were probably just chance variation. Those who continued to show high scores were invited to participate in the main training study, where ten completed at least twenty sessions on the ten-choice trainer, shown in figures 6.2 and 6.3 above, and fifteen completed at least twenty sessions on a commercially manufactured four-choice trainer by Aquarius Electronics.

The formal results of two training studies, reported in full elsewhere, were very promising. The first training study (Tart 1976) showed a probability of its total hits happening by chance of 2×10^{-25}, two times ten to the minus 25th power — yes, that's ten with twenty-five zeros after it, two in more than a million billion billion — on the ten-choice trainer and 4×10^{-4} — four in ten thousand — on the four-choice trainer. No percipient showed a decline in scoring over time (the drop-off I theorized was extinction that was so typical of parapsychological studies), and some showed suggestive signs of getting better with the feedback training. The most significant percipient made 124 hits when only 50 were expected by chance.

A later, second study had to be done with less-talented percipients, due to a lack of enough assistance for the screening stages, and it ended up showing chance scoring on the ten-choice trainer, but significant scoring on the four-choice trainer.

All in all, I felt that a good case had been made that immediate-feedback training might improve telepathic ability, but I didn't have the resources to keep following up on this line of research. Large-scale empirical studies would need to be done on how much initial psi talent was needed if learning were to overcome the inherent extinction of being right by chance, for instance. And which was the better test situation: ten-choice, four-choice, two-choice, or what? Fewer choices, for instance, meant the feedback bell showing you were correct would ring a lot, making you feel good, but most of those rings would be due to chance and thus add confusion. A many-choice test, on the other hand, would have very few false rewards due to chance, but a person might get discouraged in the long intervals between genuine psi hits.

Psychic and Didn't Know It!

What I and most of my coexperimenters found especially interesting was the apparent unconscious manifestation of psi ability. Time after time, as experimenter or sender, you'd turn on the randomly selected target so that the "ready" light came on in the middle of the percipient's console and, via closed-circuit television, you'd see the percipient immediately reach up and stop his hand right over the correct target. You'd immediately begin "mentally shouting" (no actual sounds were allowed, of course), "Push it, push it, push that button! You're right!" only to watch the percipient move his hand away to other targets, come back and hover over the correct target again and again, and then finally move his hand suddenly and push the wrong button!

All of us senders had fantasies about being able to administer electric shocks then! This would've been unethical under the social contract we had with our experimental percipients, but it was perfectly obvious that the percipient (or at least the percipient's hand) knew the correct target; how could he go and push the wrong button?

This perception that the hand "knew" could've sometimes been selective misperception on our part as senders, of course, and I tried to get grant support to do further studies where all the percipients' hand motions would be videotaped and later judged by independent raters to see if they really did "know" the target at some unconscious level. I wanted to take various bodily measures, such as galvanic skin response (the body's natural response to perceiving a new stimulus), to further see if their bodies showed more activation over correct targets, further indicating that they'd "received" the psi message at some unconscious, bodily level that just hadn't made it to consciousness. I never could get the funding to do this.[6] But this personal experience, plus a lot of other kinds of colleagues' parapsychological experiments, strongly suggests that we can unconsciously "use" psi abilities. The use they're put to may not be what we would consciously do. (We'll look at this possibility later when we discuss psi-mediated instrumental responses.)

As I hinted at the beginning of this chapter, telepathy in some form might be the "mechanism" involved in prayer, the nonphysical way of conveying intention and information from your mind to another (kind of) mind. Since, in my judgment, the experimental parapsychological evidence for telepathy, plus people's spontaneous experiences, shows that telepathy is a reality, it provides scientific support for engaging in prayer.

And insofar as a psi ability like telepathy may be used unconsciously — for example, the hands seemed to know, but the percipient's conscious mind didn't — the picture of what prayer might consist of or do gets complex. Might part of you, outside of your ordinary consciousness, be "praying for" things you don't know about — more or less effectively? It's an interesting, and somewhat scary, thing to reflect on.

Why Telepathy Is "Nonphysical"

While followers of scientism usually dismiss the evidence for the reality of telepathy a priori, without bothering to look at it since they know it's impossible, some investigators have tried to explain it within a materialistic framework.

Our brains are made of physical matter and have known physical energies — chemical and electrical — coursing within them. With German psychiatrist Hans Berger's 1924 discovery of electrical currents in the brain, some scientists immediately theorized that these electrical currents might also generate radio waves, thus making the brain a radio transmitter. If another brain could act as a radio receiver, we could have communication at a distance without the use of the usual physical senses: telepathy. The idea was very appealing: you took an exotic mystery, telepathy, and explained it "away" in terms of known scientific, physical knowledge. Insofar as this theory of telepathy is true, we should someday be able to build electronic devices that could both send and receive telepathic messages to and from human brains.

As you get more specific, though, telepathy as mental radio turns out to be a theory that doesn't account well for the facts; indeed, the empirical facts contradict it. This was clear to me when I first became interested in parapsychology, because I'd been a ham radio operator as a teenager and then studied enough electronics to pass the federal examinations to receive a first-class radiotelephone license, allowing me to work my way through college as a transmitter engineer in various radio stations. Sending and receiving by radio were very familiar matters to me.

The first problem with the telepathy-as-mental-radio theory is that communicating by radio takes enough electrical power to send a signal over the required distance. While there can be interactions with external conditions (such as the state of the electrically charged ionosphere reflecting radio waves), generally the farther you want to communicate, the stronger the radio signal you need to generate. Signal strength falls off with the square of the distance. Looking at the kind of electrical power likely to be generated in the brain, it might be feasible to transmit for a few hundred feet, but the power required to communicate over thousands of miles — some telepathy tests have been successful at that kind of distance — would be well beyond what we could expect any material brain to generate.

The second problem is that the generation of such radio waves by the brain should be easily detectable by appropriate physical instruments placed near a sender's head. For communicating over thousands of miles, the signal should be so powerful that such an insensitive detector as a fluorescent tube held near the sender's head should light up; it does not. No instrument placed near senders' heads has ever reliably detected radio waves carrying telepathic information, even of a low power.

The third problem is what engineers call signal-to-noise ratio. If you're in a very quiet room, you can hear someone whisper to you across the room. That's a high enough signal-to-noise ratio. If you're in a noisy room though, like at a cocktail party, you can hardly tell that the person's speaking, much less make out what's being said; that's a low signal-to-noise ratio. There has always been some electronic noise around anywhere on our planet due to electrical storms, but today the radio spectrum is saturated with noise from innumerable electronic devices. It's possible to pick up electrical or magnetic signals from a brain, but it not only requires our most sensitive detectors, since the electrical or magnetic radiation is so weak, it also requires that the person be in an extremely expensive metal-shielded room to keep out all this extraneous radio noise. So for telepathy as mental radio to make sense in terms of what we know about the physical world, the brain would have to generate a strong signal that should be easily detectable but never has been detected, and this signal would need to be much stronger than the extensive ambient electronic noise on our planet to convey useful information.

The fourth problem is shielding. If telepathy is indeed some kind of radio transmission, we should be able to block telepathy by putting the sender, receiver, or both in electrically shielded rooms. But the occasional use of such rooms hasn't knocked out telepathy results. Indeed, there's some evidence (Tart 1988a) that working in electrically shielded rooms that are configured in a certain way may actually make telepathy stronger, although we need much more research to solidify and refine this data. This makes no sense in terms of conventional physics. My best guess at present is that the electrical shielding may cut down interference with brain functioning from electromagnetic sources, thus producing less distraction or interference from nontelepathy tasks, allowing a sender or receiver to function more efficiently. So the shielding doesn't directly affect the telepathy; it's simply putting the human instrument who expresses telepathy, the sender or receiver, in a better physical environment and thus mental frame of mind to use this nonphysical function.

Thus what empirical data we have to date about telepathy (and other forms of psi ability) is that it's not affected by material distance or shielding. If telepathy were some form of radio communication, it would be thus affected. In this practical sense, telepathy (and other forms of psi ability) are nonphysical in nature, because they don't show the lawful characteristics associated with relevant material phenomena.

Now note carefully that I use the adjective "nonphysical" in a strictly pragmatic way. I'm not making any absolute statement about the ultimate nature of reality. How would I know? And I usually qualify "nonphysical" with the phrase "given what we know about reality and reasonable extensions of that knowledge." So what I'm saying more precisely and practically is this:

1. Given what we know about the ordinary physical universe, telepathy (and psi ability in general) doesn't follow known physical laws or reasonable extensions of those laws.
2. Telepathy (and psi ability in general) often seems to "violate" those laws.
3. The practical meaning of this lack of sense in terms of conventional physics is that it's probably a waste of time to sit around and wait for an explanation of psi phenomena and spirituality in terms of known physical laws, or reasonable extensions of known physical laws. Rather, we should investigate them on their own terms.

Certainly, we shouldn't ignore them or actively deny their reality!

How about the reasonable extensions of known physical laws? How far does "reasonable" reach?

Among some people there's certainly a hard-core adherence to materialism that insists that everything will eventually be explainable in terms of current and yet-to-be-discovered physical laws (such as quantum effects). So we can ignore psi phenomena and spirituality, and wait until progress in physics handles them?

This is certainly an attitude that people can take, but it's not science. Philosophers call this attitude promissory materialism, and it's not science, because it's not falsifiable: you can't prove that it might not be true. I could just as well claim that these phenomena will all be explained one day in terms of little green angels with four arms who mischievously avoid all our attempts to see if they're real. I guess we'd call that promissory angelism. In neither case can you prove that it won't be that way at some future time, since the future never arrives.

The Quantum Universe

If you know basic physics, you'll know I've been talking about how telepathy is nonphysical from the perspective of a classical, Newtonian, commonsense universe. But what about quantum effects? What about the entanglement of two particles speeding away from each other at the speed of light and how a change in one produces an instantaneous change in the other?

The quantum picture of the universe is indeed very interesting, and some contemporary writers have cited aspects of it as science's somehow justifying psychic and spiritual phenomena. Well maybe, and maybe not.

First, I'm skeptical of how well most of these writers actually understand quantum physics. I know enough physics to know that I don't really understand quantum physics, so I won't use my poor and possibly distorted understanding to argue for the existence of psi phenomena and spiritual phenomena. The existence of psi phenomena is more than adequately demonstrated by the empirical results of so many experiments already. I understand that this isn't enough for some people. They want to have a good reason, a good theory, to accept something, but as I've said in outlining essential science in earlier chapters, empirical evidence, data, always has priority. It's nice to have a theory to make you mentally comfortable with the data, but you can't ignore or reject data simply because you're intellectually uncomfortable.

Secondly, for all the intellectual fashionableness and excitement of quantum-theory approaches, they haven't resulted in any better psi manifestations. I have a very practical approach to essential science: usually a better theory makes things work better. If you really understand something better, you should be able to work with it more effectively. Earlier I used the example that the germ theory of disease, implying that you'd better purify the water, worked enormously better than the demon theory of plagues, which led to ringing the church bells loudly to scare off the demons. I have brilliant colleagues who are involved in thinking about psi phenomena in quantum-theory terms, but I'm required by intellectual honesty to remind them occasionally that their quantum approaches don't yield any more psi phenomena in experiments than approaches of any other sort.

I wish all theorists well, but all theories have to produce empirically verifiable results. Maybe quantum theory approaches will provide a useful theory of psi phenomena and spirituality, or maybe it'll turn out to be a fashionable but passing distraction, the way the mental-radio theory of telepathy was. And just to complicate life, it seems to be generally true that when you believe you understand something, you act more confidently and effectively because of that confidence, regardless of the literal truthfulness of your beliefs. So thinking that quantum theory justifies the reality of psi phenomena, for example, may make you a more effective psychic, just as, to use a historical example, believing in the reality of helping spirits probably made people in an earlier time more effective at using their own psi abilities.

For those who want to follow up on this, the best starting point, with great relevance to spirituality, is Dean Radin's book *Entangled Minds: Extrasensory Experiences in a Quantum Reality* (Paraview Pocket Books, 2006).

Notes

1. There are even more sophisticated statistical tests that can look for significant patterns in the data other than simply hitting (or missing) beyond chance expectation, such as shifts in the expected variance patterns, but we'll stick with simple hitting or missing here, because that's enough to make the points.

2. And yes, the evidence for learning better telepathy or better control of ESP ability from my work has also been ignored by almost everyone, including parapsychologists, for reasons I consider largely irrational. You can find references to these criticisms and my refutations of them in my works 1977b, 1978, 1979a, and 1980. I'm biased, of course, but I believe I'm right in this instance. I used to be somewhat disappointed and angry about this, but lately it's been more interesting to wonder why this kind of strange ignoring or resisting happened.

3. I simplify here since training for psi ability isn't our major focus, but those who want detailed accounts of rationale and results should see Tart 1976, 1983, and 1977b; and Tart, Palmer, and Redington 1979a and 1979b.

4. RNGs can be constructed in several ways, such as using the arrival time of cosmic rays (which is random) to trigger a Geiger counter to the simpler style used in this study, known as an "electronic roulette wheel." Why does an ordinary, mechanical roulette wheel come to an unpredictable, random stop? All the mechanical forces acting on it could, in principle, be computed and the outcome be predicted, but in practice a human's sensory ability to predict or control these forces is way too low. For a roulette-wheel type of RNG, a fast oscillator is cycling an electronic counter through its whole range (zero to nine, in this case) over and over again, hundreds or thousands of times a second. If you could control the

length of your button press to a sufficient level of accuracy, you could deliberately select the next number, but the numbers on the counter change much, much faster than your nervous system can control your muscles, so the outcome is random.

A simple demonstration is to use your digital watch as an RNG. If it has a timer function that reads out to the nearest hundredth of a second, then start the timer going, look away a few seconds, and stop it without looking at it. You might have some luck controlling the second where it stops, and you may even have a little control over the tenth of a second, but the hundredth digit will be a random choice.

5. You can't give immediate feedback of right or wrong when using a closed (a fixed number of each possibility) deck of cards as the targets, because the knowledge gained from the feedback allows the percipient to rationally improve her strategy, as in knowing what cards have already been played in ordinary card games. An electronic RNG, though, is like an infinitely large deck of cards, an open deck: knowing what has already come up doesn't affect the odds as to what might come up next, so feedback doesn't mess up the statistics.

6. Here's an "interesting" sidelight on the social dynamics of scientism's prejudice against open investigation of the paranormal: my grant application was turned down by a major scientific-funding organization. It was their practice to include the comments their anonymous referees had made in evaluating it. All the comments were negative and, to my mind, prejudiced and shallow. Months later I met a prominent psychologist at a national convention, who asked me how my grant application had gone; he'd really liked the proposal. I had no idea he even knew I'd made such an application. It turned out that he'd been one of the referees and that his response had been enthusiastic but had disappeared from the reviews by the time they were sent to me.

CHAPTER 7

Clairvoyance, or Remote Viewing

CLAIRVOYANCE (mid-19th Century [origin: French, formed as "clairvoyant"]: The supposed faculty of perceiving, as if by seeing, what is happening or exists out of sight. — SHORTER OXFORD ENGLISH DICTIONARY, *6th ed., s.v. "clairvoyance"*

REPORTING on his experience of Cosmic Consciousness (see the introduction), Bucke noted: "Among other things he did not come to believe, he *saw* and *knew* [italics mine] that the Cosmos is not dead matter but a living Presence, that the soul of man is immortal, that the universe is so built and ordered that without any peradventure, all things work together for the good of each and all, that the foundation principle of the world is what we call love and that the happiness of everyone is, in the long run, absolutely certain" (1961, 8).

The classic materialist's view is of a universe of separate objects, occasionally and meaninglessly affecting each other through material forces but basically dead matter, not linked together by some kind of living "presence." Bucke had to be deluded when he wrote the above. But are things more linked than we normally imagine?

Clairvoyance, from French words meaning "clear (clair) seeing (voyance)," is the direct perception of the state of the physical world without the use of your normal physical senses or the intermediation of another mind. That is, at the time of a clairvoyance test, no one, no human mind, knows what the relevant target information is, so any positive results can't be attributed to telepathy at that time.[1]

Figure 7.1 diagrams the basic clairvoyance-experiment procedure. This figure is almost the same as a telepathy procedure, but there's no sender or agent involved. In classical parapsychological research, to conduct a clairvoyance test an experimenter would typically take a deck of cards and, without looking at the card faces, shuffle them thoroughly to randomize their order; put the deck back in its box, still without looking at the card faces; and often further shield the target deck by putting the box into a locked desk drawer. Then the percipient would be invited into the room and, while the experimenter observed her, asked to write down the order of the deck of target cards. (There are many variations of these procedures, of course, but they need not concern us here.)

Figure 7.1 Basic Clairvoyance Experiment

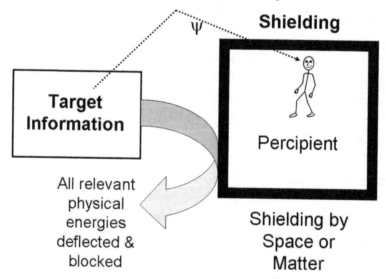

Let's look at a classic and outstanding clairvoyance study, the Pearce-Pratt experiment in clairvoyant card guessing, done at Duke University in 1933 and 1934. Hubert E. Pearce Jr. was a divinity student who had introduced himself to J. B. Rhine as someone who thought he'd inherited his mother's clairvoyant abilities, and he'd already scored exceptionally well in previous tests. J. Gaither Pratt, later a leading researcher in parapsychology, was a graduate student in psychology at Duke and a research assistant to Rhine, although he hadn't shown a particular interest in parapsychology at the time. J. B. Rhine, later founder and head of the Duke Parapsychology Laboratory, was then an assistant professor in the psychology department. Here's Rhine's description of the procedure (Rhine and Pratt 1954, 165–77):

> At the time agreed upon, Pearce visited Pratt in his research room on the top floor of what is now the Social Science Building on the main Duke campus. The two men synchronized their watches and set an exact time for starting the test, allowing enough time for Pearce to cross the quadrangle to the Duke Library, where he occupied a cubicle in the stacks at the back of the building. From his window, Pratt could see Pearce enter the library.
>
> Pratt then selected a pack of ESP cards [the Zener cards shown earlier in figure 5.2] from several packs always available in the room. He gave this pack of cards a number of dovetail shuffles and a final cut, keeping them facedown throughout. He then placed the pack on the right-hand side of the table at which he was sitting. In the center of the table was a closed book on which it had been agreed with Pearce that the card for each trial would be placed. At the minute set for starting the test, Pratt lifted the top card from the inverted deck, placed it facedown on the book, and allowed it to remain there for approximately a full minute. At the beginning of the next minute, this card was picked up with the left hand and laid, still facedown, on the left-hand side of the table, while with the right hand, Pratt picked up the next card and put it on the book. At the end of the second minute,

this card was placed on top of the one on the left, and the next one was put on the book. In this way, at the rate of one card per minute, the entire pack of twenty-five cards went through the process of being isolated, one card at a time, on the book in the center of the table, where it was the target or stimulus object for that ESP trial.

In his cubicle in the library, Pearce attempted to identify the target cards, minute by minute, and recorded his responses in pencil. At the end of the run, there was, on most test days, a rest period of five minutes before a second run followed in exactly the same way. Pearce made a duplicate of his call record, signed one copy, and sealed it in an envelope for Rhine. The two sealed records were delivered personally to Rhine, most of the time before Pratt and Pearce compared their records and scored the number of successes. On a few occasions when Pratt and Pearce met and compared their unsealed duplicates before both of them had delivered their sealed records to Rhine, the data could not have been changed without collusion, as Pratt kept the results from the unsealed records, and any discrepancy between them and Rhine's results would have been noticed. In subseries D, Rhine was on hand to receive the duplicates as the two other men met immediately after each session *for the checkup.*

(Reprinted with permission from J.B. Rhine and G. Pratt, "A Review of the Pearce-Pratt Distance Series of ESP Tests," Journal of Parapsychology 18:165-77)

How did the Pearce-Pratt experiment work out? Table 7.1 shows the results for the four subsets (where conditions varied, with approximate distances from cards to Pearce of either 100 yards or 250 yards, and Rhine being more directly involved in subseries D, as well as for the total experiment).

Note again that Pearce had been preselected from earlier work as a very talented percipient: these aren't the typical results one gets from unselected college students. He carried out a total of 1,850 calls in the combined study, scoring 558 hits when 370 were expected by chance, an average 30 percent hit rate instead of the 20 percent expected by chance with the five-choice Zener cards.

Table 7.1 Results of the Pearce-Pratt Distance Series

Subseries	Number of Runs	Hits Above Chance	Probability
A	12	+59	$P < 10^{-14}$
B	44	+75	$P < 10^{-6}$
C	12	+28	$P < 10^{-4}$
D	6	+26	$P < 10^{-6}$
Combined	74	+188	$P < 10^{-22}$

Note that these are extraordinarily significant results in terms of the odds against their being due to chance. Odds of 1 in 20 (.05) are usually called "significant" in psychology and many other branches of science, while odds of 1 in 100 (.01 or 10^{-2}) are definitively significant. Odds like 10^{-4} (1 in 10,000) are seldom reached in ordinary psychology experiments.

Clairvoyance in the Form of Remote Viewing

Since the 1970s the most interesting form of clairvoyance experiments have been what's called remote viewing (RV), a term coined by physicists Russell Targ and Harold Puthoff (1974) when they worked as researchers at the Stanford Research Institute (SRI), a prestigious, private think tank that carried out a wide variety of contract research for the government and industry.[2]) They chose the term "remote viewing" to make their research more understandable to mainstream scientists (the more general term, "remote sensing," was in wide use in the scientific and engineering communities then, to refer to all sorts of instrumental ways to detect and measure things at a distance, techniques such as radar or echo-location) and to avoid the negative "mystical" connotations many people associate with a word like "clairvoyance." I had the good fortune to be a consultant on some of these studies and see a lot of RV in action.

Puthoff and Targ once gave a report on their early RV studies at a small evening meeting of parapsychologists at my home in the San Francisco Bay Area. We were all somewhat amazed — and somewhat skeptical too — at the high quality and quantity of psi results their studies seemed to show. Most parapsychological studies yield statistically significant, but practically tiny, results. Puthoff and Targ were used to skepticism, however, and had already decided to actually conduct an informal RV demonstration at our meeting as the best way of dealing with our skepticism. One colleague left and randomly went to we knew not where. Half an hour later, we were asked to try to clairvoyantly see, or remote view, the target location where this person was, and make any notes or sketches we wanted to regarding it. Note that while this colleague was at the remote target location, we weren't asked to try to get what he was thinking but rather to describe the physical locale, an emphasis on clairvoyance, not telepathy, although telepathy isn't excluded. We'll see later how in formal RV experiments, telepathy is largely irrelevant to the results.

I had some interesting imagery come to me that involved some sort of factory or machinery, rotating drums or something, and bright colors. I wasn't impressed though; it seemed rather vague to me.

Then we were taken to the target for feedback, which turned out to be a brightly lit launderette on University Avenue in Berkeley. I wandered up and down the sidewalk a little, looking at the exterior and plate-glass window of the launderette and thinking it didn't very well match my remembered imagery that I had thought of as a factory. "Okay," I thought resignedly to myself, "ESP doesn't work really well very often; it certainly didn't seem to work for me."

But then as I stood in a new position to the right side of the window and looked in, I suddenly saw an excellent fit with my imagery: the rotating washers and dryers looked much like the rotating drums I'd seen, and bright-colored clothes were in baskets on a table. I was impressed!

But this was just an informal demonstration of procedure, nice if you experience it personally but otherwise too subjective to count very strongly as evidence for clairvoyance, so let's look at how formal RV experiments are conducted.

Figure 7.2 shows the basic procedure in the initial SRI (and many subsequent) RV studies. As a first step, a person I've sometimes thought of as the "hider," or, more formally, the beacon person or outbound experimenter, meets and gets acquainted with the person who'll serve as remote viewer. The beacon person will later go to some remote location, hidden from the ordinary senses of the viewer. At this point, though, the beacon person has no idea where he'll go, so he needn't worry about his interaction giving any cues to the viewer: there's no information to give.

Figure 7.2 Remote Viewing Procedure

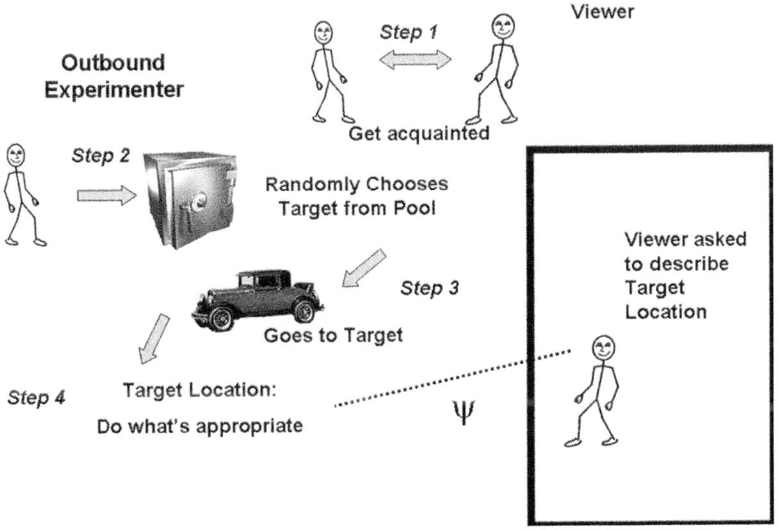

In the second step, the outbound experimenter leaves and goes to another laboratory room, where he uses an RNG to decide which of about fifty envelopes he'll remove from a locked safe. Each envelope contains the name of a target location that has visually interesting characteristics and is within a thirty-minute drive of SRI in Menlo Park, California, where the original RV research was carried out. Within a thirty-minute drive was a maximum time, but the target location could be mere minutes away, requiring the beacon person to use up a lot of time going around in circles driving to it. Given the richness of the San Francisco Bay Area, this meant that the target location could be almost anywhere; there were hundreds of thousands of sites to choose from.

At the end of the third step of traveling to the target, thirty minutes later, the outbound experimenter arrives at the target location and just hangs around in it, or does what's appropriate for people in that location, the fourth step. If the target was a fast-food restaurant, for example, the outbound experimenter would order and eat there, or if it was a playground he'd swing on the swings.

At the thirty-minute mark, the remote viewer, who has stayed in a locked laboratory with an inbound experimenter, is asked to describe what the target location is like where the outbound experimenter is. The viewer speaks into a tape recorder and, typically, makes a number of sketches of her impressions.

But "Wait," you might be thinking, "isn't this a telepathy experiment rather than a clairvoyance experiment? Couldn't the viewer be reading the mind of the outbound experimenter rather than directly perceiving the physical characteristics of the target location?"

Yes, the viewer could do that, but it wouldn't really help her score well, and might even lower her score, as you'll see when I describe the evaluation procedure. Sometimes the aspect of the target locale that was well described by the remote viewer was one that hadn't even been visible to the beacon person at the time. And it was later discovered that you didn't actually need an outbound experimenter at a target site for RV to work well anyway; this beacon person was usually a kind of psychological aid that wasn't always necessary.

There's a set period for the outbound experimenter to remain at the target, typically fifteen minutes to half an hour, and then he returns to the laboratory. The viewer's recorded verbal descriptions and sketches have meanwhile been collected by the inbound experimenter back at the lab and locked away for later formal evaluation.

Now the outbound experimenter, the viewer, and the inbound experimenter all drive to the chosen target location so the viewer can make a direct, personal comparison of her impressions with what's actually there. This comparison isn't included in the material later given to a judge for formal evaluation, since it's information gathered after the viewer knows what the target is by ordinary sensory contact while being there, but I believe this relatively fast (but not immediate) feedback to the viewer helps her hone her clairvoyant skills in the long run, learning to give more emphasis to certain kinds of feelings and impressions and less to others.

Although the results need formal evaluation, as will be described below, RV sometimes gives immediately striking results.

Figure 7.3, for example, shows a sketch (on lined paper) of an outstanding remote viewer, Pat Price, a retired police commissioner, made while remote viewing a target that turned out to be a public swimming-pool complex in Palo Alto, about ten minutes away from the laboratory. There's a formal plan drawing made later for illustrative purposes above it (again, the plan drawing was not part of the formal evaluation, in case there was any bias in creating the drawing).

In *Mind-Reach: Scientists Look at Psychic Ability*, Targ and Puthoff (1977, 52–54) report:

> ...Pat's drawing is shown...in which he correctly described a park-like area containing two pools of water:

Fig. 7.3   Swimming-Pool Complex Remote-Viewing Target

Formal plan drawing of target location

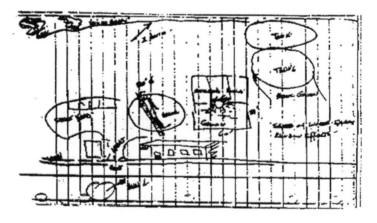

Pat Price's drawing of target location

one rectangular, 60 x 89 feet (actual dimensions 75 x 100 feet); the other circular, diameter 120 feet (actual diameter 110 feet). He was incorrect, however, in saying the facility was used for water filtration rather than swimming. With further experimentation, we began to realize that the oc- currence of essentially correct descriptions of basic ele- ments and patterns coupled with incomplete or erroneous analysis of function was to be a continuing thread throughout the remote-viewing work.

As can be seen from his drawing, Pat also included some elements, such as the tanks shown in the upper right, which were not present at the target site. The left-right reversal of elements — often observed in paranormal perception experiments — is likewise apparent.

To properly and formally evaluate RV studies, you follow the procedure shown in figure 7.4. Basically, you do a series of independent RVs with different targets. Practically and mathematically, six is the minimum number of viewings you can have in an experimental series for the statistics to be adequate, while more than nine or so gets rather complex for a judge to keep everything in mind.

Figure 7.4 Remote-Viewing Evaluation Method

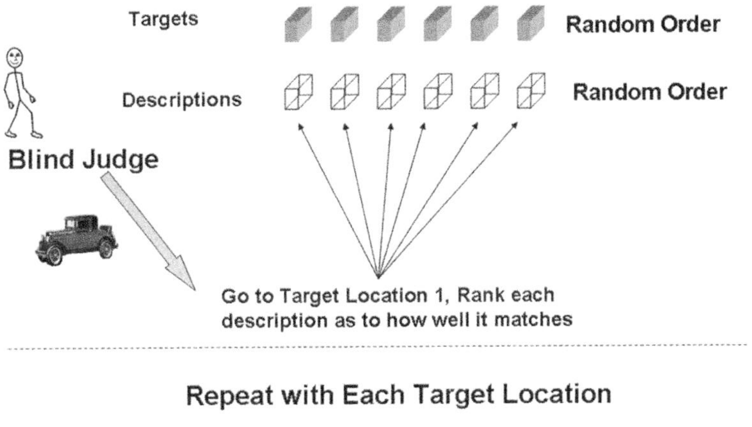

Repeat with Each Target Location

Let's say you've done six RVs in separate sessions. The materials from each — drawings and a typed transcription of the viewer's impressions — are put in six separate packets and arbitrarily labeled A through F. There's no information in each packet as to what target location the descriptions were intended to go with. The swimming-pool complex material, for example, namely the transcript and Pat Price's drawing (not the plan drawing shown above) would contain no information that this was supposed to be about the swimming-pool complex. Copies of the driving instructions to each of the six target locations used are also arbitrarily numbered 1 to 6. The twelve packets are given to a judge who doesn't know what descriptions were supposed to go with what targets, a blind judge, to use the technical term. The judge is asked to drive to each of the target locations, read all six descriptive transcripts and drawing packets while at each location, and rank each description's similarity to each target. So at target location 3, for example, the judge might decide that description F fits it best, then description B next best, and so on.

Now we can see how this kind of RV is primarily a clairvoyance experiment: the remote viewer must describe physical features of the target locations that the blind judge will later be able to notice. Passing thoughts in the outbound experimenter's mind or idiosyncratic ways of perceiving physical reality won't be of any use, because the judge has no idea what they were. Telepathy isn't ruled out; an outbound experimenter could be looking at the target location from exactly the same vantage point the judge will later have and seeing it the same way the judge is likely to see it, but telepathy from the outbound experimenter to the viewer isn't needed; clairvoyance will do. Again, it's also important to note that while the early RV experiments used beacon people, with an assumption that this would make the procedure more interesting or more successful for the viewers, many later but just as successful RV studies had no beacon people involved at all.[3]

The technically inclined reader can look up the exact statistical methods used (Tart, Puthoff, and Targ 1979), but basically the formal evaluation goes like this. If there's no clairvoyance involved, the viewer's impressions are simply guesses, and they're random and general. Some of them, especially broad generalities — "This is a big area" — will be correct, but they're just as likely to be correct for the locations that were not the target for a given viewing as for the designated target, thus giving high "hit" scores to the wrong places. If the guesses are correct and very specific, on the other hand, they're not likely to match any particular target location by chance alone. So to show a high likelihood of the involvement of genuine clairvoyance, the viewer must come up with specific items of description that are correct for the designated target but not for the other targets in the experiment, and that's what the statistics formally evaluate. It's important that the target locations used be clearly different from one another. A fast-food restaurant, a church, a playground, a fire station, a drive-in movie theater, and a redwood grove would be a good set, for instance, while six churches would have so much in common that it would take extraordinarily good RV to differentiate them enough for a blind judge to make correct matches.

To illustrate, in our example above, Pat Price gave some specifics — two pools of water, their approximate dimensions, and their shapes — that didn't match elements in the other targets in that series. So the judge easily ranked that description as the best match for that target.

The fact that the judge is blind to which descriptions were supposed to go with which targets also controls for any biases on the judge's part. A too-credulous judge will see correspondences everywhere; a too-skeptical judge will seldom see them anywhere, but a judge's credulity or skepticism won't systematically bias the evaluation of the results, except perhaps to make them less sensitive to detect genuine clairvoyance.

Is Remote Viewing of Practical Use?

Although it was classified knowledge through most of the early work, it's now well known that most RV research, especially that at SRI, was sponsored by various government agencies like the Department of Defense, the Army, or the Central Intelligence Agency, whose interests were primarily whether RV could be a useful form of supplemental intelligence gathering in the Cold War.

To become a consultant on the SRI project, I had to obtain a Top Secret security clearance and sign two contracts where I agreed not to reveal what the research found. I remember those contracts well, as agreeing to secrecy of any sort was not my usual style of life! But I believed this research was important for national security: wars tend not to start when the aggressive side believes the other side knows what its plans are. One contract stipulated the penalties for revealing secrets, namely ten years in prison and a ten-thousand-dollar fine. The other contract, which I humorously thought of as the cheap-secrets one, stipulated five years in prison and a five-thousand-dollar fine.

Fortunately for scientific knowledge, much of what was in these classified RV programs has been revealed by various authors (Schnabel 1997), who discovered them from documents recovered through use of the Freedom of Information Act, so they're no longer secrets that I have to worry about revealing. However, a good number of the most successful results used in actual intelligence operations have never been declassified.

Amusingly, the results of classified military programs aren't always what's anticipated. My colleague physicist Russell Targ, for example, one of the pioneer investigators of RV at SRI, sometimes jokes that what he found while acting as a spy for the CIA led him to find God.

Support for RV research and its practical applications for the military and intelligence agencies eventually ended when it became well known enough to be politically embarrassing. As Russell Targ (2008, 147) put it, "Shortly after that (2005), the program was declassified, and Robert Gates, now Secretary of Defense but then a CIA director, announced on the TV program Nightline that the CIA had indeed supported the SRI program since 1972, but he declared that nothing useful ever came out of it. I wondered at the time why the interviewer, Ted Koppel, didn't ask him why he supported such a stupid program for twenty-three years if indeed 'noting useful ever came out of it.'"

The Nonphysicality of Clairvoyance

As with telepathy, discussed in the previous chapter, clairvoyance, as we currently know it, is nonphysical from the perspective of a classical, Newtonian universe.

Attempts to create a physical theory of clairvoyance began with the early card-guessing test results. If such tests are done with a percipient trying to guess a single card that has been removed from the shuffled deck and is facedown on the table in front of her, the physical analogy that comes to mind is that it might be some kind of "X-ray vision," like that which Superman used in the comic books. Literal X-rays wouldn't seem feasible, because the level of radiation involved would probably give the experimenters cancer soon, but perhaps some similar form of unknown, but definitely physical, radiation accounted for clairvoyance?

But many clairvoyance tasks with cards involved leaving the shuffled pack whole, as well as often putting it back in its box, putting it in some other kind of container like a desk drawer, or both. So some kind of X-ray vision gets much tougher to imagine. If you've ever tried to look through (using ordinary light rays rather than X-rays) a stack of slides, you've seen that all the images are jumbled together so that you can't discriminate them.

Also, like telepathy, there's no indication that ordinary physicalshielding factors like distance or solid barriers have any effect on clairvoyance scores, except psychologically. But if a percipient believes a kind of barrier will create a problem, it may.

In the model of clairvoyance given in figure 7.1, the target is "shielded" from the percipient. Usually these are fairly ordinary kinds of shields, ranging from the thickness of the cardboard a target card is printed on at a bare minimum to having the target cards stacked together to shield each other while being in a cardboard box that's in a drawer and perhaps in another room with a wall between. There's one kind of known classical physical energy that could penetrate such shielding, though — although how it could "couple" to the targets to pick up the information is a mind boggler — and that is extremely low-frequency electromagnetic radiation (ELF). Eliminating ELF as a possible carrier of clairvoyant information was the outcome of a unique, albeit one-shot, experiment, Project Deep Quest. (I find it wryly amusing that we have to worry about the action of an ELF in a parapsychology experiment, but I suppose it's just a manifestation of my "elfish" sense of humor.)

Stephan Schwartz has been one of the most successful and creative investigators of RV, and was interested in the question of whether ELF might be important in RV. Through his contacts in the Navy (he had worked on many government projects in the past), in 1977 he was able to borrow the use of a deep-diving research submarine, the Taurus, which was doing its sea trials off Santa Catalina Island, near Los Angeles. Working with Hal Puthoff and Russell Targ to create target materials, Stephan and the Taurus crew took mutual friend and remote viewer Hella Hammid, an artist and photographer, more than five-hundred feet below the surface, below where it had been established that ELF waves could penetrate. This is the most thorough kind of shielding against any kind of electromagnetic radiation that you can get on our planet.

Although on the verge of nausea — it had been a rough voyage getting out to the dive site — Hammid's RV impressions were (Schwartz 2007, 58): "A very tall looming object. A very, very huge, tall tree…a cliff behind them… Hal is playing in the tree. Not very scientific."

Six sealed envelopes were then opened, one containing a photo of the correct target site (not known to anyone in the submarine), five being nontarget sites. Hammid selected the one of a large tree on the edge of a cliff, which turned out to be correct.

Later, well-known psychic and artist Ingo Swann, who's credited with creating the idea of RV in the first place, was taken out, and dived to more than 250 feet. He remotely viewed that Targ and Puthoff were then walking about in a large, enclosed space, perhaps a city hall — but no, a mall, with reddish, flat-stone flooring. It turned out that they were strolling about in a shopping mall in Palo Alto (Schwartz 2007, 61).

ELF was out. Whatever way clairvoyance works, it's very unlikely that it has anything to do with electromagnetic radiation. Applied in a rigorous way, the RV approach has yielded many interesting results. But note that a number of people have made questionable claims of being experts in RV, and offer to teach it to people for a high price. Caution is advised!

Notes

1. As with telepathy, things get more conceptually complicated. I've given you the operational definition, the procedure to define clairvoyance, namely psi perception of a shielded target when the information doesn't exist in someone else's mind at the time of the perception. Sometimes what we label clairvoyance might be precognition, though, either telepathically of the information existing in someone else's (for example, the experimenter's) mind in the future or in the percipient's own mind in the future, as described in the next chapter.

2. SRI is now officially named SRI International. While it was originally part of Stanford University, it had become an independent research center long before the RV research began.

3. Many card-guessing studies were done over the years where the exact contribution of telepathy versus clairvoyance versus precognition couldn't be assessed, so the process was simply referred to as "GESP," for "general extrasensory perception." Remote viewing with a beacon person is technically a form of GESP.

CHAPTER 8

Precognition

PRECOGNITION (Late Middle English [origin: Late Latin "praecognitio(n-)", formed as "pre-" plus "cognition"]: Antecedent cognition or knowledge; (supposed) foreknowledge, especially as a form of extrasensory perception.
— SHORTER OXFORD ENGLISH DICTIONARY, *6th ed., s.v. "precognition"*

PRECOGNITION is successful prediction of future events when such events couldn't be rationally predicted from knowledge of current conditions and the laws governing their change. Saying it will be light out tomorrow at 8:00 a.m., for instance, is not precognition: barring some cosmic catastrophe, the laws of planetary motion will result in there being light tomorrow morning. We know the causal chain that produces the sunlight tomorrow. Nor is predicting something like a prominent politician's being connected to some financial scandal next year a likely example of precognition: the event is, unfortunately, far too probable.

Figure 8.1 sketches the basic procedure for a precognition experiment. An experimenter asks a person to describe what a target situation will be at some designated time in the future. After the percipient's responses are recorded, some randomization procedure is then used to determine what the future target will be. Such a procedure might be as simple as shuffling a deck of target cards, facedown, a dozen times, for instance, or activating an electronic random generator to produce a string of target numbers after the calls have been recorded.

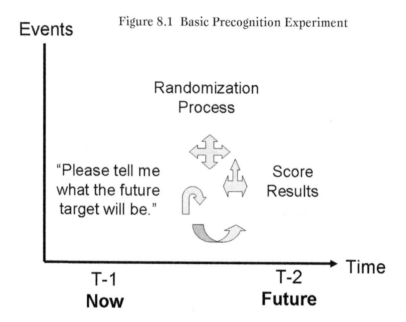

Figure 8.1 Basic Precognition Experiment

Because I have personal difficulties with precognition, as discussed later in this chapter, I survey studies of it in more detail than I've done for telepathy and clairvoyance.

One of the most impressive overviews of precognitive studies I've ever seen was an article by parapsychologist Charles ("Chuck") Honorton and psychologist Diane Ferrari, published in The Journal of Parapsychology in 1989. They carried out what has now become a sophisticated way of assessing bodies of research literature on any phenomenon, a meta-analysis. Such an analysis recognizes that various studies looked at the target phenomena in various ways, under differing experimental conditions, and with various degrees of experimental rigor and control. When you look at all the published positive and negative results obtained in this way, what's your best conclusion about the reality or lack of it of the target phenomenon?

Honorton and Ferrari looked at all the multiple-choice type precognition studies published from 1935, when the methods for testing precognition were just evolving, through 1987. (The studies of precognition in the twenty years since their analysis strengthen and extend their conclusions.) In the English-language scientific literature, they were able to find 309 separate studies, reported on in 113 articles. Sixty-two different investigators were involved, and the composite database was almost two million trials, generated by more than fifty thousand subjects. Most of the percipients were, of course, college students.[1] Many involved thoroughly shuffled decks of Zener cards, often with additional randomizing factors added after the shuffling, such as cutting the deck according to newspaper accounts of the next day's low temperature in some distant city, while others involved computer-generated target numbers.

The combined results of the studies produced odds against chance of 10 septillion to 1. What's a septillion? It's 10 with 24 zeros after it. To put it more simply, it's preposterous to believe that these cumulated precognition results were due to chance! Lots of just plain guessing was going on, certainly, but every once in a while a genuine precognitive perception of the future state of the targets occurred.

One of the common arguments for rejecting evidence for psi phenomena is what's called the file-drawer problem. We humans like success, so if a study with positive results is likely to be accepted for publication, we'll then know about it, while one with no results probably won't be accepted. "Why waste expensive journal space on a study in which nothing happened?" is the way an editor might think. Since scientists understand this attitude, they may not even submit the study for publication; they just leave their results in the file drawer.

A simple way to think about this is that if you accept the usual 1-in-20 odds against chance as a criterion for "significance," then if you do experiments in which nothing truly happens, about 1 in 20 of them will show statistical significance by chance alone. If you get that 1 published and the other 19 languish unknown in your files, a very misleading impression of reality is created.

But suppose you and your colleagues have cumulatively published 10 studies on something, each with 1-in-20 odds against chance? If indeed nothing's really happening, that means there are about 190 unsuccessful studies languishing in various file drawers. That's a lot of hidden work! So maybe it's more likely that something really is happening?

Honorton and Ferrari tested how many unsuccessful, unpublished precognition studies there would need to be to bring the cumulative results of the published precognition studies back down to chance results. They estimated it would take 14,268 studies to do so. Given that there has never been more than a few people at a time working in experimental parapsychology, there's no way there could've been so many unsuccessful studies carried out.

How about flawed studies? If there really is no precognition, we would expect any apparently successful results to be due to methodological problems like opportunities for sensory cues, improper randomization of targets, or recording and analysis errors. Honorton and Ferrari rated the studies on quality of methodology, and found that not only was it not the case that poorer quality studies were more likely to produce evidence for precognition, but also the suggestion of a relationship they found was that methodologically higher quality studies were associated with better precognition results.

Since Honorton and Ferrari's meta-analysis, many more studies have shown precognitive effects, including unconscious ones. Dean Radin's authoritative books (1997, 2006) are excellent places to see these reviewed. But let's now go on to an example of precognitive RV, precognition in action, as it were, in a situation much more like real life than a laboratory task, taken from a statistically significant formal series using the RV procedure by John Bisaha and Brenda Dunne (1979) in the Chicago area.

At 10:00 a.m. on the day of the experiment, an outbound experimenter, not yet knowing where he was going, left the laboratory and drove around randomly for twenty minutes. After the outbound experimenter had left, the remote viewer was asked to describe where the outbound experimenter would be at 10:35 a.m. The verbal description was recorded and sketches, if any, made.

At 10:20 a.m., with the viewer's description already finished and sealed, the outbound experimenter parked, used an electronic RNG to select where to go, timed his drive to arrive at the selected target location at 10:35 a.m., and did appropriate things there.

In this example, the target turned out to be a train station, and while the experimenter was there, two trains passed through, one of which stopped at the station.

Figure 8.2 Precognitive Remote-Viewing Target

Some the things the remote viewer said that allowed a judge to correctly match transcript and target location in later formal judging were (Tart, Puthoff, and Targ 1979, 114–17): "I have an image of looking at the traffic and seeing it go by really fast, speeding cars...I see a train station...I see a train coming...older building...trees... wooden planks on the floor. ... There are posters or something...

benches…tracks."

Now I should clarify that I have a personal kind of "bias" against precognition. I put bias in quotes, because it's not a bias in the usual sense of a negative intellectual concept or emotional feeling against precognition: I found the experimental evidence for precognition quite convincing when I studied it decades ago, and always lectured and wrote about precognition as one of the "big five," an effect that has so much experimental evidence attesting to its reality that no reasonable person could doubt it. Rather, my bias is that at some deep level, I find the idea of precognition, where the inherently unknowable future can sometimes be known, so incomprehensible that I just never think about precognition in a serious way. I say the words about it that the evidence logically compels me to say, but the idea doesn't really touch me or affect my way of living. And even though I've long intellectually accepted the idea that precognition could be real, I've never let it affect my living my life on the assumption that free will is a reality. To reason that we have no free will, that it's all an illusion, makes life both senseless and boring.

Precognition Sneaks into My Laboratory

I wasn't aware of this bias until I was analyzing the results of my first immediate-feedback telepathy training experiment, described in chapter 6. I was quite pleased with the large amounts of (present-time) psi ability shown by my star percipients, especially on the ten-choice trainer, and by the fact that my theory — providing immediate feedback to talented percipients would prevent the usual decline of ability and encourage learning — was holding up. Then I recalled that in many earlier ESP studies, the experimenters had often, as a secondary and exploratory analysis, scored their results for possible precognition. Just because you instructed percipients to use present-time telepathy, for instance, didn't mean they might not unconsciously use some other form of ESP, like precognition. This kind of precognitive scoring was done simply by totaling up scores where you compared the response in a series of tests at a given time to the next target coming up, rather than the current target: response 1 against target 2, response 2 against target 3, and so on.

I did this kind of analysis, and it was a real shock for me to discover that there were massive amounts of precognition in my own laboratory data! This was what made me recognize and explore my deeper attitudes about precognition, and realize that in a sense I hadn't "rejected" or "defended against" the idea of precognition; the very idea was so nonsensical to me at a deep level that I hadn't needed to actively reject or defend against it.

And just to challenge my mind further, the massive precognition in my study was in the form of psi-missing, or scoring way below what would occur by chance. The more a percipient hit on the real-time target, the more she missed on the future target just ahead.

Psi-Missing

Psi-missing is a very important concept, so let's look at it now. Recall that back in chapter 5, we discussed how calling all the cards correctly in a run through a randomized deck that was shielded from normal sensory perception was clearly fantastic, and I gave the example that in guessing red or black with a deck of 52 ordinary playing cards, with no feedback about correctness, you'd get a result that had odds of 4 quadrillion to 1 against its happening by chance. But getting 0 cards right has the same odds. You don't really need statistics in such an extreme case to know something's happening.

Suppose you carry out some kind of ESP tests, and the results are nowhere near these fantastic levels but are statistically significant, say, odds of 100 to 1 or less. But your result is not that the percipients scored more than what we expect by chance, but significantly less?

Many experiments have been done, for example, where, to succeed in the ESP test, groups of students instructed to be percipients were first given a questionnaire asking about their belief in ESP

(Schmeidler and McConnell 1958, Lawrence 1993). While there were variations in the way this was asked, basically it let you divide the students into those termed sheep, the ones who believed in ESP, and goats, the ones who didn't. Then the ESP test was given. Often, the overall mixed-group score wasn't significantly different from chance, but if you scored the sheep and the goats separately, you saw an interesting pattern.

The sheep, the ones who believed in ESP, scored abovechance, often significantly so, all on their own. The goats, those who disbelieved in ESP, scored below chance, also often significantly so, on their own, and the difference between the sheep's and goats' scores was significant. This result is, of course, after allowing for normal chance variation in scoring.

Psychologically, when individual feedback of test results was given, I think both sheep and goats were happy. After all, these are students, thoroughly indoctrinated to believe that tests usually measure what you know. The sheep believed ESP existed, they got high scores on the test, and that fitted their belief. The goats got poor scores, which made perfect sense to them since there was no such thing as ESP.

Think now: how can you score significantly below chance? I've only been able to think of one way to do this and never heard anyone propose any other way. Most of the time you may be just guessing, but once in a while you, or rather some unconscious part of you, have to use ESP to correctly identify the target and then influence your conscious mind to call anything but the correct target. It's as if your subconscious, for example, uses ESP to know the target's a five this time and then influences you to call any number but five.

Psi-missing always amazes me when I think about it. I know that in ordinary psychological functioning, we often show distorted perceptions and thoughts that uphold our beliefs and prejudices. Here, in extraordinary functioning, or psychic functioning, the mind unconsciously manifests a "miracle," ESP, to support its belief that there are no miracles and no ESP. Paralleling my theorizing about what my unconscious mind might've done in the *coup d'état* case in chapter 4, we humans are deep, subtle, and tricky.

The existence of psi-missing also illustrates why precise laboratory research can be so helpful. In many ways, lab research, especially repeated guessing at cards and the like, is very dull. Yet because we know from the mathematics precisely what chance expectation is, we can take notice when scores are significantly below chance, and discover phenomena like psi-missing or, as discussed later in this chapter, transtemporal inhibition. I can't imagine examination of ordinary-life psi phenomena leading to discovering something like psi-missing: it's pretty hard to notice what's not happening.

Back to Precognition in My Lab

If the precognition scores on the target just ahead (and they were truly just ahead in the future, for at the time of a response, the next target hadn't been created yet, the experimenter or sender hadn't pushed the button on the electronic RNG that created the next one-to-ten target) had only been mildly significant, say, with odds of twenty to one or even a hundred to one against chance, I think I might not have really been bothered by them. They would've fallen within my intellectual attitude of "Yes, precognition exists, but I don't really need to think about it on a deep level." But as well as the positive, hitting scores on the present-time targets, being very high, the missing, negative scores on that immediate-future target were also very high, although not as strong as the hitting on the present-time target. They surpassed my "gut level" threshold of needing the intellectual abstraction of statistics to theorize that something was happening to an obvious, "Something strange is happening!" What I then did is a good example of how essential science, discussed in chapter 2, is carried out.

Remember that in essential science, data is always primary over theory and belief, over expectations about what should happen. So I had to work with this data; I couldn't just ignore it because it didn't fit with my ideas of how reality worked.

One of my first lines of work was to wonder whether there was something wrong with the way we'd done the experiment: was I seeing some kind of artifact? This was straightforward science on the one hand, double-checking for possible errors and maybe a manifestation of my resistance to precognition on the other; if I could find something wrong with the experiment, I could forget about that precognition.

I checked one of the basic assumptions of any ESP experiment, namely that each target a percipient tried to call was generated in a purely random way. In this case that meant that any of the cards on the panel of the ten-choice trainer, ace through ten (see figure 6.3 in chapter 6), had an equal one-in-ten chance of being chosen on each trial and that there were no sequence effects; that is, a target selection on any given trial was independent and unaffected by previous choices. That latter requirement is why we use mechanical (thorough card shuffling in early, classical parapsychological studies) or electronic randomization procedures. Human beings are very poor randomizers; we have detectable patterns as to what we think is random, so we can't depend on a person's creating a random sequence.

It turned out that a common human belief about randomicity, namely, that random numbers seldom repeat, might have affected the experimenters' behavior. The selection button on the RNG was a "soft" button; that is, it didn't give a distinct click when you pushed it; it just got gently harder to push. So, in retrospect, I think that sometimes an experimenter might've pushed the button to generate the next target, looked at the number displayed, saw that it was the same one as previously, thought that she hadn't pushed the button hard enough to actually make it change, and so pushed it again, more deliberately. Such a result — I'm theorizing that this happened now; I don't actually know, but it fits the data — would lead to not enough target sequences of 1 to 1, 2 to 2, 3 to 3, and on up to10 to 10 for some percipients, and that's what I found. Since the percipients would likely have the same kind of bias, that "real" random numbers don't repeat, they'd avoid choosing the same target twice in a row, and this would artifactually inflate their scores above chance on present-time hitting.

For some critics of my study, this was a reason to totally throw out the entire results as invalid: the target generation was not random. But if you think about it, this kind of all-or-none, perfectly random or not-at-all random, thinking doesn't make sense. Any large set of numbers generated by truly random methods may pass the usual tests for randomness, but there could occasionally still be short patterns in the targets that might correspond to human preferences. Indeed, there's a mathematical theory that for any sequence of random numbers, no matter how long, you can actually create a formula or algorithm that would deterministically generate that set of numbers, implying that the sequence wasn't random at all. But, and this is a crucial "but," your algorithm won't predict new numbers in the sequence with an accuracy beyond chance expectation.

I think of this as a mathematical version of the principle I mentioned in chapter 2 while talking about the need to actually test the predictions of scientific theories rather than accept them just because they make intellectual sense, the Law of Universal Retrospective Rationalization, which is, in retrospect, as follows: we clever humans can always find a seemingly plausible reason why things happened the way they did; we're very, very smart pattern makers.

So the practical question for my immediate-feedback training study is, "Were the slight deviations from randomness in the target sequences enough that a clever person, taking advantage of them, could recalculate the odds as he learned about patterns from the feedback to get his high scores by this kind of estimation, rather than using ESP?" If this were so, then I could guess that the precognition scores were probably artifacts, spurious results due to the percipients' estimation abilities rather than any kind of ESP, and not have to worry about them. Indeed I could forget about the whole experiment!

This compulsive checking for possible flaws is a common procedure in essential science. You not only try to design an experiment to be flawless, but you also worry about it afterward, and if you can see, with the wisdom of hindsight, that there might have been a flaw, you test to see whether or not it was really of any importance.

To make a long story short (but the story is available in full [Tart and Dronek 1982]), I devised a way to recalculate possible biases after every trial in the experiment and come up with the most logical, mathematically probable call on that basis. When you have ten possible choices and hundreds of trials, this is formidable, to put it mildly! Working with colleague Eugene Dronek, a computer expert at the University of California, Berkeley, we embodied this logic in a program I named the Probabilistic Predictor Program (PPP), and turned it loose on the actual target data sequences of the experiment. The PPP had to be run at night, when few people were using Berkeley's main computer, because of the enormous amount of computation required.

The result? The PPP could score better than chance using the biases, but its results were way, way less than those of the real human percipients. Since the PPP could handle far more data than we would expect of any human being, while never making a computational mistake that a person might make, this pretty well eliminated the hypothesis that the main ESP scoring on the present-time target or the below-chance scoring, psi-missing, on the one-ahead precognitive target was some kind of artifact.[2] So the psi-missing had to be dealt with — whether I liked the idea of precognition or not!

Theory: Transtemporal Inhibition

In looking for processes that might account for the appearance of psi-missing, I came across the work of Nobelist Georg von Békésy (1967) on a phenomenon called lateral inhibition in neurological fields of science. First discovered in relation to the sense of touch, it turns out to be a general process applied in all our senses for sharpening information, and one now deliberately used in engineering various sensing devices to make clearer images, where the process is called by such names as edge detection, edge sharpening, and contrast enhancement.

To illustrate, take a sharp pencil and gently press down on your skin in some sensitive place, enough to dent your skin without hurting yourself. What does it feel like? It feels like a sharp point pressing down on your skin, of course.

But, in a way, that feeling doesn't make sense, given that we know we have touch receptors densely planted beneath the surface of the skin. Yes, the mechanical pressure from the pencil point is pushing down hardest, deforming the skin most that's directly under it. But the skin is elastic and stretched to the sides, and that tightened, stretched skin is stimulating touch receptors on all sides of the pencil point. Receptors give out signals that are proportional to how strongly they're stimulated, so the strongest signal should come from the receptor right under the pencil point, the next strongest from those just to the side of the pencil point, somewhat less strong signals a little farther out where the skin isn't stretched as tightly, and so forth. If what we sense is a result of all these touch receptors firing, why don't we feel a sensation of a rounded object pushing against our skin instead of a sharp point?

Figure 8.3 sketches this. Your skin is shown on the bottom, dented and stretched in a curved way, and the intensity of firing of individual touch sensors and relay neurons is shown as the density of pulses beside each one, since greater intensity of neural signals is a matter of faster firing.

What von Békésy discovered is that the touch nerves don't just transmit their signal up to the brain; they also send inhibitory signals to the touch nerves to the side of them, laterally, thus lateral inhibition. The result, shown in figure 8.3, is that while the signals from the first touch receptors, the ones actually being mechanically

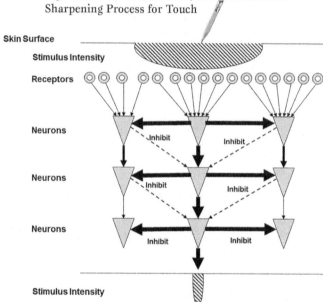

Figure 8.3 Lateral Inhibition, as an Information-Sharpening Process for Touch

stimulated, would convey the impression of a rounded object touching them, as the signals are relayed from one set of neurons to the next in the chain leading up to the brain, the most active nerve path, the one most strongly stimulated by the pencil point, is inhibiting, lessening the signals from those immediately around it, thus making it stand out more by contrast. The end result at the brain is a strong, dense signal from the most stimulated receptor and essentially nothing from the surrounding receptors: we feel a sharp point!

Parallels of this lateral inhibition process have been found in all our sensory systems. In vision, for example, this process has the effect of making objects in our visual field stand out more sharply against their background by enhancing their edges. Not that we consciously know our nervous system is doing this, of course; it's just the way we see. Some of you will have done the same process deliberately, though, as contrast enhancement or edge sharpening if you have used a photo-processing program on your computer to sharpen contrast.

Figure 8.4 Transtemporal Inhibition

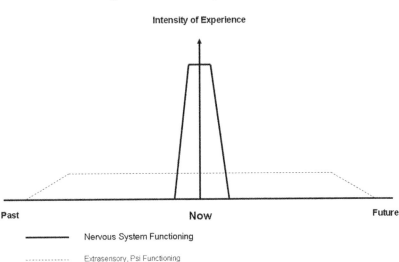

So, I wondered, if all our senses and some machines use this kind of perception-enhancement process because of its usefulness, might it be used in ESP? The result of my theorizing is illustrated in figure 8.4, where I've extended the concept of lateral inhibition through time and called it transtemporal inhibition.

Our physical, material human sensory system is very much localized in the here and the now. You can see, hear, smell, touch, and taste objects and processes that are here, in this particular location, close to and stimulating your body or in your body, and that are occurring at this time, now. But the kinds of experiences that lead us to the concept of ESP, of psi ability, in the first place, are about sensing or detecting objects and events that are neither sensorially here nor now, which we're isolated from by distance, material shielding, or time. Thus, the figure shows a short-duration physical time span of our embodied, material consciousness, centered on temporal now, to represent the physical nervous system and brain functioning. This is the "now" we ordinarily experience, and various psychological studies have shown that it's a few tenths of a second long. While, as a mathematical abstraction, "now" may be an infinitesimal point of no duration, in the nervous system it's more solid, an "artifact" or construction of our nature, as it were. This is where experience is intense; it's happening! It's intense compared to memories of the past and speculations about the future.

But because some part of our minds sometimes uses ESP to get information about the future (precognition) and the past (postcognition, a complex idea discussed later, in chapter 11, which we'll just take as a possibility for now), I theorized that this aspect of mind, something we can think of as an aspect of our spiritual nature, isn't so localized in the here and now; instead, it's more "spread out" in space and time, so it's in contact with objects and processes that aren't here and now, that are elsewhere and in the future or the past, "elsewhen." Normally we're not aware that this aspect of our minds even exists, so I show it as very low intensity in figure 8.4, but occasionally information obtained by this aspect of mind, ESP, breaks through into ordinary consciousness and we have a psychic impression: we know something that turns out to be about the "elsewhere" and "elsewhen." Because ordinary language has evolved to be about the here and now, the physical world, it's difficult to talk about what consciousness in the elsewhere and elsewhen might be like.

Let's go back to our example of lateral inhibition, when you press the pencil point into your skin. A perception that a rounded object is touching you would be, in one sense, a truer perception: your skin is being stimulated as if a rounded object were touching you. But in terms of getting along in ordinary physical reality, it's usually a lot more important to know if that's a thorn or, say, a knife against your back than a round-ended stick or a finger! That is, while this signal is processing, this lateral inhibition in all senses is artificial in some ways; it generally results in a better representation of what's actually out there in the world. Sticking with our pencil-pressed-against-your-skin example, the sensations from the stretched skin to the side of the pencil point are noise: they're confusing signals that take away from the clarity of the point perception; they're an artifact of your sensing system.

In engineering terms, lateral inhibition increases the signal-to-noise ratio of your perceptions. When you're trying to listen to a distant radio station, for example, whose signal is weak, and there's a lot of static, you have a low signal-to-noise ratio and it's hard to understand what's being said. If some process reduces the noise, even if it can't boost the signal, you can hear more clearly and understand more. There are, for example, electrical devices built in to your automobile that are designed to reduce the radio noise that any car's ignition system generates, thus increasing the signal-to-noise ratio in your radio thereby allowing you to hear weak stations you might otherwise find unintelligible.

Breakthrough Discovery or Just a Nice Idea?

So we've looked at essential science in action. I observed something unanticipated, the psi-missing, in the course of doing an experiment focused on other things, feedback learning of psi ability. This is my data. I checked that it wasn't a clear artifact of the situation, and then I created a theory of why my data took the pattern it did, namely that a basic process, lateral inhibition, was operating over time to produce transtemporal inhibition. I also went through some personal growth in seeing the deep resistance I had to the very idea of precognition.

I can't claim that when the theory of transtemporal inhibition finally clarified in my mind that I, like Archimedes, leaped out of my bathtub and ran naked down the street shouting, "Eureka! I've found it!"[3] It gelled in my mind more slowly, after going in other, fruitless directions. But I was pleased and felt very clever.

But, as I noted in describing the process of essential science and essential common sense in chapter 2, the feeling of understanding and cleverness is nice, but you don't stop there. You have to spell out the logic of your theory and then make predictions. If this is true, then under condition A, result B will be observed; under condition C, result D will follow; and then you, your peers, or both need to run tests to see if B actually results from A, D from C, and so on. If they do, your theory has gotten further empirical support; if they don't, your theory is either just plain wrong, no matter how clever it seems, or perhaps only partially adequate and needing refinement and adjustment. If you haven't made any predictions and neither you nor your peers have tested those predictions, then your theory is in limbo. It sounds good and makes "sense"; maybe it's correct and useful, and maybe it's not.

While I'd like to believe that my theory of transtemporal inhibition is a major breakthrough in understanding the process of psi ability, the reality is that it's still in limbo. It calls for strongly functioning ESP in multiple-choice test settings to even see if others observe it. I haven't done those studies, nor have my colleagues, so who's to say what's true or not at this time?

This is a good point at which to introduce a (sad) reality note. While the accumulation of more than a century of psychical research and parapsychology findings let me discuss the "big five" and "many maybes," and make a strong scientific case for the reality of some sort of basic spiritual nature for us humans, the field of scientific parapsychology has always been a taboo, rejected area, which means that very few trained scientists ever work in it; they have very few resources and a difficult time sharing the results of their work with other scientists, because mainstream journals are biased against publishing any positive psi results. So it's not as if there were a few dozen researchers conducting multiple-choice psi tests with highly talented or selected percipients, and they could just take a closer look at their vast amounts of data to see if they detected transtemporal inhibition, add new observations about it, or both. The few parapsychologists doing multiple-choice testing usually have statistically significant but very low-level psi results and wouldn't be able to see this kind of effect. And, while in principle, replication of others' findings is central in science, very few people do straightforward replication experiments in any field of science; your institution promotes you for your originality and creativity, not for replication.

I must also confess to a character quality of my scientific work that's sometimes best described as a talent, at other times as a limitation. I'm interested in many, many things, and my career has reflected this, with publications about altered states of consciousness, biofeedback, dreams, enlightenment, experimenter bias, humanistic psychology, hypnosis, hypnotic effects on nocturnal dreams, instrumentation for research, meditation, mindfulness, near-death experiences, out-of-body experiences, parapsychology, psychedelic drugs, psychophysiology, scientific method, sleep, spirituality, the ultimate nature of consciousness, transpersonal psychology, and more. I remember, in graduate school, hearing scientists described — too simplistically, of course — as generalists and specialists. At the extremes, a generalist was described as someone who knew less and less about more and more until he knew nothing about everything! A specialist knew more and more about less and less until he knew everything about nothing at all. I do move in the generalist direction.

By the time I finished my second study of feedback training for improving ESP ability, I thought I'd demonstrated its value, and others could (and ought to!) go on with extending and refining the work. I was pretty much out of resources for doing more work along this line; I'd become very interested in RV, which was much "sexier" as an experiment than repeated multiple-choice guessing; and I needed to devote a lot more time to my personal spiritual-growth work, so the theory of transtemporal inhibition still lies in limbo.[4] Perhaps this is my most important scientific discovery, or perhaps it's just an interesting idea that isn't really useful in understanding reality.

Psi-missing is a topic we'll come back to later, because it illustrates that we can use an extraordinary ability like psi ability in totally unexpected ways, including strengthening erroneous beliefs.

Does precognition mean that we have no free will? Frankly, I've never worried about this issue. Assuming I have no free will might make me feel freed of responsibility, that things happen and you can't blame me, but it also strikes me as a boring way to live.

Notes

1. Half jocularly and half seriously, for psychology students I like to define the field of psychology as the study of college sophomores by former college sophomores for the benefit of future college sophomores.

2. We also applied the PPP to the responses of the percipients, which were much more biased, as we expected, than the RNG's outputs. Interestingly, the more predictable percipients' responses were, the lower their ESP scores. This makes sense psychologically, for having biases about the way numbers behave is a restriction to opening up to ESP when the targets are indeed random.

3. While running down the street naked and shouting "Eureka!" would get you in trouble in most parts of the world, I find it amusing that since I live in California, I might be able to get away with such behavior. It's like when my Tibetan Buddhist teacher Sogyal Rinpoche once described a Tibetan growth exercise to help you break through deep inhibitions, called rushen, where you go alone to an isolated place, take off all your clothes, and run around doing crazy things! But then he reflected that in California this exercise probably wouldn't have much effect on you at all; it's too "normal."

4. My first two feedback studies were done with the assistance of student leagues, enrollees in my experimental psychology course. With considerable success, I followed a teaching philosophy that students would learn more and be more interested if they worked with me on a real experiment that could advance knowledge, rather than cut-and-dried replications of previous research. But the department stopped scheduling me to teach this course. Resistance? Perhaps. I'd also applied for a major research grant that would've opened new avenues on feedback training, but it wasn't given, and, as described in chapter 6, the apparent prejudice in denying it was discouraging.

CHAPTER 9

Psychokinesis

PSYCHOKINESIS (English, twentieth century [origin: from "psycho-" + "kinesis"]): The supposed ability to affect or move physical objects by mental effort alone. — SHORTER OXFORD ENGLISH DICTIONARY, *6th ed., s.v. "psychokinesis"*

PSYCHOKINESIS (PK), or to use an older term, *telekinesis*, is the ability of mental intentions to directly cause physical effects on the material world without any known physical mechanisms, such as muscle action, being involved. Figure 9.1 diagrams the basic model of PK. An agent is given instructions to make something happen simply by wishing for or willing it, and is physically separated from the target materials so that no ordinary physical forces are of any use.

There have always been reports that people caused resting objects, like a bottle sitting solidly on a tabletop, to move by force of will alone, but it's rare (but not unknown) to see events like this under laboratory conditions, where possible fraud or other material explanations can be completely ruled out. Many alleged PK events, for example, were produced in the darkened rooms of mediumistic séances as proof that spirits existed, but so many of these were revealed to be fraudulent when investigated closely. And yet, with a few mediums, such as Daniel Dunglas Home (pronounced "Hume," 1833–1886), major movements of physical objects occurred under good observational conditions in hundreds of cases. Putting aside for the time being the question of whether such instances proved the existence of spirits, were they paranormal?

Figure 9.1 Basic Psychokinesis (PK) Experiment

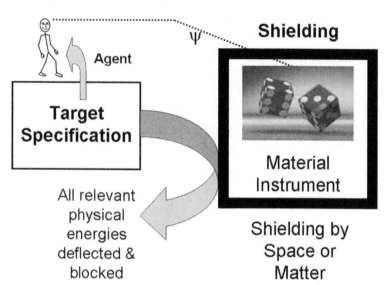

Were they PK?

I've found it psychologically interesting that most people, including most parapsychologists, find it easy to ignore all the reports about D. D. Home and other similar mediums. I've decided that there's some kind of psychological principle at work, an attitude on the order of "We moderns are so very, very smart, not like people in the old days, who were dumb and credulous, easily fooled, so if I don't like any report more than twenty years old that attests to things I don't want to believe in, I needn't go to the bother of actually finding flaws in it; I can just dismiss it as 'old' and 'anecdotal,' and forget about it."

I can't think of any good reason why an educated group of men and women a hundred years ago were any better or worse than we are at observing things under good observational conditions, so I take most of the reports about D. D. Home seriously. For example, accordions, in rooms illuminated by candles or lanterns, were often seen and heard to play recognizable tunes, even though they weren't being touched by Home or anyone else, or were being touched only with one hand. Consider this report by Sir William Crookes (1832–1919), a distinguished early scientist who investigated Home under stricter laboratory conditions than usually obtained at séances.[1]

I find Crookes's description (1926) of some accordion research with Home so charming in its language, as well as valuable, that I reproduce it at length here:

> Among the remarkable phenomena which occur under Mr. Home's influence, the most striking, as well as the most easily tested with scientific accuracy, are (1) the alteration in the weight of bodies and (2) the playing of tunes upon musical instruments (generally an accordion, for convenience of portability) without direct human intervention, under conditions rendering contact or con-nection with the keys impossible. Not until I had witnessed these facts some half-dozen times and scrutinized them with all the critical acumen I possess did I become convinced of their objective reality. Still, desiring to place the matter beyond the shadow of doubt, I invited Mr. Home on several occasions to come to my own house, where, in the presence of a few scientific enquirers, these phenomena could be submitted to crucial experiments.
>
> The meetings took place in the evening in a large room lighted by gas. The apparatus prepared for the purpose of testing the movements of the accordion consisted of a cage formed of two wooden hoops, respectively 1 ft. 10 ins. and 2 ft. diameter, connected together by 12 narrow laths, each 1 ft. 10 ins. long, so as to form a drum-shaped frame, open at the top and bottom; round this 50 yards of insulated copper wire were wound in 24 rounds, each being rather less than an inch from its neighbour. These horizontal strands of wire were then netted together firmly with strong so as to form meshes rather less than 2 ins. long by

1 in. high. The height of this cage was such that it would just slip under my dining table, but be too close to the top to allow of the hand being introduced into the interior, or to admit of a foot being pushed underneath it. In another room were two Grove's cells, wires being led from them into the dining room for connection, if de-sirable, with the wire surrounding the cage.

Fig. 9.2
Crooke's Experiments: Artist's Sketch of D.D. Home
with One Hand on End of Accordion in Shielding Cage

The accordion was a new one, having been purchased by myself for the purpose of these experiments at Wheatstone's in Conduit Street. Mr. Home had neither handled nor seen the instrument before the commencement of the test experiments. In another part of the room, an apparatus was fitted up for experimenting on the alteration in the weight of a body....

Before Mr. Home entered the room, the apparatus had been arranged in position, and he had not even the object of some parts of it explained before sitting down. It may, perhaps, be worthwhile to add for the purpose of anticipating some critical remarks which are likely to be made, that in the afternoon I called for Mr. Home at his apartments, and when there he suggested that, as he had to change his dress, perhaps I should not object to continue our conversation in his bedroom. I am, therefore, enabled to state positively that no machinery, apparatus or contrivance of any sort was secreted about his person.

The investigators present on the test occasion were an eminent physicist, high in the ranks of the Royal Society (Sir William Huggins, F.R.S.), a well-known Serjeant-at-Law (Serjeant Cox), my brother, and my chemical assistant.

Mr. Home sat in a low easy chair at the side of the table. In front of him under the table was the aforesaid cage, one of his legs being on each side of it. I sat close to him on his left, and another observer sat close to him on his right, the rest of the party being seated at convenient distances round the table.

For the greater part of the evening, particularly when anything of importance was proceeding, the observers on each side of Mr. Home kept their feet respectively on his feet, so as to be able to detect his slightest movement.

The temperature of the room varied from 68 to 70 degrees Fahrenheit.

Mr. Home took the accordion between the thumb and middle finger of one hand at the opposite end to the keys [woodcut figure omitted] (to save repetition, this will be subsequently called "in the usual manner"). Having previously opened the bass key myself, and the cage being drawn from under the table so as just to allow the accordion to be passed in with its keys downwards, it was pushed back as close as Mr. Home's arm would permit, but without hiding his hand from those next to him.

Very soon the accordion was seen by those on each side to be waving about in a somewhat curious manner; then sounds came from it, and finally several notes were played in succession. Whilst this was going on, my assistant went under the table and reported that the accordion was expanding and contracting; at the same time, it was seen that the hand of Mr. Home by which it was held was quite still, his other hand resting on the table.

Presently the accordion was seen by those on either side of Mr. Home to move about, oscillating and going round and round the cage, and playing at the same time. Dr. Huggins now looked under the table and said that Mr. Home's hand appeared quite still whilst the accordion was moving about emitting distinct sounds.

Mr. Home still holding the accordion in the usual manner in the cage, his feet being held by those next him, and his other hand resting on the table, we heard distinct and separate notes sounded in succession, and then a simple air was played. As such a result could only have been produced by the various keys of the instrument being acted upon in harmonious succession, this was considered by those present to be a crucial experiment. But the sequel was still more striking, for Mr. Home then removed his hand altogether from the accordion, taking it quite out of the cage, and placed it in the hand of the person next to him. The instrument then continued to play, no person touching it and no hand being near it.

I was now desirous of trying what would be the effect of passing the battery current round the insulated wire of the cage, and my assistant accordingly made the connection with the wires from the two Grove's cells. Mr. Home again held the instrument inside the cage in the same manner as before, when it immediately sounded and moved about vigorously. But whether the electric current passing round the cage assisted the manifestation of force inside, it is impossible to say.

The accordion was now again taken without any visible touch from Mr. Home's hand, which he removed from it entirely and placed upon the table, where it was taken by the person next to him, and seen, as now were both his hands, by all present. I and two of the others present saw the accordion distinctly floating about inside the cage with no visible support. This was repeated a second time after a short interval. Mr. Home presently reinserted his hand in the cage and again took hold of the accordion. It then commenced to play, at first chords and runs, and afterwards a well-known suite and plaintive melody, which it executed perfectly in a very beautiful manner. Whilst this tune was being played, I grasped Mr. Home's arm below the elbow and gently slid my hand down it until I touched the top of the accordion. He was not moving a muscle. His other hand was on the table, visible to all, and his feet were under the feet of those next to him....

Alas, we don't seem to have a D. D. Home around nowadays! Why? No one knows, but there has been speculation that the times have changed too much. In Home's day, many people believed in spiritualism, and this gave a useful belief and social support system for Home to work in. Anyway, we don't have any Homes, so we must work at a much less spectacular level.

In drawing the basic process diagram for PK, I showed dice as the target. The use of dice was inspired by a professional gambler, who dropped into J. B. Rhine's laboratory at Duke University in the 1930s. He told Rhine that he shot craps for a living and made a decent living at it — and he didn't cheat. But he'd recently read an article by a mathematician who showed that it wasn't possible to make a living at craps; the odds were too much against you. "So," the gambler likely asked, "how do I manage to be successful? Why do the dice come up the way I need them to so often?"

Classical parapsychological studies thus used thrown dice as the PK targets. Throwing dice is a multiple-choice-type test, like card guessing, and we can know precisely what the chance expectation is, one sixth of the desired target faces. An agent, the person attempting to mentally influence the roll of the dice, usually shielded from exerting normal influences by distance, barriers, or both from the surface where the dice were thrown, was asked to will them to come up in a certain pattern. The pattern would be something like aiming for ones for the first ten trials, twos for the second ten, and so on, equal numbers of all faces to compensate for any mechanical biases in the dice.[2] Figure 9.3 shows the highest development of this classical parapsychological technique, where the dice were tumbled about in a rotating wire cage and at some random point a timer opened the door in one end of the cage, allowing the dice to fall and bounce on the recording surface.

Fig. 9.3 Classic PK Experimental Apparatus: Motor-Driven Dice Shaker

Repinted with permission of the Rhine Research Center

Many experiments showed systematic changes in the die faces that came up. As reported in his outstanding book, *The Conscious Universe: The Scientific Truth of Psychic Phenomena* (1997), parapsychologist Dean Radin, along with psychologist colleague Diane Ferrari, performed a meta-analysis of 73 English-language publications, representing the efforts of 52 investigators from 1935 through 1987. In this half-century time span, 2,569 would-be agents altogether had tried to mentally influence the outcome of just over 2.6 million dice throws in 148 different experiments. There were also just over 150,000 dice throws in 31 control studies where no one was attempting to influence the outcomes.

To make all the experiments read on the same scale, their results were mathematically recalculated as if chance were 50 percent. The control experiments showed that empirically, dice behaved just as we'd expect them to, with a "hit" rate of 50.02 percent.

For the combined experimental studies, though, where would-e agents were attempting to get more hits, the scoring rate averaged 51.2 percent. That's not much in an absolute sense but has odds of more than a billion to one against being due to chance. The great majority of the time, the agent's wishes had no effect, but every once in a while, a tumbling die was influenced to come up the desired way.

As with the earlier meta-analysis for precognition reported in chapter 8, Radin and Ferrari considered the file-drawer problem. Were lots of unsuccessful PK studies not being published, so the successful results were really a chance artifact? Only if an astonishing 17,974 unsuccessful studies were languishing in file drawers, or to put it another way, only if 121 unsuccessful, unpublished studies had been done for each successful, published one. Nor were less methodologically rigorous studies any more successful than more rigorous ones.

Nowadays dice are almost never used, and the targets in PK experiments are most likely to be the states of electronic RNGs. It's more convenient to do them that way, because you can automate the whole experiment to preclude human errors, and the data's already in computerized form to allow for more in-depth analyses. The effects are usually small but statistically significant.

Staying with Radin's comprehensive review in *The Conscious Universe*, he and psychologist Roger Nelson at Princeton University performed a meta-analysis of 152 studies, published from 1959 to 1987. The reports covered 597 experimental PK series, where would-be agents tried to influence the RNG's outcome, and 235 control studies.

As expected, empirical results in control studies continued to meet mathematical expectation: 50 percent hits. But the hit rate in the experimental studies was 51 percent, again, small in absolute terms but with odds against chance of a trillion to one. The level of results was very similar to that of the dice-tossing studies, so we're probably dealing with the same process here: a small but significant PK effect. And as with the dice studies, poorer methodology in the earlier studies that might've produced more artifacts didn't have any significant effect, and it would take 54,000 insignificant, un-published studies languishing in file drawers to take away the significance of the published studies.

Many more PK studies with electronic RNGs have been pub-lished since Radin and Nelson's meta-analysis, the PK effect con-tinues to manifest, and analyses and theories get more sophisticated all the time. The size of the PK effect remains about the same though.

Biasing an electronic RNG slightly, by intention alone, may seem trivial compared to reports of an untouched accordion playing a tune in D. D. Home's presence. On the other hand, there's something quite mind blowing about these RNG results. What's the target? If you try to influence a tumbling die, you have an implicit, commonsense model that you need to mentally "push" with just the right amount of force at just the right angle at just the right moment on the tumbling die, and that'll force it to come up the way you want. But what do you "push" on while trying to influence electronic circuits that are sitting in a box? What level of reality are you working on? Certainly not a commonsense reality of push and shove.

A Spinning Silver Coin

My personal introduction to PK studies happened in summer 1957, between my sophomore and junior years at college, when I had a summer job as a research assistant at the Round Table Foundation in Glen Cove, Maine. Andrija Puharich, the physician and researcher who ran the foundation, was visited by some people from Virginia who claimed various psychic abilities that we tried to test. The person I'll focus on here claimed ability to psychokinetically control the spin of a coin, usually a silver dollar, so the desired side would come up as the coin slowed and finally fell to the tabletop.

I was quite suspicious of William Cantor, the man who did this. Cantor could get 80 to 90 percent of the desired target face, but he was too glib and self-assured for me, and he was the one spinning the coin, so I was sure there was some mechanical trick to the way he spun it. It looked as if the coin was spun hard and would spin for ten to fifteen seconds or more before slowing down enough to noticeably wobble, and then you could often glimpse the desired target face but not the other face as it spun. It was a fascinating visual display. But all the tricks I tried in spinning the coin myself didn't work; I got 50 percent.

I watched Cantor get strong results dozen of times, and I kept trying to figure out the trick but couldn't. I realized later that he was quite aware of my suspicions and frustration, and watched it build and build. Finally, when I was clearly very frustrated, he let me in on the secret. If you wanted the coin to come up heads, for instance, just before spinning the coin, you tilted it slightly off the vertical position so that the heads side was tilted back. I was delighted to now know the secret and have my suspicions confirmed, and I then started getting 70 to 80 percent hits on my spins!

But after a few minutes or so of this, I realized I'd already tried this particular trick before, and it hadn't worked! Indeed, using what physics I knew at the time, it seemed to me that if you gave the silver dollar a good spin, it wouldn't matter if it were tilted a little before you spun it; the momentum of a hard spin would straighten it up. (I'm not sure if this is literally true, but it's what I believed at the time.) My scores fell back to chance, 50 percent — and stayed there.

Cantor had been deliberately playing with me, letting me get very frustrated until I was desperate for a belief that would explain things for me. Then he gave me this false explanation, knowing that in my frustration, I'd grasp at it — and start getting results! He'd done it with others before.

It was a good lesson in psychology for me, whether there was any PK involved or not. Belief systems can empower us — even if they're factually wrong! Or disempower us, depending on the beliefs.

To give the flavor of experimental PK studies, I'll describe my few formal studies, inspired by this early experience.

Almost two decades later, much more mature (or so I thought) and a psychology professor at the University of California, Davis, I came back to this spinning-silver-coin puzzle, and with the help of my students Marlin Boisen, Victor Lopez, and Richard Maddock, conducted several experiments (1972). Psychologically, I felt that a spinning silver coin, like a big, shiny silver dollar, was an excellent target for PK: it was dramatic, and you could often see one face or the other, rather than a blur, as it spun, making you feel as if you were focusing on it in some mysterious fashion. Its whirring sound as it spun and the clatter as it finally lost momentum and fell drew in your attention. The whole procedure was both fascinating and fun, which I think are important conditions when you're trying to look for psi ability in the laboratory. But letting the test person, the agent, spin the coin wasn't satisfactory, since we didn't know if you couldn't influence the outcome by normal means that way. So we devised a mechanical apparatus, photographed in figure 9.4 and diagrammed in figure 9.5, to spin the coin.

Figure 9.4 Spinning Silver Coin PK Test Apparatus
in the Author's Office at the University of California, Davis

A silver dollar, selected to be as unbiased as possible, and as shiny as possible, was placed in the clear, plastic holder shown at the middle bottom of the figure. When the agent was ready for a trial, the experimenter, holding a switch attached to the apparatus by a soft, flexible cord, so that he couldn't accidentally pull on the apparatus, pushed the start button. This pulled back a little pin that held the silver dollar in place so that it now rolled down the inclined chute, pushing on a switch near the bottom of its roll. This triggering switch activated a mechanical bat arm with a padded neoprene tip, whose forceful swing hit the edge of the coin just as it rolled out of the chute, spinning it rapidly and knocking it horizontally out onto the circular tabletop. Rubber bumpers absorbed the momentum of the bat arm at the end of its swing, and then a spring returned it to its rest position.

The round table rotated very slowly (about one revolution per hour) by means of a roller and motor at its edge. This was designed to prevent uneven table wear that might affect the operation of the coin.

Figure 9.5 Apparatus for PK Test, Diagrammed,
with Spinning Silver Coin

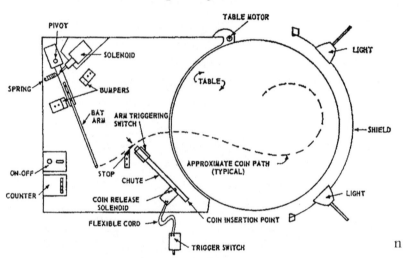

Two small, high-intensity lamps illuminated the spinning coin from the right-hand side of the machine. The subject sat or stood between these two lamps. A shield, about four inches higher than the top of the round table and extending to the floor, was between the subject and the apparatus. This shield was supported directly by the floor and had no physical connection with the apparatus. The subject was told not to touch the shield, but if he did accidentally bump it, he still wouldn't physically affect the apparatus.

The entire apparatus was shock mounted, to eliminate vibrations transmitted through the floor, in the following way.[3] A large automobile tire was laid flat on the floor, a piece of plywood laid on top of it, and then several concrete blocks were placed on it. Another automobile tire was placed on top of that, and the coin-spinning apparatus was on top of this. This inexpensive method of shock mounting was extremely effective in eliminating vibration and movement transfer. Some lead bricks were slid back and forth on the underside of the apparatus proper to level it; they also added additional mass on top of the tires for further isolation from any floor-transmitted shocks.

The subject also held a clear-plastic deflecting mask over his nose and mouth. This allowed him full physical view of the spinning coin, with no intervening materials, but prevented any effects from his exhalations. During experiments, the coin was never fired unless the subject was holding the mask over his mouth and nose. Neat, eh? As a lifelong gadgeteer, I loved this apparatus!

But, darn it — three studies, run by each of my three student colleagues, didn't show significant results, except for a possible decline effect in one. Maybe there is no PK? I didn't consider this a likely interpretation, because so many studies by others had found evidence for it, but there was no PK manifested here, perhaps because we used ordinary college students as agents rather than have someone specially selected as apparently already having PK ability?

That's one of the realities of research: you set things up with high hopes of getting interesting findings, and what you expect doesn't happen. You try to learn from what did happen, and think about why you didn't get what you expected. There's always a sense of disappointment when things don't work, but there's also satisfaction in knowing you've done a well-designed experiment.

And then, just to keep my mind from resting resignedly but peacefully, the same apparatus was later used when the well-known British psychic Matthew Manning visited my lab. He did three experimental runs with chance results and didn't want to do any more, feeling he had no psychic contact with the coin. That's quite understandable; who wants to work at something he doesn't have any success with? As we discovered after he'd left, though, the coin used showed a significant bias toward heads, 56 percent in Manning's experimental runs. But we'd calibrated the coin extensively before (and after) Manning's visit: it was a coin with a significant tails bias of 55.6 percent (Palmer, Tart, and Redington 1979). What do we make of that?

This pattern of not getting the clear evidence of psi phenomena that you expect, but getting some sort of secondary effect, is relatively common in parapsychological studies. Sometimes it's just a chance happening — if you do analysis after analysis, some will be apparently significant by chance alone. And yet sometimes, it has led some parapsychologists to think there's something inherently "perverse" about psi phenomena, that we're being "teased" by it. It's as if psi happens often enough to keep us interested, but not reliably or strongly enough for us to be certain about it or apply it very well. I've certainly felt that way at times.

Beyond the simple venting of frustration by thinking this way, though, I've sometimes had a thought that's heretical in current scientific thinking. Mainstream science and much parapsychology implicitly, if not explicitly, assumes that we, humanity, are the most, if not the only, intelligent creatures in the universe. So when we do experiments to extend our knowledge, the outcome is a function only of the natural laws governing things and our cleverness in investigating them. But suppose there is, as we consider in this book, a spiritual reality, perhaps with spiritual beings of some sort existing in it? Are the desires and qualities of these spiritual beings part of our experiments also? Is the idea of being "teased" with inconsistent but unignorable psi results more than just a metaphor?

And Speaking of Forgetting...

I wrote the preceding description of my own PK experiments with spinning silver coins largely from memory, but in putting finishing touches on this chapter, I went back and reread my original report (Tart et al. 1972) to ensure my accuracy about details. I was accurate except for one thing. Although I remembered William Cantor's psychological manipulation of me so that I apparently showed some PK for a few minutes, I had completely forgotten about the experiment Andrija Puharich and I did with him as a more rigorous test of his claimed PK ability.

In the last test before Cantor went back to Virginia, we decided to do one hundred coin-spinning trials with him. We did this in a special environment that Puharich believed enhanced ESP ability (and perhaps psi ability in general), a solid-wall Faraday cage.[4] That research is a fascinating story, too complex to go into in this book, but I've written about it and reported one confirmatory study of my own elsewhere (see Tart 1988a). Here's what happened in this PK test; I quote my earlier report (Tart et al. 1972, 143) since I don't quite trust my memory after realizing I'd totally forgotten this:

> The most well-controlled test, carried out just before W. C. [William Cantor] had to leave the foundation, was performed with an a priori agreement that there would be one hundred trials (spins of the coin), and that W. C. would try to influence the coin to fall heads on all of these. No trial was to be counted unless the coin spun for at least five seconds. It was spun by holding it vertically upright between index finger and tabletop, and flicking it on edge rapidly with the index finger of the opposite hand. The test was carried out in a small copper-shielded room (a Faraday cage) with W. C., Dr. Andrija Puharich (A. P.), and C. T. [myself] sitting around three sides of a small, glass-topped coffee table. W. C. did not touch the table or the silver dollar used at any time during the test. A. P. spun the coin, while C. T. kept a record of the number of trials and the outcome of each trial, with A. P. checking C. T.'s record of outcomes as it was made. W. C. was in perfect view at all times, and could not surreptitiously touch the table, blow on the coin, or otherwise influence it in any known, physical manner.
>
> The outcome of this test was 100 heads, the chosen target, in 100 trials. The odds against this happening by chance alone are astronomical.[5]

It's true that I now write about this fifty years later, and that's a long time, but to just forget that I saw one hundred heads in a row? Just as the unexpected appearance of massive precognitive psi-missing in my immediate-feedback training study (see chapter 8) made me aware of a deep kind of resistance to the very idea of precognition, perhaps I have some deep resistance to the very idea of PK, in spite of my intellectual acceptance of it?

My possible resistance or not, PK is one of the "big five." Sometimes the human mind can affect that state of the material world by wishing, with no known material intervention. Perhaps there's more than one kind of PK, such as a very small-sized way of biasing otherwise-random events, like falling dice or electronic RNGs, but also a much more massive kind of PK that makes accordions play when they aren't being touched.

Notes

1. Crookes was knighted in 1897 in recognition of the eminent services he'd rendered to the advancement of scientific knowledge, and was further honored in 1910 by the bestowal of the Order of Merit. In 1898 he became president of the British Association for the Advancement of Science at Bristol, and in 1913 he was elected president of The Royal Society. Once his support of the paranormal nature of D. D. Home's gifts became known, though, he was reviled in mainstream scientific circles.

2. Much thought was given to possible distortions of results due to mechanical imperfections or biases in dice, and specially machined dice have been used, but this systematic rotation of target faces handles the bias problem quite adequately. Any bias works against you as much as it might work for you.

3. I wish to thank Russell Targ, who devised this exceptionally effective shock-mounting system for his research with lasers.

4. British physicist Michael Faraday (1791–1867) discovered that electrical charges remain on the outside of metallic boxes or cages, no matter how intense they are. A Faraday cage is any electrically conducting enclosure that you put your apparatus inside of to shield it from external electrical fields. Why this should have any effect on psi ability makes no sense in terms of conventional physics, but there's evidence that it does. Since psi ability itself makes no sense in terms of conventional physics, this doesn't bother me. Empirically there seems to be an effect, one of the

many maybes, perhaps.

5. We can only approximate the precise probability figures here for the following reasons. Puharich's records of this particular experiment have been misplaced, so the data depend only on my memory of the test. I recall clearly that his mother (visiting at that time) was given the silver dollar used in the experiment and conducted several hundred trials for coin bias, trials that showed the bias of the coin to be about .55 in favor of heads, rather than a perfect .50. Some data published by Puharich, however, indicate that the bias may have been as high as .72 (Puharich 1962). Using the latter figure as a more conservative estimate of bias, the performance of 100 heads in 100 trials is still exceptionally significant, the critical ratio (unit normal deviation) being greater than 6.2, and the associated probability figure being less than about 10 to the minus 9.

CHAPTER 10

Psychic Healing:
PK on Biological Systems?

PSYCHIC (nineteenth century English [origin: Greek "psuk-hikos," of the mind or soul, from "psukhe," psyche, noun; see "-ic"]): A person who is regarded as particularly susceptible to supernatural or paranormal influence; a medium, a clairvoyant.

HEAL (Old English): To free (a person) from disease or ailment, restore to health (now chiefly by miraculous, spiritual, or psychic means). — SHORTER OXFORD ENGLISH DICTIONARY, *6th ed., s.v. "psychic" and "heal"*

FOR MANY years, when talking about parapsychological findings, I referred to the "big four," the four psi phenomena for which there was so much accumulated evidence that we could take them as the foundational findings of the field: three forms of ESP (telepathy, clairvoyance, and precognition), plus PK. Each had hundreds of well-controlled experiments supporting its existence. In the last two decades, though, enough positive studies of psychic healing have been published (see *www.stephanaschwartz.com* for an extensive, current bibliography, with abstracts) that I now speak of the "big five." There are other apparent psi phenomena, which we'll look at in later chapters, whose existence I'm not that certain about because they simply haven't been researched enough, but these big five are solid and form a firm foundation for opening us to the spiritual possibilities of people.

Fig. 10.1 Size of Wounds
Before Psychic Healing in Grad's Study

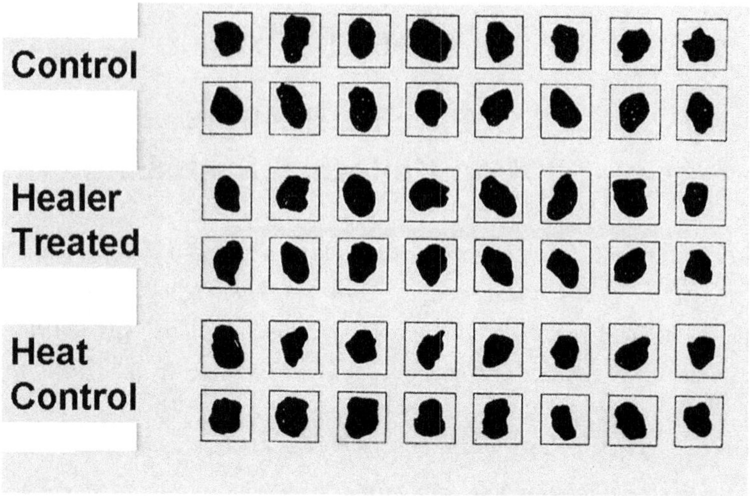

Just as telepathy, clairvoyance, and precognition might turn out someday to be three aspects of some more basic psi ability for gathering information outside of the ordinary, material senses, our current conceptual separation of PK and psychic healing, as if they were two separate processes, might change. Perhaps it's all one kind of psychic action or force, and we're merely distinguishing whether the target is dead matter, calling it PK, or living matter, calling it psychic healing. Or maybe they'll turn out to be quite distinct or perhaps aspects of something else whose existence we don't even suspect yet.

Figure 9.1, the PK diagram in the previous chapter, can be used to model psychic healing too. The target is now some living system rather than a nonliving material like dice or electronic circuits.

In ordinary life, some people claim to be psychic healers, or are acclaimed by others to be healers, and all have success stories to tell, but ill people often get better on their own, so how do we know the success stories don't really prove any special abilities of these healers? Or perhaps there's a genuine healing effect that

Figure 10.2 Size of Wounds After
14 Days of Psychic Healing in Grad's Study

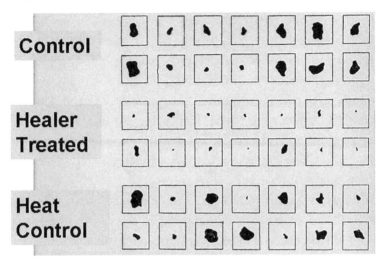

comes from a healer working on you, but it's mediated by more ordinary physical and psychological factors, rather than psi factors, as we briefly discussed in chapter 2, when considering how you'd do experiments in this area? Knowing that someone cares about you tends to stimulate your immune system, for example. If that were all there was to psychic healing, it would still be wise to learn how to train such healers and figure out the most psychologically effective way for them to work, but that could be fitted within the materialistic worldview. How do we tell if there's a psi component, a spiritual component?

For a firm basis, I like to lecture about the classical experimental work of biologist Bernard Grad, now retired, of McGill University. His was some of the pioneering, solid work that requires us to consider psychic healing as a reality.

Grad was a cancer researcher who got interested in psychic healing, especially when he met an immigrant to Canada, Oskar Estabany, who had a reputation as a healer. Estabany had discovered his gift when he was a soldier in the First World War. He was in charge of handling horses and seemed especially good at working with injured ones; they seemed to heal much quicker than they ordinarily would. He eventually found that his "laying on of hands" healing technique worked on people too, and developed a reputation as a healer.

Grad was aware of the psychological explanation of psychic healing mentioned above. If you were ill and someone was introduced to you as a healer, and then gave you a lot of careful attention and touching, you might well heal faster but simply as a matter of suggestion and placebo effects. Undoubtedly, this is useful clinically, but how could you test for a psychic component, a pure psi component of healing?

Clearly, it would help if you had "patients" who weren't suggestible in the usual human meaning of the word. Grad carried out two classic studies (1965), one in which the "patients" were wounded barley seeds, the other in which the "patients" were wounded laboratory mice. Let's look at the latter.

The laboratory mice were deliberately wounded by having a fold of their inherently loose skin plucked up and then a small chunk cut off with scissors. This produced a skin wound, which was a useful kind of illness to work with experimentally, because the size of the wound could be precisely measured by putting a piece of tracing paper over it and outlining the edges of the wound. Then a device called a planimeter could be used to objectively measure the actual area of the wound. Forty-eight mice were thus wounded and randomly assigned to three groups. The size of their wounds — the actual tracings — are shown in figure 10.1.

Aside from mental suggestion when people are the patients, we might conventionally hypothesize that the laying-on-of-hands healing might also involve some sort of chemicals emitted through the healer's skin, chemicals that might have a healing effect. This would be useful to discover if it were indeed the case for some healers, but Grad wanted to isolate his mice patients from anything but a psi healing effect. Thus each mouse received an individual treatment, but to prepare for the treatment, a research assistant (who didn't know what group the mice were to be in) would take a mouse from its cage, put it into a paper bag, and staple it shut so that the mouse was no longer handled directly. Few chemicals can readily penetrate a layer of dry paper in a short time.

Maybe just being put in a paper bag has an effect on a mouse? But all three groups of mice were put into paper bags.

For the experimental group, Estabany would then come in and hold the bagged mouse in the palms of his hands for twenty minutes twice a day, while visualizing the flow of healing energy. Estabany would leave the room, and then a research assistant would come in and put the mouse back in its cage, released from its paper bag. In the control group, once the mouse had been bagged, it sat on a shelf for the same amount of time Estabany gave healing treatments to the experimental mice. This controlled for being bagged per se.

The possibility also existed that the warmth of the healer's hands could be responsible for promoting healing, so in the third "heat control" group, another assistant, not known to have any healing abilities, held the bagged mouse for the same length of time.

Grad had decided in advance that the degree of healing of the wounds, measured by how much they had closed up, would be measured after two weeks. Besides the statistical analysis of areas, which showed significant differences, figure 10.2 shows the wound sizes. It's pretty clear to the naked eye that the controls and heat controls showed similar, moderate degrees of wound healing, but the experimental group treated by Estabany showed far more healing.

Grad's other classic study involved using "wounded" barley seeds as "patients." How do you wound a barley seed? You take a sack of them and put it in a hot oven for a while. Some of the seeds are killed by this procedure; all are partially damaged. You can then randomly separate the seeds to select your ill patients and randomly plant them in groups in a number of pots.

The healing treatment had to control for the fact that if you pray over plants, or otherwise hang out close to them, you're increasing the carbon dioxide in the air, and that will stimulate their growth. Similarly the heat of your hands or possible chemicals from them might affect the plants or seedlings, so all these possibilities must be eliminated. This was done by never letting Estabany near the actual plants. Instead, for a healing session, Estabany would be given a hermetically sealed bottle of saline solution, the slightly salty water used for transfusions in hospitals. He would hold the sealed bottle between his hands for a while, give it a healing treatment, and then leave the room. Just to eliminate any problem with heat — a held bottle would get a little warmer in Estabany's hands — the bottle was allowed to sit on a shelf so that it cooled back down to room temperature. Control bottles got no healing treatment from Estabany.

Why saline solution instead of just plain water? To keep the barley-seed patients under some stress, as an ill patient would be.

A research assistant, who was blind as to which sealed bottles had gotten a healing treatment and which hadn't, later took the bottles and watered the pots containing the barley seeds. Thus some pots were consistently watered with "healed" water, others with control water.

At the end of a preset time, fourteen days, another research assistant, blind as to conditions, measured the heights of all the sprouted seeds, and then carefully dug them up and weighed them to see how much they had grown. A statistical analysis showed that the seeds treated with the healed water were significantly taller and weighed more, and more of them had sprouted.

Figure 10.3 shows the two groups of sprouted seedlings at the end of the fourteen days. The healed seedlings are on the left. Obviously, there's a big difference, big enough to be practical, not merely statistically significant.

So when we describe some gardeners as having a green thumb, are we recognizing a possible psychic-healing ability, or growth-

Figure 10.3 Psychically Healed vs.
Control Seedlings in Grad's Study

stimulating ability, aside from gardening technique?

In an interesting case study, Grad (1965) had some bottles of saline solution that had been held by a very depressed patient later used to water seedlings. Compared to controls, fewer sprouted; they weren't as tall or as heavy. So there's a black thumb, as well as a green thumb?

Larry Dossey, a physician and one of the world's foremost experts on psychic healing once remarked to me on January 5, 2003, "You really do need to find a physician you can trust, if possible. I admire the Erma Bombeck rule: 'Never go to a doctor whose plants have died.'"

Note that successful healers come from all traditions, so spiritual healing can be real, but it doesn't prove the truth of any particular religion compared to other religions. This is a general principle applicable to all talents included in the big five and many maybes discussed in this book. They provide a support for spirituality in general but happen among followers of all sorts of religions and spiritual traditions, so there's no point in getting caught up in a "My religion's miracles are better than your religion's miracles!" kind of mind-set.

CHAPTER 11

Postcognition and Extended Aspects of Mind: The Many Maybes

MAYBE (Late Middle English [origin: from "it may be" Cf. "mayhap"]: Adverb — Possibly, perhaps. Noun — What may be; a possibility. Now rare. — SHORTER OXFORD ENGLISH DICTIONARY, *6th ed., s.v. "maybe"*

As FOR the psi phenomena in the previous chapters, the "big five," each has hundreds of well-controlled experiments supporting its existence, as well as hundreds of thousands of events reportedly happening to ordinary people in everyday life that are most likely caused by these psi functions. That sounds like a lot of evidence, but remember that scientific parapsychology is a very small-scale enterprise and it's taken decades to collect this evidence. How small? My current rough estimate is of a few dozen scientists at most, almost all of them working on parapsychological research on a strictly part-time basis. (For a more exact, if older, comparison, see Tart 1979b.) If I compared parapsychology to any mainstream research area in fields like biology, chemistry, physics, or medicine, I doubt that the total, worldwide parapsychological research in a year would equal an hour of any mainstream field's research. While we have more than adequate evidence to support the existence of the big five, there has been little definitive research, given this lack of resources, to tell us about their nature, ways of improving their operation, their implications, or the like.

Besides the big five, there are a number of possible psi phenomena I call the "many maybes" that, if they're real, have important implications for what's spiritually possible. They all have enough, even if few, studies that I find I have to consider them possible realities, but not enough to be fairly certain of their reality or to form a reliable reality basis for understanding spirituality as the big five do. I introduce some of these many maybes in this and the following chapters. Note that the iffy status of these phenomena would make some parapsychologists (of the few that exist) disagree with me about their reality status; with some thinking that some of these phenomena have pretty solid support, and others considering them to be so unlikely that perhaps I shouldn't even discuss them until there's more evidence. But just as we can't live life only on the basis of what's certain, we can't base our spirituality only on what's certain; we need to get on with life, so we have to stretch some to get a fuller picture.

Postcognition

As I mentioned earlier, I've always found the idea of precognition, that the inherently unpredictable future can sometimes be foretold by some kind of psi ability, mind boggling, to say the least. It makes no sense at all to me, which, of course, says something about the nature of my mind's organization, and not necessarily anything about reality. Yet the weight of the evidence forces me to include precognition in the big five. At a conceptual level, the reality of precognition reminds me that we understand only a little about the nature of time.

So, if the mind can sometimes get information about the future with psi ability, it implies that some psychic aspect of mind is not always stuck in the present. If this aspect of mind can view into the future, shouldn't it be able to view into the past? Shouldn't we have a logical category of postcognition?

We do have the logical category and name, but there's a real methodological problem in trying to study postcognition. Assume that the mind gets information from the past. How do we verify that this information is correct? By checking against presently existing records of the past, such as books, deeds, wills, people's memories, digging up an archeological site, and so on. If there are no presently existing records, we can't check ostensible postcognition for accuracy, and it remains merely a speculation.

But if present-time records exist that verify postcognition, how do we know that the percipient didn't use "simple," present-time ESP, clairvoyance, or telepathy, to read the records rather than contact the past or read the mind of someone who knew about the past? Or precognitively read the minds of investigators who later dug up the information about the past?

No one has thought of a satisfactory solution to this methodological problem. With precognition experiments, you can try to predict a future event that's determined by so many different factors that it's hard to imagine a mind reasoning to a correct prediction from present information, even if a good deal of clairvoyant and telepathic input about the present state of things were available, or even if some unconscious, psychokinetic manipulation of present events to try to force a particular future state occurred. For example, the classic precognition studies asked percipients to predict the future order of decks of target cards. Normal sensory knowledge or clairvoyant knowledge of the current order of the target deck wouldn't help, because that order would be destroyed and randomly reordered by thorough shuffling of the deck. Shuffling randomizes, because we can't control the small size of the cards and high speed of their motion in shuffling, in terms of our material, human senses (barring cheating by card sharks, which need not concern us here).

But suppose, through some combination of clairvoyant knowledge of where particular cards were in the deck at a given time and psychokinetic "pushes" or "alterations of friction," the unconscious mind of the ostensible precognizing percipient could influence the shuffling process to make desired cards end up in the position that had been predicted, an ace third down from the top, for example? It would only need to happen occasionally to produce statistically significant results that misled us to think we had evidence for precognition.

In point of fact, there were some classical card-guessing studies designed to test this idea. They were designated psychic shuffle studies. Experimental participants, acting as agents in this case, were given a deck of target cards, told to shuffle them, facedown, a stated number of times, while wishing or intending that the cards would come up in a certain order, say the red cards in the top of the deck and the black ones on the bottom. An experimenter supervised the shuffling, of course, to prevent agents looking at the cards or otherwise cheating. Results were generally positive; that is, significantly more of the desired cards ended up in the designated target positions than would be expected by chance (Kanthamani and Kelly 1975).[1]

The psychic shuffle is a very interesting result on its own, but because parapsychologists wanted to test precognition, not PK, further steps were added, outside what we'd think of as reasonable possibilities of manipulation by percipients or agents and experimenters, to determine the final random order of target cards. So the protocol might call for something like this:

1. Ask percipient to write down the order the deck will be in at a specified time tomorrow.
2. Send the percipient home.
3. Half an hour before that specified time, the experimenter thoroughly shuffles the facedown deck a large, pre-specified number of times.
4. The experimenter then consults that day's morning newspaper to find the high temperature in some specified location, say Kansas City, divides that number by three, counts down that number of cards in the shuffled deck, and cuts the target deck there.

5. The experimenter repeats the above step for several other locations.

When you get significant precognition results under conditions like these — and this did happen — it's really stretching it to say that this wasn't really precognition, that the ostensible percipient really was a PK agent who not only pushed cards around during later shuffling but affected the high temperature in Kansas City, and so on. You make the PK alternative more and more complex. So, we can feel highly confident in theorizing that the mind can actually get information from the future at times.

Yet things can happen that make us suspect postcognition is real, even if we can't come up with a satisfactory experimental design. For example, recall the clairvoyant RV study described in Chapter 7, where the target site was a swimming-pool complex in Palo Alto. Here, for convenience, is a repeat of figure 7.3, the plan drawing beside remote viewer Pat Price's sketch of what he thought was there.

Remember Targ and Puthoff's description (1977, 52–54):

> ...Pat's drawing is shown...in which he correctly described a park-like area containing two pools of water: one rectangular, 60 x 89 feet (actual dimensions 75 x 100 feet); the other circular, diameter 120 feet (actual diameter 110 feet). He was incorrect, however, in saying the facility was used for water filtration rather than swimming. With further experimentation, we began to realize that the occurrence of essentially correct descriptions of basic elements and patterns coupled with incomplete or erroneous analysis of function was to be a continuing thread throughout the remote-viewing work.
>
> As can be seen from his drawing, Pat also included some elements, such as the tanks shown in the upper right, which were not present at the target site. The left-

right reversal of elements — often observed in paranormal perception experiments — is likewise apparent.

All in all, this was an excellent, present-time RV, spoiled mainly by the erroneous inclusion of two water towers and the idea that the facility was used for water filtration rather than swimming. One can imagine this as imaginative overlay through associations with (correctly perceived) water or the like.

Figure 11.1 Swimming-Pool Complex RV Target
(Repeat of Figure 7.3)

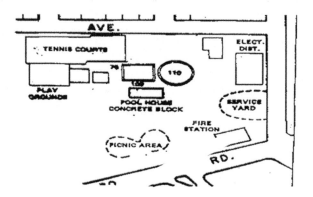

Formal plan drawing of target location

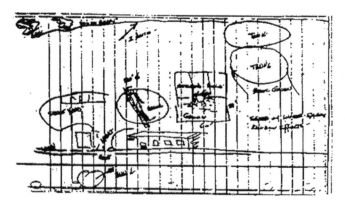

Pat Price's drawing of target location

And then many years later, long after Pat Price had died, Russell Targ, who was a resident of Palo Alto, received a routine newsletter from the city of Palo Alto. Its cover, a historical photo, showed two water towers at a long-since-gone water filtration plant. I've obtained a better-quality photo, courtesy of the Palo Alto Historical Association. Here it is.

Figure 11.2 Postcognition: Two Water Towers from Old Palo Alto Water Plant

The note on the back of the photo reads, "The city water plant with adjacent reservoir was built in 1898 at Newell and Embarcadero Roads." That's the present location of the park and swimming-pool complex. What was considered imagination or a mistake on Price's part was correct — for many years earlier.

One of the things the SRI remote-viewing experimenters gradually learned over the years from other studies than the one this example comes from, especially precognitive RV studies, was that it was a good idea to not simply ask, "Describe the place where X is," but rather "Describe the place where X is, as it looks now."

Do past things or events leave psychic traces that can be picked up in the present, is this another reminder of how little we understand time, or both?

Psychic Archeology: Postcognition?

As I noted earlier, it's conceptually frustrating to deal with the idea of postcognition, because the only way to verify its accuracy, if it is indeed real, is by checking against physical records or living people's memories, and that means that there's a source of current-time information that might account for the results, making them due to "mere" clairvoyance or telepathy. But since the existence of precognition forces us to question the adequacy of our conventional ideas about the nature of time and some ideas associated with spirituality deal with unusual conceptions of time,[2] I want to give another example of what might be postcognition — or might be "mere" clairvoyance but certainly isn't telepathy from the living. And I do have to accept the fact that just because my conceptual system has trouble with something like precognition or postcognition doesn't mean it isn't real.

In chapter 7, we looked at one aspect of Project Deep Quest, an experiment of parapsychologist Stephan Schwartz, the aspect of interest to us being how it ruled out electromagnetic radiation as a carrier of the information in RV. One of Schwartz's main interests has been the applied use of RV in archeology. Part of Project Deep Quest was the successful location of a century-old wreck lying hundreds of feet below the surface (this fascinating story is described fully in Schwartz's 2007 book *Opening to the Infinite*, which also has his comprehensive instructions on how to use RV). Postcognition? "Mere" clairvoyance? Certainly, the location was not known to any living people, nor were there any records locatable by marine-wreck experts about the wreck's location.

I'm intrigued even more, though, by one of Schwartz's Egyptian archeological projects that extends much farther back in time: the location of a specifically detailed site in the city of Marea, now buried under the desert sand. You can find a detailed report on this project online at *www.stephanaschwartz.com*, but I'll describe its highlights here.

Marea, founded several centuries before the Christian era, was a thriving trade center and regional capital, built on the shores of a large lake (Lake Maryut), with a canal to Alexandria and a river connection to the Nile. It was occupied and still functioning as a trade center as late as the sixteenth century, but today it lies hidden beneath a desert of low, semiarid hills. The lake has been reduced to isolated ponds of brackish water, none more than a few feet deep, and very little archeological work has been done on the site.

Schwartz felt Marea would be an excellent area to test the practical usefulness of remote viewing, because the only modern archeological survey, done in 1976, three years prior to Schwartz's project, found little. That survey used the then most current electronic remote-sensing technologies and search methodologies for archeology, including aerial photography, topographical survey, and proton precession magnetometer measurements. It concluded that there were lots of subsurface structures, which would be hardly surprising when you knew the ruins of a city were under the desert and that the streets were laid out in a grid pattern, like modern cities. Otherwise, it concluded that there was probably little, if anything, left under the surface but foundations. There was nothing very specific in the survey, which left lots of room for RV to add something.

Two remote viewers, George McMullen, a Canadian who'd worked extensively with another archeologist in the past (haven't you always wondered how in the world archeologists know where to dig?), and Hella Hammid, mentioned in chapter 7, the Los Angeles photographer who was originally selected as a "control," a person who thought she had no psychic abilities but turned out to be quite talented in SRI remote-viewing studies, were flown to Egypt for this project. Neither had ever heard of Marea: indeed, most archeologists have never heard of Marea; it's an obscure site.

Schwartz usually began psychic archeology projects by having viewers, working at home, look at large-scale maps of the area of interest while being instructed to "map dowse," meaning to mark on the map the areas they sensed would contain specified kinds of archeologically interesting objects. Such marked maps would then be overlaid on a light table to see where the markings of the remote viewers, who worked independently of each other, overlapped. This is a standard engineering approach for working with "noisy" signals, that is, signals that contain errors as well as correct information. Such averaging tends to cancel out errors but make the agreed items stand out. But Schwartz couldn't get any adequate maps of that area of Egypt containing Marea before going to Egypt, and even after getting there, could obtain only one map, which was on an almost useless scale.

So, Schwartz worked with Fawzi Fakharani, a prominent Egyptian professor of archeology at the University of Alexandria, who, while quite skeptical of RV, had the political connections to allow for excavation at the Marea site. On the morning of April 11, 1979, McMullen and Hammid were taken in separate vehicles to an area of desert chosen by Fakharani that was out of sight of the area of Marea, about six miles from it. After the stop, Schwartz decided to accompany McMullen during his first attempt to locate Marea, while Hammid was driven away out of sight. After they'd left, McMullen was given the following charge by Fakharani:

1. Locate the ancient city of Marea, which is somewhere within an area roughly 24 kilometers on a side, a form 576 square kilometers in size (an area roughly equal to half the city of Los Angeles, which is 15 by 15 miles or 225 square miles). After locating the city, locate a building that has either tile, fresco, or mosaic decoration in it.

2. Within the chosen building, locate the walls, windows, doors, and depth at which the floor would be found.
3. Describe any artifacts or conditions that would be found within the building site.

If, like Professor Fakharani, you were very skeptical (I would say "pseudoskeptical," as discussed in chapter 3) of the reality of RV, this was basically an impossible task and McMullen was bound to fail.

Followed by Schwartz with a tape recorder and by a camera crew, McMullen then wandered off across the sands. McMullen seemed in something of a trance state, ignoring the hundred-degree temperature, stinging winds, and sand flies, occasionally giving scattered impressions about long ago, most of which were uncheckable, but he finally reported that he knew where he wanted to go. Schwartz reports (2000):

"McMullen and the author then walked back to where Fakharani and his assistant were waiting, whereupon McMullen knelt in the sand, sketched an outline of Marea as it appears today, and described for Fakharani where the University of Alexandria's dig was located and what the area looked like...Fakharani acknowledged on camera the accuracy of the description."

Fakharani then drove the crew to Marea and his dig site. McMullen wandered around for some time suggesting other dig sites (none yet excavated; this is expensive work!) and giving unverifiable impressions of how people lived in the ancient city; only physical structure remains can be checked by archeological work, not how people lived.

Schwartz (2000) notes that once again: "McMullen was charged again by Fakharani to 'locate an important building — one with tile, fresco, or mosaic — something representative. It is for you to tell me where to dig.'"

Without hesitation, McMullen proceeded to walk up a hill on the south side of the ancient road. Once there, he did the following:

1. Quickly sketched in the outline of a building with several rooms and stated that the area described was only a part of a larger complex.
2. Located walls, one doorway, and the corners of the structure.
3. Indicated that the culture that had built this building was Byzantine.
4. Described the probable depth to the tops of the walls as being approximately "three feet" (.91 meters).
5. Indicated that there would be debris (dropped there after being taken from a different structure).
6. Said that one wall, the west one, would have tiles on it.
7. Explained the culture or cultures that had built or modified the building and its later use for storage.
8. Felt the crew should come across "a floor" of the structure at approximately "six to ten" feet (1.8 meters to 3 meters), although he confessed — somewhat distressed — "I can't see the floor" (Schwartz 2000).
9. Said that several colors would be associated with the site, but felt green was the most prevalent, since he perceived it most strongly.

And here, because I want to encourage you to read the fascinating report (*www.stephanaschwartz.com*) and I don't want us to wander too far afield from the main themes of this book, I'll simply say that basically McMullen was revealed to be correct on all those details. The corners, wall, and door were where McMullen later drove in stakes; the tops were three feet down; there was debris dumped in the site; and the funny feelings about the floor related to the fact that the tile floor had actually been almost completely removed, leaving only the white subfloor and so forth.

Is there some real sense in which the "past" still exists? If so, is it only as a kind of stored "memory"? Or, is there indeed something very unusual about the ultimate nature of time, which perhaps various spiritual traditions have hinted at, that we're a long way from understanding?

Notes

32. This sounds a lot like the card tricks that magicians do, of course, but there's a huge difference between a magician's controlling conditions to make it merely look as if things couldn't happen and an experimenter's controlling them. With respect to the classical card-guessing test results, for example, no magician has ever volunteered to come to a parapsychological laboratory and be tested in the standard ways that have evolved to eliminate trickery and sensory cues.

33. For example, "eternity," a term used in many spiritual writings, can be simplistically interpreted to mean just an infinitely long period of time, but sometimes it's probably better interpreted as referring to an entirely different way of perceiving or conceiving of time than we ordinarily do.

CHAPTER 12

Out-of-Body Experiences

OUT-OF-BODY (mid twentieth century [origin: from "out of" + "body"]): Characterized by the sensation that one's consciousness is located outside one's body. — SHORTER OXFORD ENGLISH DICTIONARY, *6th ed., s.v. "out-of-body"*

IN 1969, a UC Davis student I'll call Beth dropped by my office and reported an experience to me that she had undergone a couple of years before, when she was fifteen:

I'd had an argument with my parents, so instead of prolonging it, I left until I had cooled off. I went outside, looked up, and saw the moon; it was a very clear and beautiful night. I went onto the porch and threw myself facedown on my cot. I had my fists clenched, my teeth gritted together, and all my muscles taut. I wished I were dead.

Suddenly, I felt completely relaxed. I opened my eyes and realized I was about twenty feet above the porch roof with my house below me. I saw the dark outlines of the trees, the pond, the lawn, the stars, everything. I heard the crickets too. I just stared around at everything, which was unbelievably clear and vivid. I saw my legs and, therefore, knew I had a body.

I wanted to look at the moon, which was behind and above me, so I twisted my body — ever so easily — and looked up at it. With my "new" clear vision, it looked more beautiful than I had ever seen it. I felt so free and light.

The world seemed to be at my command. I loved this new world and wanted to explore it.

I looked toward the west and had just decided to travel out in that direction, and then just happened to glance down. I saw right through the roof to my "lifeless" body just lying there, the same way I had left it. Then an intense fear gripped me. Was I really dead? What had I done? When I'd made that wish, I really hadn't wanted it to come true.

Suddenly, I could see my parents finding me — dead. They were crying, and my mother was wringing her hands. I felt absolutely terrible and wanted to return more than anything else. I wanted to give life back to that lifeless form that belonged to me.

Then I had a very strange sensation, like the steady, very strong, overpowering pull of a taut rubber band. I didn't see anything, but I felt my "new" body being pulled downward. Then I found myself in my "old" body. They were now joined again. I told myself that's where they'd stay, 'cause I didn't want to try it again.

Since then that fear has subsided in the thrill of another possible experience.

Parapsychologists classify this kind of experience as an out-of-the-body experience (OBE).[1] Although the term is too often used rather loosely, I've defined an OBE as having two crucial aspects: (1) you find yourself experientially located at a place other than where your physical body is, and you may or may not see your actual physical body from an outside point of view; and (2) your consciousness feels clear during the experience. It may seem as clear and lucid as your ordinary waking state, and sometimes even clearer, even sharper, making the OBE, as many express it, "realer than real," more vivid and real seeming than ordinary experience. You can reason quite well during the OBE, such as reasoning that what's happening to you can't really be happening, given all we think we know about the nature of reality — but there you are, and it's obviously happening!

This second defining aspect distinguishes OBEs from ordinary dreams or other altered state phenomena: you don't look back on it from later waking consciousness and say that your mind was actually dreamy or clouded, or that you were mistaken in thinking it was clear at the time.

And, like the rest of life, some experiences happen that you're not quite sure fit the strict criteria for an OBE. So, if you've had an experience something like this, but it doesn't fit my exact definition, remember that the reality of your experience is more important than my words!

OBEs have been a major interest of mine throughout my career, although I've never personally experienced one. Clearly, the occurrence of an OBE is a major basis for a belief in some kind of immaterial soul. Is this a correct perception or delusion? These experiences are especially interesting when the person having the OBE correctly reports on some distant scene he could have no normal knowledge of. The case I introduced above is more typical in not involving any clear "external" corroboration of the reality of the experience, but the OBE is typically quite real to the person experiencing it.

In 1996 I was invited to give a lecture to the annual meeting of the International Association for Near-Death Studies (IANDS), which was meeting in Oakland, California, that year. While we'll look at near-death experiences (NDEs) in detail in the next chapter, here I speak of them only in passing but focus on one common aspect of NDEs, the OBE. Most of the attendees at the IANDS meeting were people who had personally experienced an NDE, and personal contact with them gave me a degree of feeling and intensity for the NDE I'd never gotten through the written accounts alone. What a group of people! To anticipate the next chapter, the NDE usually is a mystical experience, altered state of consciousness, or both, of which an OBE may be an initial part, while OBEs per se are usually associated with something like ordinary consciousness and thus are more amenable to description in ordinary language. (A written version of my lecture to IANDS was published in 1998 in the *Journal of Near-Death Studies* [Tart 1998b], and this chapter draws heavily on a slightly modified version of that published work.)

Because OBEs and NDEs push our worldview much harder than "mere" psi phenomena, and constitute an obvious experience of being a "spirit," I'll review some of the distinctions we've made between genuine science and scientism and then describe six studies of OBEs I've carried out over the years and some of the conclusions I've come to that may be helpful in furthering understanding and integration.

Review: Science and Scientism in the Modern World

We live in a world that has been miraculously transformed by science and technology. The results have been very good in some ways — I wouldn't still be alive except for scientific advances in medicine, like appendectomies, for example — and not in others. The negative aspect of particular concern for us is that this material progress has been accompanied by a shift in our belief systems, unhealthy in many ways, that aids the partial crushing of the human spirit by the scientism that we've discussed.

Try to always notice when I write "scientism" rather than "science." A major aspect of my personal identity is being a scientist and thinking like a scientist, and I consider science to be a noble calling that demands the best from me. I want to use genuine, essential science to help our understanding in all areas of life, including the spiritual. Scientism (Wellmuth 1944), on the other hand, is a perversion of genuine science. Scientism in our time consists mainly of a dogmatic commitment to a materialistic philosophy that dismisses and "explains away" the spiritual, rather than actually examining it carefully and trying to understand it. You who have a negative feeling whenever I mention "science" have probably gotten it from encounters with scientism. Since scientism never recognizes itself as a limited belief system but always thinks of itself as true science, or the noble search for truth, the confusion is pernicious. If someone says to you, "I believe my religion is the only truth, so I know that you're crazy and evil," your defenses quite reasonably go up, but you aren't too affected because you know that your attacker is some sort of fanatic. But if someone is identified as a scientist, supposedly an objective, well-educated truth seeker, and says, "Your quaint spiritual beliefs are old-fashioned superstitions that were long ago shown to be false, and you really ought to adjust to reality," that's a much more powerful attack for most of us.

The information I share in this book was obtained in my attempts to practice genuine science in areas of mutual interest to us. As we saw in chapter 2, genuine science is a four-part, social, continuing process of knowledge refinement that's always subject to questioning, refutation, expansion, and revision. It's a process that begins with a commitment to observe reality as carefully, humbly, and honestly as you can. Then you think about what your observations mean, and devise theories and explanations, trying to be as logical as possible in the process. The third step, though, is especially important. Our minds are wonderfully clever, so clever that they can make "sense" out of almost anything in hindsight and come up with some sort of plausible interpretation of why things happened the way we observed them to. But just because our theories and explanations seem brilliant and logical, or "intuitively obvious," or feel profoundly true, that doesn't mean that we really understand the world we observed. We could have only a wonderful post hoc rationalization. Essential science does not call for "faith" in our theories: it calls for an open-minded, rational skepticism. So the third part of the genuine scientific process is a requirement that you keep logically working with, refining, and expanding your theories and explanations, and thus make predictions about new areas of reality that you haven't observed yet. You've observed the results of conditions A, B, and C, for example, and come up with a satisfying explanation as to why they happened. Now develop your theory to predict what will happen under conditions D, E, and F; go out and set up those conditions; and test what actually happens. If you've successfully predicted the outcomes, good; keep developing your theories! But if your predictions don't come true, your theories may need substantial revision or need to be thrown out altogether.

It doesn't matter how logical, brilliant, elegant, or emotionally satisfying your theories are, scientific theories are always subject to this empirical test of predicting new observations. Indeed, if a theory doesn't have any empirical, testable consequences, it may be "philosophy" or "religion" or "personal belief," but it's not a scientific theory. A genuine scientific theory is capable of being disproven. Thus science has a built-in rule to help us overcome our normal human tendency to get cognitively and emotionally overcommitted to our beliefs.

This constant rechecking of ideas against observable reality is where scientism corrupts the essential scientific process. Because people caught in scientism have an a priori cognitive and emotional attachment to a totally materialistic worldview, they won't really look at data like psi phenomena, OBEs, or NDEs, which imply a spiritual, nonmaterial side to reality. If forced to look at some of the data, they ingeniously try to "explain it away," to trivialize it so that it doesn't really have to be dealt with. They don't recognize that their belief that everything can be explained in purely material terms should be treated like any scientific theory; that is, it should be subject to continual test and modified or rejected when found wanting. The same points can be made about believers in any particular religion or those on a spiritual path, of course; they can misperceive and mis-reason about things they don't want to deal with.

We see this kind of process in all areas of life, not just science. I focus on science here, because attacks on our spirituality from practitioners of scientism, mistakenly identified as scientists, are more harmful, due to their social prestige, than attacks from, say, politicians or salesmen. (We tend to consider someone a scientist if she has an advanced degree and works in a field considered a field of science. That's usually a reasonable way of doing it. But we tend to see "being a scientist" as a permanent condition of a person, while the reality is that a person can function one minute as a scientist by following the rules of essential science, and the next minute as a practitioner of scientism by no longer following these rules.)

This requirement of continual testing, refinement, and expansion is greatly enhanced by the fourth process of essential science: open, full, and honest communication about all the other three aspects. You fully and honestly share your observations, theories, and predictions so that colleagues can test and extend them. In principle, and often in practice — especially in parapsychology, which has been very harsh with the few investigators caught cheating — the quickest way to get thrown out of the scientific community is to be caught lying about your observations. Thus, as an individual, you may have blind spots and prejudices, but because it's unlikely that all your colleagues have the same ones, a gradual process of refinement, correction, and expansion takes place, and scientific knowledge progresses.

While I've described this formal process as essential and genuine science, need I say that it's also a quite sensible way of proceeding in most areas of life?

Inadequacy of Scientism in Dealing with OBEs and NDEs

Now let's apply these thoughts about science and scientism to OBEs and NDEs. Scientism, a dogmatic materialism masquerading as science, dismisses the OBE and NDE a priori as something that cannot be what it seems to be, that is, a mind or soul traveling outside the physical body, either in the physical world or some nonphysical world. So people's experiences are automatically dismissed as a hallucination, some kind of psychopathology, or both. One of the most effective psychological defense mechanisms to keep from being bothered by what you hear about, after all, is to think and claim that the people telling you about it are crazy. We don't need to pay any attention to what crazy people say, do we? But what if we practice actual science and look, with as objective a view as possible, at experiences like the OBE and NDE without prejudging them as impossible?

First, there's the data from a hundred years of scientific parapsychological research, using the best kind of scientific methodology, that shows us we can't simply dismiss the idea that mind is something more than just material body. In previous chapters, we've looked at that evidence for the big five: telepathy, clairvoyance, precognition, psychokinesis, and psychic healing. The reality of these psi phenomena requires us to expand our worldview from a world that's only material to one that also has mind as some kind of independent or semi-independent reality in itself, capable of sometimes doing things that transcend ordinary physical limits. So if in an OBE or NDE, a person feels that he's outside his body, or claims to have acquired information about distant events, for example, it may be an illusion in a particular case, but you can't scientifically say it must be illusion. You have to actually examine the experience, the data, and not ignore it or prejudicially "explain it away" without really paying attention or being logical.

Out-of-Body Experiences

While, as mentioned above, the term OBE is sometimes used rather sloppily, let's get more precise. Here's how I defined it early in my research: "First, let's talk about a subtype which I'm tempted to call the classical out-of-the-body experience, or d-OBE — the 'discrete out-of-the-body experience.' This is the experience where the subject perceives himself as experientially located at some other location than where he knows his physical body to be. In addition, he generally feels that he's in his ordinary state of consciousness, so that the concepts space, time, and location make sense to him. Further, there is a feeling of no contact with the physical body, a feeling of being partially or (more usually) totally disconnected from it (1974, 117).

NDEs usually have, speaking in a somewhat oversimplified way, two major aspects. First (but not always) is the locational component, the OBE component: you find yourself located somewhere other than in your physical body. Second is the noetic and altered state of consciousness (ASC) component: you know things that are unknowable in ordinary ways, and your state of consciousness functions in quite a different way as part of this knowing. I separate OBEs and NDEs, because they don't always go together. You can have an OBE while feeling that your consciousness remains in its ordinary mode or state of functioning. If right this minute, for example, your perceptions showed you that you were someplace other than where you know your body is, but your consciousness was functioning basically as it is right now, that's pretty much what a classic OBE feels like, although the OBE also often seems as real or "realer" than ordinary experience. Reality is more complex than this, of course, but this distinction between "pure" OBEs and typical NDEs will be useful for our discussion.[2]

Hypnotically Induced Out-of-Body Experiences: My First Study

I did my first parapsychological experiment in 1957, while I was still a sophomore at MIT studying electrical engineering. It was an attempt to produce OBEs with the aid of hypnosis, inspired by several old articles on the subject, especially one by a sociologist turned parapsychologist, Hornell Hart (Hart et al. 1956).

I trained several fellow students to be moderately good hypnotic subjects and then guided them to experience what I hoped would be OBEs. In individual hypnotic sessions, I suggested that the participant's mind would leave his body and go to a target area, the basement of a house several miles away, a place in a suburb of Boston he'd never physically been to, and then describe what he saw in that basement.

The target house was the home of two parapsychologists, J. Fraser Nicol and Betty Humphrey, who had deliberately arranged a very unusual collection of objects in a corner of their basement. I reasoned that if any one of my subjects gave a good description of these unusual objects, I would know that his mind had been there while out of body.[3] Note the implicit model I had of OBEs, that it was pretty much equivalent to moving your sense organs, especially your eyes, to a distant physical location. We'll question this too-simple model later.

I had also placed an electronic device called a capacitance relay, connected to a clock beside the target location, to detect and record any electrical disturbance in the properties of the space right around the targets, hoping that my hypnotized OBE participants might physically perturb the properties of space while they traveled to the targets, providing further evidence that the mind could actually leave the body. I installed the capacitance relay before Nicol and Humphrey placed any target materials on the table: I didn't want to know what the targets were; that way I couldn't inadvertently give away any clues about them.

Alas, while I wouldn't call the experiment a failure (I learned a lot from it), things didn't work out as I'd hoped. The capacitance-relay device had to be abandoned, because it went on and off every time the house furnace did. My subjects' descriptions of the target had occasional resemblances to the target materials, but the comparison was much too subjective for me to put any reliance on. A "side trip" by one of the participants, who was asked to describe my home in New Jersey, which he'd never been to, was similarly suggestive but not sufficiently so to convince me that his mind had indeed left his body and traveled south. I hadn't yet learned how essential objective ways of evaluating results in parapsychology were. We saw in chapter 7, on clairvoyance, how one can be quite objective about this in the RV experiments.

Miss Z's Out-of-Body Experiences:
My Second Study

My next study of OBEs happened through coincidence, although given some synchronicities that occurred years later (Tart 1981), I sometimes wonder if it was "Coincidence" rather than "coincidence."

While chatting about various things with a young woman who babysat for our children, I found out that, ever since early childhood, it was an ordinary part of her sleep experience to occasionally feel as if she had awakened from sleep mentally but was floating near the ceiling, looking down on her physical body, which was still asleep in bed. This experience was clearly different to her from her dreams, and usually only lasted a few seconds. As a child, not knowing better, she thought this was a normal part of sleeping. You go to sleep, dream a bit, float near the ceiling for a bit, dream a bit, wake up, get dressed, eat breakfast, and go to school. After mentioning it to friends once or twice as a teenager, she found that it wasn't "normal" and that she shouldn't talk about it anymore if she didn't want to be considered weird! She was typical in that she'd never read anything about OBEs, and this was long before Raymond Moody's book *Life After Life* (1975) was published and became a best seller, so she didn't have any idea what to make of her floating experiences. I was quite interested, because she said she still had the experience occasionally.

I told her there were two theories about OBEs: one where the experiences were basically just what they seemed to be, namely, the mind temporarily leaving the physical body and perceiving things from this outside point of view; and the other that OBEs were just some sort of hallucination. How, she wondered, could she tell the difference? I suggested that she write the numbers one to ten on slips of paper, put them in a box on her bedside table, randomly select one to turn up without looking at it before going to sleep and then, if she had an OBE during the night, look down from the ceiling, memorize the number, and then check the accuracy of her memory in the morning.

I saw her a few weeks later, and she reported that she'd tried the experiment seven times. She was always right about the number, so it seemed to her that she was really "out" during these experiences. Was there anything else interesting we could do?

Miss Z, as I've called her in my somewhat delayed primary report on our work (1968), had interrupted her college work to earn needed funds and was moving from the area in a few weeks, but before she left, I was able to have her spend four nights in my sleep research laboratory. I knew about OBEs and NDEs, although this was still long before Moody's book popularized knowledge about NDEs, so I wondered what physiological changes would take place in her body when she had an OBE: was she physiologically coming close to death? And I wanted to test her apparent ESP ability to see numbers from outside her body.

Each night, I recorded brain waves (the electroencephalogram, or EEG) in a typical fashion used in dream research, which allowed me to distinguish between waking states, drowsiness, and the four stages of sleep.[4] I measured rapid eye movements (REMs), which accompany ordinary stage-1 dreaming and are thought to represent a scanning of the dream imagery, with a tiny, flexible strain gauge taped over one eye, and I also measured the electrical resistance of her skin, which indicates activity in the autonomic nervous system, using electrodes taped to her right palm and forearm. On two of the four nights, I was also able to measure heart rate and relative blood pressure with a little device called an optical plethysmograph that shines a beam of light through a finger. The pulsing of the blood varies the transparency of the finger. Figure 12.1 diagrams the laboratory setup.

As for ascertaining whether Miss Z was, in some sense, really "out" of her body during her OBEs (Tart 1968, 8):

Figure 12.1 OBE Study with Miss Z, Lab Setup

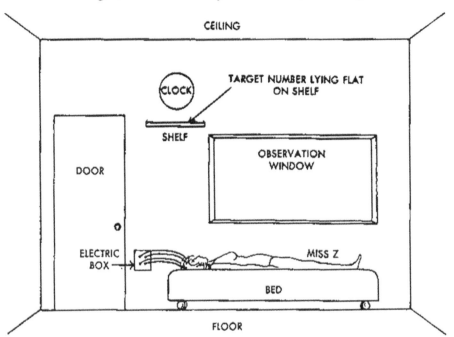

Each laboratory night, after the subject was lying in bed, the physiological recordings were running satisfactorily, and she was ready to go to sleep, I went into my office down the hall, opened a table of random numbers at random, threw a coin onto the table as a means of random entry into the page, and copied off the first five digits immediately above where the coin landed.[5] These were copied with a black marking pen, in figures approximately two inches high, onto a small piece of paper. Thus they were quite discrete visually. This five-digit random number constituted the parapsychological target for the evening. I then slipped it into an opaque folder, entered the subject's room, and slipped the piece of paper onto the shelf without at any time exposing it to the subject. This now provided a target which would be clearly visible to anyone whose eyes were located approximately six and a half feet off the floor or higher, but was otherwise not visible to the subject.

The subject was instructed to sleep well, to try and have an OBE and, if she did so, to try to wake up immediately afterwards and tell me about it, so I could note on the polygraph records when it had occurred. She was also told that if she floated high enough to read the five-digit number, she should memorize it and wake up immediately afterwards to tell me what it was.

Over her four laboratory nights, Miss Z reported three clear-cut incidents of "floating," in which she felt that she might have partly gone out of her body but the experience didn't fully develop, and two full OBEs. My general impressions of the physiological patterns accompanying her floating and full OBE experiences are that she was in no way "near death." There were no major heart-rate or blood-pressure changes and no particular activity in the autonomic nervous system. A physician wouldn't call for the crash cart to resuscitate her. This finding was reassuring: it meant we could investigate OBEs without necessarily having medical worries.

Second, floating and full OBEs occurred in a relatively discrete EEG stage of what I would technically call poorly developed stage-1 EEG, mixed with transitory periods of brief wakefulness. A sample is shown in figure 12.2. Stage-1 EEG normally accompanies the descent into sleep, the hypnagogic period, and later dreaming during the night, but these shown by Miss Z weren't like those ordinary stage-1 periods, because they were often dominated by alphoid activity, a distinctly slower version of the ordinary waking alpha rhythm, and there were no REMs accompanying these stage-1 periods, as almost always happens in normal dreaming. I had studied many sleep EEG records by then and can say with confidence that this was unusual. As to what this poorly developed stage 1 with dominant alphoid and no REMs means, that is something of a mystery.

I eventually showed the recordings to one of the world's leading authorities on sleep research, psychiatrist William Dement, and he agreed with me that it was a distinctive pattern, but we had no idea what it meant. But it has left an idea with me that I've never been able to follow up but which might still prove fruitful. If you could teach someone to produce a drowsy state and slowed alpha rhythms, say through biofeedback training, would the proper psychological procedures then make it easier to have an OBE? Indeed, I found a report of a sensory deprivation study that reported alphoid rhythms occurring and also reported some subjects feeling as if they had left their bodies (Heron 1957). I wrote to the researcher asking if these two things were associated but never received a reply. Too "far out" of a question, I guess.

Figure 12.2 EEGs of Ordinary Dreaming
and of Miss Z's OBE Alphoid Patterns

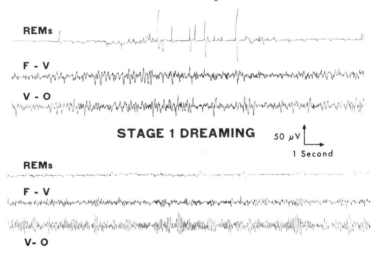

On the first three laboratory nights, Miss Z reported that in spite of occasionally being "out," she hadn't been able to control her OBEs enough to be in position to see the target number (which was different each night). On the fourth night, at 5:57 a.m., there was a seven-minute period of somewhat ambiguous EEG activity, sometimes looking like stage 1, sometimes like brief waking states.

Then Miss Z awakened and called out over the intercom that the target number was 25,132, which I wrote on the EEG recording. After she slept a few more minutes, I woke her so she could go to work, and this is what she reported regarding the previous awakening (Tart 1968, 17):

> I woke up; it was stifling in the room. Awake for about five minutes. I kept waking up and drifting off, having floating feelings over and over. I needed to go higher, because the number was lying down. Between 5:50 and 6:00 a.m., that did it...I wanted to go read the number in the next room, but I couldn't leave the room, open the door, or float through the door.... I couldn't turn on the air conditioner!

The number 25,132 was indeed the correct target number near the ceiling above her bed. I had learned something about designing experiments since my first OBE experiment, and precise evaluation was possible here. The odds against guessing a five-digit number by chance alone on one try are a hundred thousand to one, so this is a remarkable event! Note also that Miss Z had apparently expected me to have the target number propped up against the wall behind the shelf, but she correctly reported that it was lying flat.

Whenever striking parapsychological results occur, parapsychologists worry that they might've been fraudulently produced or happened through some normal sensory channel, for such things have happened historically. A visiting colleague, Arthur Hastings, who's a skilled amateur magician as well as a parapsychologist and professor at the Institute of Transpersonal Psychology, and I carefully inspected the laboratory at a later date to see if there was any chance of this. We let our eyes adapt to the dark to see if there was any chance the number might've been reflected in the plastic casing of the clock on the wall above and to the side of the target number, but nothing could be seen unless we shone a bright flashlight directly onto the numbers. Unless Miss Z had, without our knowledge, employed concealed apparatus to illuminate, inspect the target number, or both, which we had no reason to suspect, there was no normal way for anyone lying in bed, and having only very limited movement available due to the attached electrodes, to see it.[6]

I was cautious in my original write-up of these results: "…Miss Z's reading of the target number cannot be considered as providing conclusive evidence for a parapsychological effect" (Tart 1968, 18). I thought I was just making a standard statement of caution, because no one experiment is ever absolutely conclusive about anything, but overzealous pseudoskeptics have pounced on this statement as saying that I didn't think there were any parapsychological effects in this study. I've always thought that it's highly likely that some form of ESP, perhaps because Miss Z was really "out" in some real sense, is the best explanation of the results.

The most interesting criticism I've repeatedly received when describing this study comes from believers rather than skeptics. Someone usually asks me whether I knew what the target number was. When I reply that I did, their criticism is that perhaps Miss Z wasn't really out of her body but instead was merely using telepathy to read the number from my mind! I admit, with amusement, that this first study of this type was indeed too crude to rule out the counterexplanation of "mere telepathy."

As you can imagine, I was quite pleased with the outcome of this study. An unusual and important experience, the OBE was accompanied by an unusual EEG pattern, and there was evidence that Miss Z was able to correctly perceive the world from her out-of-body location. I was also greatly pleased at demonstrating that an exotic phenomenon like the OBE could be studied in the laboratory and have light cast on it, and the publication of this study stimulated a few other parapsychologists to think about doing research along these lines. I had shown you could study OBEs in the laboratory, and waited for the world to jump on the bandwagon, find their own talented people who'd had OBEs, and do larger and better studies. My personal regret was that Miss Z moved away and I was never able to track her down to do further work while I had laboratory facilities available. People who can have an OBE almost on demand are, to put it mildly, rare.

Stanley Krippner (1996) had a similar experience with a young man who reported occasional OBEs. He was tested for four nights in the laboratory with an art-print target in a box near the ceiling of the room. On the occasion when he reported having had an OBE, he gave a suggestively accurate description of the target, and had shown an unusual EEG pattern of slow waves (unlike Miss Z) about the time the reported OBE occurred. But he then went off to medical school before any further testing could be done.

With the wisdom of hindsight, I can see that I was naive in expecting that publication of my results would stimulate many other scientists to carry out similar studies so that our understanding of the physiological and parapsychological aspects of OBEs would grow rapidly. I had many other research interests and went on to other things after Miss Z moved away. I had demonstrated my main point, that OBEs could be studied in the laboratory, and got on with my many other interests. But it's too bad I never tracked her down in later years to repeat and expand this study. I did have a fleeting contact with her in a pizza parlor years later (Tart 1981) while she was visiting from out of state. Could this have been a result of my need to demonstrate a synchronicity to illustrate a paper I was working on about synchronicity? But today I don't even know if she's still alive, and being semiretired, I no longer have a research laboratory available.

As I reflect further, though, decades later, why was I satisfied that the Miss Z study had provided evidence for the "mind really goes out" theory of OBEs and shown something about possible physiological correlates of the state? Why didn't I go on, drop all my other interests, try to find the funds to fly Miss Z back to my lab, and study her intensely until I had absolute proof that she was really "out," that her OBEs could involve psychic perception of the physical environment?

Again, with the wisdom of hindsight, I can see several factors bearing on why I didn't do this. First, as previously mentioned, I was satisfied at having demonstrated my point that OBEs could be studied under laboratory conditions. Second, my other interests were real, important interests to me, and it wouldn't have been easy to neglect them. Third, it has always been difficult to raise money for research in parapsychology; there was a good chance I wouldn't succeed even if I invested a lot of time and effort, and like most people, I don't like to put energy into things I doubt I'll succeed in. Fourth, it would've been a career killer. I was early in my professional career, and given the common biases in psychology, I would've been labeled not only a kook but a determined kook threatening the status quo in the field, and advancement opportunities would almost certainly have been denied me. Since I had a family to support, this was not a minor consideration.

But it's the fifth factor that's difficult to consider but possibly very important. From a totally materialistic standpoint, my decision alone as to whether to pursue this study was the most important factor, because the other factors could've been handled to various degrees. But we're considering the possible reality of spiritual factors in this book. I use "spiritual" here in the sense of another order of reality involving its own kind of possible entities and their decisions, a spiritual order that, to an unknown extent, affects our ordinary material reality. Insofar as this kind of spiritual reality is real, how much of the decision whether or not to pursue research with Miss Z was my decision, and how much of was it a decision from another level?

Of course, most, if not all, versions of materialistic philosophy assume everything is causally determined by physical factors, operating since the beginning of the universe, modified (in a meaningless way) by random events, so I really had no free choice in the matter. (See the Western Creed exercise in chapter 1.) But most materialists ignore this aspect, and act and think as if they had some free choices in everyday life.

To even begin to think this way is quite upsetting to a lot of our current beliefs, as I briefly mentioned earlier. No scientist wants to think that the outcomes of her experiments are affected by anything other than the laws of nature and her ingenuity in setting up studies. I certainly feel that way most of the time! I am the mighty experimenter subjecting nature to my will to learn her secrets! The guy who wrote the above paragraph must be getting soft in the head! As Francis Bacon (1561–1626), one of the founders of modern science put it, "Question Nature...and torture her with experiment until she yields the truth of phenomena."

And yet logic requires me to think about the possibility that I'm only the "coexperimenter" and that sometimes I may have a "silent partner" whose actions affect what I'll see and learn and what opportunities I have.

Or perhaps this line of reasoning is a rationalization, a psychological defense on my part for not making better choices in the past? That's certainly a possibility too.

There's a long history of parapsychological experiments where powerful results were obtained in the beginning, investigators got excited, and then the results petered out for no apparent reason or the experimenter got involved in other things instead of following up on what was obviously very important. Sometimes it makes you wonder: are we being led? Baited? Intellectually teased? Given enough encouragement to think and move in certain directions but without too much success, which might inhibit a longer-term movement?

Robert Monroe's Out-of-Body Experiences: My Third Study

Some of the most interesting studies I've been able to do on OBEs have been with my friend, the late Robert A. Monroe (1915–1995), whose classic book, *Journeys Out of the Body* (1971), is well known to many with spiritual interests, as well as his subsequent books *Far Journeys* (published by Doubleday, 1985) and *Ultimate Journey* (also by Doubleday,1994). Monroe was an archetypally "normal" American businessman who was "drafted" quite involuntarily into the world of OBEs and psychic things as a result of a series of strange "attacks" of "vibrations" in the late 1950s, culminating in a classic OBE. Russell's (*The Journey of Robert Monroe: From Out-of-Body Explorer to Consciousness Pioneer*, Hampton Roads, 2007) and Stockton's (*Catapult: The Biography of Robert A. Monroe*, The Donning Company, 1989) biographies provide fascinating background material on Monroe's life. Let me quote Monroe's account (1971, 27–28) of his first OBE:

> Spring 1958: If I thought I faced incongruities at this point, it was because I did not know what was yet to come. Some four weeks later, when the vibrations came again, I was duly cautious about attempting to move an arm or leg. It was late at night, and I was lying in bed before sleep. My wife had fallen asleep beside me. There was a surge that seemed to be in my head, and quickly the condition spread through my body. It all seemed the same. As I lay there trying to decide how to analyze the thing in another way, I just happened to think how nice it would be to take a glider up and fly the next afternoon (my hobby at that time). Without considering any consequences — not knowing there would be any — I thought of the pleasure it would bring.
>
> After a moment, I became aware of something pressing against my shoulder. Half curious, I reached back and up to feel what it was. My hand encountered a smooth wall. I moved my hand along the wall the length of my arm, and it continued smooth and unbroken.
>
> My senses fully alert, I tried to see in the dim light. It was a wall, and I was lying against it with my shoulder. I immediately reasoned that I had gone to sleep and fallen

out of bed. (I had never done so before, but all sorts of strange things were happening, and falling out of bed was quite possible.)

Then I looked again. Something was wrong. This wall had no windows, no furniture against it, no doors. It was not a wall in my bedroom. Yet somehow it was familiar. Identification came instantly. It wasn't a wall; it was the ceiling. I was floating against the ceiling, bouncing gently with any movement I made. I rolled in the air, startled, and looked down. There, in the dim light below me, was the bed. There were two figures lying in the bed. To the right was my wife. Beside her was someone else. Both seemed asleep.

This was a strange dream, I thought. I was curious. Who would I dream to be in bed with my wife? I looked more closely, and the shock was intense. I was the "someone" on the bed!

My reaction was almost instantaneous. Here I was; there was my body. I was dying; this was death, and I wasn't ready to die. Somehow, the vibrations were killing me. Desperately, like a diver, I swooped down to my body and dove in. I then felt the bed and the covers, and when I opened my eyes, I was looking at the room from the perspective of my bed.

What had happened? Had I truly almost died? My heart was beating rapidly but not unusually so. I moved my arms and legs. Everything seemed normal. The vibrations had faded away. I got up and walked around the room, looked out the window, and smoked a cigarette.

(*Reprinted from* Journeys Out of the Body *by Robert Monroe, copyright ©1971, 1977 by Robert Monroe. Used by permission of Doubleday, a division of Random House, Inc.*)

Being a normally educated and socially conditioned American, Monroe went to his doctor, of course, to see what was wrong with him, but his health was fine. Fortunately, he eventually spoke to a psychologist friend, who told him that Eastern yogis had experiences like this and that he should explore them rather than worry. He didn't find this advice particularly reassuring, but he had no choice in the matter, because the vibrations and subsequent OBEs continued to occur.

I met Monroe in fall 1965, when I took a research position at the University of Virginia School of Medicine in Charlottesville. His first book, *Journeys Out of the Body*, was a finished manuscript but not yet published.[7] Monroe was having OBEs regularly by then, although he hadn't developed the Hemi-Sync techniques he later used to train others. Monroe was as curious about the nature of OBEs as I was, and also eager to try to understand his own experiences rather than be simply swept up in them. Could we test whether he was "really" at an OBE location rather than just hallucinating it? While he'd had some experiences of being at a distant earthly location where he was later able to confirm the events, frustratingly there were too many others where such confirmation was only partial or even negative, even though the experiences felt perfectly real. If there were distinctive physiological changes during an OBE, and we could learn to produce these same changes by other means in people, we might have a way of helping them to have OBEs.

I was able to have Monroe come in for eight late-night sessions (his OBEs usually began from sleep) from December 1965 to August 1966 at the University of Virginia hospital's EEG laboratory, where he tried to get out of his body. This laboratory wasn't really equipped for sleep work, so much of the time Monroe wasn't very comfortable on the cot we brought in and was unable to have an OBE. On his eighth night, however, things got interesting. Here are Monroe's notes (Tart 1967, 254–55), written the next morning:

After some time spent in attempting to ease ear-electrode discomfort, concentrated on ear to "numb" it, with partial success. Then went into fractional relaxation technique again. Halfway through the second time around in the pattern the sense of warmth appeared, with full consciousness (or so it seemed) remaining. I decided to try the "roll-out" method (i.e., start to turn over gently, just as if you were turning over in bed using the physical body). I started to feel as if I were turning, and at first thought I truly was moving the physical body. I felt myself roll off the edge of the cot, and braced for the fall to the floor. When I didn't hit immediately, I knew that I had disassociated. I moved away from the physical and through a darkened area, then came upon two men and a woman. The "seeing" wasn't too good but better as I came closer. The woman, tall, dark-haired, in her forties (?) was sitting on a loveseat or couch. Seated to the right of her was one man. In front of her and to her left slightly was the second man. They all were strangers to me and were in conversation which I could not hear. I tried to get their attention but could not. Finally, I reached over and pinched (very gently!) the woman on her left side just below the rib carriage. It seemed to get a reaction but still no communication. I decided to return to the physical for orientation and start again.[8]

Back into the physical was achieved simply, by thought of return. Opened physical eyes; all was fine; swallowed to wet my dry throat, closed my eyes, let the warmth surge up, then used the same roll-out technique. This time, I let myself float to the floor beside the cot. I fell slowly and could feel myself passing through the various EEG wires on the way down. I touched the floor lightly, then could "see" the light coming through the open doorway to the outer EEG rooms. Careful to keep "local," I went under the cot, keeping in slight touch with the floor and floating in a horizontal position, fingertips touching the floor to keep in position.[9] I went slowly through the doorway. I was looking for the technician, but could not find her. She was not in the room to the right (control-console room), and I went out into the brightly lighted outer room. I looked in all directions, and suddenly there she was. However, she was not alone. A man was with her, standing to her left as she faced me. I tried to attract her attention and was almost immediately rewarded with a burst of warm joy and happiness that I had finally achieved the thing we had been working for. She was truly excited, and happily and excitedly embraced me. I responded, and only slight sexual overtones were present which I was about 90 percent able to disregard. After a moment, I pulled back and gently put my hands on her face, one on each cheek, and thanked her for her help. However, there was no direct intelligent objective communication with her other than the above. None was tried, as I was too excited at finally achieving the disassociation — and staying "local."

I then turned to the man, who was about her height, curly haired, some of which dropped over the side of his forehead. I tried to attract his attention but was unable to do so. Again, reluctantly, I decided to pinch him gently, which I did. It did not evoke any response that I noticed. Feeling something calling for a return to the physical, I swung around and went through the door, and slipped easily back into the physical. Reason for discomfort: dry throat and throbbing ear.

After checking to see that the integration was complete, that I "felt" normal in all parts of the body, I opened my eyes, sat up, and called to the technician. She came in, and I told her that I had made it finally and that I had seen her, however, with a man. She replied that it was her husband. I asked if he was outside, and she replied that he was, that he came to stay with her during these late hours. I asked why I hadn't seen him before, and she replied that it was "policy" for no outsiders to see subjects or patients. I expressed the desire to meet him, to which she acceded.

The technician removed the electrodes, and I went outside with her and met her husband. He was about her height, curly haired, and after several conversational amenities, I left. I did not query the technician or her husband as to anything they saw, noticed, or felt. However, my impression was that he definitely was the man I had observed with her during the nonphysical activity. My second impression was that she was not in the control-console room when I visited them but was in another room, standing up, with him. This may be hard to determine, if there is a fast rule that the technician is supposed to always stay at the console. If she can be convinced that the truth is more important in this case, perhaps this second aspect can be validated. The only supporting evidence other than what might have appeared on the EEG lies in the presence of the husband, of which I was unaware prior to the experiment. This latter fact can be verified by the technician, I am sure.

(*Reprinted with permission from Charles T. Tart, "A second Psychophysiological Study of Out-of-the-Body Experiences in a Gifted Subject,"* International Journal of Parapsychology 9:251-58.)

As with Miss Z, Monroe's physiological changes were interesting but not medically exciting. He was not at all near death, just showing the relaxed body characteristics of sleep and relaxation. This fits the general pattern that emerged from many later studies by others of NDEs that shows that while being physiologically close to death may facilitate the occurrence of an NDE, it's not absolutely necessary for either NDEs or OBEs to happen.

As to exactly what was Monroe's state during OBEs, there's some general similarity to Miss Z's in that both involve a stage-1 EEG pattern that's somewhat like, but not identical to, ordinary dreaming, but the two patterns, in the limited sampling of these two studies, are not identical. Monroe had some alphoid activity but not the large amount Miss Z showed. He also showed REMs in his second OBE, in which he reported seeing a stranger with the technician. Also, in an all-night study we did with Monroe to get a baseline of normal sleep, when he wasn't trying for OBEs, he showed a normal pattern and didn't call the stage-1 REM periods that occurred there OBEs. Ordinarily he sharply distinguishes the states of consciousness of his dreams, his occasional lucid dreams, and his OBEs.

We must remember too that while there's a strong correlation between EEG stage-1 REM pattern and the psychological experience of dreaming, correlation is not causality or identity. You can't say that a dream is the physiological state of stage 1, for example. We can think of stage-1 REM as a physiological state that has evolved during the sleep of mammals. In humans, the psychological activity of dreaming can use this physiological pattern to readily manifest itself, although mental states very like dreaming may sometimes occur in other physiological conditions. The lucid dream, a dream state in which consciousness "wakes up" and feels as if it's pretty much in full possession of its waking faculties, also occurs in the physiological state of stage-1 REM (LaBerge 1985). Perhaps an OBE is also facilitated in this same physiological state.

Was Monroe really "out" when he saw the technician away from her machine and speaking with a strange man? In her notes, the technician reports (Tart 1967, 256): "In the second sleep the patient saw me (the tech), and he said I had a visitor, which I did. However, it is possible that Mr. Monroe may have heard the visitor cough during his (cigarette) break between sleeps. Mr. Monroe states that he patted the visitor on the cheeks and tried to take his hand but that the visitor avoided. Mr. X recalls that he left the cot, went under it and out the door into the recording room and then into the hallway....The patient did not see the number."

Thus we have only weak evidence that Monroe was actually "out" on this occasion, a result he found as unsatisfactory as I did.

I left the University of Virginia post after a year there to take up a position at the University of California, Davis, so our work — and I do say our, for I try (but don't always succeed) to always work with collaborators or colleagues, not "subjects" (Tart 1977b) — ended for the time being on a note both encouraging and frustrating. The scientific world had doubled its knowledge about EEG patterns during OBEs, since there were now two studies instead of none (although, as you can imagine, orthodox science has paid almost no attention to this knowledge), but a common pattern had not emerged, and the parapsychological aspects of Monroe's OBEs had not been confirmed in this study.

Second Monroe OBE Study:
My Fourth Study

Several months later, after moving to California, I wanted to have more data about whether Monroe was really "out" in his OBEs, so I decided to try an experiment in which my wife Judy and I would, for a short period, try to create a sort of "psychic beacon" by concentrating on him, to try to help Monroe have an OBE and travel to our home. If he could accurately describe our home, this would be good evidence for a psi component in his OBEs, because he had no idea what our new home was like. As in my first study using hypnosis to try to produce OBEs, I was hoping for a big effect that would be obvious evidence of ESP.

I telephoned Monroe and told him that we would try to guide him across the country to our home at some unspecified time during the night of the experiment. That was all I told him. That evening I randomly selected a time to begin concentrating; the only restriction I put on my choice was that it would be some time after I thought Monroe had been asleep for a while. The time turned out to be 11:00 p.m. California time, 2:00 a.m. where Monroe lived in Virginia. At 11:00, my wife and I began our concentration, but at 11:05, the telephone rang. We never got calls late at night, so this was rather surprising and disturbing, but we didn't answer the phone, nor did we have an answering machine, so we didn't know who'd called. We tried to continue concentrating and did so until 11:30 p.m.

The following day, I telephoned Monroe and noncommittally told him that the results had been encouraging but that I wasn't going to say anything more about it until he'd mailed me his written account of what he'd experienced. His account was as follows (Tart 1977a, 190–91):

The evening passed uneventfully, and I finally got into bed about 1:40 a.m., still very much wide awake. The cat was lying in bed with me. After a long period of calming mind, a sense of warmth swept over body, no break in consciousness, no presleep. Almost immediately felt something (or someone) rocking my body from side to side, then tugging at my feet! (Heard cat let out complaining yowl.) I recognized immediately that this had something to do with Charley's experiment, and with full trust, did not feel my usual caution with strangers! The tugging at my legs continued, and I finally managed to separate one second body arm and hold it up, feeling around in the dark. After a moment, the tugging stopped and a hand took my wrist, first gently, then very, very firmly and pulled me out of the physical (body) easily. Still trusting, and a little excited, I expressed a feeling to go to Charley, if that was where he (it) wanted to lead me. The answer came back affirmatively (although there was no sense of personality — very businesslike). With the hand around my wrist very firmly, I could feel a part of the arm belonging to the hand (slightly hairy, muscular male). But could not "see" who belonged to the arm. Also heard my name called. Then we started to move, with the familiar feeling of something like air rushing around my body. After a short trip (seemed around five seconds in duration), we stopped, and the hand released my wrist. There was complete silence and darkness. When I drifted down into what seemed to be a room...

When Monroe finished his brief OBE, he got out of bed to telephone me: it was 11:05 p.m., our time. Thus he experienced a tug pulling him from his body within one or two minutes of the time we started concentrating. The portion of his account that I've omitted, on the other hand, his description of our home and what my wife and I were doing, was quite inaccurate (for instance, he perceived too many people in the room, and my wife and me performing actions that we did not do). Looking at the description, I would conclude that nothing psychic had happened. Thinking about the precise timing, though, I can't help but wonder. Can one have an OBE in which one is really "out" in some sense yet have grossly mistaken (extrasensory) perceptions of the location one has gone to? I don't know if that was the case in this experiment, but after years of researching how much perception is a semiarbitrary construction, often badly distorted, even in our normal state (Tart 1986 and 1994), I have no doubt that perceptual distortion is possible for OBEs.

Third Monroe OBE Study: My Fifth Study

In 1968 I was able to do one further study with Monroe when he briefly visited California on a business trip. I had a functioning sleep laboratory at the University of California, Davis, far more comfortable than the University of Virginia EEG lab, and he spent an afternoon with me and my assistants (Tart 1969).

In the course of a two-hour session, Monroe had two brief OBEs, and reported awakening within a few seconds after each, allowing correlation of physiological recordings with the OBEs. EEG, eye movements, and peripheral blood flow (again with an optical ple- thysmograph) were again recorded, and he was monitored via closed- circuit TV for the first OBE.[10] Monroe was asked to try to produce an OBE, and then to travel into the equipment room where I and my assistants were and to read a five-digit target number in that equipment room.

In his first OBE, he reported finding himself in the hall con- necting the rooms for a period of eight to ten seconds at most, but then being forced to return to his body because of feelings of breathing difficulties in his physical body. In his second OBE, he reported trying to follow the EEG cable through the wall to the equipment room but, to his amazement, found himself outside the building and facing the wall of another building, still following a cable. He later recognized a courtyard on the inside of the building, which had a three-story wall and was 180 degrees opposite the equipment room as the place he'd experienced himself in.

Although he had no memory, when questioned, of ever having seen this courtyard, it's possible that he could've gotten a look at it while in my office earlier in the afternoon. There was no cable in the courtyard, at least not on the surface, although there may have been buried electrical cables under the surface connecting the wings of the building, and there were some cables from the laboratory room to my office, going most of the way toward the courtyard.

Again we have that frustrating pattern of my research with Monroe of no ESP results clear enough to be conclusive, but also results not so clearly irrelevant or inaccurate to make me feel comfortable saying that nothing at all had happened.

Technically, the EEG prior to the Monroe's reported OBE may be roughly classified as a borderline or hypnagogic state, a stage-1 pattern containing instances of alphoid activity rhythm (indicative of drowsiness) and theta activity (a normal sleeping pattern, part of stage 1). This pattern persisted through the first OBE, but was accompanied by a sudden fall of systolic blood pressure lasting seven seconds, this being roughly equivalent to Monroe's estimated length of his OBE. There was REM activity of an ambiguous nature during this period. The second OBE was reported after a period of EEG shifting between stage-1 and stage-2 sleep. This second OBE's exact duration is unknown but appears to have been accompanied by a similar stage-1 pattern and only two instances of isolated REM activity near the end. No clear-cut cardiac changes were seen on the plethysmographic recording. Monroe reported having used a different technique for producing the OBE this second time.

In general, then, Monroe's OBEs seemed to occur in conjunction with a prolonged, deliberately produced hypnagogic state (stage-1 EEG). Such prolonged states aren't usually seen in the sleep laboratory, as my experience was that people usually passed quickly through this stage into stage-2 sleep. The preponderance of theta rhythms and the occasional slowed alpha show an intriguing parallel with EEG states reported for advanced Zen masters during meditation (Kasamatsu and Hirai 1966). Modern EEG-biofeedback techniques have shown that people can learn to produce increased alpha rhythm and to slow the frequency of their alpha rhythm. If I were still actively researching this area, I would try training people to produce theta and slowed alpha rhythms, controlled drowsiness, as it were, to see if this helped them have OBEs. This is the sort of thing that Monroe worked on developing with his Hemi-Sync procedures at The Monroe Institute, which Monroe often conceptualized as putting the body to sleep while keeping the mind awake. While I've been very intrigued with some of these results, I haven't followed them closely enough to give a professional analysis of them.

Back to Hypnosis and OBEs:
My Sixth Study

The OBE study I carried out in 1970 was, like my first one in 1957, an attempt to use hypnosis to produce OBEs but on a more sophisticated level. I had done hypnosis research for more than a decade by this time, especially investigating the use of posthypnotic suggestion to influence the content and process of nighttime, stage-1 REM dreaming. I had a small group of highly selected and trained participants at the University of California, Davis (see Tart and Dick 1970 for details on selection and training), people we might justly call hypnotic virtuosos, all in the upper 10 percent of the population in terms of hypnotic susceptibility. Besides being adept at having their nighttime dreams influenced posthypnotically, they had explored various aspects of deep hypnotic states and were comfortable in the laboratory setting.

I no longer have the records available, having had to throw out a lot of old data upon retirement from the University of California for lack of storage space, so I can only describe the general results of the study, which I never found time to write up and publish. Basically, about seven of the participants had individual hypnotic sessions where they reached exceptionally deep hypnotic states, confirmed by their self-reports of hypnotic depth (Tart 1970). Each deeply hypnotized participant then received a suggestion that, while the hypnotist remained quiet for ten minutes so as to not disturb the participant and keep the person connected to her body, her consciousness would leave her physical body and cross the hall into a second, locked laboratory room, where some special target materials were displayed on a table. She was to observe these materials carefully, wander about out of body at will for a while, then return and report on her OBE to the experimenter, one of my graduate-student assistants.

All the participants reported vivid OBEs that seemed like real experiences to them. They included journeys to places they knew, like downtown Davis, which they vividly experienced, as well as clear experiences of journeying to the target room.

None of their reports of what they saw on the target table bore any clear resemblance to the targets. A formal analysis wasn't worth the trouble.

So, an OBE Is...?

So what's an OBE? Does the mind or soul really leave the body and go somewhere else, "out," or is the OBE just a special ASC that's basically hallucinatory in nature, meaning that the feeling and conviction that you're elsewhere than your physical body's location is an illusion? Perhaps, it's the latter case, with some occasional ESP thrown in to make the hallucination fit ordinary reality more closely?

After decades of reflection on the results of my own and others' research, particularly in the light of my general studies on the nature of consciousness and ASCs, I have a more complex view of OBEs that includes both of these possibilities at different times and more. Remember here that we're talking about out-of-body experiences, which are real phenomena, but we want to theorize about them, to understand what lies behind the experience.

My "best guess" theory is that in some OBEs, the mind may, at least partially, really be "out," located elsewhere than the physical body and sensing (via some form of ESP) from this extra-bodily location. This may have been the case with Miss Z. At the opposite extreme, as with my hypnotic virtuosos, whose experiences were vivid and perfectly real to them but whose perceptions of the target room showed no trace of ESP functioning, I believe that an OBE can be a simulation of being out of the body, and mind is as much "in" the physical body as it ever is. In between these two extremes, I believe we can have, as one possibility, OBEs that are basically a simulation of being out but are informed by information gathered by ESP, such that the simulation of the OBE location is accurate and veridical. As another possibility, we may have OBEs in which a person is really "out" in some sense but has a distorted perception of the OBE location, dreamlike content mixed in, or both, perhaps with perception distorted enough that we can't find any significant correlation between the actual characteristics of that OBE location and the person's description.

This is a messy situation in some ways, especially because all four of these types of OBEs may seem experientially identical to the person having them, at least at rough levels of description. While I would prefer that reality fall into simple, clear-cut categories, I've learned in life that reality doesn't care about our wishes for simplicity, though, and things are often complex.

Simulation of Reality

I want to elaborate on simulation models of consciousness here, because they're important. We all have a model, a theory, about the nature of consciousness and of the world, although it's usually implicit, so we don't consciously know that we have a theory. The theory is that space and time are real and pretty much what they seem to be, that things have a definite location in time and space, that consciousness is "in" the head, and that from that spatial position we directly perceive the outside world through our physical senses.

As a working model, this theory works quite well most of the time: if someone throws a rock toward you, for example, an automated part of this model, what's been called the ecological self (Neisser 1988), instantly calculates the trajectory of the rock, compares it to its calculated position of where you are, and makes you duck if the projected trajectory intersects your position.[11] In terms of biological survival, it's usually quite useful to psychologically identify with this ecological self and give very high priority to protecting your physical body. Indeed, it's very difficult not to automatically identify with this ecological-self process!

Looking at this in more detail, we now know, through decades of psychological and neurophysiological research, that this naive view of perception — that consciousness just perceives the external world in a straightforward way, like a camera taking a picture — is quite inadequate. Almost all perception is really a kind of rapid, implicit, and automated thinking, a set of judgments, analyses, and extrapolations about what's happening and its relevance to you. When something moves in the periphery of your visual field, for example, you'll generally actually see, say, a threatening person ducking behind a bush, rather than experience an ambiguous movement in the unfocused part of your visual field, leading to a conscious thought of "What might it be?"

Such a conscious thought, in turn, could lead to searches of memory for possible candidates that show some fit to the ambiguous perceptual data available, leading to a conclusion that a threatening person ducking behind a bush has a 45 percent chance of fitting the perceptual data, while a branch blowing in the wind has only a 30 percent chance of fitting, so that it would probably be best to get ready for action. If it really is a threatening figure, the person who sees it that way instantly has a better chance of survival by reacting faster than the one who goes through a long, sequential process of conscious analysis. It's as if there's a distinct evolutionary advantage for the organism that has instant readiness to fight or flee, even at the price of some false alarms, compared to the organism that takes too long to respond.

To jump to the end point of my and others' research, it's useful to think of our ordinary consciousness as a process that creates an ongoing, dynamic simulation of reality, a world model, an inner theater of the mind, a bio-psychological virtual reality (BPVR) (Tart 1991, 1993), "in" which consciousness dwells. The most obvious example of this process is the nocturnal dream. There we live in an apparently complete, sensory world, set in dimensions of space and time, with actors and plots. Indeed, most of the brain mechanisms that construct that dreamworld are probably by and large the same mechanisms that construct our waking world with the very important difference that in the waking state this world-simulation process must constantly deal with sensory input in a way that protects us and furthers our ends in the real physical world. This includes constantly taking social norms into account. Thus I've described the reality we ordinarily live in as consensus reality (1973), to remind us that even though we implicitly think we simply perceive "reality" as it is, it's actually a complex construction, strongly determined by the physical nature of our bodies and the world, by social consensus of our particular society about what's important, and by our own psychodynamics and conditioning.

Applying this perspective back to the study of OBEs and NDEs, we should first realize that the ordinary feeling that we're "in" our bodies (usually our heads) is a construction, a world simulation, that happens to be an optimal way to ensure survival most of the time, but that this construction isn't necessarily true in any ultimate sense. I don't know what ultimate reality is, but it's helpful to remember that, just as a person using a high-quality, computer-generated virtual reality simulator forgets where his physical body actually is and becomes experientially located "in" the computer-generated world, it might be that our "souls" are actually located somewhere else, but we're so immersed in the BPVR our brains generate that we think we're here in our bodies. This is a crazy idea, but it helps to remind us that the experience of where we are isn't a simple matter of just perceiving reality as it is. Rounding out such a theory, I'll add that our brains and bodies are telepathically and psychokinetically connected to wherever the mind is "located" (see Tart 1993 for a full exposition of this latter theory of a mechanism for interactive dualism).

So when someone has an out-of-body experience, this may well be another semiarbitrary, constructed simulation of whatever reality actually is. That reality might be that mind is located somewhere other than the physical body, and may or may not use ESP to learn about the "outside" place where it is, rather than its being completely absorbed in the brain and nervous system simulation of the physical reality around the physical body. Putting this in more traditional spiritual terms, we may have a soul, a nonphysical center of identity and consciousness, and while it's normally completely occupied with the physical-reality simulation generated by our brain and senses, sometimes it may travel elsewhere.

In a rational world, the truth or falseness of such an idea is of enormous importance to who we think we are and how we think we should live our lives, so very large amounts of resources would need to be devoted to investigating this possibility. But somehow I can't recall the mailing address for the "National Institute of Soul Research."

Notes

1. In my first publication about OBEs (1968), I coined the acronym "OOBE" for them, Out Of Body Experience. A journal editor, the late parapsychologist John Beloff, corrected me when I submitted a later article: you don't capitalize the o in "of" when you create an acronym. It was too late, though, even though I've used the proper acronym "OBE" ever since. The OOBE acronym had spread into the world, with people pronouncing it as if it were a word ("ooh-bee"), and hundreds came up to me after lectures over the years to tell me about their "ooh-bees."

2. There are more academic distinctions made in the article previously referred to, which was based on a paper I presented at a Parapsychological Association meeting, but they need not concern us here. As a humorous aside, I did create a category of pseudo-classical discrete out-of-body experience, and my friend and colleague Stanley Krippner accused me of following up my creation of the "ooh-bee" with the "Scooby Dooby."

3. I was still relatively young and new to research then and spoke of "subjects" rather than coexperimenters or percipients, following the current fashions of the time without realizing that this kind of language created particular psychological conditions and them versus us divisions that might bias studies.

4. I recorded two channels, frontal to vertex and vertex to occipital on the right side of the head, recording continuously through the night on a Grass model VII polygraph at a paper speed of ten millimeters per second.

5. There is indeed a book (RAND Corporation 1955) containing a million

random numbers. Besides making good bedtime reading for people who have trouble getting to sleep, it had many uses in generating random sequences for experiments before we all had computers that could generate pseudorandom numbers.

6. Standard sleep-laboratory procedures leave enough slack in the wires running to the electrodes on a person's head so that he can turn over with ease, but if he tries to sit up more than a little, he'll pull electrodes off, making the electrodes susceptible to picking up power-line interference, which will vibrate the recording pens so hard that they throw ink all over the recording room, as well as leave a distinctive trace on the polygraph record.

7. Indeed his manuscript had seen sitting with the literary agent he'd hired for more than a year, with no indication of any interest from publishers. I thought this was disgraceful; either publishers were overlooking an important book or his literary agent wasn't really doing enough. So I sent a copy of the manuscript to an editor I knew, Bill Whitehead at Doubleday, who later published the book. Bill later told me that he took the manuscript home to read, started it after dinner, found he was still reading, fascinated, at two in the morning, but then forced himself to stop reading. He had just reached the "how to do it" chapter, and was not at all sure that he wanted to have an OBE.

8. Monroe had already had a number of experiences where, while having an OBE, he felt he was in telepathic communication with people in the ordinary world, but they never remembered it when he asked about it later! Frustrated, he had then once pinched a friend who was in her ordinary state while he was out, hoping this would fix the memory. When he later asked her about what she had been doing at that time, she had no memory of his visit, but she did remember a sudden pain in her side and showed Monroe a bruise that had appeared.

9. Monroe had long been separating his OBEs into "local" ones in which he seemed to be someplace in ordinary reality and thus might be able to check on his perceptions, versus "nonlocal" ones where the locale was clearly not of this earth.

10. The TV monitoring equipment was already set up for other purposes, and I think we had vague hopes of seeing something ghostlike emerge from Monroe's body if he had an OBE, but we didn't see anything unusual and turned it off after the first reported OBE, because Monroe

felt uncomfortable being watched.

11. I must confess to having fun in demonstrating this theory when lecturing, as I suddenly throw a blackboard eraser toward my students and only the one or two who are actually on the trajectory duck, while the close others aren't in the least excited. It brings the point home nicely.

CHAPTER 13

Near-Death Experiences

NEAR (Middle English [origin: from "near," adverb]): Close at hand, not distant, in space or time.
DEATH (Old English): The act or fact of dying; the end of life; the final and irreversible cessation of the vital functions of an animal or plant. — SHORTER OXFORD ENGLISH DICTIONARY, *6th ed., s.v. "near" and "death"*

D ENNIS HILL earned his BS degree in biochemistry back when that was sufficient training to become a working scientist. He was employed as a consultant in environmental chemistry software when he wrote to me in 2001. Hill reported the following near-death experience (NDE) to my website, The Archives of Scientists' Transcendent Experiences (*www.issc-taste.org*). His experience occurred in November 1958 in a college infirmary in Fort Worth, Texas, although his description now incorporates descriptive terms from later spiritual seeking in life. He titled his description, "Ah, Sweet Death" (Hill 2001):

> "Damn it, woman! That hurt!" The deadly penicillin injection hits a tight knot in the muscle that the body knows is the last gesture of resistance before giving up to the insidious invader.
>
> The crusty night nurse regards me with a practiced dispassion: "Just pull up your pajamas, roll over, and go to sleep. I don't want any more trouble from you." She ambles back to her station in the otherwise unstaffed college infirmary.

I notice that something within me has become suddenly still and quiet. Has my heart stopped beating? I put my hand on my chest: nothing. I reach for the radial pulse with my other hand: nothing. Little sparkles of light dance before me as my vision begins to dim.

"Dave!" I call out to the other guy on the ward, who lives on my floor in the dorm.

Darkness sweeps in.

There is a sudden rush of expansion into boundaryless awareness. I feel utter serenity infused with radiant joy. There is perfect stillness; no thoughts, no memories. In the rapturous state, free from the limitations of time and space, beyond the body and the mind, I have no memory of ever having been other than This.

The Buddhists know about this state. They chant:

'Gaté, gaté, paragaté,
parasamgaté. Bodhi swaha!'

(Gone, gone, utterly gone, gone without recall. O freedom!)

Gone without recall? Gone beyond remembering ever having been? O freedom! It is true!

In this vast and blissful stillness there is now movement. I am drawn toward a tunnel ringed in blue radiance. Into the tunnel, through no volition of my own, I continue on around the curve in the tunnel until I see a dot of white light that grows larger as if [I am] approaching it.

Maharaj Jagat Singh writes: "As the Soul hears the sound of the Bell and the Conch, it begins to drop off its impurities. The Soul then travels up rapidly, and flashes of the distant Light begin to come into view. Connecting the two regions is an oblique passage, called the Curved Tunnel. Only after crossing this tunnel does the Soul reach the realm of the Creator. Here the attributes of the mind drop off, and the Soul ascends alone. Once it reaches

its Home, it merges in it, thereby setting the Soul free."
(Okay, so how did he know that the tunnel is curved? —
around to the left, as I recall.)

Falling into the white light, I am somehow jerked
back through the tunnel into the body. The precious
fullness of bliss and peace is juxtaposed in the limitations
of a body thumping wildly from the epinephrine injected
into my heart. The rapture is gone. I am very angry at
coming back.

The Sufi Master, Hazrat Inayat Khan, gives us this
teaching, "Die before death." The message here is to
become established in the joyous tranquility of the inner
Self so that when the body suddenly drops away, we will
not be distracted by attachments to the world. In this
way the Soul will complete its journey home. All of yoga
is preparation for the last moment before and the first
moment after leaving the body.

Next time I will be ready.

No fear, only the equipoise of the Indweller.

Hill's simple comment (2001) on his experience is, "No fear of
death. Persistent awareness of the utter stillness behind the mind
and within all activity."

Do you find that parts of this description don't quite make
sense for you? Or perhaps some part of you probably understands,
but you can't quite contact that part? That's an illustration of the
distinction I made between OBEs and NDEs in the previous chapter. A person's consciousness during a simple OBE is pretty much
like ordinary, "normal" consciousness, so she can describe it quite
comprehensibly. But in an NDE, while there may be an initial OBE
component, usually with consciousness seeming pretty much like
normal, there's usually an altered state of consciousness (ASC)
involved, so there are important changes in the way consciousness
functions. This ASC makes sense to you during the ASC, but this

sense doesn't transfer well to ordinary consciousness afterward; it's state-specific knowledge and memory.

Many people who hear about NDEs think something like, "Wow! I wish I could have that experience and that knowledge!" I certainly did when I first read about them way back in the 1950s — without the hard and scary part of coming close to death, of course!

As NDE researcher P. M. H. Atwater (1988) and others have documented, however, it's often not a simple matter that you start out "ordinary," have an extraordinary experience, and then "live happily ever after." Years of confusion, conflict, and struggle may be necessary as you try to make sense of the NDE and its aftermath, and to integrate this new understanding into your life. Part of that struggle and integration takes place on transpersonal levels that are very difficult to put into words, another part on more ordinary levels of questioning, changing, and expanding your worldview. (I'll use the term "transpersonal" rather than what would often be synonymous, "spiritual," as it has a more open connotation to it, whereas spiritual is usually associated with particular, codified belief systems. Appendix 4 elaborates on the transpersonal.) I'm not really qualified to write from a higher spiritual perspective, but I've gathered some useful information in my career about the nature of the world that may help with that part of the integration, and that's one of my primary emphases in this chapter.

Philosopher and physician Raymond Moody, whose 1975 book *Life After Life* hit the best-seller lists (there has always been a deep, spiritual hunger in people) brought the NDE out of the closet, and it's now widely known. As to actual occurrence, estimates today are that, due to modern medical resuscitation technology, millions of people may have had an NDE.

To give the general flavor of NDEs, here's the "composite case" Moody (1975) constructed out of the common elements of NDEs. No one person is likely to experience all of these elements, or always experience them exactly in this order, but the overall flavor is conveyed nicely. I've italicized brief descriptive elements.

A man is dying, and as he reaches the point of greatest physical distress, he (1) *hears himself pronounced dead by his doctor*. He begins to (2) *hear an uncomfortable noise, a loud ringing or buzzing*, and at the same time feels himself (3) *moving very rapidly through a long, dark tunnel*. After this, he suddenly finds himself (4) *outside of his own physical body but still in the immediate physical environment*, and (5) *he sees his own physical body from a distance, as though he's a spectator*. He (6) *watches the resuscitation attempt from this unusual vantage point* and is in a state of (7) *emotional upheaval*.

After a while he collects himself and becomes more accustomed to his odd condition. He notices that (8) *he still has a "body,"* but one of a very different nature and with very different powers from the physical body he has left behind. Soon, other things begin to happen. (9) *Others come to meet and help him.* (10) *He glimpses the spirits of relatives and friends who have already died* and a loving, warm spirit of a kind he has never encountered before. (11) *A being of light appears before him.* This being asks him a question, nonverbally, to (12) *make him evaluate his life*, and helps him along by showing him a panoramic, (13) *instantaneous playback of the major events of his life*. At some point he finds himself approaching some sort of (14) *barrier or border*, apparently representing the limits between earthly life and the next life. Yet he finds that (15) *he must go back to the earth* and that the time for his death has not yet come. At this point (16) *he resists*, for by now he's taken up with his experiences in the afterlife and doesn't want to return. He's overwhelmed by (17) *intense feelings of joy, love, and peace*. Despite his attitude, though, he somehow reunites with his physical body and lives.

Later (18) *he tries to tell others but has trouble doing so*. In the first place, he can find (19) *no human words adequate to describe these unearthly episodes*. He also finds that others scoff, so (20) *he stops telling other people*. Still, the experience (21) *affects his life* profoundly, especially his view about death and its relationship to life.

The fact that Moody can construct a composite case that captures so much of actual NDE cases points out one of the things most important about NDEs: the enormous similarity of NDEs across a wide variety of people and cultures. If NDEs were nothing but hallucinatory experiences, as materialists want to believe, induced by a malfunctioning brain as a person dies, then we would expect great variation from person to person, and the qualities of the experience would be largely determined by the culture and beliefs of the each person experiencing the NDE. Instead, we have great similarity across cultures and belief systems, arguing that there's something "real" about the NDE rather than its being nothing but a hallucination. Indeed aspects of the NDE often contradict the (previous) belief systems of the people experiencing them. (Former) atheists, for example, are embarrassed by meeting a being of light who's so godlike, yet their descriptions of the being are very similar to people with other beliefs.

There are many things in life we believe, for example, not because we've had direct experience of them, but because others' reports of their experiences are so similar. I've never been to Rome, for example, but am quite content to believe that Rome exists because of such consistency in others' accounts. The NDE, then, is what we call psychologically an archetypal experience, a possibility if you're human, whether your culture has prepared you for it or not.

The Pam Reynolds Case

A standard reason for materialistic pseudoskeptics to dismiss NDEs, when they pay any attention to them at all, as nothing but brain-based hallucinations is to emphasize the "near" part of NDE, noting that the person experiencing it wasn't really dead. The person may have looked dead from the outside if she showed no obvious signs of a pulse or respiration, and may have even been declared dead by a doctor, but the fact that she recovered later tells us that she wasn't really dead. Maybe there was still a lot of brain functioning going on. This is an important point, and one of the things we'd like to know about NDEs is just how "dead" was the person experiencing it? What exactly does "dead" mean?

Ideally we'd like sophisticated physiological measures taken on people who've just died and might revive and report an NDE. Realistically, though, most NDEs don't take place in medical settings, and when they do, the emphasis, to put it mildly, is on resuscitating the patient as quickly as possible (the longer they're without a pulse, the more probable the chances of brain damage), not on conducting an accurate physiological study of their bodily and nervous system state. In principle, for example, it would be useful to measure brain-wave activity (EEG) to see if there is any, but it takes a while to properly attach the needed electrodes for this, during which time oxygen starvation is continuing in the brain — and then the first massive electrical shock applied to the chest in an attempt to restart the heart would completely destroy the expensive EEG machine!

There's one dramatic NDE case, though, where we know a great deal about what was happening in the patient's brain, that of Pam Reynolds (pseudonym), written about by cardiologist Michael Sabom (1998). (48)

Pam Reynolds, singer and musician, needed surgery for a giant basilar artery aneurysm. This was a weakness in the wall of a large artery at the base of her brain, which had caused it to balloon out much like a bubble on the side of a defective automobile tire. If it burst — and it could at any time — Pam would die in minutes. Unfortunately, the aneurysm was located in a place so difficult to access and so close to vital brain functions that normal surgery techniques were too risky; they could cause the rupture that would kill her or inflict permanent brain damage. So her doctor referred her to one of the few places in the world where appropriate surgery might be possible, the Barrow Neurological Institute in Phoenix, Arizona. Its director, Dr. Robert Spetzler, had developed a new surgical procedure termed hypothermic cardiac arrest. As Sabom (1998, 37) starkly puts it, this procedure would require that "... Pam's body temperature be lowered to sixty degrees, her heartbeat and breathing stopped, her brain waves flattened, and the blood drained from her head. In everyday terms, she would be dead."

I must admit that I find just reading about this is a little frightening. It brings back memories for me, as it probably will for many readers, of having surgery, lying on that cold table with an intravenous line inserted. There's an interesting part then, in my own memories, where I'm having an intellectual conversation with the anesthetist about the nature of anesthesia (it's a professional interest to me how consciousness can be so altered as to feel no pain, and I'd rather think about my technical interests and competences than about what's going to happen to me soon on that table!), and suddenly, to my perception, I'm coming back to consciousness in the recovery room, having gone unconscious midsentence, without even feeling sleepy first. Pam remembered intravenous lines being put in, and I'm sure she was much more worried than I, since she had a life-threatening situation.

General anesthesia was begun, and various instruments were connected to Pam's body to monitor her condition. (I've examined Pam's anesthesia records, courtesy of Dr. Sabom. For us laypeople, we can say that she was very heavily sedated.) Blood pressure and blood flow from her heart were continuously monitored, as well as blood oxygen levels. Temperature sensors were placed in her esophagus and bladder to monitor her core body temperature, and her brain temperature was also monitored. Conventional EEG electrodes on her scalp would measure cortical brain activity, and the auditory nerve center in her brain stem would be monitored. This involved putting molded earphones in both her ears and continuously playing hundred-decibel clicks (the amount of sound that a full symphony orchestra, all playing loudly, can put out, or like being beside a jackhammer — loud!), while looking for an averaged evoked electrical response from this deep brain-stem level.

After about an hour and a half of preparation, Dr. Spetzler began the surgery by opening a flap of scalp, exposing Pam's skull. The anesthesiologist would have indicated that she was adequately unconscious for doing this. Spetzler then used a bone saw to open her skull. This pneumatically powered saw gave off a loud buzzing noise as it ran.

In her later account to Dr. Sabom (1998, 41), Pam reported: *"The next thing I recall was the sound: It was a natural D. As I listened to the sound, I felt it was pulling me out of the top of my head. The further out of my body I got, the more clear the tone became. I had the impression it was like a road, a frequency that you go on...."*

Recall that Pam had molded earphones in both ears, effectively blocking outside sound, and hundred-decibel clicks repeating several times a second, but the sound or vibration of the bone saw could have reached her inner ears through direct bone conduction. That she would have or recall any experience with this degree of anesthesia is remarkable, though. Pam goes on (Sabom 1998, 41): *"I remember seeing several things in the operating room when I was looking down. It was the most aware that I think that I have ever been in my entire life...."* (Note that describing experiences as especially clear isn't what you normally expect from patients on sedative drugs or nitrous oxide, but this is common in NDEs.)

The account continues (Sabom 1998, 41): *"I was metaphorically sitting on Dr. Spetzler's shoulder. It was not like normal vision. It was brighter and more focused and clearer than normal vision.... There was so much in the operating room that I didn't recognize, and so many people."*

Over twenty doctors and nurses were present in the operating room, although we don't know how many of them were present before Pam was anesthetized. Pam goes on (Sabom 1998, 41): "I thought the way they had my head shaved was very peculiar. I expected them to take all of the hair, but they did not."

She then noticed what was making the sound, and described it as looking like an electric toothbrush, with a dent in it and a groove at the top where the saw blade appeared to go into the handle, and also that the saw had interchangeable blades that were stored in what looked like a socket-wrench case. Sabom has sketches of the bone saw and its case for blades in his book, and describing them this way strikes me as quite accurate for a layperson who was trying to make sense of something she was seeing for the first time under what were, to put it mildly, unusual conditions!

While Dr. Spetzler was opening Pam's head, a female cardiac surgeon had located the femoral artery and vein in Pam's right groin. But they turned out to be too small to handle the large flow of blood that would be needed to feed the cardiopulmonary bypass machine if the blood had to be drained from Pam's body, so she got the left-side artery and vein ready for use. Pam later recounted (Sabom 1998, 42): "Someone said something about my veins and arteries being very small. I believe it was a female voice and that it was Dr. Murray, but I'm not sure. She was the cardiologist [sic]. I remember thinking that I should have told her about that.... I remember the heart-lung machine. I didn't like the respirator.... I remember a lot of tools and instruments that I did not readily recognize."

This suggests that Pam's mind was using psi ability to perceive what was happening in the operating room. She wouldn't have been able to see anything even had she been conscious, as her eyes were taped shut, nor hear any doctor's voice because of the molded earphones excluding outside sound and the hundred-decibel clicks masking any really loud sound that did manage to get through. But note that while Pam was heavily anesthetized — certainly deeply enough to feel no pain from the cutting and sawing on her scalp and skull — she was not "dead," as she would be later.[1]

Dr. Spetzler found, as had been feared, that it was too dangerous to operate directly on the aneurysm, so they would have to induce hypothermic cardiac arrest, that is cool Pam's body, stop her heart, and drain the blood from her body to keep the aneurysm from bursting. Through tubes inserted into her femoral artery and vein, warm blood was then drawn from Pam and cooled in a special machine.

By 11:00 a.m. her body temperature was down by twenty-five degrees Fahrenheit, and her heart was going into ventricular fibrillation. She was given a massive dose of intravenous potassium chloride to completely stop her heart before the fibrillations could irreversibly damage it. After her heart stopped, her EEG flattened into nothing measureable, and her deeper brain-stem functions, measured by the click stimulation, weakened. By 11:20 a.m. her core body temperature was down to sixty degrees, with her heart still stopped and her brain stem showed no activity. The operating table was tilted up, the blood bypass machine turned off, and the blood drained from her body. By usual medical criteria, Pam was dead.

Pam, meanwhile, was continuing her NDE. She told Dr. Sabom (1998, 43–44): "There was a sensation like being pulled but not against your will. I was going on my own accord, because I wanted to go. I have different metaphors to try to explain this. It was like The Wizard of Oz — being taken up in a tornado vortex, only you're not spinning around like you've got vertigo. You're very focused and you have a place to go. The feeling was like going up in an elevator real fast. And there was a sensation, but it wasn't a bodily, physical sensation. It was like a tunnel, but it wasn't a tunnel."

This difficulty in finding words adequate to describe the experience is typical of the altered-state aspect of NDEs. New kinds of sensations and experiences can occur that we have no accurate words for and ordinary language wasn't designed to deal with (Sabom 1998, 44–45):

> At some point very early in the tunnel vortex, I became aware of my grandmother calling me. But I didn't hear her call me with my ears…. It was a clearer hearing than with my ears. I trust that sense more than I trust my

own ears. The feeling was that she wanted me to come to her, so I continued, with no fear, down the shaft. It's a dark shaft that I went through, and at the very end, there was this very little, tiny pinpoint of light that kept getting bigger and bigger and bigger.

The light was incredibly bright, like sitting in the middle of a lightbulb. It was so bright that I put my hands in front of my face fully expecting to see them, and I could not. But I knew they were there. Not from a sense of touch. Again, it's terribly hard to explain, but I knew they were there.

I noticed that as I began to discern different figures in the light — and they were all covered with light; they were light and had light permeating all around them — they began to form shapes I could recognize and understand. I could see that one of them was my grandmother. I don't know if it was reality or projection, but I would know my grandmother, the sound of her, anytime, anywhere.

Everyone I saw, looking back on it, fit perfectly into my understanding of what that person looked like at their best during their lives.

I recognized a lot of people. My Uncle Gene was there. So was my great-great-Aunt Maggie, who was really a cousin. On Papa's side of the family, my grandfather was there....They were specifically taking care of me, looking after me.

They would not permit me to go further.... It was communicated to me — that's the best way I know how to say it, because they didn't speak like I'm speaking — that if I went all the way into the light, something would happen to me physically. They would be unable to put this "me" back into the body "me," like I had gone too far and they couldn't reconnect. So they wouldn't let me go anywhere or do anything.

I wanted to go into the light, but I also wanted to come back. I had children to be reared. It was like watching a movie on fast-forward on your VCR: you get the general idea, but the individual freeze-frames are not slow enough to get detail.

With no blood in Pam's body, it was relatively easy for Dr. Spetzler to remove the aneurysm and seal off the artery. Then the blood-bypass machine was turned back on, and warmed blood sent back into her body. Her brain stem and then the higher levels of her brain began to show electrical activity (Sabom 1998, 45): "Then they [Pam's deceased relatives] were feeding me. They were not doing this through my mouth, like with food, but they were nourishing me with something. The only way I know how to put it is something sparkly. Sparkles is the image that I get. I definitely recall the sensation of being nurtured and being fed and being made strong. I know it sounds funny, because obviously it wasn't a physical thing, but inside the experience, I felt physically strong, ready for whatever."

It's tempting to think that this "feeding" experience corresponded with the warmed blood flowing back into Pam's body, but we don't have any precise timing marker in the later parts of her NDE as we seemed to have with her perception of the remark about her veins being too small.

At noon, though, the previously inactive heart monitors showed the disorganized activity of ventricular fibrillation, and it wasn't corrected with just more warming of her blood. This fibrillation could kill Pam within minutes. Her heart was shocked, without effect, then shocked a second time, which finally restored a normal heart rhythm.

Meanwhile, but again we don't have markers for precise timing, Pam's NDE continues (Sabom 1998, 46):

My grandmother didn't take me back through the tunnel,
or even send me back or ask me to go. She just looked up

at me. I expected to go with her, but it was communicated to me that she just didn't think she would do that. My uncle said he would do it. He's the one who took me back through the end of the tunnel. Everything was fine. I did want to go.

But then I got to the end of it and saw the thing, my body. I didn't want to get into it....It looked terrible, like a train wreck. It looked like what it was: dead. I believe it was covered. It scared me and I didn't want to look at it.

It was communicated to me that it was like jumping into a swimming pool. No problem, just jump right into the swimming pool. I didn't want to, but I guess I was late or something because he [the uncle] pushed me. I felt a definite repelling and at the same time a pulling from the body. The body was pulling and the tunnel was pushing....
It was like diving into a pool of ice water....It hurt!

Given that by ordinary criteria, Pam was still heavily anesthetized, one wonders how it could hurt.

By a little after 12:30, Pam was stable enough to be disconnected from the blood-bypass machine. Dr. Spetzler left the operating room, because his younger assistant surgeons normally closed the various surgical wounds. They turned off the classical music Dr. Spetzler usually enjoyed in the background during surgery, and played rock music as background to their task. Pam later told Dr. Sabom that when she came back, they were playing the hit song "Hotel California," by the Eagles, which has a famous line about how a person can check out but somehow never be able to really leave. Pam felt that this was an amazingly insensitive thing to play in an operating room (Sabom 1998, 47)!

One can argue about the timing in Pam's NDE — if time in an altered state is experienced more rapidly than in an ordinary state, for example, could her entire NDE have taken place while there was still activity in her living brain, before she was brought to a standstill? — such that her NDE did not really occur while she was technically dead? But that's an argument that itself pushes a lot of our ideas about what time is, so it certainly looks, by ordinary standards, as if parts of Pam's NDE happened after she was physically dead.

Essential science likes to collect a lot of evidence about something before getting too serious in theorizing about what might have happened. It would be wonderful if we had more cases like this, but so far we don't.[2] But let's do a little theorizing now based on the big five and many maybes we've reviewed so far.

A Model of Mind That Opens to Noetic Knowledge

Almost all of you who've had your own OBEs, NDEs, or both know, on some very deep level, that your mind or soul is something more than your physical body. Our everyday, automatic, psychological identification of who we are with our physical bodies, with the simulation constructed by the ecological self we discussed in chapter 12, is a useful working tool for everyday life but not the final answer. As discussed earlier, though, integrating this experiential knowledge with your ordinary self in the everyday world is not always easy, especially when the too dominant climate of scientism constantly tells you that your deeper knowledge is wrong and that you're crazy to take it seriously.

My small contribution toward integration is the message that, using the best of essential scientific method rather than scientism, looking factually at all of the data rather than just what fits into a philosophy of physicalism, the facts of reality require a model or theory of who we are and what reality is that takes psi phenomena; OBEs; NDEs; and noetic, ASC knowledge seriously. Certainly we all make mistakes in our thinking at times, but you're not deluded or crazy to try to integrate this kind of knowledge with the rest of your life. You're engaged in a real and important process!

I can schematize my best scientific and personal understanding of our nature at this point with a diagram I created years ago (1993).

Figure 13.1 Transpersonal Realm

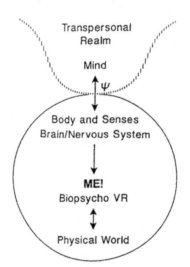

Being a product of older Western culture, which makes me think that the spiritual realm is "higher," I've put a transpersonal or spiritual realm at the top of the figure, and I've shown it as un-bounded in extent. (Perhaps the transpersonal realm should be drawn at the bottom — basis of all, or totally surrounding — nature of all, the rest of the figure, depending on what aspect you want to symbolically represent.) Those of you who've had OBEs, NDEs, or other transpersonal experiences know, to some degree, of what realm of experience I speak here, even if ordinary words can't describe it well. A part of that transpersonal realm, designated as "Mind" in figure 13.1 is in intimate relation with our particular body, brain, and nervous system. As I mentioned briefly earlier, although this "mind" is of a different nature from ordinary matter, I believe that psi phenomena like clairvoyance and PK are the means that link the transpersonal and the physical; that is, our mind has an intimate and ongoing relationship with our body, brain, and nervous system through what I've termed auto-clairvoyance, where "mind" reads the physical state of the brain, and auto-PK, where "mind" uses psychokinesis to affect the operation of the physical brain.

The result of this interaction is the creation of a bio-psychological virtual reality, or BPVR, an emergent system labeled "ME!" in the figure, to stand for "Mind Embodied." The bold type and exclamation point remind us that our identification with and attachment to ME! is almost always intense! We may have lofty philosophical beliefs about how the spirit is so much more than the merely material, but if somebody shoves our head underwater and holds us down, the beliefs and needs of ME! will manifest quite strongly!

This ME! is a simulation, derived from and expressing our ultimate, transpersonal nature, our physical nature, and the external physical world around us. We ordinarily live "inside" this simulation; we identify with it and mistake it for a direct and complete perception of reality and ourselves. But those of you who've been "out" in various ways know, as we've just discussed, our ordinary self is indeed just a specialized and limited point of view, not the whole of reality.

We need an immense amount of research to fill in the details of this general outline, of course, but I think this conveys a useful general picture.

If you've never had an OBE or NDE, dear reader, let me suggest you try to meet someone who has — not someone filled with ideas and convictions based on thinking or emotions, but someone who has actually had the experience and is willing to talk about it.

Summing Up So Far

Here are some of the key points of this wider model of human nature, taken from what we've discussed, that will help set the stage for the remaining chapters:

- There's no doubt that the physics and chemistry of body, brain, and nervous system (the BBNS) are important in affecting and (partially) determining our experience. Further conventional research on these areas is vitally important, especially if it's done without the traditional scientistic arrogance that physical findings in, for example, neurology automatically "explain away" psychological and experiential data. Sometimes they do; sometimes they don't, but we have to discriminate which is which.

- The findings of scientific parapsychology force us to pragmatically accept that minds can do things — perform information-gathering processes like telepathy, clairvoyance, and precognition (ESP), and directly affect the physical world with PK and psychic healing — that cannot be reduced to physical explanations, given current scientific knowledge or reasonable extensions of it. So it's vitally important to investigate what minds can do in terms of mind, not faithfully (faithful to dogmatic materialism) wait for these phenomena to be explained (away) someday in terms of brain functioning. The firm belief that they'll be thus explained away is a form of faith that, as mentioned earlier, philosophers have aptly called "promissory materialism," and it's indeed mere faith since it cannot be scientifically refuted. You can never prove that someday everything won't be explained in terms of a greatly advanced physics — or a greatly advanced knowledge of angels, dowsing, stock market movements, or whatever. Recall that if there's no way of disproving an idea or theory, you may like it or dislike it, believe it or disbelieve it, but it's not a scientific theory.

- The kind of research on the nature of mind called for above is vitally important, because most forms of scientism have a psychopathological effect on too many people by denying and invalidating the spiritual or transpersonal longings and experiences that they have. This produces not just unnecessary individual suffering but also attitudes of isolation and cynicism that worsen the state of the world. You can review my Western Creed exercise in chapter 1 for elaborations of this point, and also some of the consequences I would see for my life (and your life) if the Western Creed were true, which I discuss in a later chapter.

- Two of the most important kinds of transpersonal, spiritual experiences people can have are OBEs and NDEs. They have major, long-term effects on the attitudes toward life of those experiencing such phenomena. People experiencing both of these psi phenomena from the inside have what to them is a revelation of a truer or higher understanding of who we really are. While this is usually a positive feeling and psychologically gratifying, it's also important to extensively investigate these phenomena more deeply, because they themselves may be, at least partially, simulations of even higher-order truths as well as distortions of reality. Remember, just because something feels deeply true does not make it true. The essential scientific approach to such feelings, then, is to take them seriously indeed but to, with humility and dedication, (1) try to get clearer data on their exact nature; (2) develop theories and understandings of them (both in our ordinary state and in appropriate ASCs, along the lines of state-specific sciences that I've proposed elsewhere) (1972, 1998a); (3) predict and test consequences of these theories; and (4) honestly and fully communicate all parts of this process of investigation, theorizing, and prediction.

Genuine and open scientific inquiry has much to contribute to our understanding of our spiritual nature.

Notes

The account of the Pam Reynolds case is taken from *Light and Death* by Michael Sabom. Copyright 1998 by Michael Sabom. Used by permission of Zondervan.

1. One critic (Augustine 2007) has argued that she might have been able to hear the doctor's statement with her normal hearing because she was inadequately anesthetized. As I responded (Tart 2007), I tried listening to hundred-decibel music with ordinary muff-type headphones while my wife spoke loudly in the room beside me, and although I was fully conscious, with no disadvantage of clouding of any sort by drugs, I couldn't make out a word she said. I have normal hearing but a hundred decibels is literally deafening.

2. It looked as if a second comparable case had appeared just at the time of this writing (Hamilton 2008), but rumors in the parapsychological community are that this is a composite case rather than an actual one, and so of no evidential value. My attempts to contact Dr. Hamilton have received no reply.

Chapter 14

Postmortem Survival:
After-Death Communications

POSTMORTEM (origin: Latin): (1) adverb: After death.
(2) adjective: Taking place, formed, or done after death or
(colloquially) after the conclusion of a matter. — Shorter
Oxford English Dictionary, *6th ed., s.v. "postmortem"*

Sogyal Rinpoche, Tibetan lama and author of the best seller
The Tibetan Book of Living and Dying (1992, 7–8), writes:

When I first came to the West, I was shocked by the contrast between the attitudes to death I had been brought
up with, and those I now found. For all its technological
achievements, modern Western society has no real understanding of death or what happens in death or after death.

I learned that people today are taught to deny death,
and taught that it means nothing but annihilation and
loss. That means that most of the world lives either in
denial of death or in terror of it. Even talking about death
is considered morbid, and many people believe that simply
mentioning death is to risk wishing it upon ourselves.

Others look on death with a naive, thoughtless cheer-
fulness, thinking that for some unknown reason death
will work out all right for them, and that it is nothing to
worry about.

When I think of them, I am reminded of what one Tibetan master says: "People often make the mistake of being frivolous about death and think, 'Oh well, death happens to everybody. It's not a big deal; it's natural. I'll be fine.' That's a nice theory until one is dying."

All the greatest spiritual traditions of the world, including, of course, Christianity, have told us clearly that death is not the end. They have all handed down a vision of some sort of life to come, which infuses this life that we are leading now with sacred meaning. But despite their teachings, modern society is largely a spiritual desert, where the majority imagines that this life is all that there is. Without any real or authentic faith in an afterlife, most people live lives deprived of any ultimate meaning.

I have come to realize that the disastrous effects of the denial of death go far beyond the individual: They affect the whole planet. Believing fundamentally that this life is the only one, modern people have developed no long-term vision. So there is nothing to restrain them from plundering the planet for their own immediate ends and from living in a selfish way that could prove fatal for the future....

Fear of death and ignorance of the afterlife are fueling that destruction of our environment that is threatening all of our lives. So isn't it all the more disturbing that people are not taught what death is, or how to die? Or given any hope in what lies after death, and so what really lies behind life? Could it be more ironic that young people are so highly educated in every subject except the one that holds the key to the entire meaning of life, and perhaps to our very survival?[1]

I resonate strongly with Sogyal Rinpoche's point of view but, being a modern Westerner, recognize how difficult it is for us moderns to simply accept religious or spiritual teachings about death or otherwise resolve this issue, especially with a built-in biological fear of death lurking in the background of our more rational and conscious attempts to deal with it. Being sensible and rational about death is a fine aim, but I doubt we ever completely get there.

I'm sure it's psychologically rewarding and useful to have a firm, spiritually oriented set of beliefs that include postmortem survival, reincarnation, or both for a possibility of long-term evolution of the individual and the world. That adds long-term meaning to life. But in these days when scientism has so thoroughly undermined the capacity for religious belief in so many, most of us need something more than teachings on what spiritual systems believe: we need supportive, empirical, scientific evidence for giving energy to spiritual ideas. Part of this undermining is irrational faith in materialism as a total worldview, but part is also genuine science showing that a wide variety of traditional religious views about reality are factually wrong; they just don't stand up to empirical tests. Many of these religious ideas may have been the best people could do at the time to try to make sense of life, but tenaciously holding onto them after they've been superseded by scientific theories with much more evidence to support them, such as the earth's age being hugely more than the five thousand years extrapolated from biblical scholarship, leads to unnecessary suffering and conflict.

As we've discussed in various places, that's the main thrust of this book, looking at scientific evidence that makes it a reasonable strategy to invest in spirituality.

When we come to the topic of death — you and I, after all, are going to die someday — probably the most important question ever looked into by psychical research is the question of postmortem survival. Does our consciousness or mind, in some form, survive physical death? Or is such hope deluded and futile? Remember how Bertrand Russell (1923, 6–7) put it in this quote first given in Chapter 1?

That man is the product of causes which had no prevision of the end they were achieving; that his origin, his growth, his hopes and fears, his loves and his beliefs, are but the outcome of accidental collocations of atoms; that no fire, no heroism, no intensity of thought or feeling, can preserve an individual life beyond the grave; that all the labours of the ages, all the devotion, all the inspiration, all the noonday brightness of human genius, are destined to extinction in the vast death of the solar system; and the whole temple of Man's achievement must inevitably be buried beneath the debris of a universe in ruins — all these things, if not quite beyond dispute, are yet so nearly certain, that no philosophy that rejects them can hope to stand. Only within the scaffolding of these truths, only on the firm foundation of unyielding despair, can the soul's habitation henceforth be safely built.

I personally find this materialistic idea quite depressing — an admission that, to materialists, will simply show that I have neurotic hopes and lack the courage to face the facts. If I believed that there's no hope of any kind of survival, I would adapt as much as possible by becoming more "normal" in this materialistic age. That is, I would show excessive concern for my health, promote research that supports health and increases our life spans, and avoid taking any unnecessary risks that might endanger my health or my life, while otherwise trying to maximize my pleasure and minimize my pain. Psychologically, I would try not to think about the depressing reality and finality of death, work on distracting myself with constant pleasurable pursuits, and if the above steps weren't enough, find a doctor who would prescribe mood-altering medications so I wouldn't feel depressed.

Hmmm… doesn't this sound like what a lot of people already do? Is there widespread, but largely suppressed, depression resulting from our materialistic outlook? Yet the way to effectively treat depression is not to pretend it isn't there.

We can get chemical protection from emotional lows (and highs), but too often we give up the possibility of rich and vivid lives for the apparent safety of dull ones.

We'll return later to questions about what differences good evidence for or against some kind of survival would make in people's lives. But now let's look at some of the existing evidence: first the indirect kind and then the more direct kind.

Psychic Creatures More Likely to Survive Death

The *a priori* materialistic dismissal of the possibility of survival of any aspect of mind after death rests on the simple equation: mind equals brain.

If this is all there is to it, of course, mind couldn't survive death. The brain shuts down its electrical activity within a few seconds of being deprived of oxygen, which happens when the heart stops beating. After a few minutes, at most, of being deprived of oxygen, the brain cells become irreversibly damaged. With physical death, the damage is complete and permanent, and the brain decays into mush. The usual materialistic analogy is that the mind is like a personal computer. Once the computer's parts are destroyed, any programs it ran are gone forever. How could any aspect of mind survive the destruction of the brain?

But we've looked at many aspects of psychic functioning in previous chapters, psi phenomena that don't seem limited by the known laws of the physical world. Telepathy and clairvoyance aren't affected by any of the physical-shielding materials or physical distances that have been studied to date, for instance. PK and psychic healing don't have any known or likely classical physical basis. Precognition (and perhaps postcognition, if it indeed is a distinct, real phenomenon) doesn't seem limited by time as known physical energies are. One way of bringing this data into our worldview is to admit that, while ordinary mind and consciousness are strongly affected by the brain, you can't totally equate them.

You must say that in some real sense, mind does not equal brain, or, more positively: ordinary mind equals brain plus something else.

Thus the various psi phenomena open a possibility of survival of some aspect of mind. If mind is something (and the "thing" in "something" is probably misleading in its concreteness) more than simply brain, it's reasonable to ask if that "something more" survives bodily death or has "spiritual" characteristics.

Basic psi phenomena, then, the big five, provide indirect evidence of possible postmortem survival.

OBEs and NDEs

From one point of view, OBEs and NDEs, discussed in chapters 12 and 13, provide more-direct evidence of postmortem survival. That kind of experience is usually conclusive from the viewpoint of the person experiencing it. After direct, personal experience of mentally functioning while experientially separated from your physical body, the typical attitude is something like, "I don't just believe I'll survive death; I know it. I've been there and had my preview." Belief or disbelief is an inference, a theory, made from a lack of enough direct data, or direct experience. I might believe that, say, vanilla ice cream tastes sweet if I've never had any, judging from reports of what others have said, but since I've actually tasted it, I know it tastes sweet.

From the point of view of those of us who haven't had an OBE or NDE, of course, we can certainly accept as data that those experiencing these phenomena claim that they have direct knowledge of survival; it's their (from our perspective) belief, but we can rationally accept it only as evidence, of varying quality, not final proof. After all, none of these people having OBEs or NDEs was really dead. The person's brain functions later, so perhaps it was functioning in some fashion during the OBE or NDE, even if we don't see that it was? Maybe the Pam Reynolds case in Chapter 13, where her psi perception of things during an NDE while there was no blood in her brain wasn't really what it seemed to be? The idea that people who've had NDEs weren't really dead is a reasonable objection in many ways. That's why I usually present information about OBEs and NDEs as more direct evidence for survival than psi phenomena in general, but still indirect evidence, supporting but not proving postmortem survival.

After-Death Communications

As far back as recorded human history goes, and undoubtedly farther, people have experienced what they've called ghosts, spirits, and apparitions, and many have taken these as evidence of some kind of postmortem survival. Sometimes it seems as if these experiences are deliberately produced from the "other side" as a form of communication, thus the modern acronym ADCs, after-death communications. When looked at dispassionately and closely, many, if not most, of these reports aren't very evidential and may well be hallucinations, but a significant number require more serious consideration.

Here's an impressive case from my website, The Archives of Scientists' Transcendent Experiences (*www.issc-taste.org*). The contributor, Joseph Waldron, received his Ph.D. in psychology from Ohio State University in 1975, has been a professor of psychology, and was a Distinguished Research Professor at Youngstown State University in Ohio when he sent in this personal experience. He's well known for many contributions to rehabilitative medicine and research on one of the most widely used psychological tests, the Minnesota Multiphasic Personality Inventory. I mention this background information to remind us that many reports of psi experiences come from people we would expect to be the best kinds of observers, not from careless, superstitious people.

I've shortened this account somewhat to keep our focus, but other fascinating details are available in the original account on the TASTE website (Waldron 2000).

And She Came Back: Rene

Rene and I were married during 1966. Twenty-six years later (1992), we had three beautiful daughters and a wonderful marriage. In April she was diagnosed with cancer. She died November 19, 1992.

The last eight months were among the best and the worst of times. We seemed to be more and more in love as she slowly slipped away. We were rarely apart. While Rene knew she was dying, she did not want to know about the nitty-gritty of it. She wanted me to take care of "all that palliative stuff," and so I did. During her last seven days I never left her side except to use the bathroom. And then she was dead. We were both confirmed agnostics: she was a former Presbyterian, and I was a Roman Catholic until I turned atheist at age fifteen. By twenty-five I was an agnostic, because it was the only reasonable position. Death, we agreed, was probably the best night's sleep a person ever got. According to her wishes, she was cremated in something like a cardboard box, and we remembered Rene as she lived — not in death. Out of respect for her wishes, there was no memorial service. I cite these behaviors and ideas to indicate the firm belief we both had in agnosticism. However, as any good agnostic would do, I said to her two days before she died and while she was conscious that if she continued after death, I would sorely want to hear from her. I anticipated a very long, lonely road. Rene, in her usual, somewhat humorous way, raised one eyebrow as she looked at me in the way she would do when she nonverbally queried if the other person seriously meant what they said. We did not discuss it any more than that.

Two weeks after her death, I was going through the motions of acting as though life had meaning. Two of our daughters were still at home and "Dad" was needed to be there for them. Our family is about as close as five people could be, and Rene had been the center of our collective universe. I was sleeping a lot, as depressed people are likely to do. I knew I was clinically depressed, fought it for the girls' sake, and tried to live a normal life — under the circumstances. I entertained no notions of seeing or hearing from Rene again. The black hole was deep and appeared to be never ending. I was learning to accept the idea that the major part of my life was over, and only cleaning up was left to do.

As best I can remember, I was lying on the couch [at] about 11:00 p.m. I was probably in a hypnagogic state when I got up to answer a knock at the front door. The girls were young adults, and I expected any twenty-something male or female at that time of night. I opened the door and was startled, surprised, taken aback. There stood Rene in the long, red velvet cape I had bought several years ago. I loved her in that "Red Riding Hood" cape. She was statuesque, regal, and commanded attention whenever she walked into a room. I was proud just to be with her when she wore that cape. Need I say that she only ever wore it at my insistence

My stupid comment was, "What are you doing here at the front door?" The thought in my mind was, "You are dead; how can you be here?" But I was trying to be tactful. She answered with, "You know why; I don't live here anymore." There was a smile of love and kindness, and also of hesitancy. She turned and walked across the porch to leave.

I was dazed, confused, and "came to" [while] standing in the living room. I had closed the door but do not remember doing it. The event was unbelievably real, "more real than real," as the people who have near-death experiences say.

By the next morning I had pretty well dismissed the whole event. [It] [h]ad to be some kind of hallucination — though I have never, to my knowledge, hallucinated or suffered anything worse than the depression I was now in. It seemed that maybe I had better straighten up and get on with my life before my daughters noticed how strange their father had become. And yet, every memory of it was as though it were real. To say I was confused is to put it mildly. Over the next few days I seemed to become more confused, more depressed. Think of the possibilities: maybe she still lived in another world; maybe I would see her again after I died. No, the dead were — well — dead. This hallucination, if that is what it was, was more torturous than not having it. Was she alive; was she not alive? Does she love me; does she not? Like picking the petals on a daisy, though far more painful than such adolescent musings, I was contemplating the center of my universe. By turns I was elated, hopeful, a little giddy, and alternatively deeply depressed missing her, anticipating a dismal future, helpless and hopeless. I felt like I was going around the proverbial bend. "Definitely a sharp left turn," I said to myself.

About ten days later I was in my study/therapy office. Our home was in the country, and I had a separate wing for my research and practice. This night, as had been common over the last few weeks, I slept wherever I found myself. I just could not bring myself to sleep in our bed. I had worked all day, and I had worked hard to try and lose myself in something other than my own depression. By 11:00 p.m. I was literally falling asleep as I sat reading on the couch. I nodded once, opened my eyes, and there stood Rene where it was impossible for her to stand, in a six-inch space between two file cabinets. In front of her was the wheelchair that I had pushed around for the last four months (in reality the chair had been returned to the supply company). Somehow the chair was now gone, and we were in a long embrace that seemed to last 20–30 minutes. I have never felt so loved and cared for in my life. We did not talk about anything of consequence. In fact I don't really remember what we said. I do know that the conversation was not in words, and I also knew she was "dead" and I was not.

Eventually a woman got my attention and said she wanted to show me something that Rene had made. The lady was kind; I did not want to be rude, so I walked into the other room so she could show me whatever it was. She showed me some sort of other-world crystal carving of a butterfly or something similar. I tried to be polite, said it was beautiful [footnote omitted] (which it was) but that I had to get back to the other room. When I got back, Rene was gone. During this whole interaction I was aware of someone else in another corner of the room where Rene and I met: A man who seemed to be there to help Rene do what she wanted to do (see me) and make sure that everything went as it should. He never spoke or communicated in any way, but I sensed he was there to help her in some way unknown to me. In (later) thinking about the presence of this other person, I have the idea that his function was to insure that I did not remember some of the things that Rene and I discussed. I know we talked about the kids and loving each other. I am also sure that I would have had a million questions about what it was like to be dead. However, I do not remember any of the content of our discussion, and that is not like me. In some way, completely unknown to me, this other person had the ability to make sure that Rene and I could get together and that I would take away from that meeting only the information presented here.

All this could be a hallucination or a dream, and indeed if I were to hear it in my clinical practice, I would place much emphasis on the hypnagogic state on both occasions. However, it happened to me, and I know it was real as well as I can know anything. The ramifications have been long acting, for now all of my nonteaching time is spent in studying after-death experiences. In the last seven years I have read and studied more about parapsychology, after death, near death, and dying than I ever read for a Ph.D. in developmental psychology....

To me these experiences are real. So real they have changed my life. My depression was gone, absolutely lifted, after the second instance. I have never looked back. I know she lives on somewhere and that life after what we call death is far too important a topic to leave for softheaded people to think about.??

Now from a hardball scientist who teaches multivariate statistics, research methods, and one who wrote computerized diagnostic software, I have joined the paranormal set. I am sure that some of my colleagues think I have indeed gone round that bend when they hear about my public talks and workshops exploring the issues as we in the sciences are prone to do.

And that little agnostic side of me creeps in and says, "Even if you are deluded, the positive effects of after-death experiences are too therapeutic to ignore." They sure can be life changing.

As we noted in discussing OBEs and NDEs, this kind of ADC experience is directly evidential and convincing to those who've had the direct experience, but is still indirect evidence for those of us who haven't.

Like most people in our culture, I've always implicitly assumed that these kinds of ADCs are rare, that I knew of them only because of my extensive reading of the exotic psychical research literature. A colleague who's a well-known grief counselor, Louis LaGrand, assures me that having ADCs after losing a loved one is actually common (1998). In fact, a majority of people have had them! By and large, they never talk about them to others, knowing they'd be considered crazy as a result of their grief. By never talking about them, they help maintain the belief that it's not "normal" to have such an experience.

Table 14.1 will give you some general idea of what ADCs are like. Bill and Judy Guggenheim (1997) have charted the characteristics and types of ADCs based on interviews with 2,000 people, yielding 3,300 accounts.

Table 14.1
Qualities of After Death Communications

Sensing a presence
Distinct feeling that deceased loved one is nearby.
Feeling is often discounted with culturally approved beliefs
that it's just imagination.

Hearing a voice
May seem like an external, physical voice or may be
n internal, telepathic voice.

Feeling a touch
Affectionate touches like pats, hugs, and caresses.

Smelling a fragrance
Smelling loved one's favorite perfume or cologne,
personal scent, or favorite food.

Visual appearances

Ranging from head and shoulders to full body;
transparent mist to full, solid visual reality.

Visions

Loved one in a scene, like seeing a slide show
or movie in the air.

Altered-state experiences

In the hypnagogic (falling asleep) or hypnopompic (coming
awake) state, or while meditating or praying.

Sleep-state ADCs

Vivid experiences of contact during sleep,
not confused with ordinary dreams.

OBE ADCs

Contact with loved one while having an OBE, at his or
her "level" or "place." Typically more "real" than "real."

Telephone calls

Answer phone and hear loved one's voice giving a message.
Sometimes two-way conversations.

Physical phenomena

Physical manifestations such as paranormal movement
of objects taken as a sign from deceased loved one.

Symbolic ADCs

Something happens in response to the bereaved's request
for a sign from the deceased loved one that reassures the
bereaved that deceased loved one is okay.

Like OBEs and NDEs, ADCs carry powerful convictions that (at least some part of) consciousness can survive physical death, and ADCs have been experienced by enormous numbers of people, rather than being comparatively rare as with OBEs and NDEs. Some ADCs, like OBEs and NDEs, may be purely subjective phenomena, but some have psi components that don't allow us to dismiss them as "merely" subjective.

Now let's look at the most direct evidence that some aspect of consciousness may survive physical death.

Notes

1. From the *Tibetan Book of Living and Dying* by Sogyal Rinpoche and edited by Patrick Gaffney and Andrew Harvey. Copyright © 1993 by Rigpa Fellowship. Reprinted by permission of HarperCollins publishers.

CHAPTER 15

Mediumship: Experimental Approach to Postmortem Survival

MEDIUM (origin: Latin, literally "middle," "midst"): (1) A person acting as an intermediary, a mediator, rare. (2) (Plural: "-iums") A person thought to be in contact with the spirits of the dead and to communicate between the living and the dead.

MEDIUMSHIP (noun): (1) The state or condition of being or acting as a spiritualistic medium; (2) intervening agency, intermediation. — SHORTER OXFORD ENGLISH DICTIONARY, *6th ed., s.v. "medium" and "mediumship"*

THE MOST direct kind of evidence bearing on possible postmortem survival comes from studies with spiritualist mediums. A medium is someone who believes she can serve as an intermediary to convey messages to and from whatever aspect of people survives death, usually in a special session termed a séance. We know far less about the psychology of mediumship than we need to, but there's a lot of variation in how it's done. In the classical days of studying mediumship (mid and late 1800s through early and middle 1900s), the most interesting mediums went into "trances," ASCs of which they usually remembered nothing after coming back to normal, but during which they believed they were temporarily "possessed" or controlled by a guiding spirit who controlled access by other spirits, deceased spirits, or both so that they could perform their role as a communications medium. Such deep-trance mediums are rarer nowadays, and contemporary mediums usually remain in pretty much an ordinary state of consciousness while getting impressions (visual and auditory images) of what the deceased spirits want to communicate.

There have always been people like this in all human societies that we know of, often playing a central role in the societies' religious systems. Christian culture deliberately suppressed such people, calling mediumship and related areas the "work of the devil," and more-modern psychiatric diagnoses of it as inherently pathological further suppresses it. Who wants to be regarded as crazy? There may be a lot of people around with a natural talent for mediumship who are thus inhibited from developing it.

In its present Western form, mediumship began in December 1847, in Hydesville, New York. Three sisters, two of them still teenagers, Margaret, Leah, and Kate Fox, heard strange rapping sounds that seemed to come from the walls. Soon neighbors visited to hear the sounds, and by using a code of various numbers of raps for yes or no, apparent communication with deceased spirits occurred. The story of what happened to the Fox sisters over their lives is fascinating and complicated (Weisberg 2005), especially as to whether a "confession" that Margaret had faked it all, obtained from one sister but later repudiated, was the real truth or a desperate sellout for money from an old, destitute, and, by then, alcoholic woman. What matters to us is that those 1847 raps fed into religious yearning and inspired social movements in America and then Europe, which rapidly led to Spiritualism's becoming a major (and always highly controversial) religious movement.

At its best, Spiritualism had (and still has) an attitude quite congruent with essential science. Like the science of its time (and today), it recognized that a lot of received religious beliefs had been shown to be false by science. Beliefs, like scientific theories, should, as much as possible, be based on evidence, not unrecognized emotions or hopes and fears. So Spiritualists didn't ask anyone to believe in postmortem survival or what the spirits communicated and taught. They asked, quite reasonably, that you consider the possibility that there might be such survival and then look at the evidence for it. Go to a good medium, they would say, ask her (mediums are of both sexes, but women usually predominated) to contact a deceased relative or friend, and then ask that ostensible spirit sufficient questions to establish whether he is or isn't who he claims to be. Perfection wasn't expected, because the communication channel of the medium was recognized as noisy and as distorting transmission sometimes, like a poor, long-distance telephone or cell-phone connection, and the spirits themselves often complained that they could not get their messages across accurately. But if there were lots of good answers, then you could believe that this was indeed the spirit of your deceased relative. If not, you certainly shouldn't believe it.

Another aspect was physical mediumship, where spirits apparently proved their existence by performing psychokinetic feats, such as levitating tables, speaking aloud from midair, and so on, but this is a very complex area, sometimes involving deliberate fraud, and we won't go into it here, because the evidence for survival it produced wasn't as direct as the information from ostensible spirits. D. D. Home, discussed in chapter 9, was an example of an outstanding physical medium.

Of course, what evolved, Spiritualism as an organized religion, has added, like any human activity, a great deal of accumulated belief that may overshadow this basic scientific, investigative function.

Figure 15.1 diagrams how mediumship is theorized to work according to general Spiritualist beliefs.

The medium and the person seeking communication, the sitter, are together communicating via their physical bodies and senses, the sitter asking questions or responding to the medium's statements, and the medium supposedly communicating what the spirits are telling her. That's at the ordinary, material level. At a mind or soul level, though, the medium's soul is using some kind of telepathy to communicate with the soul of the departed spirit. Ordinary

Figure 15.1 Mediumship from the Perspective of Spiritualism

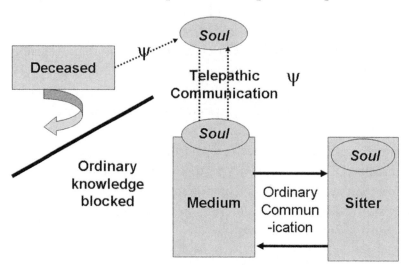

knowledge about the deceased is blocked, the deflected arrow in the figure, since ideally the medium didn't know the deceased or have access to any ordinary knowledge about him.

The materialist's model of mediumship rules out any possibility of postmortem survival of any aspect of consciousness, of course, as well as psi ability in general. It could be represented in Figure 15.2.

Here the deceased is simply gone, and there are no souls of the deceased, the medium, or the sitter to engage in any kind of communication. If there's any resemblance between the deceased's qualities and what the medium says, we must attribute it to some combination of deliberate, conscious fraud on the medium's part, coincidence, conscious or unconscious cold reading by the medium as some part of her mind imitates the deceased, or all of these. "Cold reading" (Nelson 1971) is the technical term used by magician mentalists and fraudulent psychics to mean ways of faking a psychic reading, based on close observation of physical characteristics of the sitter and her responses to leading questions.

Figure 15.2 Materialist's Model of Mediumship

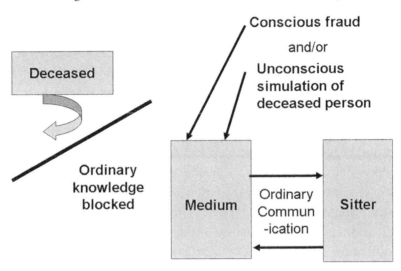

I haven't personally investigated mediumship in an active way but have, rather, contented myself with extensive reading of and thinking about my colleagues' studies. Why not look into it personally? Partly I've simply been too busy with my many other interests, and partly I've recognized what a complex area it is and that I'd have to give up too many of my other interests to get adequately involved in mediumship studies; it may be partly temperament or because I have little interest in the future, being content to take life as it comes. Who knows why? Perhaps I have some unacknowledged fear of death that I subconsciously deal with by avoiding too close contact with mediums? But here I'll sketch the picture of what fairly extensive evidence collected by others shows.

The most solid finding that I think all investigators who try to be objective and scientific would agree on is that the results of most mediumistic séances do not provide strong evidence for (or against) survival. Almost all séances are held to provide comfort to the bereaved; they usually do this, and it's an important psychological function. Bereaved people may want evidence that a loved one has survived and is continuing a happy existence, but emotional need makes them poor judges of evidence. If the sitter asks the medium to contact Uncle Joe, for instance, and Uncle Joe "proves" his identity to the sitter by telling him, "You know I always loved you, even when I couldn't show it very well," that may be emotionally convincing to the bereaved sitter and may perhaps even be true, but it won't impress others. It's far too vague and general.

Just as in the evaluation of descriptive statements about distant target locations in remote-viewing experiments, discussed in Chapter 7, for significance we need correct and specific statements about the intended targets without a lot of generalities that apply to many other targets diluting them. (The blind judging and statistical evaluation techniques developed for remote viewing would be excellent for studying mediumship, but very little has been done so far.) A nonemotionally involved observer will want the Uncle Joes of séances to produce specific, verifiable facts particular to their earthly lives, specific facts that wouldn't be known to the mediums through normal means, or readily deduced from the appearances or actions of the sitters. And deliberate fraud must be ruled out. Like any area of human activity where money and power can be gained, there are many who prey on others, ranging from the mild forms of "cold readings" to impress the bereaved with psychological trickery based on sensory observations and psychological manipulations, to serious swindling schemes where private detectives track down information about deceased relatives to make the faked communications from the spirits look genuine, so when substantial "donations" are asked for, they're likely to be gotten (Keene 1976).

But there have been many honest and outstanding mediums who've given much more impressive results than vague generalities to comfort the bereaved. I'll give two examples here to illustrate both the richness and the complexity of this material.

I had the privilege of meeting Eileen J. Garrett (1893–1970), one of the world's outstanding mediums, while I was still an engineering student at MIT, back in 1955 and 1956. She lectured several times in Boston, and I was invited to small receptions with her afterward. While she'd been a medium most of her life, she was also honestly puzzled and curious about what she did and, through her Parapsychology Foundation, was a major supporter of research in parapsychology.

Mrs. Garrett was investigated by several researchers and was familiar with all the attempts to explain mediumship, both pro and con. When asked, toward the end of her life, whether she believed that she really communicated with spirits, she replied that on Mondays, Wednesdays, and Fridays she was certain of it. On Tuesdays, Thursdays, and Saturdays, though, she thought that the psychologists were probably right, that it was just her unconscious mind making it up, with a little ESP thrown in for veracity. On Sundays she didn't give a damn!

The *Challenger* Disaster of Its Time

In 1930, Mrs. Garrett was unexpectedly involved in a very impressive mediumship case. She lived in London at the time, and all of Britain had been excited for months over the forthcoming launch of a new dirigible, the R-101, by the British military. There was controversy, too, as some people thought the airship hadn't been tested enough, and both Mrs. Garrett and some other psychics had experienced warnings that there would be some kind of disaster. She gave a personal warning of these predictions she'd received through her spirit control, while in trance, to Sir Sefton Brankner, director of civil aviation at the Air Ministry, more than two weeks before the airship's scheduled departure. His answer was, "We are committed." The flight had to be made, for prestige purposes, before the October Imperial Conference of Dominion Prime Ministers. Naturally, the government didn't pay attention to warnings from psychics!

Fig. 15.3 R-101 Airship, Moored

The excitement then was comparable to our excitement at the beginning of the first manned launches into space. This giant airship was to be a triumph of technology, introducing a way of flying from Britain to India instead of the long sea voyage.

The R-101 left Cardington Aerodrome as scheduled at 7:36 p.m. on October 4, 1930, bound for India. At 2:05 a.m. that night, she crashed into a hill in France and exploded. Forty-eight people died in the crash. One of those who died was the wife of Sir Sefton Brankner. The world was shocked, and grieved! Its effect on people was comparable to the U.S. 1986 Challenger space-shuttle disaster.

Three days later, October 7, an already scheduled séance was held for a visiting Australian journalist, Ian Coster, and British psychical researcher Harry Price. The prearranged aim was to try to contact Sir Arthur Conan Doyle, the creator of the Sherlock Holmes detective stories, who'd died three months before. An expert stenographer noted everything that was said.

Mrs. Garrett went into her usual trance, with her usual control spirit, Uvani, working through her, and was working on contacting Doyle, when suddenly (Fuller 1979, 224):

...Eileen became agitated. Tears rolled down her cheeks. Her hands clenched. Uvani's voice became hurrying. "I see I-R-V-I-N-G or I-R-V-I-N. [Flight Lieutenant H. C.

Figure 15.4 R-101 Airship, Crashed

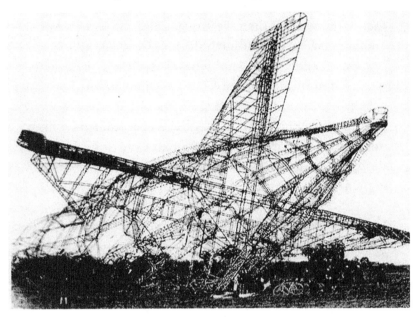

Irwin was captain of the R-101.] He says he must do something about it. Apologizes for interfering. For heaven's sake, give this to them. The whole bulk of the dirigible was too much for her engine capacity. Engines too heavy.... Gross lift computed badly. And this idea of new elevators totally mad. Elevator jammed. Oil pipe plugged [more technical details]....Almost scraped the roofs at Achy."

Achy was an obscure railroad junction in France, not shown on regular maps, but it was on dirigible navigation maps.

The following is from notes reconstructed the day after another session, with Major Oliver G. Villiers, an Air Ministry Intelligence officer (Fuller 1979, 251):

Communicator Irwin: "One of the struts in the nose collapsed and caused a tear in the cover. It is the same strut that caused trouble before and hey know... (sitter believes reference was to officials in Air Ministry). The wind was blowing hard, and it was raining. The rush of wind caused the first dive. And then we straightened out again. And another gust surging through the hole finished us."

Sitter Villiers: "Tell me, what caused the explosion?"

Communicator Irwin: "The diesel engine had been backfiring because the oil feed was not right. You see the pressure in some of the gas bags was accentuated by the undergirders crumpling up. The extra pressure pushed the gas out. And at that moment the engine backfired and ignited the escaping gas."

In a somewhat amusing aftermath once this material was published, two Royal Air Force Intelligence officers came to interview Garrett. It turned out that they suspected Garrett of having had an affair with one of the R-101's officers: there were too many correct but militarily classified technical details in her account!

As to these technical details, Mrs. Garrett's granddaughter, Lisette Coly, assures me that Mrs. Garrett was not at all a technical type of person; it was hard for her to operate a TV set without help. Andrew MacKenzie (1980) also notes that it's usually quite difficult to get technical details in mediumistic sittings.

Complexity: The German Diplomat Case

In this R-101 example of high-quality, mediumistic communications, we have plenty of specific detail, correct for the particular situation and not likely accessible by ordinary means. Let's look at another high-quality case that will further illustrate both the possible quality of mediumistic readings and their complexities. This case is from the personal experience of Rosalind Heywood (1964), a British psychic investigator:

After the war I went to a Scottish medium to see if she could pick up something about a friend, a German diplomat whom I feared had been killed either by the Nazis or the Russians. I simply didn't know what had happened to him. The medium very soon got onto him. She gave his Christian name, talked about things we had done together in Washington, and described correctly my opinion of his character. She said he was dead and that his death was so tragic he didn't want to talk about it. She gave a number of striking details about him and the evidence of personality was very strong....

Who wouldn't be impressed with this kind of material? Indeed, many investigators say evidence of personality, little quirks about a communicator that embody the deceased's style, can often be more impressive than simple factual data.

However, Heywood goes on (1964 as quoted in Roll 1985, 178–79):

If I had never heard any more, I would have thought it very impressive. But after the sitting, I set about trying to find out something about him. Finally the Swiss foreign office found him for me. He was not dead. He had escaped from Germany and had married an English girl. He wrote to me that he had never been so happy in his life. So there I think the medium was reading my expectations. She was quite wrong about the actual facts but quite right according to what I had expected.

There are no exact statistics on the occurrence of mediumistic communications that are impressive in terms of apparent psi elements but quite incorrect about the person's being dead. The impression of a number of my colleagues is that these cases are uncommon but not extremely rare. That this sort of thing can happen at all, though, means that we must theorize that, in at least some, if not all, cases, there might not be any actual postmortem survival but, rather, that the high-quality evidence can be alternatively explained by a theory of unconscious impersonation plus unconscious psi phenomena. That is, some aspect of the unconscious mind of the medium imitates the deceased and, in addition to generalities and pleasantries that make the sitter feel good, adds occasional veridical information obtained by psi ability. Since this veridical information is often extensive and highly specific, compared to the statistically significant, but practically tiny, amounts of psi ability seen in most laboratory studies, this kind of psi phenomena is referred to as super-psi phenomena.

Figure 15.5 diagrams the unconscious impersonation plus superpsi theory as an alternative explanation of what happens in good mediumship. By some combination of unconscious clairvoyance of physical traces of information about the deceased, plus telepathic access to the sitter's (and other people's) knowledge about the deceased, a plausible simulation of a surviving spirit is constructed.

Figure 15.5 Alternative Explanation of Mediumship Data:
Super-Psi and Simulation by the Living, but
No Communication with the Dead

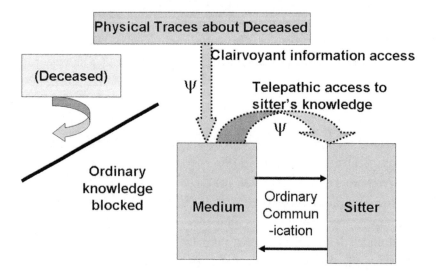

This is a rather amazing alternative theory if you think about it. Unconscious impersonation, unconscious use of psi ability, and high-level super-psi ability: how plausible is it?

Unconscious impersonation of another personality is a generally accepted psychological phenomenon. When I was extensively involved in hypnosis research at Stanford University back in the 1960s, for instance, one of the standard items on our regular hypnotic susceptibility scale for talented subjects included such a suggestion, and stage hypnotists often amuse audiences by picking some obviously shy-looking volunteers from the audience, subtly selected among them for those having high hypnotic talent, hypnotizing them, and then suggesting that they're a famous rock star or similar performer. The theatrical, extroverted performances as they sing are usually pretty impressive! This kind of thing is routine for stage hypnotists, so the idea of unconscious impersonation by mediums is plausible. In our cultural setting, this is "obviously" a demonstration of hypnosis and the powers of the unconscious mind. In other cultural settings, this sort of thing might be an "obvious" example of "spirit" possession.

How about unconscious use of psi ability? How plausible is that? In a general way, unconscious use of psi ability has been demonstrated repeatedly for decades in parapsychological experiments as the sheep-goat effect, introduced in chapter 8. This effect, discovered by psychologist Gertrude Schmeidler in 1942, is unusual and important enough to discuss in further detail. A multiple-choice ESP test, such as a card-guessing test, telepathic or clairvoyant, is given to a group of percipients. Before the actual ESP test, they fill out a questionnaire asking, among other things, about their belief in ESP or their personal ESP abilities. The sheep are those who believe in ESP, the goats those who don't.

The ESP test is given, its results recorded and then scored separately for the sheep and the goats. The sheep usually score above chance expectation, often significantly so. The goats, in contrast, usually score below chance expectation, often significantly so.

Almost all of these sheep-goat studies have been done with highly educated people, usually college students. There's a belief implicitly drummed into us over and over again through our schooling by its repeated occurrence: tests measure what you know. The more you know, the higher your test scores; the less you know, the lower. They wouldn't give us all those tests unless it meant something, would they?

The sheep believe in ESP: they take a test to measure ESP, tend to get a "good," above-chance score, and therefore are happy. They're good sheep, properly herded by their shepherd, the experimenter. Their beliefs have been confirmed: there is ESP and their scores showed it. The goats, on the other hand, the stubborn ones not following the shepherd's leadership, don't believe in ESP, there's nothing to be measured on the test, and sure enough, they get low scores, which seems to verify their beliefs that there's indeed nothing to measure. Everybody who believes that tests measure what you know is happy.

Of course, these aren't statistically sophisticated people who realize that below-chance scoring can be just as significant as above-chance scoring. I don't believe anyone has ever done a sheep-goat experiment with statistically sophisticated people.[1]

So how do you score significantly below chance? The only possible way I've ever thought of or heard anyone else mention is that while you're undoubtedly just guessing most of the time, every once in a while you unconsciously use some form of ESP to correctly know what the next test card is, and then your unconscious mind influences your conscious mind to guess anything but that correct answer.

I find this a marvelous demonstration of the power of the human mind: we can unconsciously use ESP in the service of our needs, in this case to support our belief that there is no ESP! Our clever minds (mistakenly) produce a "miracle" to demonstrate that there are no miracles!

Returning to the super-psi hypothesis as an alternative explanation for accurate mediumistic results, the answer is yes; it is plausible that, at least occasionally, a medium, believing in spirit survival, might unconsciously use psi ability to get valid information that increases the believability of her unconscious imitation of a deceased person.

Sometimes I wonder about the place of unconscious, unrecognized psi ability in life. When we think about the long-term possibilities of investigating spirituality and add psi phenomena into the equation, you can see that these kind of results, while arguing for some kind of reality to spirituality in a general sense, also mean that those future investigations may require a lot of sophistication if people can unconsciously use psi ability to support the particulars of their belief systems.

Psi-Mediated Instrumental Responses

Here's another example of unconsciously using psi ability in support of our needs. Parapsychologist Rex Stanford thought about people who were "lucky." What exactly did being "lucky" mean? Some events attributed to luck are really the deliberate use, consciously or unconsciously, of skills; it's just not obvious to us how this was done. And clearly some luck is just coincidence; a person just happens to be in the right place at the right time for something good to happen. Yet it often seems that some people are persistently lucky rather than that instances of good luck are uniformly spread across the population.

Stanford devised a theory of psi-mediated instrumental responses (PMIRs) (1974), and he and his colleagues carried out a number of experiments to test his theory that at least sometimes, we unconsciously use psi ability to scan our world, detect a situation coming up that it would be lucky to be involved in (or avoid), and our unconscious influences our conscious mind to just happen to be at the right place at the right time. Being at the right place at the right time is the instrumental (effective) response in psychological jargon. The person manifesting the PMIR has no idea she's using psi ability in this way; for example, she suddenly feels like taking a walk around the block and "just happens" to meet a person who does something that benefits her. Indeed she can be a person who doesn't believe in weird things like psi ability, yet still benefits from her unconscious, instrumental use of it.

Stanford and his colleagues conducted several studies of potential PMIRs, and in one (Stanford et al. 1976), forty college-age men were individually tested by an attractive female experimenter. No mention of the PMIR hypothesis was made to these percipients. Each person participated in a short word-association test; the experimenter would say a word from a list and the percipient would respond with the first word that came to his mind. The experimenter recorded the time it took the percipient to make each response. To all appearances, this was a straightforward psychology experiment of a kind that had been done hundreds of times before in mainstream psychology.

None of the percipients knew that there was a sealed decision sheet (a different one for each of them) on which one of the words of the association list had been randomly selected as a psi target. For half (randomly selected) of the men, if their fastest (or tied for fastest) response was the target word, they would go on to participate in a much more interesting ESP experiment after the word-association test was finished. The other half of the group had to give their slowest (or tied for slowest) response for the key word. Stanford believed that this wouldn't work as well because he theorized it would be easier for psi ability to speed up a response on such a test than to inhibit one.

The experimenter giving the association test did not, of course, know what the key word was until the test was completed, so she couldn't make biased scoring errors. The percipients had no idea (by ordinary means) that their responses in the first part of this experiment would affect what happened in the second part, or even that there would be a second part to the experiment.

The favorable experiment consisted of participating in a picture-perception ESP task under pleasant, relaxed conditions, with positive suggestions. The female experimenter conducted this task, which would presumably be quite pleasant to the male percipients. The less interesting experiment consisted of sitting alone in a straight-backed chair in the experimental room doing card-guessing tests for twenty-five minutes. (I've always wondered what it said about the psychology of many classical parapsychology experiments that this kind of card-guessing test was used as a kind of punishment.)

The results supported Stanford's PMIR hypothesis. In the fast group, the correct associations occurred significantly faster than they would by chance. As expected, the speed increase in the fast-response condition was larger than the speed decrease in the slow-response condition.

In the favorable second experiment of another PMIR study (Stanford et al. 1976), college-age men participated in a picture-rating task of attractiveness showing college-age women in varying degrees of undress. In the unfavorable condition, they participated in a vigilance task with a pursuit rotor. This was a device developed in the early days of psychology to measure motor skill. You had to hold a stylus over a small patch of light on the pursuit rotor (a rotating disk), but it was set to rotate at such a slow speed that the task was very easy, unskilled, very boring, and physically tiring. The percipient had to keep this up for twenty-five minutes. Again, word-association times were significantly changed.

So we have good evidence that two of the three aspects of the alternative theory, unconscious impersonation and unconscious use of psi ability, can happen in other situations. Whether this happens rarely, often, or always in mediumship is still a wide-open question.

The third aspect of this alternative theory, the "super" in super-psi ability, creates big problems though. If you really make the possible psi ability super, able to pull out large amounts of specifically correct information, you not only require much larger amounts of psi ability than living percipients usually show when they deliberately try to use psi ability in various laboratory tests, you also get beyond the limits of science. Recall that when we discussed essential scientific method in chapter 2, one of the characteristics of a scientific theory was that, in principle, it was disprovable; that is, it could logically lead to predictions of outcomes that, when tested, did not occur, and so the theory could be rejected. When you vaguely allow psi ability to be super, though, when you have no limits on what it might do, you can't disprove it. If we allow super-psi ability, for example, we might say that right now you're mistaken in thinking that you're sitting in a chair reading this book. Actually you're long dead, with no physical body and no location in the material world; you're just unconsciously hallucinating this world and using various forms of super-psi ability to create an ongoing, consistent hallucination of being embodied and reading this book. With no limits on your unconscious, psychic abilities, how could you disprove that?

For those who like clear, neat, and tidy outcomes of their research, the super-psi explanation of mediumship results is a great disincentive to bother doing research. With a few major exceptions, such as psychologist Gary Schwartz's recent ingenious work at the University of Arizona (2003), and intermittent work under the auspices of the Society for Psychical Research in England, for example, the fascinating work on physical mediumship of the Scole group (Keen, Ellison, and Fontana 1999), there's little research on survival via investigation of mediumship going on today. Almost all of what we know comes from the older research. Why did it die out (no pun intended)?

Primarily, of course, in the mainstream scientistic world, post-mortem survival research is a taboo topic. The mind is nothing but the brain, which turns to mush when we die; survival is thus *a priori* impossible, so only fools, charlatans, and crazies would want to research it.

The world of psychical research, where the mediumship work took place, was (and still is, unfortunately) a very small world, with almost no full-time, trained scientific researchers and only a few dozen part-timers like me. Resources are extremely limited, and most of the part-timers, like me, tend to be scholars who study the older work rather than active researchers. And conceptually, as noted previously, the super-psi hypothesis to explain mediumship put a lot of inhibition on the motivation to study postmortem survival. Why collect more evidence for survival when it not only might be nothing but unconscious impersonations plus super-psi ability but when you also can't figure out a way to distinguish the two?

Personally I'm not too bothered by an alternative, super-psi explanation of the good mediumship evidence. A creature who can use super-psi ability actually sounds like the kind of creature who's not so dependent on his or her physical body and thus might survive death. Such a creature might even be described as spiritual.

Notes

1. My testing to see if immediate feedback would increase ESP scores accidentally produced a fascinating case study of this. A young woman who didn't believe in ESP nevertheless made enough almost hits, interesting-looking displacements, that her experimenter wanted to give her individual test sessions in the second phase of the study. She was tested, and on the ten-choice trainer scored a little below chance on correct hits, but well above chance if you looked at either her clockwise or counterclockwise spatially displaced responses; that is, if the target was, say, an eight, she was low on calling eights but high on sevens and nines. Her scores were so significant this way that her experimenter invited her to take part in the formal training study, figuring she could learn to correct her displacements. She was shocked to be asked back; she didn't believe in ESP and thought her low scores confirmed her belief. When told she had spatially displaced plus or minus one, she buckled down in the study and, not realizing we would explore all displacements rather than just plus or minus one, now showed a displacement pattern as far away as possible from the correct targets (Tart 1976).

CHAPTER 16

Reincarnation

REINCARNATION (mid-nineteenth century [origin: from "re-" plus "incarnation"]): (1) Renewed incarnation, especially (in some beliefs) the rebirth of a soul in a new body. (2) A fresh embodiment of a person. — SHORTER OXFORD ENGLISH DICTIONARY, *6th ed., s.v. "reincarnation"*

REINCARNATION or rebirth is the belief, held by a large proportion of the world's population, that some essential aspect of one's living self, the soul, survives physical death and, after some period of varying length in an afterlife state, is reborn as the soul of a new being. Beliefs in reincarnation usually include a belief in some form of karma, a psychic law of cause and effect, so that actions in one lifetime will eventually, when circumstances are ripe, have effects in a later lifetime. In classical Hinduism and Buddhism, for example, a person who performs virtuous actions and grows spiritually in one life is more likely to be reborn in happy circumstances and have good things happen to her as she interacts with others. Someone who lived an evil life, on the other hand, is likely to be reborn in difficult circumstances or even, in some belief systems, as an animal or other kind of being.

The typical flavor that comes with belief in reincarnation in the East is negative: you suffer in this life, and unless you get enlightened, you'll suffer in future lives as your karma ripens, you unskillfully generate more negative karma, or both. My own bias, what I'd like to be true, as a Westerner believing in progress, is positive: there's so much to learn in life, so many interesting things, that one lifetime isn't anywhere near enough to make much progress on this. So I look forward to returning to "school" many times until I finally have a "master's degree." That's just my personal bias, of course, which has no bearing on the important question as to whether reincarnation is real. Remember, as a scientist my strong desire is to know the truth, whether or not it accords with what I'd like it to be. Part of having a better chance of learning the truth is to know what biases you have in approaching issues.

If reincarnation is established for any cases, then we can some-day deal with more refined questions like these: Does it happen to everybody or just to some? Does karma actually work? If so, how? How would I live my life more effectively and with a longer-term view if I thought reincarnation was likely? Meanwhile, our basic task remains to assess what evidence we have for reincarnation rather than just blindly believe or disbelieve in it.

Although I'd read about apparent cases of reincarnation that had some evidential value while I was still a teenager, devouring what literature I could find on psychical research and parapsychology, my first serious involvement with a case occurred in fall 1956, while I was a student at MIT. I was browsing in the student bookstore one day. Because I had very little money for anything but essentials, most of my browsing was done at the remaindered books table, and I found one hardcover book for a dollar that intrigued me, *The Search for Bridey Murphy*, by Morey Bernstein (1956). The title didn't attract me, and I don't know why I picked it up and looked at it more closely, because it sounded like some kind of novel. But I saw from the jacket that it was about hypnosis and reincarnation, and since I'd already read extensively about hypnosis, I was intrigued and gambled my dollar.

It was a good gamble, because I ended up fascinated with the story and felt that the whole thing had been well researched. I little suspected, as did the publishers, that the book I'd found being re-maindered on the dollar table would soon become a best seller!

Morey Bernstein, the author, was a prominent Colorado businessman who experimented with hypnosis as a hobby. An "amateur hypnotist," in the sense that he wasn't trained in psychology or medicine and didn't charge for what he did, he had a decade of experience using hypnosis in a variety of ways, and I could tell from my own reading that he was quite knowledgeable about the scientific literature on hypnosis. Bernstein had become interested in hypnotic regression, where you suggest to a hypnotized subject that it's much earlier in time than the present, the subject's fifth birthday, for example, and often find the subject, especially if she's hypnotically talented, then beginning to speak and behave like her earlier self. Often the subject talks about things long forgotten, making you wonder if hypnosis can increase memory in a dramatic way.

Bernstein had heard stories of people being regressed to previous lives but was quite skeptical about them. He finally tried it himself, arranging to have six recorded sessions over the course of several months with a casual social acquaintance who was a talented hypnotic subject to whom he gave the pseudonym Ruth Mills Simmons. She was later identified by the press as Virginia Burns Tighe.

I'll now briefly summarize the case, not to prove or disprove the reality of reincarnation — that would take many books in and of itself to begin to adequately weigh the evidence — but to give the flavor of this kind of material.

I'd read the Bernstein book and put it aside, thinking it definitely provided some good evidence for reincarnation but, like any real case, had possible flaws and questionable points. A while later, I had to reread it though, for the book had hit the best-seller lists and so much was being written about it. Yet what was being written really puzzled me; so much was on the order of "Bernstein made this (ridiculous) claim and that (ridiculous) claim." I didn't remember those claims, so I had to check my memory of the book.

This was a great lesson for me about resistance to knowledge, for it soon became clear that the very idea of reincarnation was so upsetting to many people in the culture of the fifties that they lost what sense they had and got kind of crazy! This was even true for writings by people I had regarded, based on their previous published work, as scientific authorities on hypnosis: they made fools of themselves in the course of criticizing and ridiculing Bernstein over things he hadn't said! In retrospect, I saw that it was a good lesson for a young man to start getting skeptical of authorities, but it was quite shocking to me at the time that people who were supposed to be paragons of truthfulness and accuracy could be so far off.

The discrepancy between what Bernstein had written and claimed (quite modest claims, really) and what was attributed to him and attacked was so great that I've somewhat jokingly expressed it as the idea that there must've been two books called *The Search for Bridey Murphy* written by authors named Morey Bernstein and published at about the same time. Clearly I'd read only one of them, and the raging debunkers, the pseudoskeptics, had read the other.

To my pleasure and edification, I met Morey Bernstein and his wife Hazel a few months later when I worked in parapsychology research at physician Andrija Puharich's Round Table Foundation in summer 1957. It saddened me to hear the inside story of just how vicious and personal so many of the attacks on the book and its author were. Bernstein was especially angry at a Chicago paper that claimed that Virginia Tighe actually spent a lot of time as a child with a neighbor who was Irish and had regaled her with tales of Ireland. According to Bernstein, the neighbor, who never made herself available to be interviewed by any other investigators, was the mother of the publisher of a newspaper whose editor was very angry at Bernstein for not giving his paper early rights to the story, and had told Bernstein he would get back at him!

So what was all the fuss about? Neither Morey Bernstein nor Virginia Tighe had ever visited Ireland, but when she was told to go back to a life before this one, Virginia started to recount memories of a life in which she was named Bridey (Bridget) Kathleen Murphy. She was an Irish girl who claimed to have been born in Cork, Ireland, in 1798. Her father was a Protestant Cork barrister named Duncan Murphy, and her mother was named Kathleen.

Virginia, speaking with an Irish accent, reported that she'd gone to a school run by a Mrs. Strayne and that she had a brother, Duncan Blaine Murphy, who eventually married Mrs. Strayne's daughter, Aimee Strayne. Bridey also had another brother, but as was too common in those days, he died while still a baby.

When she was twenty, Bridey recounted getting married in a Protestant ceremony to a Catholic, one Brian Joseph McCarthy, the son of another Cork barrister. The couple then moved to Belfast, where her husband received more schooling and, Bridey claimed, eventually taught courses in law at Queens University.

Protestantism versus Catholicism was an issue of great importance then (and today) in Ireland, so the couple married again in a second ceremony by a Catholic priest, Father John Joseph Gorman, of Saint Theresa's church. Bridey and Brian had no children.

Bridey lived, Virginia recalled, to age sixty-six and then was, to use her own expression, "ditched" — that is, buried — in Belfast in 1964.

Virginia made many statements, some about commonplace things that anyone would know about Ireland, some uncheckable, some found to be incorrect, and some correct and unlikely to be known by most people (Ducasse 1960, 5).

Evaluating a case like this is much more complex (and interesting!) than the laboratory studies described earlier, which established the existence of the five major kinds of psi ability: telepathy, clairvoyance, precognition, psychokinesis, and psychic healing. We can't come up with some precise mathematical statement that the odds our results are due to chance are one in ten (which we'd regard as no evidence), one in twenty (the traditional level in psychology at which the results are considered "significant," unlikely to be due to chance), or even less probable. What is "chance" in a case like this? Certainly that an Irishwoman would be named Murphy is not at all improbable, but suppose the term "ditched" for being buried, certainly not in use in America or Ireland at the time of the experiments, turns out to be true (as it did)? How significant is that?

Or when, while regressed, she sneezed once and spontaneously asked for a "linen," how likely is coincidence when you find out that "linen" was a term used for handkerchief way back then? How do you evaluate the fact that evidence can be found for her claimed husband's existence as a clerk but not as a barrister, so perhaps she was actually recalling a past life but inflating her social status in a way that might've been typical in such a past life? Or is this just an example of imagination and it's only the desire to believe that makes some people see this kind of thing as evidential?

I recommend reading *The Search for Bridey Murphy* for those interested in reincarnation, for the wealth of detail we have no space to go into here. There's still a recording available of some of the sessions; as we discussed in the case of mediumship, the style of communications can sometimes seem more evidential than the "facts" involved. When you weigh all the information about Bridey Murphy, I think the rational conclusion is that the evidence it provides for possible reincarnation is strong enough that it would be foolish to just disregard it because of a priori convictions that reincarnation can't be possible, but it would also be foolish to feel that it "proves" the reality of reincarnation.

This case also illustrates a general problem in investigating reincarnation with modern people: by the time we're adults or even teenagers, we've been exposed to an enormous amount of information about the past. Just as the unconscious impersonation theory of mediumship has been put forward as an alternative to believing that spirits survive death (perhaps with a bit of psi ability, if not super-psi ability, to add verisimilitude to the simulation), perhaps an adult recalling a previous incarnation is simply believing a simulation, a kind of dream, concocted by his unconscious mind.

When hypnotic regression is involved — and many techniques for recalling past lives that aren't formally called "hypnosis" may indeed be a kind of hypnosis — we must remember that, in general, hypnotized subjects have a great desire to please the hypnotist.

Thus when there's a suggestion that a person will remember a time before her birth, from a previous life, it's quite reasonable to assume that, at least some of the time, the material "recalled" is actually a fabrication by her unconscious mind. But this is a "fabrication" that seems quite true to the subject; there's no conscious imagination or lying involved. The recaller has no conscious memory of having read the books or seen the documentaries about past times that provide convincing evidence, but he might have done so; it's hard to prove someone has never been exposed to certain kinds of material.

For example, I recall a fascinating case reported by psychiatrist Ian Stevenson (1983) in which a Mrs. Crowson (pseudonym) participated in Ouija board séances with a friend, resting one hand on the movable planchette, and thus capable of (unconsciously) influencing it. A lot of excellent, fact-filled communications were received from ostensibly deceased persons, and the details were easily verified in the obituary columns of the London Daily Telegraph. In fact, the material was almost exclusively what you could find in the obituaries, causing Stevenson to wonder if Mrs. Crowson had read them, even if she'd consciously forgotten that she'd done so. She did not read the paper, but her husband read it and also did the crossword puzzles in it, which were on the same page, such that when the paper was folded for convenience in doing the puzzles, there were obituaries visible around it. Mrs. Crowson sometimes finished off crossword puzzles her husband had been unable to complete, so she was visually exposed to the relevant material even if she didn't consciously look at it. Thus cryptomnesia (concealed recollection, or hidden memory) was the likely normal explanation rather than communication from the deceased.

My own best guess at present is that if you have a hundred cases of past-life recall in adults, by whatever method, there might be some genuine cases among them, but probably some are indeed unconscious fabrications. I wish we had the data to specify what "some" means here, but we don't.

One partial way around the problem of adults unconsciously

knowing so much about the past and being motivated, especially when hypnosis is involved, to please the hypnotist or reincarnation investigator, is to look for instances of young children who spontaneously recall past-life material. While we may not be absolutely certain, we can often be much surer about whether a child has been exposed to certain kinds of factual material compared to an adult.

Psychiatrist Ian Stevenson devoted a major part of his career to looking for and investigating such cases of children who spontaneously claimed to remember past lives, and the laboratory he left behind at the University of Virginia in Charlottesville, after his recent death in 2007, now has thousands of such cases. This allows for broadscale analyses of patterns, as well as checking on individual cases. Stevenson never claimed that he'd "proven" reincarnation but only that he'd found sufficient evidence that it needed to be looked at seriously. In this way he was practicing essential science, where you never get so attached to any theory that you claim that it's proven, only that you have certain kinds of evidence for and against it, and that your best guess, given the evidence so far, is.... An excellent introduction to Stevenson's work is Thomas Shroder's book, *Old Souls* (Fireside, 2001).

Psychiatrist Jim Tucker, one of the leading scientific investigators of reincarnation, starts his excellent book on this kind of research, *Life Before Life* (2005, 1–3), with the following case report, drawn from this collection of ostensible reincarnation cases at the University of Virginia Division of Perceptual Studies, which Stevenson founded:

> John McConnell, a retired New York City policeman working as a security guard, stopped at an electronics store after work one night in 1992. He saw two men robbing the store and pulled out his pistol. Another thief behind a counter began shooting at him. John tried to shoot back, and even after he fell, he got up and shot again. He was hit

six times. One of the bullets entered his back and sliced through his left lung, his heart, and the main pulmonary artery, the blood vessel that takes blood from the right side of the heart to the lungs to receive oxygen. He was rushed to the hospital but did not survive.

Figure 16.1 Reincarnation of John McConnell?

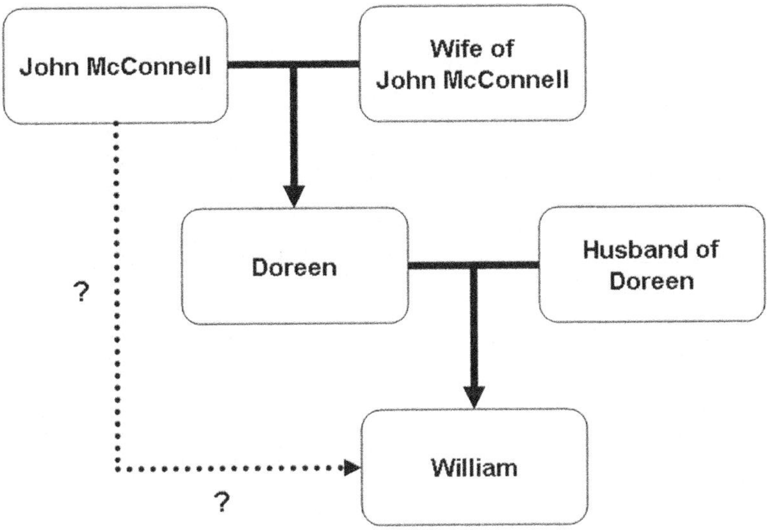

John had been close to his family and had frequently told one of his daughters, Doreen, "No matter what, I'm always going to take care of you." Five years after John died, Doreen gave birth to a son named William. William began passing out soon after he was born. Doctors diagnosed him with a condition called pulmonary-valve atresia, in which the valve of the pulmonary artery has not adequately formed, so blood cannot travel through it to the lungs. In addition, one of the chambers of his heart, the right ventricle, had not formed properly as a result of the problem with the valve. He underwent several surgeries. Although he will need to take medication indefinitely, he has done quite well. [I've sketched the relationship between various people in this case in figure 16.1 to make it easier to follow.]

William had birth defects that were very similar to the fatal wounds suffered by his grandfather. In addition, when he became old enough to talk, he began talking about his grandfather's life. One day when he was three years old, his mother was at home trying to work in her study when William kept acting up. Finally, she told him, "Sit down, or I'm going to spank you." William replied, "Mom, when you were a little girl and I was your daddy, you were bad a lot of times, and I never hit you!"

His mother was initially taken aback by this. As William talked more about the life of his grandfather, she began to feel comforted by the idea that her father had returned. William talked about being his grandfather a number of times and discussed his death. He told his mother that several people were shooting during the incident when he was killed, and he asked a lot of questions about it.

One time, he said to his mother, "When you were a little girl and I was your daddy, what was my cat's name?" She responded, "You mean Maniac?"

"No, not that one," William answered. "The white one."

"Boston?" his mom asked.

"Yeah," William responded. "I used to call him Boss, right?" That was correct. The family had two cats, named Maniac and Boston, and only John referred to the white one as Boss.

One day, Doreen asked William if he remembered anything about the time before he was born. He said that he died on a Thursday and went to heaven. He said that he saw animals there and also talked to God. He said, "I told God I was ready to come back, and I got born on Tuesday." Doreen was amazed that William mentioned days since he did not even know his days of the week without prompting. She tested him by saying, "So, you were born on a Thursday and died on Tuesday?" He quickly responded, "No, I died Thursday at night and was born Tuesday in the morning." He was correct on both counts: John died on a Thursday, and William was born on a Tuesday five years later.

He talked about the period between lives at other times. He told his mother, "When you die, you don't go right to heaven. You go to different levels: here, then here, then here," as he moved his hand up each time. He said that animals are reborn as well as humans and that the animals he saw in heaven did not bite or scratch.

John had been a practicing Roman Catholic, but he believed in reincarnation and said that he would take care of animals in his next life. His grandson, William, says that he will be an animal doctor and will take care of large animals at a zoo.

William reminds Doreen of her father in several ways. He loves books, as his grandfather did. When they visit William's grandmother, he will spend hours looking at books in John's study, duplicating his grandfather's behavior from years before. William, like his grandfather, is good at putting things together and can be a "nonstop talker."

William especially reminds Doreen of her father when he tells her, "Don't worry, Mom. I'll take care of you."[1]

Coming back to general patterns, initial analyses of the University of Virginia collection indicate that a typical case starts with a preschool-age child spontaneously claiming to be someone who has died recently. While this is more likely to be noticed in cultures that accept the idea of reincarnation, such as India, it's often not a welcome development for the parents, especially if the claimed incarnation is of a lower social status or caste than the current family! While such claims are liable to be ignored at first — the child must be imagining things or just playing — they eventually become persistent or dramatic enough, in the cases we hear about, that parents will begin investigating whether it was possible. Was there truly a person named so and so who lived in such and such place and died recently?

There are often behavioral indications that the child might be a reincarnation of someone else, such as markedly different diet preferences than those of his actual biological family and sometimes scattered words, even occasionally the use of a language the child has not learned in this life but which fits the claimed reincarnation.

The child frequently wants to "go home," to be reunited with his real family, especially his spouse from the previous incarnation. When a reunion is finally arranged, there are sometimes dramatic instances of the child's accurately picking out particular people from a crowd of onlookers, although this is sometimes hard to tell in the confusion surrounding the reunion.

Some of the most dramatic cases Stevenson and his colleagues collected are about biological markers, where the child has unusual birthmarks that correspond to the wounds that killed the previous personality. A child may show a small, roundish darkened area on his chest, for instance, and a much larger, irregular darker area on his back behind it, while claiming to be someone who was killed by a shotgun blast to the chest. Shooting wounds have small entrance holes and much larger exit holes. It's as if the trauma of a violent death carries through strongly enough to affect biological development in the next life, and indeed, there are a few cultures that accept reincarnation, especially within families, that deliberately mark the corpse of a deceased person to see if a baby born later will bear those marks.[2]

Indeed there are enough cases in which children claiming previous incarnation showed unusual birthmarks and the previous personality had been violently killed that Stevenson used to joke that if you wanted to remember this incarnation in your next one, the best advice he could give you was to die a violent death. Stevenson documented many such cases in a massive two-volume work (1997a, 1997b).

Usually by the early school years, the memories of the previous life slip away and the child becomes "normal."

Notes

1. From *Life Before Life*, by Jim B. Tucker. Copyright © 2005 by the author and reprinted by permission of St. Martin's Press.

2. I once suggested to the investigators carrying on Stevenson's work that it would be quite interesting to start marking a lot of corpses with the equivalent of bar codes, so that if any children later claimed to have been incarnations of these folks, we would have a clear biological marker. I wasn't sure, nor were they, whether I was serious or indulging in black humor.

CHAPTER 17

So What Have We Learned?

REVIEW (origin: French "reveue" (now "revue"), from "revoir," from "re-" and "voir"): A general survey or reconsideration of some subject or thing (frequently in "in review," "under review"); a retrospect, a survey of the past. — SHORTER OXFORD ENGLISH DICTIONARY, *6th ed., s.v. "review"*

BEFORE moving on, let's do a quick review of what we've covered so far. We began by facing up to what's probably the most profound problem of life once you've adequately handled basic issues of physical survival and social relationships, namely, questions about our real spiritual nature, and we looked at some of the difficulties we moderns face in trying to deal with such questions. Although all ancient traditions see us as basically spiritual creatures, and some current psychological work reveals the great importance of spirituality in life — people who belong to a church tend to live longer, for example — we're conflicted about it and have a hard time putting consistent energy into spiritual practice, for science apparently tells us that there's nothing but material reality. Ideas of the spiritual are superstitions and delusions from earlier times, perhaps needed by the dumb and cowardly who can't face reality, but certainly not by intelligent, educated modern people. Because we like to be considered intelligent, educated, and modern, and since science has been so enormously successful in so many other areas of life, we can't help but take this objection to spirituality quite seriously. That's just at a conscious level. Semiconsciously and unconsciously, we've all been subjected to great

amounts of belittlement of spirituality by scientists and other prestigious thinkers, so there's unconscious, as well as conscious, resistance to spirituality and the emotional issues around it.

So here we are, spiritual creatures in historical and experiential
senses — people do have spiritual experiences, whether they're considered nonsense or not — who doubt, suppress, ridicule, and "explain away" many of our own deepest experiences.

With deeper inquiry into essential scientific method, we saw
that the problem is not a conflict between science per se and spirituality, but between scientism and spirituality. Scientism, attached
to the enormous success of the physical sciences, presumes a philosophy of total, materialistic monism. Everything can and will be
fully explained by studying space, time, matter, and energy with
physical instruments, and we can dismiss the spiritual a priori without wasting our time by looking at it seriously.

Essential, genuine science, radical empiricism, insists, though,
that we look at all data, all experience, not just those things that
make us happy because they fit the beliefs and theories we've already adopted. People have always had and keep right on having
experiences that simply do not fit into current materialistic frame-
works or reasonable extensions of them. My *coup d'état* experience,
described in chapter 4, exemplified such experiences, as did other
accounts in this book, and the interested reader can find literally
thousands and thousands of such experiences from intelligent,
educated people. My TASTE website, The Archives of Scientists'
Transcendent Experiences (www.issc-taste.org), for example,
describes many such experiences that living scientists have had.

When we apply the methods of essential science to look at
these kinds of experiences, which are ignored in materialistic
scientism, we discover paraconceptual phenomena, paranormal
phenomena as they're usually called, apparent transcendences of
the usual limitations of space and time that happen to so many
ordinary people that the "normal" in paranormal is actually
misleading. If what happens to a majority of people is "normal,"

then those who haven't personally had some sort of paranormal experience are not up to normal; they're subnormal or abnormal.

When we look at paraconceptual phenomena in detail, in the science of parapsychology we find, grouped for convenience, two categories. Group one, the big five — telepathy, clairvoyance, precognition, psychokinesis, and psychic healing — are psi phenomena whose existence is supported by hundreds of rigorous experiments for each phenomenon. Group two, the many maybes, are phenomena that have enough evidence that it would be foolish to simply dismiss them as unreal, but not enough evidence, in my estimate, to make them foundational realities for further research as the big five are. The many maybes that we've surveyed (which certainly aren't all of them) in this book are postcognition, out-of-body experiences (OBEs), near-death experiences (NDEs), after-death communications (ADCs), and postmortem survival in some kind of afterlife as evidenced through mediumship and reincarnation.

The big five paint a picture of humans as beings who are more than just their physical bodies, beings who can sometimes communicate mind to mind, sometimes clairvoyantly know the state of the physical world, sometimes predict an inherently (by physical laws) unpredictable future, sometimes affect physical objects by thought and intention alone, and sometimes affect, for the better, other biological systems, as in psychic healing. Traditional spiritual systems in general tell us that ordinary, physical life is only part of reality; there's a larger, more encompassing spiritual reality beyond ordinary space, time, and embodiment, and the big five can readily be seen as glimpses of mind operating in this larger reality.

The many maybes bear even more directly on the general spiritual idea that we have some essence or soul that's the core of the real self. OBEs are almost always interpreted by the people who have them, for example, as a direct experience of existing as a (temporarily) disembodied soul, and we have a little evidence that someone who's had an OBE can sometimes give us correct information about ordinarily inaccessible aspects of physical reality, suggesting that something is really "out," rather than that the person is just vividly imagining being out. NDEs add an altered state of consciousness (ASC) dimension to the experience of being out of the body, suggesting that what we consider to be ordinary consciousness is a compound of some more basic mind that's beyond the body, with the particular amplifying and limiting characteristics of the physical body, brain, and nervous system. Both those who've had OBEs and NDEs almost always know afterward that they'll survive physical death in some form, so these experiences have huge effects on people's lives.

OBEs and NDEs are, at this time, as "far out" as one can go and still remain a living person. Those having such experiences may know they'll survive death in some form, but we who haven't experienced such phenomena do have to consider the fact that they weren't really dead, since "dead" means permanently dead in ordinary language. It's nice for them that they have a deep conviction that they'll survive, but will they, really?

ADCs, which happen to enormous numbers of people, tell us that in spite of the automatic scientistic dismissal of such a possibility, apparent contacts between loved ones and the recently deceased are actually rather frequent. But while the feeling of being contacted is wonderfully reassuring to grieving loved ones, this isn't much evidence of any reality to the contact when assessed by the scientific parts of our minds. Is there any solid evidence that our being might actually survive physical death in some real form?

This is where mediumistic communications provide the most direct evidence. While many such communications are, like ADCs, emotionally satisfying but not very evidential to the rational mind, some, like the R-101 case we looked at, are quite specific and correct, providing information known to the deceased but not to the living. My own personal assessment of this evidence can be expressed in two statements. First, after I die I won't be surprised if

I regain consciousness in some form. Perhaps there'll be temporary unconsciousness, as happens ordinarily in sleep, and without a body to continuously shape and support ordinary consciousness, the consciousness I regain may be an altered state compared to my ordinary, embodied consciousness. So second, I'll be surprised if I regain consciousness. I expect that my sense of "I," of who I am, will definitely change.

So the better mediumistic phenomena suggest some kind of survival of consciousness after bodily death. Questions about the form of this survival, such as how long it lasts, what it means in terms of how we live this life, and so on, are, to my mind, vastly important but unable to be answered in any satisfactory way with our present data. The descriptions of the afterlife given by ostensible surviving spirits have undoubtedly been distorted by the hopes and fears of both mediums and sitters, and we need a lot more research to learn how to ask these kinds of questions in ways more likely to get useful answers. And, as I mentioned earlier, the fact that we don't support any research to speak of that deals with the reality or lack of it of postmortem survival and the nature of the afterlife is an incredible lack in modern culture. Probably our fear of death has a lot to do with this total avoidance, but pretending that problems aren't there has never been a very useful way to solve them.

One possibility is some kind of temporary postmortem survival in a disembodied state and then an incarnation, a reincarnation, to a new body. As with the other many maybes, there's enough evi0 dence that the possibility must be taken seriously, and it's just plain crazy that we aren't devoting enormous efforts to studying this sort of thing.

Interesting creatures, aren't we?

CHAPTER 18

If I Believed the Western Creed

MATERIALISM (English, eighteenth century [origin: from "material" plus "-ism"]): (1) Philosophy. The doctrine that nothing exists except matter and its movements and modifications. Also, the doctrine that consciousness and will are wholly due to the operation of material agencies. (2) A tendency to prefer material possessions and physical comfort to spiritual values; a way of life based on material interests.
— SHORTER OXFORD ENGLISH DICTIONARY, *6th ed., s.v. "materialism"*

IN CHAPTER 1 we looked at (and hopefully did aloud, to get a deeper experiential feel) my Western Creed exercise, a way of seeing more deeply some of the possible implications of scientistic materialism for our own and others' lives. I shared some of my students' reactions to this deeper look into our common beliefs in that chapter but held my own in reserve, even though you can deduce some of them implicitly in the way I constructed the creed. I think it would be useful to share more of my personal reactions to scientistic materialism at this point to help illustrate some of the possible take-home lessons of this book.

On the next page, the Western Creed again, for convenience:

THE WESTERN CREED

I BELIEVE — in the material universe — as the only and ultimate reality — a universe controlled by fixed physical laws — and blind chance.

I AFFIRM — that the universe has no creator — no objective purpose — and no objective meaning or destiny.

I MAINTAIN — that all ideas about God or gods — enlightened beings — prophets and saviors — or other nonphysical beings or forces — are superstitions and delusions — . Life and consciousness are totally identical to physical processes — and arose from chance interactions of blind physical forces — . Like the rest of life — my life — and my consciousness — have no objective purpose — meaning — or destiny.

I BELIEVE — that all judgments, values, and moralities — whether my own or others' — are subjective — arising solely from biological determinants — personal history — and chance — . Free will is an illusion — . Therefore, the most rational values I can personally live by — must be based on the knowledge that for me — what pleases me is good — what pains me is bad — . Those who please me or help me avoid pain — are my friends — those who pain me or keep me from my pleasure — are my enemies — . Rationality requires that friends and enemies — be used in ways that maximize my pleasure — and minimize my pain.

I AFFIRM — that churches have no real use other than social support — that there are no objective sins to commit or be forgiven for — that there is no divine retribution for sin — or reward for virtue — . Virtue for me is getting what I want — without being caught and punished by others.

I MAINTAIN — that the death of the body — is the death of the mind — . There is no afterlife — and all hope of such is nonsense.

So if I fully believed the Western Creed: I would rationally — as far as rationality is possible for us complex humans — understand that I live in a universe composed entirely of physical objects and forces, physical matter and physical energy. Although many spiritually inclined people cite modern quantum mechanics as making room for spirituality, I'm not convinced of that, nor are many quantum physicists. Quantum approaches turn apparently solid objects into fuzzier and fuzzier manifestations of energy, but nevertheless the scientistic picture of the world remains one of insentient, object-like "things" being acted upon by insentient forces with no reason, purpose, or destiny inherent in this universe. Some quantum physicists (Stapp 2007) see consciousness as an inherent property of the universe, as fundamental as matter and energy, but the majority doesn't see the need for such an idea.

The best treatment of possible relationships between quantum physics and parapsychology that I know of is Dean Radin's *Entangled Minds: Extrasensory Experiences in a Quantum Reality* (2006). The treatment is thoughtful and creative, and comprehensible by non-physicists. At the very least, Radin makes a convincing case that the Newtonian, classical-physics universe that seems to rule out psi phenomena in principle is really only a special case of a larger physical reality, where psi phenomena might have a place. But a lot of details need to be filled in on that "might."

Given this inherently meaningless world, it's still my biological nature — again with no inherent reason for it; it just happened or evolved that way — to seek pleasure and avoid pain. Since my ability to do this well depends on my biological integrity, health, and intelligence, which are applied to make the best of whatever situations I find myself in, it's essential that I ensure my physical health and safety, and use my intelligence as effectively as possible.

Physical Safety and Health as Number One Priority

If I fully believed the Western Creed, obviously my first priority must be my physical or biological safety. This physical body

is all I've got, and while reason compels me to accept the fact
that eventually all physical bodies — including mine, damn it! —
sicken and die, I want to maintain my good health and put off my
death as long as possible. (Although if my health gets really bad,
I'm constantly suffering, and there's no medical hope of any improvement, suicide is the logical course: why continue when there's
nothing but suffering?)

I would engage in no risky actions then, nothing that significantly raises my risk of serious injury or death. I see a child
drowning, for example, and I could jump in and probably rescue
her. Well, is it a sure thing, given my swimming ability and the
situation? If there's any real risk to me, forget it! If I'm criticized,
I can always use the excuse (true or not) that I can't swim well.
If I feel guilty about letting the kid drown, there's always rationalization, cynicism, tranquilizing drugs, or any combination of these.

If others see me rescue her (assuming it's safe for me), it will
raise my social capital, so that argues for it, but if there's no one
around to see me or realize I had the opportunity to rescue her,
why bother?

As to maintaining my health, I would certainly get a reasonable
amount of exercise, especially of forms that I enjoy, eat a good diet,
as revealed by contemporary science, and avoid vices, like smoking,
that are very costly to the body. Not that it makes any difference
in scientistic materialism whether I die young or old, since it's a
purposeless universe, but I do seem to be stuck with this biological
drive to keep living, so as the popular phrase put it, I'll look out for
"number one."

While only I matter from this perspective, the fact remains that
my survival and pleasure is heavily dependent on my society, so
while at a rational level I don't give a damn what society likes or
dislikes, at a practical, Machiavellian level, I want to be seen as a
good citizen, deserving of aid and all social benefits. Particularly I
want my society to invest in the medical research that will maintain and improve my health and longevity — others' health and

longevity are quite secondary — and invest in things that will increase my safety from injury or death. That's where my and everyone else's taxes should go! Yes, the practicalities are complex: we have to support medical schools to train the future doctors (who'll help me), for example, rather than spend it all directly on my health and safety.

As to using my intelligence most effectively in the service of my biologically given needs, I would want to solve any problems in habits of thinking and feeling that interfered with optimal use of my reasoning ability, especially with the "obviously illogical" vestiges of superstitions and spiritual beliefs that I have. To be logical, all my beliefs should fit together and not contradict each other. So thoughts and actions like prayers, for example, would have to go. Not only would explicit prayers to the God of my childhood — clearly a neurotic leftover from childhood conditioning from the perspective of scientistic materialism — have to go but even vague, half-articulated thoughts that I hope "someone up there" or "to whom it may concern" would do something to make things turn out for the best (for me). My capacities and habits of thought and feeling should maximize my survival, health, and pleasure, and minimize suffering and danger.

There's the neurochemical-approach aspect to my life, of course, ranging from legal drugs my doctors could prescribe, which would dull down any remaining worries I have, to currently illegal but relatively safe drugs that would produce nice fantasies, conducive to pleasure. Rationality would require avoiding dangerous and addictive drugs, like heroin or crack, since the physical debilitation and earlier death is too high a price to pay for enhanced pleasure.

Long-term, I really needn't worry about the degradation of the planet, global warming, overpopulation, and so on. I'll probably, even with reasonable advances in medical science, only live another twenty or thirty years, so I'll likely be dead when civilization collapses. So I'll use resources to make myself happy now and not worry about the distant future. If I feel any guilt about this or worry about my descendants, that's meaningless social conditioning and biological built-ins manifesting; I should ignore them and get on with looking out for number one.

My personal reaction to these lines of thinking is one of revulsion, but then I'd just be thinking like lots of other "rational" people, wouldn't I?

CHAPTER 19

Bringing It All Back Home: Personal Reflections

When I was a child, I spoke as a child, I understood as a child, I thought as a child; but when I became a man, I put away childish things. — I Corinthians 13:11

GOD: A superhuman person regarded as having power over nature and human fortunes; a deity. Also, the deity of a specified area of nature, human activity, and so on.

SKEPTIC (late sixteenth century [origin: from Greek "skeptikos," plural "skeptikoi," from "skeptesthai," look about, consider, observe]: (2) A person who doubts the validity of accepted beliefs in a particular subject; a person inclined to doubt any assertion or apparent fact. (3) A person seeking the truth; an inquirer who has not yet arrived at definite convictions. — SHORTER OXFORD ENGLISH DICTIONARY, *6th ed., s.v. "god" and "skeptic"*

WHEN I'm functioning as a scientist, I try to be as objective as possible. I report the data, the facts of what I and others have observed, as completely and accurately as I can, and I work hard to keep my own hopes and fears, desires, and aversions out of reporting data or formulating possible explanations. When I theorize and present ideas about what this data means, I try to make it clear that this part is my or someone else's theory, not the data. This attitude carries over into the rest of my life too. It's not that I would be described as a "cold fish"; I don't habitually suppress my emotional and bodily responses to life: indeed I've devoted great effort to sensitizing, honoring, and educating my emotional and bodily "brains," to use Gurdjieff's term (1986), as part of developing my full humanity. But I take care not to confuse my ideas and feelings with the facts, insofar as I'm able.

But the material we've been discussing in this book isn't simply intellectually interesting, isn't mere facts; it has enormous personal implications for all of us.

Am I a meaningless accident in a meaningless cosmos, the result of zillions of meaningless molecular collisions that just happened to turn out this way? A meat-based computer that will soon die, whose life doesn't really matter to anything or anyone but my illusion of a self? Are you?

Or am I some sort of spiritual creature, potentially in touch with something greater and higher, as well as my biological and physical existence? Are you?

Should I live in accordance with that possibility? Should you?

So, how have I ended up after all this scientific and personal searching and thinking about our possible spiritual nature? Yes, I'm a scientist and a spiritual seeker, and many other things, each of which is just a part of being a whole human being. How do I see the world now, how do I live, given the kinds of things we've discussed in this book? It's not that I'm the model for how people should live — different strokes for different folks, as the saying goes — but sharing the views relevant to this book that I've worked out may be helpful for some readers as you formulate or modify your own views.

Let's start back at the beginning: When I was a child, I thought and felt as a child. My wonderful, loving grandmother, my Nana, took me to Sunday school and church, and if those places were good enough for someone as wonderful as her, they were good enough for me. If God was anything like my Nana, a source of unconditional love, comfort, and treats, he was indeed wonderful, and both Nana and my mother, although she didn't go to church herself, said it was so.

It was a simple but basically understandable worldview to my child mind, which, like most child minds, thought in absolutes. God had created the world and set up "the rules." We were to obey the rules. If we did, we were rewarded and, after death, went to heaven. If we didn't, we were punished and went to hell.

But it did get rather complicated at times. I can remember a kind of moment of awakening, being taught in Sunday school over and over that God was a god of love but also that he was a jealous and wrathful god, punishing not only sinners but also, as I recall it, the sinner's children and the sinner's children's children down to the seventh generation. Wow! This God fellow could really hold a grudge! (My memory was a bit exaggerated, because the Bible says that God visits the sins of the fathers on the children, even to the third and fourth generation [Exodus 20:5, 34:6–7; Deuteronomy 5:9] but not the seventh. Still, how incredibly mean!) I could almost never stay mad at anyone after a night's sleep. But this holding of grudges and retribution was a manifestation of God's love? And how could God be so incredibly mean as to punish innocent children? Something didn't compute.

As I mentioned earlier, by the time I was in my teens, I faced a serious struggle between my childhood religion (Lutheran) and modern thought and science. My grandmother had died, so I was no longer receiving that unconditional love to smooth over the rough spots of life. My mother was loving but not in an unconditional way, as my grandmother had been. I'd read extensively in science by then and loved it, but it was clear that a lot of the "facts" science had discovered didn't fit with my religion. I knew by then that many scientists dismissed all religion as primitive and psychopathological superstition that we'd be better off without, and it seemed clear that science was right about at least some of this. Like most teenagers I had also become very good at spotting the hypocrisy of adults, and too many of the adults in my church weren't living the beliefs they preached. Discovering psychic research and its modern form, parapsychology, was my vehicle for working toward a satisfactory resolution of religion or spirituality and science, as I hope this book has demonstrated in various ways.

It was not that there was some simple and final resolution of the conflict between science and spirit, but rather, a process of investigation and discrimination began for me that continues as central to my life. Learn as much as I can about many things; separate the wheat from the chaff when I can; the essential, valid, and nourishing from the superfluous, false, and toxic; and try to fit the knowledge together. Here are the claims of religions A, B, and C, and here's modern science and psychology: how do they cast light on each other?

Here's an example from my young adulthood: Freud and other psychoanalytic investigators demonstrated quite convincingly that some (they tended to claim all, but I'm always skeptical about any claims that something explains everything) of our feelings toward God are unconscious, emotionally driven manifestation of our feelings as young children toward our parents, projected outward onto the idea of God. There's clearly a lot of truth here. When we were infants and young children, our parents were amazingly superior to us, knowing so much, capable of doing such incredible things compared to us in our ignorance and helplessness. Naturally we loved and admired them (and perhaps feared and hated them too), and they were as gods to us.

But is our search for a god or worship of one nothing but a projection of these childhood feelings? Certainly such projections are likely to be there as part of our spiritual seeking, but might this be a distorting obstacle to overcome, rather than a reason for totally dismissing the spiritual?

I can remember a dramatic personal breakthrough one evening in the 1970s, while doing psychological work as part of my efforts toward spiritual growth: I suddenly realized that my childhood image of my mother was interposed on and relatively dominant over my conception of what God might be like! Particularly, my mother — bless her soul — was a perfectionist. But in this world, nothing ever quite comes up to the standards of a perfectionist, so it's one disappointment after another. I'd been implicitly thinking of God that way: I had to try and try to do my best, but nothing would ever be good enough to satisfy God. I had to recognize that aspect of my projection.

This was a very liberating insight, because I realized I actually knew nothing about the actual characteristics of whatever or whoever God might be, and I could look at that whole direction of spiritual reality anew, afresh, instead of with the implicit assumption that I would always fail to please a too perfectionistic mother-god. And just to make things more puzzling and interesting to me, this was a very unusual insight; it didn't feel like my regular psychological insights, which came from the usual "place" inside me where all my thoughts and feelings came from. This one experientially "zoomed in" from outside of me, to my left, as if something outside myself were giving me this insight, even though I was doing a psychotherapeutic process designed to provoke insight.

This is not to say, though, that we're completely full of irrational childhood ideas and feelings that must always be harshly uprooted and exterminated. A lot of our basic energy — and, I believe, spiritual nature and energy — is rooted in our childhood, and my best understanding is that we need to honor it, understand it, and do some selective weeding and fertilizing, not wholesale plowing up. This is personally hard for me, because I picked up a lot of my mother's perfectionism and thus tend to be hard on myself, but for me, at least, a gentler style of discovery and understanding works better than harsh rejection.

Returning to my personal story of trying to accommodate both religion and science, as I grew into adulthood, I trained in the sciences, first with the intention of becoming an electrical engineer — I had already learned enough electronics on my own to pass Federal Communications Commission examinations and become a licensed radio engineer with a First-Class Radiotelephone license — then to become a psychologist. In my psychological training I learned more and more about how to do science properly and, since I took a lot of clinical courses, more and more about psychopathology and the various ways we easily fool ourselves.

I'd like to say that I've learned enough now about how I fool myself and how others fool themselves that I never do it anymore. But while I can think of many instances in my life, such as the one just mentioned, where I've seen such distortions and eventually stopped or transcended them, by definition I can't see the ones I don't know about yet; I can only be alert to the possibility of distortion, to the signs that I might be fooling myself, such as finding I'm a lot more emotional about some idea or situation than it reasonably calls for, or that I have funny body feelings. The personal picture I'll draw next, then, while it's my best current understanding of myself and the world, is always open to revision if new facts, new understandings arise.

God

So what "happened" to God or, rather, to my conception of God, in my life? First, I've realized that while there might indeed be a greatly superior being (or perhaps lots of them), compared to me, I haven't had any direct experience of such a being, and thus must realize that what I think and feel about superior beings or God is largely just that, my ideas and feelings. Put in scientific terms, I have lots of theories and beliefs, as well as lots of descriptions of and theories about experiential data collected and experienced by others, but I don't have any direct data myself. In accordance with essential scientific practice and common sense, I need to hold my own theories and understandings lightly. And, especially important, I need to be aware of my emotional investments in various ideas about God if I hope to learn anything about this aspect of spirituality, rather than just cling to my own emotional hopes and fears.

A part of me has always longed for direct experience of contact with God or higher beings. Like all of us, I am a weak, vulnerable biological being in a big universe, and it would be nice to have some direct reassurance, beyond doubt, that everything will turn out all right, as Bucke had in his Cosmic Consciousness experience. Some people have experiences that give them such reassurance, and their descriptions of such experiences are data that I've studied. At the same time, I realize it's a certain kind of advantage that I haven't had such personal experiences: since my main work has been building bridges between essential science and essential spirituality, I can do it more effectively by being a practical, grounded scientist, because, out of prejudice, too many scientists and laypeople might automatically dismiss my work and arguments without really thinking about them if I were a "mystic."

At the same time I don't take my lack of direct, experiential certainty to mean I should live some sort of pale, wishy-washy life, where, believing I don't understand any ultimate truths, I don't commit myself to doing what I think is right. Understanding and accepting the tentativeness of my knowledge is one thing, and turning it into a psychological or spiritual defense mechanism to excuse avoiding grappling with the hard parts of life is quite another.

Second, while honoring and nourishing the child in me, that basic part of my being on which so much was constructed, my inner child still needs to be nourished and educated. An important part of this education and training is to learn to discriminate which parts of my childhood (and current) spiritual longings are actually spiritual longings and which parts are psychological needs that could be more healthfully satisfied on a more ordinary psychological level. When they're confused, we tend to debase the spiritual and overvalue the ordinary. Here's an example:

When I was nineteen, I saw Cecil B. DeMille's "The Ten Commandments" and was very moved by it. In my forties I saw the movie again but had meanwhile done a lot of psychological and spiritual growth work on myself, so I saw it with new eyes. And I was embarrassed! I especially loved the scene where Moses got angry with the Israelites and cast down and broke the tablets of the Commandments, with all hell threatening to break loose! Why was this scene so appealing to me? I realized I still had a lot of unresolved childhood anger at people who'd been cruel to me, and I wanted to hurt and punish them! But since I thought of myself as a good and spiritual person, a desire for revenge wasn't an allowable feeling. But righteous wrath, as Moses showed, was good! Some part of me was misusing my childhood spiritual feelings to justify feeling angry and wanting revenge on those damned sinners, those people who'd been cruel to me. I could have my cake and eat it too; I could punish those I didn't like while still feeling spiritual.

It was a sobering revelation. I had to learn to accept the fact that, of course, I'm human, and I don't like people who are cruel to me; nobody does. Of course, I would get angry and want to get back at them! Accepting this, then I could decide whether or not to act on those feelings and take responsibility for whatever I did, but I could stop fooling myself that I was somehow being spiritual and justly participating in the wrath of God unleashed on guilty sinners who deserved it.

Third, I've had to realize that I've projected a lot of my unresolved childhood conditioning on God in the form of automatically thinking of God as male, with lots of cultural reinforcement for that, unfortunately. After doing a lot of psychological growth work on my relationships with my parents, I've faced up to a lot of what I perceived as inadequacies on my father's part — not to mention my own! — such that I wanted or needed a powerful father figure in my life, and thus projected a lot of what I wanted onto my ideas of and feelings about God, the big "he." The rise of feminism in my lifetime has helped my attitudes and understandings, but I'm still working on semiconscious feelings here.

Fourth, I often have to look at my idea of what spiritual growth or enlightenment is, to bring my semiconscious and unconscious ideas about it to consciousness, so that they stop working in the background as biases that might distort my view of reality.

For example, in the last few years I've gotten an increasingly clear picture of my expectations of what a mystical "enlightenment" experience for me should be like, given the childhood roots of my spirituality. Since it involves (my ideas about) God and sets standards for God to live up to, one of my insights is to see the unconscious arrogance involved. "Look, superior being, this is how you should do it in order to come up to my standards." I learned from my perfectionist mother, it's no problem at all to set standards for God. When I can just look at these expectations as my personal psychological preferences and needs, though, not as arrogant, automatic injunctions, they're much less of a problem, because I can remember that reality is what it is and I'm reasonably good at coping with reality, even when it doesn't meet my "standards."

What were some of the expectations I discovered? They included that I would (1) have a mystical experience that solved all my problems, but (2) while it would be spiritually and emotionally overwhelming, it would come on gradually so as not to frighten me, while (3) it gave me the absolutely correct answers to all life's questions, "the rules," so that I'd never be in doubt about "the right thing to do." This would include, of course, (4) direct reassurances from God that I was okay, as well as (5) a guarantee that nothing would ever hurt or upset me in any way ever again, and that (6) everyone would recognize my spiritual superiority and respect me. Given how much I've always identified with being a good student, this revelatory experience would probably also (7) include getting some sort of certificate or diploma testifying to my enlightenment and spiritual superiority.

When I look at these expectations rationally, from my adult perspective, they're kind of embarrassing and ridiculous, as well as amusing. I doubt very much that real spirituality works that way or that I can make demands on an order of reality (I try to transcend the connotations of using the word "God" here) way beyond me as to how it should manifest. And yet they do represent longings from my childhood, still relevant in some ways, so I need to gently respect them even if I shouldn't hold onto them too tightly.

So what's my current working view of the spiritual and material nature of reality? It's a "working view" in the sense that it's not fixed or absolute; it's the best I can come up with at this time, but it's always open to change as I learn more.

How do I say these things? I don't want to say "I believe," because that has too much absolutism about it. "I postulate" sounds much too formal and stuffy. "I think that" seems kind of weak and evasive, and "My working hypothesis is" sounds much too formal. How about, "My current best bet is...?" That conveys the openness of my understanding to growth and change, while simultaneously making it clear that there are consequences from thinking and feeling about reality this way; it's a bet that there are stakes, that my life and happiness (and that of others) are on the line; it's not just idle speculation.

Spiritual Beings, Purposes, and Realities

My current best bet is that there's a real spiritual realm, as real or perhaps even "more real" (in some sense that's hard to understand in our ordinary state of consciousness) than ordinary material reality. My current best bet is that this spiritual realm has purpose and is intelligent and loving in some profound sense. My current best bet is that our human nature partakes of this spiritual nature. The deep experience of many mystics that we are one with all of reality, including spiritual reality, is about something vital and true. The several psychic ways we occasionally connect with each other (telepathy) and the material world (clairvoyance) are partial manifestations of this inherent connection with all of reality, spiritual as well as material.

Moving toward traditional specifics, how about God? Or gods? Angels? Demons? We're incredibly arrogant in regarding ourselves as so intelligent that we can dismiss the idea of the existence of any intelligent being who is superior to us in any way, so I'm betting that we should be open to such possibilities and actually investigate them, not just believe or disbelieve on the basis of conditioned childhood belief systems or reactions to them, rather than with any real looking at the data. At the same time we have to understand the numerous psychological functions such ideas can play in allowing us to be intellectually lazy (God or the devil did it, so I don't have to think about it) or morally irresponsible (it's God's will, it's the devil's work, or it's karma).

My current best bet is that there might be independently existing spiritual beings, and I work with two mutually helpful attitudes toward this possibility, one from Buddhism and one from G. I. Gurdjieff (1886?–1949).

Buddhism accepts the idea that there are all sorts of gods, goddesses, angels, demons, extraterrestrials, and so on. Everybody believed that during the period when the Buddha taught. But just because such beings are different and superior in some ways and inferior in others, before we try to get very involved with them, we have to ask, "Are they enlightened?" A being might have godlike powers but be quite neurotic and unenlightened. Buddhism generally doesn't put much emphasis on such beings, because its doctrines regard most of them as unenlightened.

The goal of Buddhism is for each of us to become enlightened, to eliminate all the psychological qualities that create useless suffering in us and others, and to discover our true spiritual nature. That nature is that we're all actually Buddha in essence, just "asleep" to our real nature at this time, caught up in our delusory dreams but able to wake up, end our personal suffering, and help each other. We can learn from enlightened beings, but we have to do the work ourselves; no other being can do the work of enlightenment for us. If help comes from a spiritual level or being, great; accept it, be thankful, and get on with the work of enlightenment. But don't mistake spiritual or psychic experiences per se as enlightenment. Even the gods, in Buddhism, are not enlightened, and eventually suffer as a consequence of their unenlightened behavior.

Gurdjieff expressed his advice here in a lovely, somewhat para-doxical form, by admonishing his students to work as if everything depended on work but pray as if everything depended on prayer.

The work admonition reminds us of the Buddhist injunction that enlightenment, rediscovering our true nature, comes from work, hard work and lots of it. Give such work your best efforts as if every-thing depends on it, as if nothing else matters. The second part cries out for and accepts help from a spiritual level when it's given. Pray as if nothing matters but divine grace. Holding both injunctions in mind, which isn't easy, can remind us to be humble, that we need help and guidance, but it also reminds us to keep doing our best to learn, grow, and manifest our spirituality.

So my current best bet is that there may well be spiritual beings that may help us, and I pray that they do exist and will help us, but meanwhile I focus on what I know how to do and what I can do for myself and others.

Survival of Death

The evidence for survival, in some sort of postmortem psychic or spiritual state, as reincarnation, or both, is among the many maybes as I've currently bet on it. Belief in some kind of survival is a psychologically dangerous idea in some ways, because it so readily provides a rationalization to not do your best or to not be adequately concerned about the conditions of ordinary life. So the poor suffer and are exploited? No problem; they'll get their reward in heaven if they obey the rules, or perhaps it's just their karma from past lives and there's nothing I can do about it. This kind of thinking is a too-convenient excuse for ignoring or exploiting others.

Nevertheless I'm betting that some sort of postmortem survival is possible and, importantly, that the kind of postmortem existence you have is strongly dependent on the way you live your life now. That is, I'm betting on causality, on karma, which is causality carr-ied from one lifetime to another, as part of the survival package. So I try to live a moral life, mainly for the inherent satisfaction in it, but also for the possibility that I'm creating karma for future lives.

I've expressed this bet on survival in an earlier chapter in the form of two expectations. First, I won't be surprised if, after the initial shock and confusion of death (I hope there's not too much of that!), I regain consciousness and am still existent. Second, I'll be quite surprised if I, my ordinary self, regains and maintains consciousness. That is, I'm quite impressed by our current evidence for postmortem states and reincarnation, even if I still list it among the many maybes, so I won't be surprised if I regain consciousness after I die, which, of course, will be very interesting to me and answer all sorts of questions I've wondered about. But, both my professional studies of psychology and my personal explorations have shown me just how much my sense of self, my particular "I," is shaped by and at least partially dependent on having a physical body in this material world. How much can "I" remain unchanged when my physical body no longer functions, shaping my experience? So "something," some deeper part of who I am — I think of it and experience it as my basic ability to be aware — may go on after death, but I don't think Charles T. Tart will persist too long as the being he is now, which is scary in some ways, because I like myself. In other ways, it's a quite liberating idea: may the worst parts fall away and the best parts go on in some form! Benjamin Franklin's self-written epitaph expresses my hopes quite well.

Benjamin Franklin's Final Epitaph

The body of

B. Franklin, Printer,

(Like the Cover of an Old Book,

Its Contents torn Out,

And Stript of its Lettering and Gilding)

Lies Here, Food for Worms.

But the Work shall not be Lost;

For it will (as he Believ'd) Appear once More

In a New and More Elegant Edition,

Revised and Corrected

By the Author.

You might notice that my current best bet on postmortem survival is a safe bet in an important way. Thinking that something interesting will happen after death makes current life more interesting and lowers my fear of death. But if I'm wrong and death is truly the end of consciousness, I'll never have to suffer the embarrassment of knowing that I was wrong.

There's also a psychological advantage to my attitude, based on what I've termed the Law of Experience. Given my engineering background, I think of it as

$$(Q)E = f(R,A)$$

Put simply, the quality of our experience, Q of E, is a function of the interaction between the actual reality we're experiencing, R, and our attitude, A, toward that experience. To take a simple example, if I hoped to win a big lottery and got a hundred-dollar win on my dollar ticket, I might curse my luck for not hitting the million-dollar jackpot and the whole experience would be one of suffering. A lot of people might see a hundred-to-one gain as quite positive. Applying this law to dying, if my attitude is that death is the absolute end, that all I've learned and accomplished in life is now lost, I suspect my dying will be experienced as much more painful than whatever its reality actually is, whereas if my attitude is that this process will be interesting, even if painful, and I'm probably going to get answers to all sorts of important questions once I reach the other side, I think I'll have a much better death.

I've left out one of the most widespread ideas about what happens after death, of course, and that is the idea of hell. I'm an optimist by nature and an idealist by choosing. If there's any kind of superior being such as God, then this being must be superior to me. I'm nowhere mean and petty enough to condemn anyone to eternal punishment, knowing how difficult it is to do the right things in this life, and I wouldn't expect it of God (which shows I'm rather like my mother; I have standards for God to live up to). Yes, there are hellish experiences in this life, some from actual physical suffering, many from psychological attitudes that distort our experience. Since my current best bet is that something like karma is real, that our past and current actions are constantly shaping our future — not totally determining it since we often can make new choices — perhaps there are even afterlife periods that seem hellish but still offer opportunities for learning and growth, and thus lead on to a better existence. Purgatory? Bardos? My bet is that I'll have some direct experiential data on this some day.

As I write this, I have a new insight: I'm really angry at the people who have such petty and warped conceptions of God that they made him into a blown-up version of an insecure, petty tyrant, ruling by force and needing to be praised all the time to soothe his insecure ego. All the useless psychological suffering such ideas have created! Okay, there probably have been lots of kings and despots who were like that and, unfortunately, lots of parents who were like that, but let's not confuse them with the idea of a truly superior being.

Organized Religions

Back in the introduction, I distinguished basic spirituality from organized religion. This book has been almost exclusively about basic spirituality, about the fact that we humans have certain kinds of experiences that point toward a larger, nonmaterial order of reality, and we have a lot of rigorous scientific data telling us to take these signs seriously; it's not just wish-fulfilling imaginings. We also looked at the four ways of knowing — experience, authority, reason, and revelation — and discussed that very useful way of combining them, through refining knowledge, resulting in essential science. So what do we make of organized religions then? Suppose we ask the question, has there been any progress in spirituality, as there has been in all the physical sciences in the last few centuries?

I'm inclined to argue that, by and large, the answer is no. Religions start from the way of experience: a founder has profound spiritual or psychic experiences, or both. While there are small numbers of people in all religious traditions who try to work from this basis, by themselves having and expanding the basic kinds of experiences that started it all, their efforts are swamped by the theoreticians, the people who make some kind of intellectual and emotional "sense" of the experiences. These people too often have had no direct experiences themselves, but they're smart people, capable organizers, creative theorizers. The way of reason is very attractive! I know from far too much personal experience how seductive a good idea can be!

So far the process is fairly parallel to essential science, but now a major change in direction takes place. The organizers of most religions make their theories into doctrines, too often doctrines that must be believed or you'll be damned! The scientists, in contrast, delight in their clever theories that make sense of the data, of their experiences, but then submit (even if grudgingly) to the discipline of essential science that these theories may be the best that they can think of at the moment, but they're always subject to further tests, refinement, and possible rejection.

There are innumerable human complexities in both these processes, of course. Both religions and science, for example, become embedded in the social structure in ways that reinforce themselves. Children are taught the dominant religion at home, in church or temple, and in special schools. The public schools in most Western countries teach the findings of science, as they're known at the time. Shaping children's minds can both implicitly and consciously shape the way they perceive the world to fit the doctrines and theories of religion and science. The difference is that religion is almost never taught with the attitude, "This is the best sense we can make of these things so far; we hope you find it useful, but ask questions and stay open to your own experience, and perhaps you can come up with a better understanding." Science, when properly taught, is taught with exactly that attitude. Religions are too often taught with an attitude that you must not question the doctrines and that you're a bad person if you do and you'll be punished. Properly, science is taught in a way that stimulates wonder and questioning.

Progress in spirituality and progress in religion — will we develop experimentally oriented spiritual systems and religions that can respect and profit from old ideas, the way of authority, but go on to test, refine, reject, and expand our basic knowledge of spirituality?

That's a very big question, beyond the scope of this book, although I've worked at it a little in Appendix 4, on transpersonal psychology.

Back to Death

We've looked at various kinds of evidence suggesting that some aspect of our consciousness might survive bodily death. Examining evidence involves evaluation, rationality, and thinking, but as we discussed earlier, this is much more than a "rational" issue, for at some level or levels we're usually terrified at the thought of, much less the reality of, death. How rational can we be about it? Can we get beyond the extreme of unquestioned religious faith, on the one hand, and just as rigid a materialistic denial of the possibility of any kind of survival on the other? Most would suspect that this fear of death is built into the hardwiring of our nervous systems, so we can never really get beyond it. Does any evidence of survival, no matter how strong, really overcome such innate fear of death?

Thinking about this recently, I remembered something that happened or, more accurately, didn't happen, when I came close to death a few years ago. For several years now, I've had chronic atrial fibrillation, A-fib, a heart condition where the upper chambers of the heart, the atria, have chaotic and rapid electrical firings. Since the main pumping chambers, the ventricles, receive the overly rapid electrical signals from the atria, a fast and erratic heartbeat occurs. If the atrial fibrillation rate can be controlled, it's usually not much of a problem. When the rate isn't well controlled, one can get light-headed and even lose consciousness. The most worrisome complication of atrial fibrillation is due to its propensity for blood clots to form in the heart, which can lead to a stroke if the clot were to travel to the brain.

Sound a little scary? I certainly understood it to be that way when I was initially hospitalized for it and then told I had to be on blood-thinning medication for the rest of my life to reduce the chance of clots, as well as other medication to try to control the A-fib itself. It was a powerful reminder of my mortality! My heart, not some abstract heart, could go on me! Not that I panicked or brooded too much about it — I'm usually not that type — but I gave it serious attention.

While my cardiologists were trying to find the best medication to control my A-fib, I read about a treatment that European doctors had found very helpful, although it hadn't been used much yet in America. There's a drug called Flecanide that tends to regularize the heart rate in A-fib, and some people take regular daily doses of it for this purpose. I didn't like the regular-doses idea, because I read about a lot of possible undesirable side effects of daily usage. The European treatment, which they called a "pill-in-the-pocket" approach, was not to take Flecanide regularly but to carry some of the drug with you at all times and, if you had a strong A-fib episode, take triple what the normal daily dose would be. They reported that in almost all cases the A-fib attack quickly subsided and there were no recurrences for some time.

That sounded like a good idea to me, but Flecanide is a potentially dangerous drug in some people, so it has to first be administered while you're hospitalized, with your heart continuously monitored, to be certain you don't have an adverse reaction to it before it will be prescribed for daily use. My then cardiologist — let's call him Dr. A — arranged a day's hospitalization so we could see if I had an adverse reaction to the drug. I didn't, so he wrote me a prescription for it. On examining the prescription and my hospital record, though, I found that Dr. A had not tested me at the triple dose of the pill-in-the-pocket approach but at the usual daily dose for regular use the rest of my life, and thus was expecting me to take the drug daily.

I was angry. I had made it clear to Dr. A on several occasions that I didn't want to chance the potential nasty side effects of the daily-dose approach and he was supposed to be testing the safety of the pill-in-the-pocket approach. Because both my wife and I had already noticed several times that Dr. A had a strong tendency to not hear what I was saying but be caught up in his "expert opinion," that was the last time I consulted him.

Fortunately, I'd already gotten a second opinion from another cardiologist, Dr. B, who listened, as well as applied his expertise. He checked with several American colleagues, who agreed that the pill-in-the-pocket approach looked promising. Since I was scheduled to see Dr. B for a routine appointment in a few weeks and the Flecanide seemed to be safe for me at the normal dose, when my appointment with Dr. B came up, I took the triple dose an hour before it, even though my A-fib was mild at the time, figuring that if there were any mild adverse effects from the higher dose, it was much better to experience them when Dr. B would be examining me than when I was off on a trip somewhere (my wife and I camp a lot), far from medical attention. But I expected no problems, given what I knew and the "okay" result at the usual daily-dose level in the earlier hospitalization.

By the time I saw Dr. B, my body felt weird. He took a quick recording of my heart's electrical activity and, after looking at it, got me in a wheelchair in seconds and pushed me through the hospital corridors to the emergency room! I was in ventricular tachycardia, the main pumping chambers of my heart beating at more than two hundred beats per minute. This heart arrhythmia can easily degenerate into ventricular fibrillation, a lethal heart rhythm. I was rushed into emergency, a medical team of a half-dozen doctors and nurses seemingly appeared from nowhere, an intravenous line was inserted in me, electrodes were taped to my chest, and a mild sedative and analgesic drug, Brevitol, was shot into my veins. I don't remember the actual shocking, because the Brevitol knocked me out temporarily, but the shocking stopped the ventricular tachycardia and restored a normal heart rhythm.

What I found rather amazing, not at the time but with the clarity of hindsight, is that I didn't get very excited by all this. Yes, it was quite clear to me that I was having a potentially fatal reaction to the Flecanide and that the odds were high that I might die before the medical staff could do anything about it. But until the Brevitol made me stupid, I was alert, calm, and cooperative, and asked questions of the doctors and nurses, because I was interested in what they were doing. I was practically oriented, such as making sure that my wife, who was out in the cardiology clinic waiting room, was informed about what was happening to me, because I didn't want her to worry that I was in the clinic for such a long time. Not that the news that I was being rushed to the ER would be an improvement, but she would want to know. I thought about the possibility that some part of my mind might survive if I did die and figured it would be very interesting to finally have a direct, personal answer to such questions, but I also knew that I enjoyed life and felt that there was a lot I'd still like to do (like writing this book), including activities that might help people. So I definitely preferred not to die at that time, but tried to maintain an attitude of, "Thy will be done"; meanwhile there was no reason not to be present, alert, helpful, and cheerful.

Being this way seemed quite normal and appropriate during the experience. It's only in retrospect that I wonder why I didn't panic. That would've been quite "normal"! Why did I stay in clear contact with everything happening in and around me instead of tuning out to try to avoid realizing I might be dying? Why in the world was I finding my real chance of dying interesting?

Insofar as I understand myself, I have to give part of the credit for my clarity and calmness to the psychological training in meditation and mindfulness that I've been involved in over the years. But part of the credit must go to my knowledge of the research on postmortem survival. I wasn't convinced that if I died, the scientistic materialist's "final failure" experience awaited, nothingness, but rather that I might well be able to continue living, growing, and serving. That was a comforting thought.

This is all a retrospective look at a personal experience, of course, and I could be reading things into it that don't really support my thesis that knowing about the evidence for survival can be helpful in facing the stress of impending death, but what way do we have of making sense of life and preparing for death other than working with our own and others' knowledge and experience?

This personal experience doesn't carry the kind of weight and deep conviction that a personal OBE or NDE would that I'll definitely survive death in some form, the feeling those experiencing such phenomena have that they "know" they'll survive rather than "believe" they will, nor does it guarantee that I won't panic or otherwise have a miserable time the next time I come close to death. I can't help but envy those lucky people who've had such OBE and NDE experiences, and transcended the fear of death so deeply. If you're such a person, don't worry; I'm not "jealous" in any negative sense, I'm happy that you've been blessed this way. For you this book has probably been too mild, too conservative. But for the many like me, who haven't had this kind of life-changing psychic or mystical experience, who need to make the best guesses about life and the way to live it that we can, based on our own and others' knowledge and experience, I hope this survey of why it's sensible to be both scientifically oriented and spiritually inclined will help to smooth the path of your life.

Science, Spirit, and Reality

I've always been very curious about many things, and while I can handle it, I don't like to be fooled, either by others or, more embarrassingly, by myself. Essential science, as a disciplined way of investigating and thinking, as a systematic refinement of common sense, has thus served me well both personally and professionally. Observe the facts as clearly and objectively as possible, come up with possible explanations, make some predictions from those explanations, and test them against new observations. Share all this with peers you respect, and listen to their feedback. Do this with a humility that recognizes that you can be wrong and fixated in your error, but do prefer truth over just sticking to your opinions. Slowly, sometimes erratically, as we do get sidetracked by our limitations and biases, but in the long run steadily, we develop understandings of reality that work better and better.

I've shared with you my five decades of observing and collecting facts that have consequences for trying to understand the spiritual. These have been largely the basic facts of parapsychology, the solid and some of the not so solid, but possible, the big five and the many maybes.

So reality is, in many understandable and useful ways, "material" in a classical, Newtonian sense, a bunch of "things" that bump into each other and cause reactions. But this material reality leaves the existence of mind itself a great puzzle and has no room at all for "spiritual" things or beings. Modern physics, though, with its quantum phenomena, has the solid Newtonian materiality as a special case, not the be-all and end-all, and suggests a "nonlocal" world with mysterious, instantaneous connections all through the universe. I haven't discussed quantum views here and their implications — again, I highly recommend Dean Radin's book for that (2006) — because I know how little I understand quantum physics and I don't want to misrepresent it. But I do know the data of parapsychology, and this data soundly shows that Newtonian materiality and its lack of a place for spiritual possibilities is not enough. The human mind sometimes behaves as if it's "nonlocal," connected to other minds and the material world through telepathy and clairvoyance, connected to the future with precognition, perhaps to the past with postcognition, and sometimes able to affect the material world (and other minds?) through PK and psychic healing effects. That's the sort of mind that would be basically "spiritual," a mind that involved the brain but was more than the brain, a mind that transcended the usual limits of ordinary matter, a mind intimately connected to other minds at some level, and a mind that was open to — ah yes, open to what?

And Where Might Science and Spirituality Go?

Open to what, exactly? This is a nice phrase, and a meaningful one for those who are curious and those who are scientifically inclined. One of the things I like about essential science is that it's based on data as the primary source, so no matter how satisfied or fulfilled you are by a particular theory or explanation, that theory is always open to upgrading or rejection or modification if new data comes in that requires it.

I've tried to show with this book that it's sensible and reasonable to be both scientifically inclined and serious about seeking the spiritual. Given the enormous amount of unnecessary suffering people have undergone who think science has shown all their spiritual impulses and experiences to be nonsense, if I've helped anyone feel better about being both ways, scientific and spiritual, I'm quite pleased.

But that's only the beginning, of course. If we developed sciences that were not only open to spirituality but also wanted to help advance spirituality, and spiritual systems that were not only open to science but also wanted to help advance science, where might this openness take us?

Advance spirituality? Sometimes, as I mentioned earlier, I enjoy asking spiritually inclined friends, partly teasingly but really very seriously, "Has there been any progress in spirituality in the last few centuries?"

I don't mean surface things like spiritual ideas being more widely available or the number of believers in particular religions increasing; I have a practical orientation. Are spiritual or religious training systems significantly more efficient than they used to be in making people more intelligent, wise, and compassionate?

If you asked this kind of question about medicine, for example, or just about any other field where essential science has been applied, the answer is a resounding yes! Diseases that were fatal a century or two ago are now routinely cured, for example. But are there any spiritual systems that can say something like, "It used to be that only N percent of our students reached such and such levels of performance, enlightenment, or salvation, and now it's three times as high." You hear a lot of complaints in spiritual circles about the degenerate times we live in — certainly that's part of reality — but that kind of thinking, regardless of what truth value it has, can also serve as an excellent way of not facing up to a lack of progress.

Thinking about spiritual progress is a whole book in itself, but as a final note in this book, I'll give one example of where we might go, a "dream project" I've hoped would come about for a long time, although it's too late in my life for me to start it. This dream is to make spirituality more "efficient" by improving one of its principal methods, meditation.

A spiritually inclined life is much more than just practicing some special technique like meditation, of course, but let's focus on that here.

Some years ago I was talking with my friend and colleague, Shinzen Young, who is, in my not-so-humble opinion, one of the best meditation teachers in the world. A native of Los Angeles, he's proficient in several Asian languages and spent many years as a monk studying under various masters in the East before returning to the United States to teach and continue his own development. He also knows a great deal about how Buddhism, his primary interest, had to adapt itself to the various cultures it moved into in the course of its history, and has tried many experiments to make the basic meditation technique he teaches, insight meditation, or vipassana, work more successfully for Western students. Take a look at his website (*www.shinzen.org*) if you're interested; there's fascinating material there.

During the course of our conversation, we got on to the question of how well meditation "works" for most people, and Shinzen's observation shocked me. He noted that when he taught a course or workshop introducing Westerners to meditation, it worked well enough that just about everyone indicated that he or she would make meditation a regular part of life. If he came back a year later, though, and 5 percent were still meditating, he felt quite successful as a meditation teacher.

I couldn't believe it! My model of teaching is Western educational institutions. If we admitted students and 80 to 95 percent were still enrolled for the second year, we'd be doing well, pretty much as expected. But a 95 percent dropout rate? Unheard of! With such a rate, I'd be convinced that we, the faculty, were rotten teachers! Something was badly wrong with our educational program! Certainly a few would drop out because they didn't have enough motivation, and a few would drop out because they didn't have the needed talent, but 95 percent? And here I thought Shinzen was an excellent meditation teacher.

Shinzen noted that this was not just his personal experience; it was also the experience of the many Western meditation teachers he knew. Further, it was like that among the venerable Eastern teachers — and they didn't worry about it. If they thought about it, the enormous dropout rate was attributed to karma. If you had enough positive karma from your past lives, you came around seeking meditation instruction. If you had even more good karma, you stuck around and learned; if not, you drifted off. If you accumulated more good karma in the future, maybe you came around again a few lifetimes down the road.

Well, maybe. Maybe reincarnation and karma are real, and

the vast majority who show an interest in meditation don't have enough good karma or personal development to stick with it. But this idea can also function as a great rationalization for teaching very ineffectively. "I'm teaching just fine; there are no faults with me; it's the poor karma of my students."

Shinzen has been experimenting with more effective teaching methods for years and has, I believe, had some notable successes. Also, people who learn meditation today as the only effective way to deal with chronic-pain problems, a whole new Western development (Young 2005, Kabat-Zinn 1990), stick with it much better, because they have the motivation of enduring horrible pain if they don't.

So here's the problem: one of the principal methods of spiritual development, meditation, apparently can't be taught effectively to the vast majority of Westerners.

I'd been given meditation instruction by a number of teachers over the years and, until I met Shinzen, I'd long ago decided that whatever special talent it took to be a meditator, I didn't have it, so I'd given it up. I'd also heard many spiritual teachers talk about how their system was individualized for particular students to get best results, but I often have the impression that it's generally a one-size-fits-all approach: a given teacher teaches the way his teacher taught. Was my own failure, or that of many others, to get anywhere with meditation really a function of my bad karma (I could theorize that my karma might be much worse than I can imagine, but who knows?) or more that the teaching methods don't match the needs of individual students in our times?

If friends or students come to me saying that they want to become more spiritual and asking what they should do or what teacher or system they should study with, my honest answer is that I don't know. I don't know what's best in general, and I certainly don't know what's best for individuals. They'll just have to try a variety of systems and see what happens in each (I have some more detailed advice along those lines in my *Waking Up* book [published by iUniverse, 1988]). The risk is that, at best, they'll waste a lot of time doing spiritual practices and meditations that really aren't suitable for who they are and, at worst, get discouraged or be damaged by unsuitable practices.

So back to my dream project. We take some very large number, say a hundred thousand, of people who are starting down various spiritual paths, and we give them extensive psychological testing. We don't know enough yet to know what psychological tests would really be effective for what we want to know, so we just give an awful lot. And then we follow these students up every few years and collect statistics. How many people of personality type P went into Zen, say? How long did they last? Were any hurt? Do any feel they have made significant spiritual progress? Were any enlightened? Did any go nuts? Don't even ask at this point how in the world we'll measure enlightenment! But we can work toward it. Some might find a technical discussion of some of the dimensions of "enlightenment" useful (Tart 2003).

When we've collected many years of such data, we can do brute-force, empirical correlations and develop a way of testing that can give people more specific individual guidance. Then a student asks me what spiritual path to try, and I have her take the developed test, and I end up giving answers on the order of, say, "For your type, avoid Zen; there's a 2 percent enlightenment rate after fifteen years but a 12 percent psychosis rate; that's a pretty high risk. Sufism, on the other hand, has a 15 percent strong spiritual growth rate for your type with only a 1 percent psychosis rate."

A dream? Yes. But in the long term, we do need to use science to help our spirituality and vice versa. I'll say some more about these kinds of possibilities in appendix 4. I hope some of you dreamers out there will help make this kind of progress real!

A Final Ending or a Beginning?

Let me end by sharing a beautiful Tibetan prayer* usually done at the end of periods of spiritual practice, to dedicate whatever merit the practice has created to the betterment and ultimate enlightenment of all beings. This is Sogyal Rinpoche's translation (1992). The bulk of my "spiritual practice" is the research and writing I've been doing, and while I'm not too impressed with the "power" of my practice, it does aim toward truth, so in the spirit of this dedication prayer, I pray:

By the power and the truth of this practice,

May all beings have happiness,

And the causes of happiness,

Be free of sorrow,

And the causes of sorrow,

And never be separated from the sacred happiness,

Which is sorrowless.

May they live in equanimity,

Without too much attachment

Or too much aversion,

And live, believing

In the equality

Of all that lives.

From the Tibetan Book of Living and Dying *by Sogyal Rinpoche and edited by Patrick Gaffney and Andrew Harvey, Copyright © 1993 by Rigpa Fellowship. Reprinted by permission of HarperCollins publishers.*

CHAPTER 20

Returning to Mystical Experience

MYSTICAL (English, eighteenth century [origin: formed as "mystic"; see "-ical"]): (1) Having an unseen, unknown, or mysterious origin, character, or influence; of hidden or esoteric meaning. (2) Chiefly Christian church. Having a spiritual character or significance that transcends human understanding. (b) Designating or pertaining to the branch of theology relating to direct communion of the soul with God. Also, of, pertaining to, or characteristic of mystics; relating to or of the nature of mysticism. — SHORTER OXFORD ENGLISH DICTIONARY, *6th ed., s.v. "mystical"*

I WISH I could leave you, dear reader, with final, absolutely certain and wonderful answers to all our questions about science and spirituality, the ultimate meaning of life, and what to do about it — but I don't know these answers. I do believe in (the possibility of) progress, though, and that each of us individually, as well as collectively, can learn enough to enrich our lives, to make them more fulfilling and interesting, and to move slowly ahead in knowledge. I hope I've aroused your curiosity, as well as provided an interesting look at this area of science and spirituality, and I want to end by circling back to a most interesting and vital experience or knowing that's potentially available to us.

In the introduction, we looked at Richard Maurice Bucke's 1872 Cosmic Consciousness experience and asked some questions about it, questions that are of vital importance for human life.

Here's his experience again (Bucke 1961, 7–8):

> It was in the early spring at the beginning of his thirty-sixth year. He and two friends had spent the evening reading Wordsworth, Shelley, Keats, Browning, and especially Whitman. They parted at midnight, and he had a long drive in a hansom (it was in an English city). His mind, deeply under the influences of the ideas, images, and emotions called up by the reading and talk of the evening, was calm and peaceful. He was in a state of quiet, almost passive enjoyment. All at once, without warning of any kind, he found himself wrapped around, as it were, by a flame-colored cloud. For an instant he thought of fire, some sudden conflagration in the great city; the next he knew that the light was within himself. Directly afterwards came upon him a sense of exultation, of immense joyousness, accompanied or immediately followed by an intellectual illumination quite impossible to describe. Into his brain streamed one momentary lightning flash of the Brahmic Splendor which has ever since lightened his life; upon his heart fell one drop of Brahmic Bliss, leaving thenceforward for always an aftertaste of heaven. Among other things he did not come to believe, he *saw* and *knew* that the Cosmos is not dead matter but a living Presence, that the soul of man is immortal, that the universe is so built and ordered that without any peradventure, all things work together for the good of each and all, that the foundation principle of the world is what we call love and that the happiness of everyone is, in the long run, absolutely certain. He claims that he learned more within the few seconds during which the illumination lasted than in previous months or even years of study and that he learned much that no study could ever have taught.
>
> The illumination itself continued not more than a few moments, but its effects proved ineffaceable; it was impos-

sible for him ever to forget what he at that time saw and knew; neither did he, or could he, ever doubt the truth of what was then presented to his mind.

I presented this account as data, as a conscientious report of an experience of a fellow human being. Essential science, proper science, begins with data, theorizes about it — "what does it mean?" — and comes back to data to check on the usefulness of theories. Does my theory usefully predict and account for new data? Data is supreme.

The theoretical explanation of Bucke's spiritual experience from the viewpoint of materialistic scientism is quite straight-Forward: psychiatrist or not, there was something wrong with him. His brain malfunctioned in some way and gave him a deep conviction of the truth of things, which is obviously false. We have no souls, we're not immortal, there's no inherent meaning in the universe, much less all things working together for the good of each and all, and so on. Bucke's account doesn't really deserve the name of data; it's nonsense and it and similar reports can be disregarded.

Essential science, proper science, as opposed to scientism, doesn't cavalierly throw out data just because it makes no "sense" in terms of the theories we're intellectually (and emotionally) attached to. If the data is reliable — comes from trustworthy sources and shows consistency — it must be worked with.

So was Bucke just having some sort of odd brain stroke, a unique and peculiar malfunction? Or was his Cosmic Consciousness experience at least a basic possibility of human experience, regardless of how we want to assess its value in telling us about the nature of reality?

Let's jump ahead more than a century to a life-changing experience of my friend and colleague Allan Smith. In 1976 Allan was a young physician and anesthesiologist, devoting himself to research. He had a secure university position, had already won a national prize for his research, and had a brilliant career ahead of him. An atheist, he had no interest in religious or spiritual matters and certainly had never heard of Richard Maurice Bucke or Cosmic Consciousness. Like many California professionals in the 1970s, he had occasionally tried marijuana, without ever experiencing anything like a "mystical experience," and had never tried more-powerful, psychedelic drugs. And yet, here's what "spontaneously" happened to him (Smith and Tart 1998, 97–98)(55):

> My Cosmic Consciousness event [he later learned the classical name for this experience] occurred unexpectedly while I was alone one evening and was watching a particularly beautiful sunset. I was sitting in an easy chair placed next to floor-to-ceiling windows that faced northwest. The sun was above the horizon and was partially veiled by scattered clouds, so that it was not uncomfortably bright. I had not used any marijuana for about a week previously. On the previous evening I probably had wine with dinner; I do not remember the quantity, but two glasses would have been typical. Thus, we would not have expected any residual drug effects.
>
> The Cosmic Consciousness experience began with some mild tingling in the perineal area, the region between the genitals and anus. The feeling was unusual but was neither particularly pleasant nor unpleasant. After the initial few minutes, I either ceased to notice the tingling or did not remember it.
>
> I then noticed that the level of light in the room as well as that of the sky outside seemed to be increasing slowly. The light seemed to be coming from everywhere, not only from the waning sun. In fact, the sun itself did not give off a strong glare. The light gave the air a bright, thickened quality that slightly obscured perception rather than sharpened it. It soon became extremely bright, but the light was not in the least unpleasant. Along with the

light came an alteration in mood. I began to feel very good, then still better, then elated. While this was happening, the passage of time seemed to become slower and slower. The brightness, mood elevation, and time slowing all progressed together. It is difficult to estimate the time period over which these changes occurred, since the sense of time was itself affected. However, there was a feeling of continuous change, rather than a discrete jump or jumps to a new state. Eventually, the sense of time passing stopped entirely. It is difficult to describe this feeling, but perhaps it would be better to say that there was no time, or no sense of time. Only the present moment existed.

My elation proceeded to an ecstatic state, the intensity of which I had never even imagined could be possible. The white light around me merged with the reddish light of the sunset to become one all enveloping, intense undifferentiated light field. Perception of other things faded. Again, the changes seemed to be continuous. At this point, I merged with the light. and everything, including myself, became one unified whole. There was no separation between myself and the rest of the universe. In fact, to say that there was a universe, a self, or any "thing" would be misleading — it would be an equally correct description to say that there was "nothing" as to say that there was "everything." To say that subject merged with object might be almost adequate as a description of the entrance into Cosmic Consciousness, but during Cosmic Consciousness there was neither "subject" nor "object." All words or discursive thinking had stopped and there was no sense of an "observer" to comment or to categorize what was "happening." In fact, there were no discrete events to "happen," just a timeless, unitary state of being.

Cosmic Consciousness is impossible to describe, partly because describing involves words, and the state is one in which there were no words. My attempts at description here originated from reflecting on Cosmic Consciousness soon after it had passed and while there was still some "taste" of the event remaining.

Perhaps the most significant element of Cosmic Consciousness was the absolute knowingness that it involves. This knowingness is a deep understanding that occurs without words. I was certain that the universe was one whole and that it was benign and loving at its ground. Bucke's experience was similar. He knew, "...that the universe is so built and ordered that without any peradventure, all things work together for the good of each and all, that the foundation principle of the world is what we call love and that the happiness of every one is, in the long run, absolutely certain" (8). The benign nature and ground of being, with which I was united, was God.

However, there is little relation between my experience of God as ground of being and the anthropomorphic God of the Bible. That God is separate from the world and has many human characteristics. "He" demonstrates love, anger, and vengeance, makes demands, gives rewards, punishes, forgives, etc. God as experienced in Cosmic Consciousness is the very ground or "beingness" of the universe and has no human characteristics in the usual sense of the word. The universe could no more be separate from God than my body could be separate from its cells. Moreover, the only emotion that I would associate with God is love, but it would be more accurate to say that God is love than God is loving. Again, even characterizing God as love and the ground of being is only a metaphor, but it is the best that I can do to describe an indescribable experience.

The knowingness of Cosmic Consciousness permanently convinced me about the true nature of the universe.

However, it did not answer many of the questions that (quite rightly) seem so important to us in our usual state of consciousness. From the perspective of Cosmic Consciousness, questions like, "What is the purpose of life?" or "Is there an afterlife?" are not answered because they are not relevant. That is, during Cosmic Consciousness ontologic questions are fully answered by one's state of being, and verbal questions are not to the point.

Eventually, the Cosmic Consciousness faded. The time changes, light, and mood elevation passed off. When I was able to think again, the sun had set and I estimate that the event must have lasted about twenty minutes. Immediately following return to usual consciousness, I cried uncontrollably for about a half hour. I cried both for joy and for sadness, because I knew that my life would never be the same.

Reflecting on the long-term effects of his Cosmic Consciousness experience, Allan writes (Smith and Tart 1998, 101–02):

Cosmic Consciousness had a major impact on the course of my life. I had received a national prize for my research and had a grant funded for five years, but any interest I had in becoming a famous academician evaporated. My research seemed more like an interesting puzzle than work of immense importance to the world. I left my secure and successful university faculty position and supported myself as a part-time freelance clinician. I needed time to explore spirituality and to integrate the Cosmic Consciousness experience into my life. Those explorations included theology, psychology, mysticism, stern religion, parapsychology, consciousness studies, and holistic health. Eventually, I earned a MA in Consciousness Studies and another in Theology. Since Cosmic Consciousness, I have not had a "career" in the usual sense of the word.

One important aftereffect of Cosmic Consciousness that I soon discovered was the ability to create a subtle shift in consciousness. By quieting myself within, my inner mental chatter almost stopped, and I became calm and present centered. Perception of the world and myself were both especially clear. The world seemed benign and "right" with everything as it was "supposed to be." There was a great sense of inner peace. As the years passed since Cosmic Consciousness, my ability to attain this state at will has diminished. When it does occur, it seems less profound than previously. I am personally very sad at this loss.

Cosmic Consciousness did not make me into an instant saint or enlightened being. I still occasionally lose my temper, worry, judge people, and need ego support. But from the time immediately following Cosmic Consciousness, there were lasting personality changes. My general anxiety level was considerably reduced and remains low. I do not (usually) strive at living but truly enjoy it. When I do "lose it," there is a subtle way in which I can mentally "step back" and see the real significance (or lack thereof) of whatever disturbed me. I have not been able to return to Cosmic Consciousness, although I have a real longing to do so. However, I can usually recall enough of the experience to know that the world is benign and that my ordinary consciousness phenomenal experience can only hint at the true nature of reality.

The Cosmic Consciousness experience occurred in 1976. I did not make any notes until about a month later. Unfortunately, those original notes are lost. Even so, I feel quite confident that my memory of the essential aspects of Cosmic Consciousness is accurate. There are several reasons for this belief. (1) The Cosmic Consciousness experience was the most powerful event of my life, and such a momentous experience is not possible to forget. (2) From the early weeks afterwards, I compared my experience to published accounts of Cosmic Consciousness. The comparisons constitute an independent way to stabilize the memory. (3) I frequently review the experience as a technique to achieve inner peace. (4) My remembered accounts are similar to the accounts reported in the literature. In addition, many other Cosmic Consciousness experiencers have reported that their experiences have remained fresh after the passage of many years (James 1925, Bucke 1961). We cannot claim that memory is infallible, and the long period between the events and the report is unfortunate. However, we do believe it very likely that the above phenomenal report has not been significantly distorted by the passage of time. Furthermore, my belief that my memory is accurate is data: Cosmic Consciousness produces that feeling.

Besides the beauty of Smith's account, I was impressed, on first hearing it, with its close parallels to Bucke's account when Smith had, back in 1976, never heard of Bucke or anything like it. It is similar to the way NDEs seem to have some kind of archetypal reality, because there's so much core similarity in them among people from different cultures and religions. Thus the NDE didn't seem accountable for a simple hallucination based on a person's religious upbringing. Similarly the parallels between Bucke's and Allan Smith's accounts, a century and massive cultural change apart, as well as similar accounts by others, impress me: Cosmic Consciousness is an archetypal human potentiality, regardless of how we otherwise interpret it. I think it's time we applied essential science to studying things like Cosmic Consciousness: what is its nature, how can it be induced, what kinds of effects does it have on people's lives, how can the experience be healthfully integrated into ordinary life, and so on. That's how science and spirituality will aid each other in ways that will benefit us all!

Our main concern in this book has been the useless and unnecessary suffering caused by personally internalized scientistic models of humanity that completely reject the spiritual, that see us as nothing but meat computers in a meaningless material universe. I've argued that rigorously using the same scientific method, essential science, that has led to such great success in understanding and engineering the material world, leads us to a picture of humans having a nonmaterial, spiritual aspect to our reality. I'm proud to be both a scientist and a spiritual seeker. If you're a scientist, I hope you can be both scientist and spiritual seeker. If you're not a scientist by profession but, like most moderns, value real scientific method over scientism, I hope you, too, can be both "scientist" and "spiritual seeker."

When we first looked at Bucke's experience, I raised some questions. What if...

- ...Bucke's (and Smith's) experience is literally true?

- ...the cosmos is indeed not dead matter but a living presence?

- ...we have souls that are immortal?

- ...the universe is so built and ordered that, without any peradventure, in spite of all the apparent evil in the world, all things work together for the good of each and all?

- ...the foundation principle of the world is what we call love?

- ...and the happiness of every one of us is, in the long run, absolutely certain?

My best guesses at this stage of my knowledge — remember, I have no absolute truths to give, just my best judgments — about them is as follows.

What if Bucke's (and Smith's) experience is literally true?
As to the literal truth of Bucke's and Smith's experiences, well, I try
to never take anything literally, as if the particular description given
of something were the best possible, absolutely true description
of its reality. I place a high value on these descriptions — Bucke
and Smith are intelligent people doing their best to describe what
happened to them — but we're all creatures of our times, our
culture, our beliefs, our hopes and fears, and the limits of our
language. Indeed I think a lot of the unnecessary suffering of our
world comes from people who take the descriptions of spiritual
experiences and insights by the founders of various religions as the
literal truth, instead of those founders' sincere attempts to express
things as well as they could. But those founders were also creatures
of their times, their cultures, their beliefs, their hopes and fears,
and the limits of their languages.

In spite of the need to stay open minded, be aware of my own
biases, and consider alternatives, I do believe that Bucke and Smith
are somehow expressing important truths.

**What if the cosmos is indeed not dead matter but a living
presence?** As a human being, I don't feel arrogant enough to make
any final judgments about the whole cosmos being alive, but given
that with present knowledge, we can't put any limits on psi phenomena, maybe. That is, we have no evidence that any information
about reality is not available to our psychic faculties, and that
supports the idea that perhaps life and consciousness do indeed
pervade much or all of reality.

What if we have souls that are immortal? Immortality suggests eternity, and I don't know about eternity, but, as we've looked
at in chapters 12 through 16, there's strong evidence that some
aspects of our human minds may survive death.

**What if the universe is so built and ordered that, without
any peradventure, in spite of all the apparent evil in the world,
all things work together for the good of each and all?** I hope so!
But I don't know, and I'm not sure how you would scientifically

test this as a human being. This might be one of the ideas that would be better investigated by some state-specific sciences (Tart 1972, 1998a) of the future.

What if the foundation principle of the world is what we call love? And what if the happiness of every one of us is, in the long run, absolutely certain? Again, I hope so! And while the absolute truth or falseness of these last three ideas may not be open to any clear test, even in more highly developed sciences of the future, there are certainly practical, psychological, and sociological consequences of believing in these ideas that can be studied. After all, how will you live your life and affect others if, on the one hand, you think that life is a meaningless accident and we die anyway, rather than that love is the primary factor in the universe, and aligning yourself with it and expressing it is your main function in life?

There's so much more information I want to share, but it will have to wait for another book or my online writing:

http://blog.paradigm-sys.com/

APPENDIX 1:

Recommended Reading in Parapsychology

As I mentioned earlier, it's best to read about parapsychology and related areas with discrimination, because the accuracy and quality of the material, and its adherence to basic rules of scholarship and essential science, vary a great deal. That's a polite way of saying that some of what you'll find is about as accurate as one can get with the present state of our scientific knowledge, some is considerably slanted and tailored to promote particular belief systems, some is just plain wrong, and some is fantasy pretending to be fact.

You can't be very discriminating at the beginning, of course, when you're just learning about the material and ways of studying it; you do have to depend on authorities to get started. Next is a list of books — some recent, some more classical, compiled by me and my parapsychologist colleagues — that we consider generally accessible to the nonspecialist, interesting, and accurate. My thanks to Alexander Imich, Bryan Williams, Andreas Sommer, Carlos Alvarado, Dean Radin, Eberhard Bauer, Gary Schwartz, Guy Playfair, Jim Carpenter, Larry Dossey, Loyd Auerbach, Michael Sudduth, Nancy Zingrone, Neal Grossman, Peter Mulacz, Ruth Reinsel, Sally Rhine Feather, Stephan Schwartz, Vernon Neppe, and William Braud. My colleagues were so enthusiastic about recommending good books that I had to eventually just call a halt to keep this list from getting out of hand.

This is in no way of making a "complete" listing of good books on parapsychology; that could take forever. But any of these books are good starts and overviews. Some of these books are out of print and some are reprints of the originals, but the Internet makes it so easy to find both used and new books now, not to mention the availability of interlibrary loan, that I haven't worried about citing original printings versus reprintings and later editions. If you read several of these books, you'll be much better informed about parapsychology than the vast majority of people.

Some of these books are older than I would prefer, but as we discussed, support for scientific parapsychology is so meager that progress is very slow, so there's no change in much of what the older books say.

You can find other lists of reliable books on parapsychology at various websites, listed in Appendix 2, as well as in the reference list.

At the end of the list I've referenced a few books that are "skeptical" of the findings of parapsychology. They do contain some valuable material on the ways in which we can fool ourselves, but they also tend to be in the pseudo-skeptic tradition discussed earlier; that is, there is often such a zealously strong commitment to materialism as the complete and final explanation of everything that they become scientistic rather than scientific.

Almeder, R. 1992. *Death and Personal Survival: The Evidence for Life After Death*. Lanham, MD: Littlefield Adams Quality Paperbacks.

Alvarado, C. S. 2002. *Getting Started in Parapsychology*. New York: Parapsychology Foundation.

Arcangel, D. 2005. *Afterlife Encounters: Ordinary People, Extraordinary Experiences*. Charlottesville, VA: Hampton Roads Publishing Company.

Auerbach, L. 1986. *ESP, Hauntings, and Poltergeists: A Parapsychologist's Handbook*. New York: Warner Books.

— . 1996. *Mind Over Matter*. New York: Kensington Books.

— . 2004. *Hauntings and Poltergeists: A Ghost Hunter's Guide*. Oakland, CA: Ronin Publishing.

Barrington, M. R., I. Stevenson, and Z. Weaver. 2005. *A World in a Grain of Sand: The Clairvoyance of Stefan Ossowiecki*. Jefferson, NC: McFarland.

Bauer, H. H. 2001. *Science or Pseudoscience: Magnetic Healing, Psychic Phenomena, and Other Heterodoxies.* Champaign, IL: University of Illinois Press.

Beloff, J. 1993. *Parapsychology: A Concise History.* New York: St. Martin's Press.

Benor, D. J. 2002. *Healing Research Volume I: Spiritual Healing — Scientific Validation of a Healing Revolution.* Southfield, MI: Vision Publications.

Blum, D. 2006. *The Ghost Hunters: William James and the Search for Scientific Proof of Life After Death.* New York: The Penguin Press.

Braud, W. 2003. *Distant Mental Influence: Its Contributions to Science, Healing, and Human Interactions.* Charlottesville, VA: Hampton Roads Publishing Company.

Braude, S. E. 1979. *ESP and Psychokinesis: A Philosophical Examination.* Philadelphia: Temple University Press.

— . 1997. *Limits of Influence: Psychokinesis and the Philosophy of Science.* London: Routledge and Kegan Paul, Ltd.

— . 2003. *Immortal Remains: The Evidence for Life After Death.* Lanham, MD: Rowman and Littlefield Publishers.

— . 2007. *The Gold Leaf Lady and Other Parapsychological Investigations.* Chicago: University of Chicago Press.

Broad, C. D. 1962. *Lectures on Psychical Research.* New York: Humanities Press.

Broderick, D. 2007. *Outside the Gates of Science: Why It's Time for the Paranormal to Come in from the Cold.* New York: Thunder's Mouth Press.

Broughton, R. S. 1991. *Parapsychology: The Controversial Science.* 1st ed. New York: Ballantine Books.

Cardeña, E., S. J. Lynn, and S. Krippner, eds. 2000. *The Varieties of Anomalous Experience: Examining the Scientific Evidence.* Washington, DC: American Psychological Association.

Collins, H., and T. J. Pinch. 1979. The construction of the paranormal: Nothing unscientific is happening. In *On the margins of science: The social construction of rejected knowledge*, ed. R. Wallis, Sociological Review monograph 27. Staffordshire, UK: University of Keele.

— . 1982. *Frames of Meaning: The Social Construction of Extraordinary Science.* London: Routledge and Kegan Paul Ltd.

Cornell, T. 2002. *Investigating the Paranormal.* New York: Helix Press.

Darling, D. J. 1995. *Soul Search: A Scientist Explores the Afterlife*. New York: Villard Books.

Dilley, F. B., ed. 1995. *Philosophical Interactions with Parapsychology: The Major Writings of H. H. Price on Parapsychology and Survival*. New York: St. Martin's Press.

Doore, G., ed. 1990. *What Survives? Contemporary Explorations of Life After Death*. Los Angeles: Jeremy P. Tarcher.

Dossey, L. 1993. *Healing Words: The Power of Prayer and the Practice of Medicine*. San Francisco: HarperSanFrancisco.

Duncan, L., and W. Roll. 1995. *Psychic Connections: A Journey into the Mysterious World of Psi*. New York: Delacorte Press.

Dunne, J. W. 1973. *An Experiment with Time*. London: Faber and Faber.

Eisenbud, J. 1989. *The World of Ted Serios: "Thoughtographic" Studies of an Extraordinary Mind*. Jefferson, NC: McFarland.

Feather, S., and M. Schmicker. 2005. *The Gift: The Extraordinary Experiences of Ordinary People*. New York: St. Martin's Press.

Fenwick, P., and E. Fenwick. 2008. *The Art of Dying*. London: Continuum.

Fontana, D. 2005. *Is There an Afterlife? A Comprehensive Overview of the Evidence*. Hants, UK: O Books.

Gauld, A. 1982. *Mediumship and Survival: A Century of Investigations*. London: Heinemann.

Gauld, A., and T. Cornell. 1979. *Poltergeists*. London: Routledge and Kegan Paul Ltd.

Graff, D. E. 1998. *Tracks in the Psychic Wilderness: An Exploration of Remote Viewing, ESP, Precognitive Dreaming, and Synchronicity*. Boston: Element Books.

Gregory, A. 1985. *The Strange Case of Rudi Schneider*. Metuchen, NJ: Scarecrow Press.

Griffin, D. R. 1997. *Parapsychology, Philosophy, and Spirituality: A Postmodern Exploration*. Albany, NY: State University of New York Press.

Grim, P., ed. 1990. *Philosophy of Science and the Occult*. Albany, NY: State University of New York Press.

Gruber, E. R. 1999. *Psychic Wars: Parapsychology in Espionage — and Beyond*. London: Blandford Books.

Hastings, A. 1991. *With the Tongues of Men and Angels: A Study of Channeling*. New York: Harcourt.

Henry, J., ed. 2005. *Parapsychology: Research on Exceptional Experiences.* East Sussex, UK: Routledge.

Hess, D. J. 1993. *Science in the New Age: The Paranormal, Its Defenders and Debunkers, and American Culture.* Madison, WI: The University of Wisconsin Press.

Inglis, B. 1984. *Science and Parascience: A History of the Paranormal, 1914–1939.* London: Hodder and Stoughton.

Irwin, H. J., and C. A. Watt. 2007. *An Introduction to Parapsychology.* 5th ed. Jefferson, NC: MacFarland.

Kelly, E. F., E. W. Kelly, A. Crabtree, A. Gauld, M. Grosso, and B. Greyson. 2006. *Irreducible Mind: Toward a Psychology for the 21st Century.* Lanham, MD: Rowman & Littlefield Publishers.

LaGrand, L. E. 2001. *Gifts from the Unknown: Using Extraordinary Experiences to Cope with Loss and Change.* Lincoln, NE: Authors Choice Press.

LeShan, L. 1974. *The Medium, the Mystic, and the Physicist: Toward a General Theory of the Paranormal.* New York: Viking.

MacKenzie, A. 1982. *Hauntings and Apparitions: An Investigation of the Evidence.* London: Heinemann.

Mayer, E. L. 2007. *Extraordinary Knowing: Science, Skepticism, and the Inexplicable Power of the Human Mind.* New York: Bantam Books.

McMoneagle, J. 1997. *Mind Trek: Exploring Consciousness, Time, and Space Through Remote Viewing.* Charlottesville, VA: Hampton Roads Publishing Company.

— . 2002. *The Stargate Chronicles: Memoirs of a Psychic Spy.* Charlottesville, VA: Hampton Roads Publishing Company.

Mishlove, J. 1975. *The Roots of Consciousness: Psychic Liberation Through History, Science, and Experience.* 1st ed. New York: Random House.

Mitchell, E. D. 1974. *Psychic Exploration.* New York: G. P. Putnam's Sons.

Monroe, R. 1985. *Far Journeys.* 1st ed. New York: Doubleday.

— . 1994. *Ultimate Journey.* New York: Doubleday.

Pilkington, R. 1987. *Men and Women of Parapsychology: Personal ? Reflections.* Jefferson, NC: McFarland.

— . 2006. *The Spirit of Dr. Bindelof: The Enigma of Séance Phenomena.* San Antonio, TX: Anomalist Books.

Radin, D. 1997. *The Conscious Universe: The Scientific Truth of Psychic Phenomena.* San Francisco: HarperOne.

— . 2006. *Entangled Minds: Extrasensory Experiences in a Quantum Reality*. New York: Paraview Pocket Books.

Rhine, L. E. 1961. *Hidden Channels of the Mind*. New York: William Morrow.

Ring, K. 1984. *Heading Toward Omega: In Search of the Meaning of the Near-death Experience*. New York: William Morrow.

Rogo, D. S. 1975. *Parapsychology: A Century of Inquiry*. New York: Taplinger Publishing Co.

Roll, W. G. 1976. *The Poltergeist*. Metuchen, NJ: Scarecrow Press.

Roll, W., and V. Storey. 2004. *Unleashed: Of Poltergeists and Murder — The Curious Story of Tina Resch*. New York: Paraview Pocket Books.

Russell, R. 2007. *The Journey of Robert Monroe: From Out-of-Body Explorer to Consciousness Pioneer*. Charlottesville, VA: Hampton Roads Publishing Company.

Schoch, R. M., and L. Yonavjak. 2008. *The Parapsychology Revolution: A Concise Anthology of Paranormal and Psychical Research*. New York: Tarcher.

Schwartz, G. E. 2003. *The Afterlife Experiments: Breakthrough Scientific Evidence of Life After Death*. New York: Atria Books.

Schwartz, S. A. 1978. *The Secret Vaults of Time: Psychic Archaeology and the Quest for Man's Beginnings*. New York: Grosset & Dunlap. (Rev. ed., Hampton Roads Publishing Company, 2005.)

— . 1983. *The Alexandria Project*. New York: Delacorte Press/Eleanor Friede.

— . 2007. *Opening to the Infinite*. Buda, TX: Nemoseen Media.

— . Forthcoming. *Mind Rover: Explorations with Remote Viewing*. Buda, TX: Nemoseen Media.

Shroder, T. 1999. *Old Souls: The Scientific Evidence for Past Lives*. New York: Simon & Schuster.

Sidgwick, H. 1894. Report on the census of hallucinations. *Proceedings of the Society for Psychical Research* 10:25–422.

Sinclair, U. 1930. *Mental Radio*. Preface by Albert Einstein. New York: A. & C. Boni.

Smith, P. H. 2005. *Reading the Enemy's Mind: Inside Star Gate, America's Psychic Espionage Program*. New York: Tom Doherty Associates.

Stevenson, I. 2001. *Children Who Remember Previous Lives: A Question of Reincarnation*. Jefferson, NC: McFarland.

Stockton, B. 1989. *Catapult: The Biography of Robert A. Monroe*. Norfolk,

VA: The Donning Company Publishers.

Stokes, D. M. 2007. *The Conscious Mind and the Material World: On Psi, the Soul, and the Self*. Jefferson, NC: McFarland.

Storm, L., and M. A. Thalbourne, eds. 2006. *The Survival of Human Consciousness: Essays on the Possibility of Life After Death*. Jefferson, NC: McFarland.

Swann, I. 1991. *Everybody's Guide to Natural ESP: Unlocking the Extrasensory Power of Your Mind*. Los Angeles: Tarcher.

Targ, R., and K. Harary. 1984. *The Mind Race: Understanding and Using Psychic Abilities*. New York: Villard Books.

Targ, R., and H. Puthoff. 1977. *Mind-Reach: Scientists Look at Psychic Ability*. New York: Delacorte Press/Eleanor Friede.

Tart, C. 1975. *Transpersonal Psychologies*. New York: Harper & Row.

— . 1988. *Waking Up: Overcoming the Obstacles to Human Potential*. Longmead, England: Element Books. Currently in print through www.iuniverse.com.

— , ed. 1997. *Body Mind Spirit: Exploring the Parapsychology of Spirituality*. Charlottesville, VA: Hampton Roads Publishing Company.

— . 2001. *Mind Science: Meditation Training for Practical People*. Novato, CA: Wisdom Editions.

Tart, C., H. Puthoff, and R. Targ, eds. 1979. *Mind at Large: IEEE Symposia on the Nature of Extrasensory Perception*. New York: Praeger.

Taylor, E. 1999. *Shadow Culture: Psychology and Spirituality in America*. Washington, D.C.: Counterpoint.

Tucker, J. B. 2005. *Life Before Life: A Scientific Investigation of Children's Memories of Previous Lives*. New York: St. Martin's Press.

Tyrrell, G. N. M. 1947. *The Personality of Man: New Facts and Their Significance*. New York: Penguin Books.

Ullman, M., S. Krippner, and A. Vaughan. 1989. *Dream Telepathy: Experiments in Nocturnal ESP*. Jefferson, NC: McFarland.

Vasiliev, L. L. 1962. *Experiments in Mental Suggestion*. New York: Dutton.

Warcollier, R. 2001. *Mind to Mind: Studies in Consciousness*. Charlottesville, VA: Hampton Roads Publishing Company.

SKEPTICAL BOOKS

Alcock, J. E. 1990. *Science and Supernature: A Critical Appraisal of Parapsychology*. Buffalo, NY: Prometheus Books.

Carter, C. 2007. *Parapsychology and Skeptics: A Scientific Argument for the Existence of ESP*. Pittsburg, PA: SterlingHouse Publisher.

Hansel, C. E. M. 1989. *The Search for Psychic Power: ESP and Parapsychology Revisited*. Buffalo, NY: Prometheus Books.

Hyman, R. 1989. *The Elusive Quarry: A Scientific Appraisal of Psychical Research*. Buffalo, NY: Prometheus Books.

Kurtz, P., ed. 1985. *A Skeptic's Handbook of Parapsychology*. Buffalo, NY: Prometheus Books.

Wiseman, R. 1997. *Deception and Self-Deception: Investigating Psychics*. Buffalo, NY: Prometheus Books.

Zusne, L., and W. H. Jones. 1989. *Anomalistic Psychology: A Study of Magical Thinking*. Hillside, NJ: Lawrence Erlbaum Associates.

APPENDIX 2:

Online Sources of Scientific Information About Parapsychology

There's a huge amount of information available on the Internet about parapsychology, and it varies enormously in quality. Some of it is just plain factually wrong, some is personal ideas inaccurately presented as if they were backed by scientific research, and some is stimulating and accurate. In this appendix I present a list of websites that are likely to be accurate and informative. I say "likely," because websites can change rapidly and I can't keep monitoring them for accuracy. I compiled this list in 2006 with the help of many parapsychologist colleagues, and the Rhine Research Center updated my original compilation in 2008. As with print material, read with discernment!

Items are listed in several categories. I want to give much more praise about so many of these but am trying to keep it brief! Please note that URLs are subject to frequent change, and some of those listed here may be out of date. If so, you can usually relocate the indicated resources with an internet search.

COMPREHENSIVE INFORMATION ON PARAPSYCHOLOGY AND RELATED TOPICS

Lexscien (Library of Exploratory Science) (www.lexscien.org) An online library containing the searchable full text of many of the major journals in the field:

> **Journal of the Society for Psychical Research** (JSPR),
> **Proceedings of the Society for Psychical Research** (ProcSPR),
> **Journal of Parapsychology** (JP),

Journal of Scientific Exploration (JSE),
European Journal of Parapsychology (EJP),
Research in Parapsychology (RIP) (abstracts of papers presented at various meetings of the Parapsychological Association),
Revue Métapsychique (RM), and various classic books. More sources are being added. There's a subscription fee.

PEER-REVIEWED JOURNALS

The most recent research in any scientific field almost always appears first at professional conferences, then in the field's technical journals. It can be years before this information makes its way into books. The following are peer-reviewed journals, meaning that potential articles are almost always vetted by at least two experts in the field to be sure that the methodology and conclusions of studies are reasonably sound. Peer-reviewed articles are thus generally accurate and reliable, although the peer review system does tend to filter out revolutionary articles.

ELECTRONIC JOURNALS AND NEWSLETTERS

European Journal of Parapsychology (http://ejp.org.uk/) Focus on experimental and theoretical work in parapsychology.

International Journal of Parapsychology (www.parapsychology.org/dynamic/070103.html) Experimental, theoretical, philosophical, and scholarly articles.

Journal of Humanistic Psychology (http://www.ahpweb.org/index.php?option = com_k2&view = item&layout = item&id = 32&Itemid = 34Occasional psi-relevant articles within the larger context of human-potential work.

Journal of Near-Death Studies (www.iands.org/journal.html) Primary journal for scientific and scholarly work on near-death experiences (NDEs).

Journal of Parapsychology (www.http://rhinecenter.org/what-we-do/journal-of-parapsychology.html) Primarily experimental work, as well as scholarly overviews.

Journal of Scientific Exploration (www.jse.com/) Anomalous research in general but with frequent parapsychology articles.

Journal of the American Society for Psychical Research (www.aspr.com/jaspr.htm) Experimental, theoretical, philosophical, and scholarly articles. No issues have appeared for several years; may be defunct.

Journal of the Society for Psychical Research (www.spr. ac.uk/expcms/index.php?section = 41) Experimental, theoretical, philosophical, and scholarly articles. The original, English-language journal for the field.

Journal of Transpersonal Psychology (www.atpweb.org/ journal.asp) Broad context, scholarly articles on spiritual potentials, with psi phenomena usually implicitly taken for granted, occasional psi-specific articles.

Luce e Ombra (http://www.bibliotecabozzanodeboni.it/evleo. htm)

Metapsichica (www.metapsichica.it/Frame1.htm)

Quaderni di Parapsicologia (http://cspbo.altervista.org/b/ qp.htm)

Argentine Journal of Paranormal Psychology (www.alipsi. com.ar/english.asp)

Subtle Energies and Energy Medicine Journal (www.issseem. org/journal.cfm) Potential applications of psi ability to the healing arts as well as basic, psi-related research.

The Humanistic Psychologist (http://www.apadivisions.org/ division-32/publications/journals/index.aspx) Primarily humanistic psychology, occasional articles on parapsychology and transpersonal psychology.

Zeitschrift für Anomalistik (Journal for Anomalistics) (www.anomalistik.de/zfa.shtml) The journal is published in German with English abstracts. Its scope is similar to that of the SSE's Journal of Scientific Exploration with about 50 percent of its contents being devoted to issues immediately related to parapsychology.

Zeitschrift für Parapsychologie und Grenzgebiete der Psychologie (www.igpp.de/german/libarch/info.htm#zfp)

ORGANIZATIONS AND CENTERS WITH A MAJOR FOCUS ON PARAPSYCHOLOGY

American Society for Psychical Research (www.aspr. com/) The oldest organization in America for promoting research in parapsychology ("psychical research" is the older term) has occasional lectures in New York City and publishes the *Journal of the American Society for Psychical Research*. (At the time of this writing, late 2008, the journal is several years behind in publishing.)

Anomalistic Psychology Research Unit (www.goldsmiths. ac.uk/apru/)

Association for Humanistic Psychology (www.ahpweb.org) Primary professional psychological organization of the human potential movement.

Association for Transpersonal Psychology (ATP) (www. atpweb.org) The premier organization for everyone interested in spiritual (transpersonal) psychology (see appendix 4). ATP publishes the *Journal of Transpersonal Psychology* and holds an annual meeting every other year with both professional and experiential presentations. Mostly relevant to questions about possible implications of psi data rather than primary research reports on psi phenomena.

Associazione Italiana Scientifica di Metapsichica (www. metapsichica.it/Frame1.htm)

Australian Institute of Parapsychological Research (www. aiprinc.org/who_are_we.asp)

Austrian Society for Parapsychology and Border Areas of Science (http://parapsychologie.ac.at/eng-info.htm)

The Scientific and Medical Network (www.scimednet.org/) British organization to investigate and disseminate information about alternative medicine and related spiritual and parapsychological issues. Publishes a newsletter.

Centre for Parapsychological Studies, Bologna (http://cspbo. altervista.org/)

The Laboratories for Fundamental Research (www.lfr.org/) Run by physicist Dr. Edwin May, this site provides valuable information about parapsychology.

Consciousness Research Laboratories (www.psiresearch.org/) Solid parapsychology information and online tests by parapsychologist Dr. Dean Radin.

Esalen Center for Theory & Research (www.esalenctr.org/) This is the more conceptual branch of the Esalen Institute. They hold invited conferences in cutting-edge areas and publish proceedings, some on their website. Material from several invited conferences on research on the possibility of survival of the mind after bodily death is on the site.

Exceptional Human Experience Network (www.ehe.org) The Exceptional Human Experience Network studied the personal and transformative meaning at the core of all types of anomalous experiences (335 types to date on the website), such as mystical, encounter, psychic, healing, death-related, peak, healing, desolation or nadir experiences, and exceptional human performance. Especially interested in their aftereffects, the most common being a sense of the connectedness of all things. They have developed an EHE autobiography technique to help potentiate this and other core realizations such as reverence for all life and a sense of planetary stewardship.

Firedocs Remote Viewing Collection (www.firedocs.com/remoteviewing/) Essential material by Palyne Gaenir and must reading for those really interested in remote viewing.

Fondazione Biblioteca Bozzano-De Boni (http://www.bibliotecabozzanodeboni.it/)

Institut für Grenzgebiete der Psychologie und Psychohygiene (Institute for Border Areas of Psychologie and Mental Hygiene) (www.igpp.de/english/welcome.htm Interdisciplinary research concerning insufficiently understood mental and physical phenomena, as studied by parapsychology, and other anomalies at the frontiers of current scientific knowledge. These include altered states of consciousness; mind-matter relations; and their social, cultural, and historical contexts from the perspectives of the humanities, social sciences, and natural sciences. The IGPP maintains a broadly conceived program offering information, education, and counseling for people with paranormal and exceptional experiences, a comprehensive special library (about fifty thousand volumes) and a historical archive including personal papers of prominent German parapsychological researchers. The IGPP cooperates with numerous German and international universities and research institutions. It contributes to the education of undergraduate and graduate students.

Institut Métapsychique International (www.metapsychique.org) For French speakers, a valuable source of information on the paranormal.

The Institute of Noetic Sciences (IONS) (www.noetic.org/) IONS is a membership organization devoted to promoting research and education in areas like alternative medicine, parapsychology, human potential, creativity, and so on. Membership is an excellent way of keeping up with these areas through IONS's publications.

Institute of Transpersonal Psychology (now Sofia University) (www.sofia.edu/) A highly recommended program for those seriously interested in careers in transpersonal psychology. (See also my career advice letter at www.paradigm-sys.com/ctt_articles2. cfm?id = 56/.) (My web site is being revised, so URL may differ.) Offers Western Association of Schools and Colleges (WASC) accredited MA and Ph.D. programs in transpersonal psychology, both in residential and distance programs. Note that I teach there, so I may be biased.

  Instituto de Psicología Paranormal (Institute of Paranormal Psychology) (www.alipsi.com.ar/english.asp)

  The International Association for Near-Death Studies (www.iands.org) An organization of scientists who research near-death experiences (NDEs) and those who've experienced them. A vital contact point if you've had an NDE!

  International Association of Spiritual Psychiatry (http://www.art.ridne.net/dir/node-2465.html/).

  International Society for the Study of Subtle Energies and Energy Medicine (ISSSEEM) (www.issseem.org/) Besides offering their journal, the ISSSEEM holds yearly professional meetings.

  International Society of Life Information Science (ISLIS) (www.soc.nii.ac.jp/islis/journal.htm).

  Intuition Network (www.intuition.org/)

  Koestler Parapsychology Unit (University of Edinburgh) (http://www.koestler-parapsychology.psy.ed.ac.uk/) Ph.D. in psychology program at the University of Edinburgh with specialization in parapsychology. One of the very few such programs.

  Laboratoire de Parapsychologie de Toulouse (http://geepp. or3p.free.fr/index_800.htm)

  Mind-Matter Unification Project (www.tcm.phy.cam. ac.uk/ ~ bdj10/mm/top.html) Nobel Laureate physicist Brian Josephson's material on parapsychology and related topics.

  Online Noetics Network (www.noetic.org/)

  Near Death Experience Research Foundation (www.nderf. org/)

  Pacific Neuropsychiatric Institute (www.pni.org/research/ anomalous/) Research by Dr. Vernon Neppe on anomalous experiences.

  Parapsychological Association (PA) (www.parapsych.org/) The PA is the scientific and scholarly organization in the field. Election to full membership in the PA comes with demonstrated scientific and scholarly contributions to the field. Student or associate membership is available also.

Parapsychology Foundation (PF) (www.parapsychology. org/ and www.pflyceum.org/131.html) The PF is the publisher of the *International Journal of Parapsychology*. The PF also provides small grants for scientific parapsychology and has one of the best libraries on the subject.

PEAR Publications (www.princeton.edu/ ~ pear/publications. html) Princeton Engineering Anomalies Research (PEAR) was one of the world's foremost parapsychology laboratories.

Perrott-Warrick Research Unit, University of Hertfordshire (www.answers.com/topic/perrott-warrick-research-unit).

Rhine Research Center (www.rhine.org/) Long the major research center in the United States, it continues the work started by Dr. J. B. and Louisa Rhine at Duke University in the 1930s. Publishes the *Journal of Parapsychology*, one of the essential scientific journals for keeping up with the latest developments in parapsychology.

Society for Psychical Research (SPR) (www.spr.ac.uk/expcms/ index.php?section = 1) Founded in 1882 by leading British intellectuals, the SPR was dedicated to investigating those kinds of phenomena that suggest that we humans are something more than mere biological machines, phenomena such as telepathy, clairvoyance, precognition, psychokinesis, and postmortem survival. Publishes essential reading in parapsychology, including the *Journal of the Society for Psychical Research*, as well as conducts programs in Britain. Occasionally publishes longer reports as proceedings.

Society for Scientific Exploration (www.scientificexploration. org/) The society's journal is one of the essential scientific journals to read if you want to keep up with the latest developments in parapsychology and other areas in science that might be considered "fringe" or "cutting edge." Yearly meetings.

Spiritual Emergence Network (http://www.spiritualemergence. info/) The Spiritual Emergence Network (SEN) tries to find professional help for those disturbed by unusual experiences, and turn such experiences into spiritual growth instead of pathologizing them. Also educates mental health professionals about these areas.

The Archives of Scientists' Transcendent Experiences (TASTE) (www.issc-taste.org/index.shtml) Transcendent, spiritual, psychic, or all such experiences of people recognized as scientists.

The Forge Institute (www.TheForge.org) The Forge Institute is working to bring transformative, trans-traditional spirituality into society. Its programs include a professional organization, The Forge Guild of Spiritual Leaders and Teachers; a for-credit college course taught at several universities; local spiritual growth communities for seekers, Forge Hearths; and a public initiative to bring spirituality into discussions of social issues.

Global Consciousness Project (http://noosphere.princeton. edu/).

University of Virginia Division of Perceptual Studies (www. healthsystem.virginia.edu/DOPS) The leading scientific research center for topics like reincarnation, out-of-body experiences, near-death experiences, and other aspects of parapsychology.

WEBSITES OF PROMINENT RESEARCHERS WITH INTERESTS AND WORK IN PARAPSYCHOLOGY

Loyd Auerbach (www.mindreader.com) Auerbach is both a parapsychologist and a magician and psychic entertainer, a rare combination.

Daryl Bem (http://dbem.ws) Prominent psychologist who has conducted parapsychological research.

Dick Bierman (www.parapsy.nl) For those who speak Dutch, physicist Bierman has conducted many parapsychological studies.

William Braud (www.integral-inquiry.com) Professor Braud, of the Institute of Transpersonal Psychology, is one of the world's leading transpersonal psychologists and parapsychologists. He created this site as part of a course on dissertation writing for ITP students. It has many valuable resources on transpersonal psychology and parapsychology.

Steven Braude (http://userpages.umbc.edu/ ~ braude/ or www. jazzphilosopher.com/) Philosopher Braude is one of the most incisive thinkers dealing with parapsychological matters.

Etzel Cardena (http://www.lu.se/o.o.i.s/23839) Research on hypnosis and altered states as well as parapsychology. Professor Cardena accepts graduate students with parapsychological interests at Lund University in Sweden.

Michael Grosso (www.parapsi.com) Sections on philosophical musings, parapsychology of religion (the effectiveness of prayer; the existence of God, spirits, and demonic forces; reports of miraculous phenomena; and what parapsychology has to say about this), death and consciousness, books and book reviews and articles, and a gallery of

Michael Grosso's metaphysical paintings.

Erlendur Haraldsson (www.hi.is/~erlendur/) Professor at the University of Iceland and prominent parapsychologist.

Brian Josephson (www.tcm.phy.cam.ac.uk/~bdj10/) Nobel laureate physicist Brian Josephson has a long-standing interest in parapsychology and the nature of consciousness.

Stanley Krippner (www.stanleykrippner.com) Psychologist and professor at the Saybrook Institute, Krippner has done outstanding research in many parapsychological and related areas.

Louis LaGrand (http://www.extraordinarygriefexperiences.com/) Information on after-death contacts experienced by those mourning the death of a loved one and how the experience can be used in coping with the loss.

Robert McConnell (www.parapsychologybooks.com).

Joanne McMahon (www.DrGhost.com)

Joseph McMoneagle (www.mceagle.com/) Joe McMoneagle was one of the outstanding remote viewers in the classified U.S. Army program and does remote viewing today as a private consultant.

Rosemarie Pilkington (www.AreSpiritsReal.com).

Dean Radin (www.psiresearch.org/ and www.deanradin.com) Dean Radin is one of the leading experimental parapsychologists.

Stephan Schwartz (www.stephanaschwartz.com) Outstand-ing parapsychologist with special interests in remote viewing and arche-ological applications of psi ability.

Rupert Sheldrake (www.sheldrake.org) A comprehensive overview of Rupert Sheldrake's experiments on telepathy and the sense of being stared at. Online experiments may be available.

James Spottiswoode (www.jsasoc.com/) Remote viewing work, both experimental and conceptual.

Michael Sudduth (www.homestead.com/mscourses/worldreligionsSFSUSpring06.html and www.homestead.com/mscourses/EastBayWRspring06.html) Course materials for Professor Sudduth's course on postmortem survival, currently taught at San Francisco State University.

Russell Targ (www.espresearch.com) Very useful guides to parapsychology by one of its leading remote-viewing researchers.

Charles Tart (www.paradigm-sys.com/cttart) Published articles and so forth.

Jim Tucker (http://www.medicine.virginia.edu/clinical/

departments/psychiatry/sections/cspp/dops/home-page Reincarnation research at the University of Virginia by Dr. Tucker, who is a psychiatrist.

Jessica Utts (http://www.ics.uci.edu/ ~ jutts/ Professor Utts, of the University of California, Davis, is a leading authority on statistical analyses as applied to parapsychology.

Sylvia Hart Wright (www.sylviahartwright.com/) Includes first chapter of Professor Wright's book, When Spirits Come Calling, and other info on ADCs.

MISCELLANEOUS

After-Death Communications Project (www.after-death. com) This started with a book by Bill and Judy Guggenheim reporting hundreds of experiences of ordinary people's communications from loved ones who had died, and has expanded into a variety of resources for information about the possibility of survival of death. Excellent links also.

Parapsychology Sources on the Internet (www.homepages. ed.ac.uk/ejua35/parapsy.htm)

Parapsychology, Anomalies, Science, Skepticism, and CSICOP (www.blavatskyarchives.com/zeteticism.htm) A very large collection of articles debunking parapsychology, illustrative of what I call "pseudo-skepticism."

PSI-Mart.com: Online Parapsychology Bookstore (www. psi-mart.com/home.php) Useful offerings from the Parapsychology Foundation.

Sergio Frasca's Parapsychology Resources on Internet (www. roma1.infn.it/rog/group/frasca/b/parap.html).

Skeptical Investigations (www.skepticalinvestigations.org) Excellent factual data on the pseudo skeptics and how they treat parapsychology.

Public Parapsychology (http://publicparapsychology.blogspot. com/2006/12/mind-over-matter-study.html) A Web blog dedicated to public parapsychology, run by Annalisa Ventola, former Summer Study Program student at the Rhine Center.

APPENDIX 3:

The Archives of Scientists' Transcendent Experiences (TASTE)

One of the themes we've constantly dealt with in this book is the popular, but false, idea that science long ago showed that spirituality was nonsense. If this were true, it might follow, perhaps, that scientists, being highly intelligent and rational people, would certainly not have spiritual or psychic experiences themselves, yes?

Well, Richard Maurice Bucke was a physician, which meant that he'd had a lot of the best scientific training of his time; Joseph Waldron was an experimental psychologist; and Allan Smith was also a scientifically trained physician in modern times. Perhaps they were exceptions?

In reality, over the years many scientists, once they've realized I'm a safe person to talk to, have told me about unusual and transcendent experiences they've had. Too often I'm the first and only person they've ever spoken to about their experiences, for fear of ridicule from their colleagues and of adverse, prejudicial effects on their careers. Such fears have, unfortunately, too much of a basis in fact. There are a lot of scientists with negative intentions deliberately trying to suppress their colleagues, even if it's mainly the automatic manifestation of the social conditioning of our times rather than deliberate nastiness. A real interest in, much less actual research in, the spiritual and the psychic has too often been a career killer in the academic and scientific worlds (Hess 1992). I wanted to start to change that, and this appendix points you toward a small step in that direction.

As we've discussed, scientists today often occupy a social role like that of "high priests" in earlier cultures, telling laypeople and each other what is and isn't "real," and, consequently, what is and isn't valuable and sane. Unfortunately, the dominant materialistic and reductionistic psychosocial climate of contemporary science, scientism, rejects and suppresses both having and sharing transcendent, transpersonal, and altered-state (or "spiritual" and "psychic" experiences, to use more common words, in spite of their often too vague connotations) experiences.

From my perspective as a psychologist, though, this prejudicial suppression and rejection psychologically harms and distorts both scientists' and laypersons' transcendent (and other) potentials, and also inhibits the development of a genuine scientific understanding of the full spectrum of consciousness. Irrational denial and suppression of any aspects of our nature, whatever their ultimate reality status, is never psychologically or socially healthy.

The Archives of Scientists' Transcendent Experiences (TASTE), a website I created in 1999, is intended to help change this restricted and pathological climate by operating in journal form, allowing scientists from all fields — anthropology, botany, mathematics, physics, psychology, and zoology, to name just a few — to share their personal transcendent experiences in a safe, anonymous, but quality controlled, space that almost all scientists and the general public have ready access to.

TASTE, to various degrees:

- Allows individual psychological growth in the contributing scientists by providing a safe means of expression of vital experiences
- Leads toward a more receptive climate to the full range of our humanity in the scientific professions, which, in turn, would benefit our world culture at large
- Provides research data on transcendent experiences in a

highly articulate and conscientious population, scientists
- Facilitates the development of a full-spectrum science of consciousness by providing both data and psychological support for the study of transcendent experiences
- Helps bridge the unfortunate gaps between science and the rest of culture by illustrating the humanity of scientists

As an example of how this gap can be bridged, the site was given the Science Social Innovations Award for 2000 by the Institute for Social Inventions.

If you want to see the range and often amazing character of scientists' transcendent experiences, take a look at the TASTE site, psychology.ucdavis.edu/tart/taste (or, if the UC Davis psychology server is off-line, visit www.issc-taste.org). There are fuller versions of Joseph Waldron's ADC experience and Allan Smith's Cosmic Consciousness experience there. If you find it valuable, please pass this information on to friends and colleagues. I have no budget for advertising and thus must depend on word of mouth to get the information that's on the TASTE website out to the world.

If you have a website of your own that would be suitable to link to TASTE, thank you! Feel free to copy one of the TASTE experiences as an example on your website, if you like.

In terms of more conventional, slower publicity, if you can recommend any journals I should send notices to, please let me know. If you're the editor of any publication, you have my permission (and thanks!) to print this notice in your publication.

At the time of this writing (November 2008) I've frozen the TASTE site in the sense of not accepting new experience submissions, for lack of time to work on it, but the earlier experiences are there for the reading. I hope to someday get an assistant to manage the TASTE site so that it can be open for submissions again.

APPENDIX 4:

Transpersonal Psychology

Although it opens into a far too huge and too important area than I can deal with in this book, and goes way beyond the fundamental essential-science data that gives a basic reality to the spiritual, I want to give a few hints in this appendix about the directions an essential science of spirituality could go in.

Readers of this book may reasonably think of me as a parapsychologist or as a psychologist with a special interest in parapsychology, but when I'm asked, I usually describe myself as a transpersonal psychologist, reflecting a field I had the privilege of helping to launch in 1975 with my book *Transpersonal Psychologies*. "Transpersonal psychologist" is a larger, more inclusive identity for me to work with than "psychologist" or "parapsychologist." What is this field, then?

Transpersonal psychology is a quite new branch of psychology — thirty years or so old, depending just how you count — that will, in the long run, apply the findings of parapsychology as well as those of other sciences to our spiritual nature, and both give us a clearer understanding of that nature and develop more effective practices for realizing it. Psychologist Abraham Maslow was the primary founder of the field, beginning with his insistence that psychology shouldn't look only at the worst in human behavior, psychopathology but, at the best, the functioning of exceptionally mature people (Maslow 1964). The field concerns itself with ultimate questions about human existence: "Transpersonal psychology is concerned with expanding the field of psychology to include the study of optimal psychological health and well-being. It recognizes the potential for experiencing a broad range of states of consciousness, in some of which identity may extend beyond the usual limits of the ego and personality" (Vaughan and Walsh 1980, 16).

The applied side of transpersonal psychology, transpersonal psychotherapy, is similarly defined by psychiatrist Walsh and psychologist Vaughan as follows:: "Transpersonal psychotherapy includes traditional areas and concerns, adding to these an interest in facilitating growth and awareness beyond traditionally recog-nized limits of health. The importance of modifying consciousness and the validity of transcendental experience and identity is affirmed (1980, 16).

Transpersonal, transcendent experiences, like those of Bucke (see the introduction) or Smith (see chapter 20) are the basis for this new field, rather than philosophical or religious convictions. While philosophical, religious, or ethical beliefs, for example, might argue that we ought to treat each other as if we were interdependent, with each's individual well-being intimately connected to the welfare of all, transpersonal psychology would emphasize the fact that sometimes people have profound experiences, usually in altered states of consciousness, where they deeply experience being at one with other, sometimes all other, living beings. Regardless of how we retrospectively interpret or theorize about such experiences, they aren't abstract, merely "mental" ideas but often feel "realer than real," and thus can profoundly change people's orientation and behavior. Just as it makes no sense to hurt yourself, it then makes no sense to hurt others, and it makes perfect sense to help and cherish them.

Transpersonal psychology is not a religion, theology, or philosophy. It's distinguished from such fields by its desire to base itself in empirical study, essential science, and by the incorporation of modern psychological and neurophysiological knowledge, rather than having a dogmatic a priori belief system that experience is forced to fit into. There are no beliefs or doctrines that must be accepted, only an openness to studying transpersonal and psychic experiences as if they might be about important realities, rather than dismissing them a priori as scientistic materialism does. If a person reports interior conversations with a benevolent spirit, for example, let's find out more about the nature of that experience and what consequences if has for the person's life, and perhaps wonder if there will someday be a way to prove or disprove the independent existence of that spirit, rather than automatically declare that person crazy and give him medications to make the experience go away. If our investigations of a particular person show the experience to probably be largely or wholly delusory, and it's having bad effects on the person's life, then we give him conventional psychological or psychiatric treatment, but that course of action isn't an automatic, prejudicial action.

The late Anthony Sutich (1907–1976), founder and editor of the *Journal of Transpersonal Psychology*, listed topics of central empirical interest in transpersonal psychology as including (from the first page of the journal for most of its first decade) "individual and species-wide meta-needs, ultimate values, unitive consciousness, peak experiences, being-values, ecstasy, mystical experience, awe, being, self-actualization, essence, bliss, wonder, ultimate meaning, transcendence of the self, spirit, oneness, cosmic awareness, individual and species-wide synergy, maximal interpersonal encounters, sacralization of everyday life, transcendental phenomena, cosmic self-humor and playfulness, maximal sensory awareness, responsiveness, and expression."

When I read this list, my reaction is usually, "Phew! Wonderful! Too much! Crazy!" Hmmm, how would we study this or that?

Here's a more formal and coherent definition of the field that I created in 1995, with refinement from my colleagues at the Institute of Transpersonal Psychology:

> Transpersonal psychology is a fundamental area of research, scholarship, and application based on people's experiences of temporarily transcending our usual identification

with our limited biological, historical, cultural, and personal self, and, at the deepest and most profound levels of experience possible, recognizing/being "something" of vast intelligence and compassion that encompasses/is the entire universe. From this perspective our ordinary, "normal" biological, historical, cultural, and personal self is seen as an important but quite partial (and often pathologically distorted) manifestation or expression of this much greater "something" that is our deeper origin and destination.

We are forced to use imprecise terms like "something," because ordinary language, as a partial manifestation of our ordinary self, which is itself a partial manifestation of our deeper transpersonal "self," is of only partial use in our research and practice in transpersonal psychology, and needs to be supplemented with other expressive and communicative modalities.

Transpersonal experiences generally have a profoundly transforming effect on the lives of those who experience them, both inspiring those experiencers with an understanding of great love, compassion and nonordinary kinds of intelligence, and also making them more aware of the distorting and pathological limitations of their ordinary selves that must be worked with and transformed for full psychological and spiritual maturity.

Because people ordinarily identify primarily with the personal, which tends to separate us, rather than with the transpersonal, which experientially impresses us with our fundamental unity and oneness with each other and all life, intelligent knowledge of and/or contact with the transpersonal can thus be of great potential value in solving the problems of a world divided against itself.

Conventional scholarly disciplines and activities are thus subsets of the general transpersonal perspective, important and useful in themselves, but limited. Transpersonal psychology, as both an area of scholarly and scientific study and as an area of therapeutically applied discipline, is one of these subsets, focused on the psychological factors that either facilitate or inhibit contact with and understanding of the transpersonal and the effects of transpersonal experiences on the rest of life. Transpersonal psychology draws knowledge and practices from mainstream psychology, anthropology, history, sociology and other disciplines when helpful and needed, and tries to understand them from the more inclusive transpersonal perspective.

As a field of work, transpersonal psychology is still quite small and in its infancy, and much of our knowledge base is more hint and intimation, mixed with generous amounts of what we'll probably someday see as only partial truths or mistakes, than highly factual data. Similarly, transpersonally oriented therapy is more art than science at this time. Since some of the deepest and most enduring human experiences and values are treated in this area of psychology, however, its extensive development is vital to a full understanding of human life.

An excellent Internet guide to transpersonal psychology can be found at *atpweb.org*.

Since taking early retirement from the University of California in 1994, I've had the privilege of working at the foremost — and, unfortunately, the only one in its class — institution for promoting transpersonal psychology, the Institute of Transpersonal Psychology (ITP), in Palo Alto, California (*www.itp.edu*). Founded by psychologist and high-ranking Aikido teacher Robert Frager in 1975 and cofounding psychologist Jim Fadiman, this accredited graduate school awards master's and doctoral degrees in transpersonal psychology, in both residential and distance-learning programs.

Unlike conventional graduate schools, which train on an almost exclusively intellectual level, ITP also educates its students' emotional, spiritual, physical, social or relational, and creative sides. Residential doctoral students, as just one example, take courses in the martial art Aikido, learning to be calm and peaceful, present and resourceful under the stress of being physically attacked, while effectively but nonaggressively defending themselves. I studied Aikido for many years before joining the ITP faculty, and personally know how useful it can be in training what Gurdjieff called the "intelligence of the body" (see my book Waking Up [1986], for example), and promoting a mindfulness and caring for others in real life and under stress that is slow to develop from classical sitting-meditation procedures.

Those of you who've been through conventional graduate training, but have worked on developing your potentials afterward, will realize how unique the ITP program is. My own graduate-school training was, as is "normal," strictly intellectual. Fortunately it didn't completely crush my emotional, spiritual, physical, social or relational, and creative sides, but I had to get basic education in them through my own efforts, often misdirected, for decades afterward — and still don't feel very educated in these areas.

Besides training doctoral students, ITP produces many knowledge contributions to the field of transpersonal psychology through the research projects students carry out for their dissertations, as well as research by the faculty. To give some examples of how empirical, scholarly, and scientific research can help us learn more about our spiritual sides, here are titles of a couple of dozen ITP dissertations. A fuller listing, in alphabetical order by author, is available at *www.itp.edu/academics/phddissertations.cfm*. I'm proud to have served on the dissertation committees of some of these students! (See next page.)

Exploring self-transformation through the spiritually positive resolution of mental health crises, by Guy Albert (2004)

A phenomenological investigation of the decision-process of a woman trusting herself in making a spiritual commitment that is contrary to the wishes of a significant person or persons, by Joan Andras (1993)

A phenomenological study of channeling: The experience of transmitting information from a source perceived as paranormal, by Kathleen Wise Barrett (1996)

Jungian psychology and the Mahamudra in Vajrayana Buddhism, by Chayim Douglas Barton (1990)

Four dimensions of experiencing Sat-Guru Adi Da's spiritual Heart-Transmission (Hrdaya-Saktipata): Phenomenological, lasting-effects, setting (internal and external), and personality set, by Harley Michael Bennett (2000)

When children witness the sacred: Spiritual and psychological impacts, lifelong aftereffects, and disclosure aspects of religious apparitional encounters, by Irene Ann Blinston (2005)

The effects of EEG biofeedback on hypnagogia, creativity, and well-being, by Tracy B. Boynton (2000)

A sourcebook for helping people in spiritual emergency, by Emma Bragdon (1987)

Reported effects of Holotropic Breathwork: An integrative technique for healing and personal change, by Gilles Brouillette (1997)

An investigation of the modern day vision quest as a transformative spiritual experience, by Jennifer Clements (1992)

The impact of recorded encounters with a ghost or haunting: An examination of 12 experiences, by Margaret Ann Cochran (2004)

Implications of mandated celibacy for the psychospiritual development of Roman Catholic clergy: A qualitative inquiry, by Douglas E. Dandurand (2001)

Eastern religion for Western people: A phenomenological inquiry into the experience of Tibetan Buddhist practices in the lives of six western people, by Tracy Deliman (1989)

Coming home to nature through the body: An intuitive inquiry into experiences of grief, weeping or other deep emotions in response to nature, by Jay P. Dufrechou (2002)

Spirited flesh: An intuitive inquiry exploring the body in contemporary female mystics, by Vipassana Christine Esbjorn (2003)

Using past-life regression as a tool to reduce feelings of hopelessness in individuals who experience suicidal ideation, by Carolyn Frances Ethridge (1996)

The awareness response: A transpersonal approach to reducing maladaptive emotional reactivity, by Frederick Christian Fehrer (2002)

Mutual hypnosis: An exploratory multiple-case study, by Elizabeth Ferguson (2001)

Dance as a spiritual practice: A phenomenological and feminist investigation of the experience of being-movement, by Jan Fisher (1996)

Business people who meditate: the impact of the practice on their experience in the workplace, by Julie Forbes (1999)

The history of the Goddess and the transpersonal significance of her decline and re-emergence in the West, by Vocata Sue George (1986)

Student experiences of betrayal in the Zen Buddhist teacher/ student relationship, by Caryl Reimer Gopfert (1999)

Kundalini: A study of eastern and western perspectives and experiences and their implications for transpersonal psychotherapists, by Bonnie Lynne Greenwell (1988)

Awakening spirit in the body: a heuristic exploration of peak or mystical experiences in the practice of aikido, by Brian Heery (2003)

Fascinating, isn't it? These dissertations are examples of how we can start increasing our useful knowledge and understanding of spiritual aspects of our nature if we start to apply intelligence and essential science to questions about our psychic and spiritual nature.

Most of our ITP graduates, though, will go on into service positions as therapists and spiritual guidance counselors rather than researchers continuing to expand our knowledge. It's wonderful that they'll serve individuals and communities like that but sad that the infrastructure, the jobs and funding, isn't there yet to support them as researchers.

ITP's core faculty have longer-term research programs and, in spite of support resources that are still way too small compared to the enormity and importance of the questions to be answered, have produced hundreds of journal publications and many books. To give you some idea of faculty interests, here are some transpersonally oriented book titles, not counting my own, published by ITP faculty:

Celtic Oracles: A New System for Spiritual Growth
Changes of Mind: A Holonomic Theory of the Evolution of Consciousness
Changing Images of Man
Distant Mental Influence: Its Contributions to Science, Healing, and Human Interactions
Forgive for Good: A Proven Prescription for Health and Healing
Foundations of the Buddha's Teachings: Abhidhamma and Its Causation, Correlation, and Liberation
Health for the Whole Person
Heart, Self, and Soul: The Sufi Psychology of Growth, Balance, and Wholeness
Love Is the Wine: An Introduction to Sufism
Personality and Personal Growth
Stress Free for Good: 10 Scientifically Proven Life Skills for Health and Happiness
Sufi Akbar: The First Mogul Interfaith King
Transcendent Sex: When Lovemaking Opens the Veil
Transpersonal Research Methods for the Social Sciences: Honoring Human Experience
Who am I? Personality Typologies for Self-Discovery
With the Tongues of Men and Angels: A Study of Channeling

I can't emphasize enough that getting better answers to questions about who we really are, our spiritual natures, is vital if our civilization is to survive and grow. Unchecked materialistic greed, combined with institutionalized religious intolerance and ignorance, are ruining our planet. But if, as scientistic materialism tells us, we're nothing but chemical accidents whose existence has no inherent meaning anyway, why not try to get all you can right now? Who cares about other people or future generations? We'll all be long dead by then.

Telling us we should treat each other like one big human family is nice, but doesn't carry much weight when pitted against human greed, resource shortage, scientistic materialism, and the like. But when someone like Richard Maurice Bucke or Allan Smith has a deep, transpersonal experience of Cosmic Consciousness and our essential-science studies of parapsychology tell us that this could be about realities, not just pleasant fantasies — well, things change drastically. I know that saving the world is a huge and complex problem, but my personal conviction is that developing a large-scale, well-supported transpersonal psychology, sorting the true from the false in spirituality and religion, and learning how to help people have direct experiences of our essential spiritual nature and relatedness are the most important parts of saving it.

But, as I mentioned earlier, transpersonal psychology is still a new and tiny field of psychology, and ITP, the leading institution, in spite of an enviable record of faculty and student productivity, is limited in its resources to promote research.

Earlier I asked whether there has been any progress in spirituality. You could break that into more specific questions like:

- Are more people seriously embarking on a spiritual growth path?
- Has such training become more effective, such that a higher proportion of people grow from the training?
- Are we producing more wise, compassionate individuals who are of service to others?
- Are we reducing the number of dropouts and people who are hurt by outmoded or unsuitable (for them) spiritual training practices?

To get more positive answers to any of these kinds of questions, we need the research, both theoretical and applied, that will create progress in spirituality. If we had major support for transpersonal psychology, I can imagine enormous leaps forward in the depth and effectiveness of spiritual practice.

I'll devote the remainder of my career to advancing transpersonal psychology. That's part of being, and being proud of being, both a spiritual seeker and a scientist.

References

Atwater, P. M. H. 1988. *Coming Back to Life: The After-Effects of the Near-Death Experience.* New York: Ballantine.

Augustine, K. *2007.* Does paranormal perception occur in near-death experiences? *Journal of Near-Death Studies 25(4): 203-236.*

Begley, S. *2007. Train Your Mind, Change Your Brain: How a New Science Reveals Our Extraordinary Potential to Transform Ourselves.* New York: Ballantine Books.

Bekesy, G. von. *1967. Sensory Inhibition.* Princeton, NJ: Princeton University Press.

Bernstein, M. *1956. The Search for Bridey Murphy.* New York: Doubleday.

Bisaha, J. P., and B. J. Dunne. 1979. Multiple subject and long-distance precognitive remote viewing of geographical locations. In *Mind at Large: IEEE Symposia on the Nature of Extrasensory Perception,* ed. C. T. Tart, H. E. Puthoff, and R. Targ. New York: Praeger.

Bucke, R. M. *1961. Cosmic Consciousness: A Study in the Evolution of the Human Mind.* New York: University Books, Inc.

Crookes, *W 1926. Researches in the Phenomena of Spiritualism.* Manchester, England: The Two Worlds Publishing Company, Ltd. Quoted in *1964,* R. G. Medhurst and K. M. Goldney, William Crookes and the physical phenomena of mediumship, *Proceedings of the Society for Psychical Research* 54:10-14.

Dalai Lama. *2005. The Universe in a Single Atom: The Convergence of Science and Spirituality.* New York: Broadway Books. Quoted in Begley *2007.*

Dossey, L. *2003.* Personal communication, January 5.

Ducasse, C. 1960. How the case of the search for Bridey Murphy stands today. *Journal of the American Society for Psychical Research* 54:3-22.

Eisenbud, J. 1970. Psi *and Psychoanalysis: Studies in the Psycho-analysis of Psi Conditioned Behavior.* New York: Grune & Stratton.

Eisenbud, J. 1982. *Paranormal Foreknowledge: Problems and Perplexities.* New York: Human Sciences Press.

Fuller, J. G. 1979. *The Airmen Who Would Not Die.* Books.

Grad, B. 1965. Some biological effects of the "laying on of hands": A review of experiments with animals and plants. *Journal of the American Society for Psychical Research* 59:95-127.

Guggenheim, B., and J. Guggenheim. 1997. *Hello from Heaven: A New Field of Research-After-Death Communication Confirms That Life and Love Are Eternal.* Paperback ed. New York: Bantam Books.

Hamilton, A. J. 2008. *The Scalpel and the Soul: Encounters with Surgery, the Supernatural, and the Healing Power of Hope.* New York: Jeremy P. Tarcher/ Penguin.

Harner, M. J. 1980. *The Way of the Shaman: A Guide to Power* San Francisco: Harper & Row.

Hart, H., and colleagues. 1956. Six theories about apparitions. *Proceedings of the Society for Psychical Research* 50:153-239.

Heron, W 1957. The pathology of boredom. *Scientific American* 196:52-56.

Hess, D. J. 1992. Disciplining heterodoxy, circumventing discipline: Parapsychology, anthropologically. In *Knowledge and Society: The Anthropology of Science and Technology,* eds. D. J. Hess and L. L. Layne, 9:223-52. Greenwich, CT: Jai Press, Inc.

Heywood, R. 1964. ESP: *A Personal Memoir.* New York: Dutton. Quoted in W Roll, Will personality and consciousness survive the death of the body? An examination of parapsychological findings suggestive of survival. Ph.D. diss., University of Utrecht, The Netherlands, 1985, 178-79.

Hill, D. 2001. "Ah, Sweet Death." The Archives of Scientists' Transcendent Experiences, Collected Archives. *www.issc-taste.org.*

Honorton, C., and D. C. Ferrari. 1989. Future telling: A meta-analysis of forced choice precognition experiments, 1935-1987. *Journal of Parapsychology* 53:281-308.

Kabat-Zinn, J. 1990. *Full Catastrophe Living: Using the Wisdom of Your Body and Mind to Face Stress, Pain, and Illness.* New York: Dell Publishing.

Kanthamani, H., and E. F. Kelly. 1975. Card experiments with a special subject II: The shuffle method. *Journal of Parapsychology* 39 (3):206-21.

Kasamatsu, A., and T. Hirai. *1966*. An electroencephalographic study of the Zen meditation (Zazen). *Folia psychiatrica et neurologica japonica* 20 *(4):315-36*.

Keen, M., A. Ellison, and D. Fontana. *1999*. The Scole Report. *Proceedings of the Society for Psychical Research 58* (Part *220,* November): 149-452.

Keene, M. L. *1976*. *The Psychic Mafia: The True and Shocking Confessions of a Famous Medium.* New York: St. Martin's Press.

Krippner, S. *1996*. A pilot study in ESP, dreams, and purported OBEs. *Journal of the Society for Psychical Research* 61 *(843):88-93*.

LaBerge, S. *1985*. *Lucid Dreaming.* Los Angeles: Tarcher.

LaGrand, L. *1998*. *After Death Communication: Final Farewells.* 1st ed. St. Paul, MN: Llewellyn Publications.

Lawrence, T. *1993*. Gathering in the sheep and goats: A meta-analysis of forced choice sheep-goat ESP studies, 1947-1993. *Proceedings of Presented Papers of the Parapsychological Association 36th Annual Convention*, 75-86.

MacKenzie, A. *1980*. Review of *The airmen who would not die. Journal of the Society for Psychical Research* 50 *(783):314-16*.

Maslow, A. H. *1964*. *Religions, Values, and Peak-Experiences.* Columbus, OH: Ohio State University Press.

Maslow, A. H. *1966*. *The Psychology of Science: A Reconnaissance.* New York: Harper & Row.

Monroe, R. *1971. Journeys Out of the Body.* Garden City, NY: Anchor Books.

Moody, R. A. *1975*. *Life After Life: The Investigation of a Phenomenon-Survival of Bodily Death.* Atlanta: Mockingbird Books.

Neisser, U. *1988*. Five kinds of self-knowledge. *Philosophical Psychology* 1 *(1):35-59*.

Nelson, R. A. *1971*. *The Art of Cold Reading.* Calgary, Alberta, Canada: Hades Publications (distributed by Tannen's Magic, New York).

Palmer, J., C. T. Tart, and D. Redington. 1979. Delayed PK with Matthew Manning: Preliminary indications and failure to confirm. *European Journal of Parapsychology* 2:396-407.

Puharich, A. 1962. *Beyond Telepathy.* Garden City, NY: Doubleday.

Puthof, H. E., and R. Targ. 1976. A perceptual channel for information transfer over kilometer distances: Historical perspective and recent research. *Proceedings of the Institute of Electrical and Electronic Engineers* 64 (3):329-54.

Radin, D. 1997. *The Conscious Universe. The Scientific Truth of Psychic Phenomena.* San Francisco: HarperOne.

Radin, D. 2006. *Entangled Minds: Extrasensory Experiences in a Quantum Reality.* New York: Paraview Pocket Books.

RAND Corporation. 1955. *A Million Random Digits with 100,000 Normal Deviates.* Glencoe, IL: The Free Press.

Rhine, J. B., and J. G. Pratt. 1954. Review of the Pearce-Pratt distance series of ESP tests. *Journal of Parapsychology* 18:165-77.

Russell, B. 1923. *A Free Man's Worship.* Portland, ME: Thomas Bird Mosher.

Sabom, M. B. 1998. *Light and Death: One Doctor's Fascinating Account of Near-Death Experiences.* Grand Rapids, MI: Zondervan Publishing.

Schmeidler, G. R., and R. A. McConnell. 1958. *ESP and Personality Patterns.* New Haven, CT: Yale University Press.

Schnabel, J. 1997. *Remote Viewers: The Secret History of America's Psychic Spies.* New York: Dell.

Schwartz, G. E. 2003. *The Afterlife Experiments: Breakthrough Scientific Evidence of Life After Death.* New York: Atria Books.

Schwartz, S. A. 2000. The location and reconstruction of a byzantine structure in Marea, Egypt, including a comparison of electronic remote sensing and remote viewing. http://www.stephanaschwartz.com/wp-content/uploads/2010/03/Marea.pdf.

Schwartz, S. A. 2007. *Opening to the Infinite: The Art and Science of Nonlocal Awareness.* Buda, TX: Nemoseen Media.

Shor, R. E. 1959. Hypnosis and the concept of the generalized reality-orientation. *American Journal of Psychotherapy* 13:582-602.

Sidgwick, H. 1882. Address by the president at the first general meeting. *Proceedings of the Society for Psychical Research* 1:7-12.

Smith, A. L., and C. T. Tart. 1998. Cosmic consciousness experience and psychedelic experiences: A first person comparison. *Journal of Consciousness Studies* 5 (1):97-107.

Sogyal Rinpoche. 1992. *The Tibetan Book of Living and Dying.* San Francisco: HarperSanFrancisco.

Stanford, R. 1974. An experimentally testable model for spontaneous psi events I. Extrasensory events. *Journal of the American Society for Psychical Research* 68 (1):34-57.

Stanford, R., and A. Stio. 1976. Associative mediation in psi-mediated instrumental response (PMIR). In *Research in Parapsychology 1975,* ed. J. Morris, W Roll, and R. Morris. Metuchen, NJ:

Stanford, R., A. Stio, D. O'Rourke, F. Barile, J. Wolyniec, J. Bianco, and C. Rumore. 1976. Motivational arousal and self-concept in psi-mediated instrumental response. In *Research in Parapsychology 1975,* ed. J. Morris, W Roll, and R. Morris. Metuchen, NJ: Scarecrow Press.

Stapp, H. P. 2007. *Mindful Universe: Quantum Mechanics and the Participating Observer.* New York: Springer.

Stevenson, 1. 1983. Cryptomnesia and parapsychology. *Journal of the Society for Psychical Research* 52 (793):1-30.

Stevenson, I. 1997a. *Reincarnation and Biology: A Contribution to the Etiology of Birthmarks and Birth Defects: Volume 1-Birthmarks.* Westport, CT Praeger.

Stevenson, I. 1997b. *Reincarnation and Biology: A Contribution to the Etiology of Birthmarks and Birth Defects: Volume 2-Birth Defects and Other Anomalies.* Westport, CT. Praeger.

Targ, R. 2008. *Do You See What I See? Memoirs of a Blind Biker.* Charlottesville, VA: Hampton Roads Publishing Company, Inc.

Targ, R., and K. Harary. 1984. *The Mind Race: Understanding and Using Psychic Abilities.* New York: Villard Books.

Targ, R., and H. Puthoff. 1974. Information transmission under conditions of sensory shielding. *Nature* 252:602-07.

Targ, R., and H. Puthoff. 1977. *Mind-Reach: Scientists Look at Psychic Ability.* New York: Delacorte Press/Eleanor Friede.

Tart, C. 1967. A second psychophysiological study of out-of-the-body experiences in a gifted subject. *International Journal of Parapsychology* 9:251-58.

—. 1968. A psychophysiological study of out-of-the-body experiences in a selected subject. *Journal of the American Society for Psychical Research* 62:3-27.

—. 1969. A further psychophysiological study of out-of-the-body experiences in a gifted subject. *Proceedings of the Parapsychology Association* 6:43-44.

—. 1970. Self-report scales of hypnotic depth. *International Journal of Clinical and Experimental Hypnosis* 18 (2):105-25.

—. 1972. States of consciousness and state-specific sciences. *Science* 176:1203-10.

—. 1973. States of consciousness. In *Human Action: An Introduction to Psychology,* ed. L. Bourne and B. Ekstrand. New York: Dryden Press.

—. 1974. Some methodological problems in out-of-the-body experiences research. In *Research in Parapsychology* 1973, eds. W Roll, R. Morris, and J. Morris, 116-20. Metuchen, NJ: Scarecrow Press.

—. 1976. *Learning to Use Extrasensory Perception.* Chicago: University of Chicago Press.

—. 1977a. Psi: *Scientific Studies of the Psychic Realm.* New York: E. P. Dutton.

—. 1976b. Toward humanistic experimentation in parapsychology: A reply to Dr. Stanford's review. *Journal of the American Society for Psychical Research* 71:81-102.

—. 1978. Comments on the critical exchange between Drs. Stanford and Tart: Dr. Tart's reply to Dr. Gatlin. *Journal of the American Society for Psychical Research* 72:81-87.

—. 1979a. Randomicity, predictability, and mathematical inference strategies in ESP feedback experiments: Discussion of Dr. Gatlin's paper. *Journal of the American Society for Psychical Research* 73:44-60.

. 1979. A survey of expert opinion on potentially negative uses of psi, United States government interest in psi, and the level of research funding of the field. In *Research in Parapsychology 1978,* ed. W G. Roll. Metuchen, NJ: Scarecrow Press.

—. 1980. Are we interested in making ESP function strongly and reliably? A reply to J. E. Kennedy. *Journal of the American Society for Psychical Research* 74:210-22.

—. 1981. Causality and synchronicity: Steps toward clarification. *Journal of the American Society for Psychical Research* 75:121-41.

—. 1983. Learning to use psychokinesis: Theoretical and methodological notes. In *Research in Parapsychology 1982,* ed. W G. Roll, J. Beloff, and R. A. White. Metuchen, NJ: Scarecrow Press.

—. 1986. *Waking Up: Overcoming the Obstacles to Human Potential.* Boston: New Science Library.

—. 1987. The world simulation process in waking and dreaming: A systems analysis of structure. *Journal of Mental Imagery* 11:145-58.

. 1988. Effects of electrical shielding on GESP performance. *Journal of the American Society for Psychical Research* 82:129-46.

—. 1993. Mind embodied: Computer-generated virtual reality as a new, dualistic-interactive model for transpersonal psychology. In *Cultivating Consciousness: Enhancing Human Potential, Wellness, and Healing,* ed. K. R. Rao. Westport, CT: Praeger.

—. 1994. *Living the Mindful Life: A Handbook for Living in the Present Moment.* Boston: Shambhala Publications.

—. 1998a. Investigating altered states of consciousness on their own terms: A proposal for the creation of state-specific sciences. *Ciencia e Cultura, Journal of the Brazilian Association for the Advancement of Science* 50 (2-3):103-16.

—. 1998b. Six studies of out-of-body experiences. *Journal of Near-Death Studies* 17 (2):73-99.

—. 2003. Enlightenment and spiritual growth: Reflections from the bottom up. *Subtle Energies and Energy Medicine* 14 (1):19-59.

—. 2007. Commentary on "Does paranormal perception occur in near death experiences?" *Journal of Near-Death Studies* 25 (4):251-56.

INDEX

Printed in Great Britain
by Amazon

26862865R00238